History's Locomotives

HISTORY'S LOCOMOTIVES

Revolutions and the Making of the Modern World

Martin Malia

Edited and with a Foreword by Terence Emmons

Yale University Press
New Haven & London

Set in Postscript Electra by Tseng Information Systems, Inc.
Printed in the United States of America.

Library of Congress Cataloging-in-Publication Data
Malia, Martin E. (Martin Edward)
History's locomotives : revolutions and the making of the modern world /
Martin Malia ; edited and with a foreword by Terence Emmons.
p. cm.
Includes bibliographical references and index.
ISBN-13: 978-0-300-11391-4 (cloth : alk. paper)
ISBN-10: 0-300-11391-9
1. Revolutions—Europe—History. I. Emmons, Terence. II. Title.
D210.M28 2007
303.6′4094—dc22   2006012932

A catalogue record for this book is available from the British Library.

The paper in this book meets the guidelines for permanence and durability
of the Committee on Production Guidelines for Book Longevity of the
Council on Library Resources.

10 9 8 7 6 5 4 3 2 1

Contents

FOREWORD

The essential insights informing this book on revolutions in the making of the modern world were already present in a paper Martin Malia delivered at the annual meeting of the American Historical Association in 1975: that the numerous revolutions of the twentieth century have deep roots in European history, specifically; and that revolutionary thought and action underwent a process of *radicalization* from one "great" European revolution to the next, culminating in the Bolshevik Revolution of 1917 in Russia. That revolution established on the ruins of one of the last surviving European old regimes a revolutionary regime devoted, in theory for seventy-four years and in practice into the late 1930s at least, to the total transformation of human relations under the banner of Communism. Malia's aim in this book, as he wrote in one outline of the project, "is to show that the Russian case, for all its uniqueness, is also a logical, though extreme, culmination of the long revolutionary tradition in European civilization as a whole." If we add to this his conviction that revolutions in modern history can be compared fruitfully only as elements in an ongoing international or transnational process—that is, historically, *in media res*—we have the rationale for the writing of this book.

By the same token, this book may be considered a primer on a properly historicist approach to comparative history based on consideration of cognate developments within a space and time continuum, an approach that links Malia's work to an intellectual tradition whose outstanding exponents included, in the twentieth century, the historian Marc Bloch and, in the nineteenth, that great historical sociologist *avant le mot*, Alexis de Tocqueville.

There can be little doubt that a great stimulus to the writing and design of this book was the collapse of the Communist regimes in the Soviet Union and

Eastern Europe in 1989–1991. All of a sudden, these truly historic events demonstrated that the terminus ad quem of Malia's thematic inquiry, the "institutionalized revolution" which was the Soviet regime, was itself at last over. His response to these events is an apt illustration of a point he makes repeatedly in discussing the historiography of the various revolutions treated in this book: that historians' interpretations are inevitably shaped by the context—political, cultural, ideological—in which they operate. If nineteenth-century historians worked under the spell of the French Revolution and twentieth-century historians (those of the "short twentieth century," 1914–1991) worked under the spell of the Bolshevik Revolution, so latter-day historians can only be profoundly influenced in their interpretations of past revolutions (and not only revolutions) by the collapse of the Communist-utopian experiment. For Malia, to paraphrase an historian he admired, François Furet, "the Russian revolution is over."

As he notes in the Introduction below, before he returned to the revolutionary tradition that culminated in the Russian Revolution, Malia wrote two books, one arguing his views on the nature of the Soviet regime and its collapse, and another exploring the origins of "the uniqueness and inverted nature of the Soviet regime" in the context of "modern European development since the Enlightenment." He was then free, as it were, to return to the theme of the long historical tradition that lay behind Russian developments. The new, "post-Soviet" context provoked him to recast this theme in significant ways. I quote from a paper he presented to the Historical Society in Boston in 2000: "What does [the failure of Communism] do to the problem of revolution as such? In essence, it inverts the problem's very nature. The last century's preoccupation with the route from the bourgeois to the socialist revolution has turned out to be a false problem. What remains instead is the problem of the route leading *to* 1776, and especially 1789. And just as important, we confront the new task of explaining the two-century long illusion of 1789's Second Coming as Socialism." What began as an effort to reconceptualize the Russian Revolution focused at first on the "great revolutions": the English Revolution of the seventeenth century, and the American and French revolutions of the late eighteenth century, especially the French Revolution and its reverberations throughout the nineteenth century up to Red October. In the present study, in keeping with the first of his prescriptions in the passage quoted above, Malia's analysis of the great revolutions is preceded by a detailed discussion of their religious and political-institutional origins in late medieval and early modern Europe (Chapters 1–5), an exercise that is essential to his argument about the specifically European origins of the "modern revolutionary impulse" in general. The second prescription is fulfilled by his extensive critique of modern social-science theories of revolution and ongoing discussion of the ideological underpinnings of the many and various historiographies he confronts along the way in his study of the European revolutionary tradition.

At the time of Martin Malia's death on November 19, 2004, the text of *History's Locomotives* was essentially complete. The author's general aim of analyzing the revolutionary tradition leading to the Communist revolutions of the twentieth century was accomplished in the eleven finished chapters of the present book. Nothing of significance in those chapters has been changed. None of the author's ideas or even his phrasing has been altered. Changes to the manuscript amount only to copy editing, reference checking, internal referencing, and a few stylistic changes of a sort the editor knows from experience would have elicited no objection from the author. In a few cases, some material appended by the author to the end of individual chapters, usually in the form of rephrasings or elaborations, has been added or made to replace existing portions of text at the editor's discretion.

The material presented here in Appendix I (Revolution: What's in a Name?) and Appendix II (High Social Science and "Staseology") served as the Introduction and Chapter 1, respectively, of the original manuscript. These "chapters" have been removed to appendices in order to make room for a proper introduction describing the main themes and methods of the work immediately preceding the historical narrative. The new Introduction consists of the author's own summary description of his work and methods drawn from several papers and book prospectuses.

While Martin Malia's central aim in this project remained constant—to explain the origins and nature of Red October and the "institutionalized revolution" to which it gave rise—he considered the idea of adding chapters on interwar fascism and on "The Cloning of October: East Asia and Latin America, 1945–1975." He discussed this possibility with several colleagues, included the chapter titles in a draft table of contents, and produced some material, ranging from bare bibliographical references to elements of the arguments to be developed, under these rubrics. This material has not been included as a whole in the present text. Some of the arguments presented there, supplemented by Malia's published writing on the same themes (as referenced in the notes), appear in the book's Conclusion and Epilogue.

Malia's own working title for this book was "The Pattern and Escalation of Western Revolution: From the Hussites to the Bolsheviks, 1415–1991 (or The Western Revolutionary Process, 1415–1991)." The present title, beginning with

Marx's famous designation of revolutions, *History's Locomotives*, which the author cites several times in his text, was provided by the editor.

All English translations of foreign-language sources in this book are the author's unless otherwise noted.

Terence Emmons

HISTORY'S LOCOMOTIVES

INTRODUCTION

Delineating the Problem

Revolution, together with global war, was the defining characteristic of the twentieth century. Indeed, most of the events in world history that customarily qualify as "revolutions" have occurred since 1914. With Communism's demise, the modern revolutionary phenomenon seems to have run its course. Is this, in fact, likely to be the case, or does revolution spring eternal in human affairs? Both to answer this question and to understand the century's drama, it is necessary to trace the roots of modern revolutionary phenomena far back into the past of Western society.

But does the subject of revolution as such exist? War has certainly existed as a distinct phenomenon from earliest times, and as the subject of historical investigations since Herodotus and Thucydides. By analogy, it seems, we suppose that revolutions can occur in any place or time if appropriate conditions are present. My argument is that this supposition is mistaken, and that what we call revolutions are a historically specific phenomenon—in fact, specific to Europe and, during the last century, the area of European influence.

Therefore, I will not begin by offering a definition of revolution and then comparing it with a list of cases. Rather, I will proceed the other way around, building from specific problems and events to more general propositions. And my approach will not be structural; it will be historical. This means tracing the radicalization of the European revolutionary process from what I consider to be its beginnings with the fifteenth-century Hussites to the twentieth century, with special emphasis on the two pivotal instances of modern revolution, France in 1789 and Russia in 1917.

And my key questions are: Is there a basic pattern—structure, if you will— of European revolution? Is there an overall European revolutionary process in which this pattern escalates over time? Finally, is there an underlying revolutionary impulse acting throughout the last millennium?

My interest in the problem of revolution goes back many years. It began as an effort to "re-conceptualize" the Russian Revolution, which fitted into none of our usual theories of revolution. Most of these posited that revolution is a process with a clear beginning, middle, and end, whereas the Russian Revolution, once the Bolshevik-Jacobins had seized power, was fixed in a seemingly unending ultra-radical movement, which in fact lasted seventy-four years (it was as if the original Jacobins had held power from 1793 to 1867). Similarly inapplicable to Communist Russia are such comparative categories as "Thermidor" and "Bonapartism," such explanatory ones as "proletariat" versus "bourgeoisie," or such excessively broad concepts as "modernization" and "development." None of these categories gets at the uniqueness of the Russian case. For, after October 1917, Russia offered the unprecedented spectacle of an inverted world in which the ideology determined the political structure (Party hegemony), and the political structure determined the economic order (a command economy), while there was no society (that is, no "civil society"), since all components of the system lived in subordination to Party purposes and control—the whole structure justified by the great cause of building, then defending, Socialism. And it was because there was no real society or autonomous economy in Soviet Russia to counteract the total state that October could be frozen in place until the meltdown of 1989–1991.

These views regarding the uniqueness and inverted nature of the Soviet regime were argued extensively in my *The Soviet Tragedy: A History of Socialism in Russia, 1917–1991*.[1] The origins of this paradoxical phenomenon were then explored in the context of modern European development since the Enlightenment in *Russia Under Western Eyes: From the Bronze Horseman to the Lenin Mausoleum*.[2] What I wish to do now is to show that the Russian case, for all its uniqueness, is also a logical, though extreme, culmination of the long revolutionary tradition in European civilization as a whole. Russia will not figure prominently in this book, but it will enter in as the terminus ad quem of an all-European development. This book's main subject is the European revolutionary tradition.

Seven general considerations define the approach of this book.

1. Revolution is a European phenomenon in origin—just as modern civilization overall is a European creation, however unfair this may be to the rest of humanity. Until the twentieth century, outside the European cultural orbit (which includes, of course, the Americas) there was nothing that may plausibly be called a revolution—nor, for that matter, was there anything resembling democracy,

constitutionalism, or philosophies of the pursuit of individual liberty or social equality as supreme social goods; nor were there words for such concepts outside of European languages. Thus, the origin of the revolutionary phenomenon must be sought in specifically European institutions and cultural norms.

2. As a consequence of this Eurocentricity, revolution must be studied in the first instance historically, in specifically Western terms, rather than structurally and "trans-culturally." The American social sciences are, by and large, structural in orientation; that is, they operate in terms of the "social system" or "society," whose basic structure is assumed to be the same in all times and places, from France to China and from the twelfth century to the twentieth.[3] History, by contrast, operates in terms of the particular and the temporal, a perspective in which differences in time and place have a great deal to do with the differing structures we find across the globe.

The most prominent of all theories of revolution, Marxism, offers a combination of structural and historical elements. It is structural insofar as it holds that all "history is the history of class struggle," and class is universally defined in terms of relationships of production leading to relationships of exploitation: thus, whether we are talking about such significantly different "ruling classes" as Chinese mandarins, Hindu Brahmins, Roman slaveholders, Western feudal lords, or American planters, we are always talking essentially about "exploiters." Yet Marxism is also historical in that class struggle develops over time in intensity and self-consciousness, as the mode of production becomes ever more advanced and exploitative. Nonetheless, in Marxism historical movement itself is structured, since there is only one, logically phased line of social development, in all civilizations, from slaveholding to feudal to capitalist society. Further, there is no significant place in Marxism for the autonomy of either politics or culture, both of which are reduced to the status of a mere "superstructure."

In short, Marxism, though recognizing historical differences over time, is not really comparative because it reduces all history to a single set of socioeconomic factors arranged in an escalating continuum. Thus, historical materialism, though it proclaims that "Europe shows the rest of humanity its future," can hardly explain why it was only the European "class struggle" that produced those revolutions that are "the locomotives" of universal history. Yet a diffuse Marxism remains far and away the most important influence in the contemporary social sciences.

3. A Western revolution is in the first instance a political and ideological transformation, not a social one. And on this subject the best guide is Weber, taken as a general methodological antidote to Marx, for Weber has nothing to say directly about the phenomenon of revolution. The relevant point here is that Weber, as a

genuine comparativist, sought to explain why Marx's capitalism was born in Europe, rather than in some other culture; and he answered that it was the distinctiveness of European religion, particularly Calvinism, that made Europe more dynamic than rival civilizations.[4]

But there is more to European religion than the Lutheran doctrine of this-worldly calling and the Calvinist principle of double predestination which Weber singled out. There was, in the first instance, the sacramental and sacerdotal system of the early church and the Middle Ages; and there was the principle developed from Constantine onward that the church was coextensive with society; a church-society called by the Carolingians Christendom. In this sacred world the spiritual and the secular swords were inextricably linked, with the former of course being the higher of the two. Thus revolt, if not yet revolution, began in Europe with the redefinition of the sphere of the spiritual: that is, with heresy.

Specifically, since eternal salvation depended on sacraments, and since these might be invalid if the priest were unworthy, European heresy perennially tended toward antisacerdotalism and antisacramentalism. Over the long years after the Gregorian reform of the eleventh century, it eventually emerged that the ultimate consequence of this position was the abolition of both clergy and sacraments in favor of direct contact of the believer with God. The culminating expression of this was the Münster Anabaptist revolt of 1534–35.

Moreover, in this sacred world any challenge to the ecclesiastical hierarchy was automatically a challenge to the secular hierarchy. Religious dissent and heresy, therefore, furnished the first impulse to radical social change, and ultimately leveling, in Western culture, and they remained the primary force for egalitarianism until the eighteenth-century Enlightenment. Furthermore, even the church's own efforts to reform itself tended to generate a millenarian expectation of the reign of the Holy Spirit on earth. These and other, more temperate, forms of religious protest were brought into the center of politics by the Reformation; and the secularization of religious values is clearly one component of the Western revolutionary tradition, acting to diffuse power in a manner similar to the fragmentation of political authority by feudalism. The radical political consequences and the egalitarian social implications of medieval and Reformation heterodoxy have received their most impressive theoretical formulation by Weber's colleague Ernst Troeltsch.[5]

These insights, and their application to the Middle Ages and Reformation, will be the subject of the first part of the book. The three "escalating" cases involved are: Hussite Bohemia, Lutheran Germany, and the Dutch Revolt.

4. The same cultural distinctiveness may be claimed for European political forms and philosophies, for it is only the Western world—first in Greece and

Rome and then in medieval representative assemblies and their modern descendants — that has known participatory politics and the legal and philosophical reflection such arrangements generate. And this political culture thoroughly encapsulates the Western "class struggle."

Thus, although there are numerous examples in European history of acute social conflicts, whether urban revolts such as that of the Ciompi in Florence in 1385, or rural uprisings such as the *jacquerie* during the Hundred Years' War or the German Peasants' War of 1525, none of these led to general revolutions like 1640 or 1789. Such social struggles, therefore, are the necessary but not the sufficient cause of major revolution. For the latter type of event to occur there first must exist the framework of a *unitary state* to focus all political, social, and other forms of protest in a single set of institutions. And this focus on the transformation of state structures, and the concomitant challenge to existing state legitimacy, is what gives to a general revolution both its explosive character and its political-ideological nature.

Historically speaking, these European state forms originated in feudal monarchies. These proto-national institutionalizations of the secular sword, like the parallel organization of the spiritual sword into a clergy-laity ecclesiology, were strictly hierarchical bodies; in fact, the two hierarchies meshed in the system of the three orders or estates: those who pray, those who fight, those who work. Formed between 1100 and 1300, these feudal monarchies were slowly centralized to where by the sixteenth century they became what historians later called "absolute" monarchies, and which after 1789 everyone called *anciens régimes*. The feudal origin of these state forms is of paramount importance because feudal relationships everywhere mean a division of power, which would later form the basis for the separation of powers and the checks and balances of modern constitutionalism.

5. A European "grand revolution," then, is a generalized revolt against an Old Regime. Moreover, such a transformation occurs *only once* in each national history, since it is also the founding event for the nation's future "modernity." Western revolutions thus acquire their distinctive character from the Old Regime constitutional and cultural structures *against which* they are made, thereby producing each time related patterns of revolutionary action. And that against which European revolutions were made, from 1400 to 1789, was the sacred commonwealth of the two swords and the three orders.

6. Western revolutions do not simply repeat the basic pattern of revolt against the Old Regime; rather each revolution learns from the experience of its predecessor, and so escalates that pattern each time to a more intense level of radicalism. (And let it be recalled that everywhere east of the Rhine modified Old

Regimes existed until World War I—in Prussian Germany, Austria-Hungary, and Russia.) This progression is, schematically, as follows:

a. The English or Puritan Revolution, though the same in its basic pattern of action as the French, was still half-religious in character, and so never thought of itself as a revolution. When it was finished its heirs obliterated from the national consciousness the fact that they had made a revolution. At the time, the revolution's concluding episode, the Glorious Revolution of 1688, meant a "restoration." (The original meaning of revolution is a return to a point of origin.)[6]

b. The American colonists began what they indeed called their "revolution" (in the 1688 sense) as an effort at the "restoration" of their historic rights as Englishmen. But when they got through, they had created a new nation and a republic, an outcome that was obviously "revolutionary" in the modern sense of post-Old Regime.

c. This modern sense emerged fully in the course of the French Revolution. Although similar in its basic pattern to its English predecessor, the French Revolution was the first to occur in a predominantly secular culture: the Enlightenment. Seventeen-eighty-nine therefore quickly escalated into a frontal assault on the whole of Europe's thousand-year-old ancien régime: monarchy, aristocracy, and church. As a result, revolution now came to mean a creatively violent process ushering in a new world-historical epoch, and the creation of a "new man." Thus, the French events generated, for the first time in the West, a cult of revolution as the way history works; or at least it did so on what now became known as "the left."

d. Then came the turning point of 1830–1848. Since the French Revolution failed to complete its task of human emancipation, after the July overturn of 1830 its more radical heirs took to anticipating a second, and final, 1789. On the far left, this Second Coming was expected to escalate the revolutionary agenda from political liberty for the rich and the few to social justice and equality for the impoverished many, a creed variously called socialism or communism; its maximal program was the abolition of private property, profit, and the market, an "exploitative" system for which the term "capitalism" was coined toward the end of the century. This socialism was of course this-worldly in orientation, indeed often militantly anti-religious, just as the Enlightenment had been. Nonetheless, the new movement in fact often reproduced medieval and Reformation millenarian expectations in secular guise, from the Saint-Simonians' New Christianity to Marx's edenic "classless, stateless society," a filiation often directly claimed by the movement's leaders. Marx, the basis of whose system was laid by 1845, was only the most prominent of these theorists of *revolutionary anticipation*. Moreover, the link between his communist vision and Reformation eschatology can be clearly traced through Hegel's historicist metaphysics. Engels, indeed, deemed Thomas Müntzer to be Marx's direct predecessor.

Tocqueville, in the same years, made a kindred point in more sober fashion: once "democracy," in the sense of social equality, had "destroyed monarchy and aristocracy," there was no reason to "believe that it would stop short before the bourgeoisie and the rich." Thus he defined democratic revolution as the unavoidable fate of the modern world, and the great political problem of modernity was how to make it compatible with individual liberty; and this, not the chimera of integral socialism, is indeed the practical political and social problem of modern politics. Tocqueville, further, plausibly traced the origins of modern liberty back to feudal "liberties," and the modern leveling impulse back to the monarchical state's struggle against those same aristocratic liberties. Tocqueville, finally, is a genuine comparativist: in order to understand why the most explosive of European revolutions broke out in France, he compared the French case with cognate Old Regimes that did *not* produce revolutions so as to "isolate the variable" peculiar to France; and the answer, of course, was that this variable was the anti-nobility, leveling monarchy. All of these insights will be used in this study and applied to the hundred and fifty years of revolutionary history since Tocqueville.

e. The would-be new 1789, when it at last materialized in 1848, disappointed the anticipations of all stripes of revolutionary, whether liberal, socialist, or nationalist, by bringing to power the likes of Napoleon III and Bismarck, thus producing the first revolution won by conservatives. But revolutionary anticipation hardly disappeared. To be sure, in industrialized Western Europe there were no more working-class uprisings after the Paris Commune of 1871; and after 1889, the Marxist Second International tended increasingly to seek its goals though elections, thus becoming by 1914 social-democratic reformism, in fact if not in formal doctrine. Still, Socialism as full noncapitalism remained the stated goal of the international workers' movement, and crisis could easily give it a new life.

f. At the same time, maximalist revolutionary anticipation moved east to backward Russia. In 1917 this one-time bastion of European reaction unexpectedly produced the Second and Final Revolution, anticipated yet constantly thwarted farther west from 1830 to 1871. From the victorious high ground of October, Marxism-Leninism then reinjected into part of the Western left the cult of revolution, whose specter would dominate so much of twentieth-century politics everywhere.

7. The Western revolutionary tradition moves not only from the primacy of political liberty to that of eliminating social inequality, and from relative moderation to extremism, but from more advanced societies to more backward ones. Thus, it spreads from the economically developed and politically complex Old Regimes of the Atlantic West, to the simpler and more predominantly military Old Regimes of Prussia and Austria, to the crudest and most brutal of them all, Russia. That is, it moves along what Germans call the "West-East cultural gradient." This factor also contributes to the radicalization of the revolutionary process, for modernity's movement eastward leads to the telescoping of historical stages, and after 1917 to the inversion of the Western development. Finally, once this tradition has achieved its "final," inverted embodiment in Russia, it then expands in the twentieth century to much of the Third World, thus making the twentieth century the world-historical locus of revolution. (This view of Europe as a spectrum of graded zones owes much to Alexander Gerschenkron.)[7]

These various considerations at last permit a comprehensive definition of the method employed here. This method is, first, to follow Tocqueville's procedure of comparing only cognate cases within the same culture. By extension, this means pursuing comparisons of contiguous cases in a sequential temporal continuum: that is, cases of partial overlap, as well as of partial divergence, between earlier and later instances of a brusque break in European history. Indeed, such a genetic and incremental approach is the grand axis of historical method. And historical investigation, after all, is not primarily about structures; it is about appropriating the human experience under the ordinance of change and continuity over time.

Programmatically, the overall aim of this investigation is to generalize Tocqueville's insights into the workings of the modern democratic impulse, and to do so both forward and backward in time. Tocqueville explained the escalation of egalitarianism down to 1789 by the action of Old Regime absolute monarchy on feudal structures going back to the year 1000. But it is obvious that the egalitarian impulse thereby generated continued to escalate after 1789 to yield the increasingly radical, leveling revolutions of the twentieth century. Moreover, although Tocqueville spoke often of the clergy, he said little about religion itself, beyond noting that it was the indispensable moral cement of society.

A second fundamental aspect, then, of the approach used here is to apply to Tocqueville's problem Weber's sensitivity to the social role of Christianity. This means linking both Christianity's doctrinal content and its institutional structures to the political and social process of democratic escalation. To do so, it is necessary to go back again to Tocqueville's starting point in the year 1000, and thus to relate Christian theology and ecclesiology to both feudalism and early-modern Old Regime successors. Weber himself, of course, never attempted such an effort; nor was he interested in the problem of revolution. But the aspect of European uniqueness he was interested in, capitalism, clearly was not the source of that other uniquely European phenomenon, escalating revolution — as the perverse twentieth-century fate of Marxism amply illustrates. Nonetheless, a religious approach to Tocqueville's political problem is a legitimate extension of Weber's assessment of the historical decisiveness of culture.[8] For it is indeed from this long-term political-cum-cultural background that the insatiable and Faustian revolutionary tradition of Europe springs.

To illustrate the birth of this-worldly radicalism out of otherworldly faith, let us recall that before the watershed of 1776–1789 Europeans lacked the modern concept of revolution as a clean break and new departure. But recall also that the first European revolution now considered modern, the English Revolution of 1640–1660, was fought in terms of a religious ideology, thus earning it the label Puritan. Yet, the culmination of this "revolution of the saints" in the monarch's ritual execution links it to the next grand upheaval in the standard series — the unambiguously secular and democratic French drama of 1789–1799. This pair of revolutions thus clearly offers two species of the same historical genus. Until now, modern "staseology" has usually followed this organic development forward to the twentieth century. The first step here, however, will be to follow it *backward* to the medieval matrix of a distinctive European civilization in the period 1000–1300. For it is in those remote centuries that the European revolutionary impulse first appeared; and it was directed, not against the state, which did not yet exist, but against the church, which was the only all-embracing unit of European society. The revolutionary impulse, indeed, first appears in the sacred sedition of heresy, particularly in its millenarian or apocalyptic form.

From this base, the continuum of European radicalism will be followed forward as it escalates from religious to political sedition and on to overt revolution; and then from the political revolutions of the seventeenth and eighteenth centuries to the "scientific" millenarianism of twentieth-century social revolution. Thus did the Western revolutionary tradition traverse the millennial trajectory from salvation religion as surrogate politics to salvation politics as surrogate religion.

For seventy-odd years, social science "staseology" has been in pursuit of the grail of a universal (standard) model of revolution, and the dominant approach, inevitably, has been comparative. Unfortunately, this method has usually been treated as a one-way street designed to lead us to *similarities*. In fact, though, as between any two cases there always exists at least as many differences as similarities, and so the longed-for "model" has never appeared. Now seven decades into the quest, the search has ended in a clear cul-de-sac. So why not try the other side of the comparative street, and collect *differences* as well? This indeed was the tried-and-true method practiced by Tocqueville and Weber in order to isolate the decisive political and cultural variables from one case to another. And when it comes to a *historical*, as opposed to a sociological, investigation, might not these differences, when shuffled in with the similarities, yield a different kind of model, one of incremental-revolutionary change over time? That making comparisons should yield differences as well as similarities is no doubt a platitude. Yet it is surprising how many great minds have missed this elementary point—Marx, for example, for whom all "bourgeois revolutions" must ultimately be the same.

In the nineteenth century, "revolution" was a problem in political history. In the twentieth century, it became a problem in social history. After two centuries of inconclusive pursuit of both approaches, it has now become clear that revolution must in the first instance also be considered a problem in the history of ideas. This is true on two accounts, first, because the historiography of both the various revolutionary "cases" and revolution-as-such is so self-contradictory that our understanding of either subject must initially be approached as a branch of intellectual history; and second, because this historiography reveals that both the political and the social content of our various cases has been crucially molded by ideas. The present study, therefore, is above all an investigation of revolution as a history of ideas. Accordingly, each revolutionary case examined here will begin with a survey of its historiography.

So much for the generalities; now for the historical narrative.

HISTORIC EUROPE

The Medieval Matrix and Its Internal Contradictions, 1000–1400

Therefore, despite the development that [socialist] theories have undergone . . . I
still see on the stage only two great facts, two principles, two actors, two persons:
Christianity and the Revolution. . . . The Revolution continues Christianity, and
contradicts it. It is at the same time Christianity's heir and its adversary.
—JULES MICHELET, *History of the French Revolution*, 1847

And I saw an angel come down from heaven, having the key of the bottomless pit.
. . . And he laid hold on the dragon, that old serpent, which is . . . Satan, and bound
him a thousand years. . . . And when the thousand years are expired, Satan shall be
loosed out of his prison. And shall go out to deceive the nations which are in the
four quarters of the earth. . . . [But then] fire came down from God out of heaven,
and devoured them. And the devil that deceived them was cast into the lake of fire
and brimstone.

And I saw a new heaven and a new earth: for the first heaven and the first earth
were passed away. . . . And I John saw the holy city, new Jerusalem, coming down
from God out of heaven, prepared as a bride adorned for her husband. And I heard
a great voice out of heaven saying, Behold, the tabernacle of God is with men. . . .
And God shall wipe away all tears from their eyes; and there shall be no more
death, neither sorrow, nor crying, neither shall there be any more pain: for the
former things are passed away. . . . And he carried me away in the spirit to a great
and high mountain, and shewed me that great city, the holy Jerusalem, descending
out of heaven from God.
—*Revelation of Saint John*, 20–21

We begin with the problem of definition: what do we mean by Europe or the
West? How did a geographical term come to designate a civilization? When did
this civilization begin? How far does it extend in space, particularly to the East?
What, finally, are its defining characteristics? This last question, of course, is not

directed to anything metaphysical, to finding some enduring cultural essence, as in the usage common to a Toynbee or a Spengler or an Alfred Weber.[1] What is involved, rather, is a matter of empirically grounded delineation.

A broad definition would put Europe's beginnings in Greece and Rome. Indeed nothing in modern Western civilization, from its art and literature, its laws and politics, its languages and philosophies, can be understood without the continuity of this heritage. Yet this ancient Europe itself is not a self-contained cultural unit; for the dominant religion of both late antiquity and the modern West, Christianity, had its origins in Judaism and in a geographic East extending on to Babylon and Persia, and of course to African Egypt.[2] But such a tri-continental, tri-millennial entity is too vast to constitute a single civilization. What such a search for ultimate roots in fact indicates is that there are no absolute beginnings in history.

There are, however, relatively clear turning points or caesurae in human affairs, and one of these is the fall, or fading away, of the Western Roman Empire between the fifth and the eighth centuries. Indeed, some would argue that it was medieval Europe's great good fortune that the empire fell in the West, thereby sparing it the autocratic fate of the East under Constantinople—or of the eternally renewed Celestial Empire of China. For in this dissolution the Latin West received the chance for a new beginning.

Europe's beginning limit in time, its terminus a quo, therefore, is for present purposes taken as the moment the inhabitants of that West began to think of themselves as a community distinct from other communities, a self-consciousness, moreover, expressed in a set of common, enduring institutions. Such a collective self-awareness, with a minimum of corresponding institutions, emerged when the Carolingian world first defined itself as "Christendom" over against the worlds of pagan barbarians and Muslim infidels. This division was given enduring status by the eighth-century Arab conquest of the southern half of the Roman world, for the first time culturally separating the European peninsula from the unitary Mediterranean *oecumene* of ancient Rome. This religious definition of the West would not be displaced by the more secular term "Europe" until the end of the seventeenth century.[3]

It is necessary to insist that the founding age of Europe as a civilizational entity falls between 800 and 1000, for since the eighteenth century Western history has largely been seen in a tripartite pattern of ancient, medieval, and modern. In this perspective, the Middle Ages are viewed as a long parentheses of ignorance and superstition in the rise of true "Western civilization," which began in Greece and became fully itself only in the Renaissance and Reformation.[4] To be sure, it was not until the sixteenth century that Europe thrust itself outward to eventual hegemony over the planet. But this feat would have been impossible had it not been for the economic, institutional, and cultural capital accumulated between 1000 and 1400. Despite the darkness overhanging the Carolingian backwater at the start of the second Christian millennium (the first time the centuries were so numbered), it is the year 1000, not the discovery of the Americas or the sea route to the Indies and Cathay, that marks Europe's takeoff on the road leading to its terminus ad quem in modernity.[5]

For by the time Europe, after 1492, began its outward thrust, its accomplishment had gone well beyond those of previous civilizations. Indeed, it is Europe's dynamism that invented the modern world (the new hegemon, America, would later mass-produce it). To be sure, present historiography now emphasizes that Europe accomplished so much only by pillaging and enslaving the other continents. But pillage and slavery are the common practice of civilizations; and it was largely Europe's latter-day concepts of human rights and democracy, as they spread around the globe, that made it possible to counterbalance pride in its accomplishments with recognition of its crimes.

The present chapter is devoted to illuminating the sources of this dynamism. And since one aspect of this dynamism was constant expansion, the emergence of historic Europe will be traced here not just for its western end, as is usual, but for its full geographical area, from the Atlantic to the Urals, a broader zone which is in fact a genuine historical unit. For over the long haul, this broader unit would constitute the theater of the ever-escalating European revolutionary drama, which culminated at the continent's eastern end with Russia's Red October.

EXTENT IN TIME AND IN SPACE

The first self-definition of what is now Europe was the *Romanitas* of antiquity, meaning the politically defined *oecumene* of the Roman Imperial state. The *Christianitas*, or Christendom, of the Carolingians and the year 1000, of course, had its origins in this older Romanitas, from which it derived its imperial ambitions, its religion, its central institution, the Church, and its written language, Latin, as well as what little it conserved of higher culture. This new imperium, however, was no longer primarily defined in political terms; it was rather a society that fused the political and the religious into one.

Yet it was not alone in proclaiming such a self-definition. By the year 800 the Eastern Empire too had become a sacred institution, though with the *basileus* clearly paramount. As already noted, in the seventh century the nomads of Arabia had conquered the southern half of the Mediterranean world, thereby making the Latin West a backward rump of old Rome. At the same time, these invaders were the bearers of a new monotheism syncretized from Judaism and Christianity, thus confronting the surviving Christian lands with a rival and irreconcilably hostile religious-political oecumene. As if in compensation, the reduced Latin West expanded on the northern frontier of the crumbling Roman world to convert the region's nomadic barbarians—the Germans first, in the fifth and sixth centuries; then, around the year 1000, the Scandinavians, the Western Slavs, the Hungarians; and on the easternmost ricochet, those Scandinavian-Slavs, the Varangians (also called Russes).[6]

The conversion of the northern barbarians furnished the first substratum of historic Europe. All its modern nations made their appearance in history when Mediterranean missionaries baptized a barbarian warrior chief—in the first round, from Clovis the Frank in 497 to Ethelbert the Saxon, king of Kent, in 598; then, in the round of 1000, Saint Olaf of Norway, Saint Steven of Hungary, Mieszko of Poland, and in 988 Saint Vladimir of Kiev. True, conversion from Constantinople rather than from Rome represented a significant difference. For the Eastern church, operating as it did in a region of old developed civilizations, had always used the local vernacular alongside Greek as the liturgical language, a policy extended to such new converts as the Armenians and the Slavs. This fact would later make an enormous difference in the fates of Orthodox and Catholic Europe: the frontier between the two is visible to this day from the Balkans to the Baltic, and indeed in current projects for expanding NATO and the European Union.[7] At the time, however, the difference was insignificant: so in the mid-eleventh century, Henry I of France married Anne of Kiev in a kind of Franco-Russian alliance against the Germanic Holy Roman Emperor. This melding of Roman, Christian, and barbarian elements in a zone extending into Russia was the founding act of a continuing Europe.

The driving force of historic Europe, however, would not be its first, broad substratum of Christian-barbarian proto-nations; it was the smaller but more dynamic world of the Latin West, as first organized by the Carolingians. The basic innovation, already noted, of that ephemeral imperium was to call itself "Christendom," thereby defining itself by its religion, something that the still classical Roman empire of Constantine and Theodosius had never done. It implemented this project by introducing a calendar that counted the years from the birth of Christ; it spread Christianity, an urban religion in antiquity, to the pagan peasantry by organizing the countryside into parishes; and it forged an alliance with the papacy and Benedictine monasticism, thereby imposing the Catholic orthodoxy of Rome throughout the West and at the same time making the secular power sacred.

Of course, the self-consciousness of this world as a coherent unit did not extend to the Orthodox East. In fact, the emergence of a Carolingian Western empire produced a religious schism with Constantinople that would culminate in 1064.[8] This development, to be sure, did not put the Greek East in the same category as pagans or infidels; but it did create a duality within Christian Europe that would not be overcome until Peter the Great in the early eighteenth century. And some would maintain that it was not overcome even then.

When the Frankish empire crumbled under the second wave of Barbarian attacks—from the Vikings, Hungarians, and seaborne Saracens of the ninth and tenth centuries—Latin Christendom's political unity was ended for good. The highest secular authorities that survived were the kingdoms descended from the barbarian *gentes*, even though one such nation, the Saxons, after 962 revived the Carolingian imperial tradition in the form of the Holy Roman Empire of the German Nation, whose effective sway extended from the mouths of the Rhine and the Elbe to the city of Rome. Indeed, the German emperor's ambition to control central Europe from Rome to the North Sea was a chief cause of the empire's failure to develop into a national monarchy. Still, this policy made sense in medieval conditions: since the emperors were dependent on nonhereditary church fiefs for support and administrative personnel against the hereditary princes of the empire, it was only prudent for them to seek control of the church's center in Rome. Prudent but not practical; for feudal administrative means were inadequate for controlling the sprawling German-Italian domain. And so, by the mid-thirteenth century the combined resistance of papacy, German princes, and Italian communes, all with local power bases, had destroyed the most ambitious imperial house, the Hohenstauffen, and with them the effective power of the empire itself.

In the chaos of the age, minimal security could be achieved only by the militarization of society at the local level. There thus emerged, in the zone between the Loire and the Rhine and in Burgundy along the Saône, a nobility of warrior lords and dependent vassals bound by a contract of mutual fealty and support. Unlike the ancient Romans, these nobles fought with metal armor and on horseback, they shoed their horses and used stirrups to mount them—techniques brought to the west by steppe barbarians. And in a rural world, this nobility lived off the labor of manorial peasants to whom they in return owed protection. By the year 1000, this feudal society, as we now call it, had gone far toward restoring internal order in westernmost Europe. Under the influence of the church, the activity of these rude warriors was "ethicized" as knighthood and chivalry. These knights, moreover, were more or less converted to observing ecclesiastical injunctions for a Truce of God, or better still a Peace of God.

Easternmost Europe, however, knew no such stability. The great corridor of horse-borne barbarians that runs from Mongolia and Central Asia across the Ukrainian steppes to the Hungarian plain became increasingly active from 1100 onward, culminating in 1240 with the arrival of the Mongols.[9] And no military force anywhere in the settled world was capable of resisting them. If the Latin West was spared, it was because the Mongols, after crushing a German-Polish host at Liegnitz in Silesia in 1241, turned homeward on learning of their Great Khan's death. In the meantime, however, most of Russia had become their tributary.

Thus, like Spain for some five hundred years after the Arab conquest of 712, or Hungary for almost two hundred after the Turkish conquest of 1526, Russia for nearly three hundred years was detached from the Christian world. Or more exactly, Kievan Rus after 1240 was partitioned between its western lands in present-day Ukraine and Belarus, which were absorbed into the Polish-Lithuanian Commonwealth, and Muscovy, which alone experienced the "Tatar yoke." Yet, unlike Spain or Hungary, Muscovy was not occupied or colonized; and, contrary to widespread opinion, no Mongol institutions were implanted there. Muscovite institutions remained essentially the prince and his comitatus of boyars (*druzhina*), which until the late fifteenth century functioned under a contractual regime of what may be fairly called incipient feudalism.[10]

THE WESTERN TAKEOFF

It was in the heartland of Latin Christendom, relatively secure after 1000 under the protection of consolidated feudalism, that historic Europe first developed its enduring dynamism.[11] The process began with an agricultural revolution, a transformation that rested on the technology of the deep plow, on the horse collar to put the nobles' mount to the baser use of drawing that plow, and on the three-field-system of cultivation.[12] By 1300, this revolution had made transalpine Europe richer and more populous than the Mediterranean world of antiquity had ever been. It also ended serfdom, an institution that had first emerged in Europe in the late Roman period, under Diocletian and Constantine. With this new wealth, commerce revived and manufactures appeared. From the Mediterranean to the North Sea, towns grew both in number and in size, even along the Baltic shore as far as Russian Novgorod.

With the feudal organization of power and an expanding economy, the conditions were created for the building of a strong institutional framework for Latin Christendom. It emerged from the top down, through a radical reform in what had been the weaker half of the Carolingian system, the monastic and papal church, thereby giving medieval Europe the closest thing it ever had to a single "government." The properly religious aspect of this transformation will be examined shortly. For the moment, it is sufficient to sketch a part of its impact on society at large.

In exercising its leadership of society, this pan-European theocracy sponsored a revival of higher learning. It developed a sophisticated legal system based on the revival of Roman law, and professionalized church administration. Moreover, many of the achievements of this ecclesiastical government, as well as the trained clerics it produced, were employed by the nascent monarchies of England and France to give their realms an order higher than that of raw feudalism.[13]

The twelfth and thirteenth centuries were the period of consolidation and flowering of this first Europe. The traces of its institutions are still present in the representative assemblies and the legal systems of the major European states, as they are in the organization and philosophical vocabulary of its universities. Its material work is still visible in the limestone Romanesque and gothic churches of Europe's villages, often cleared from the forest in the wake of the year 1000; and it can be seen in the irregular street patterns and soaring cathedrals of its cities. The same work is present, though more feebly, in the brick gothic churches of Hanseatic cities from Lübeck to Tallinn. Even in remote Muscovy, the contemporary landscape was given enduring focus by the twelfth-century stone churches of Byzantine derivation.

THE EASTWARD GRADIENT

The original Europe of the year 1000 did not remain fixed in its exiguous Carolingian heartland, nor did it develop as a uniform bloc. It underwent a process of constant expansion and mutation, which by 1300 had doubled its size and diversified its internal composition. In 1066 a ready-made, mature feudalism, together with a closer subordination to papal Rome, was exported by conquest to England. Slightly later, other Norman barons detached southern Italy from the Byzantines and Sicily from the Saracens. In the same years, the *Reconquista* of Iberia commenced its two-century course, aided by contingents of Frankish knights. And the most spectacular, if also the most ephemeral, aspect of this expansion, was of course the Crusades.

At the same time, German colonization crossed the old Carolingian frontier along the Elbe and Saale rivers, the Bohemian forest, and the Inn (roughly where the Iron Curtain descended in 1945). Indeed, it was this pressure that led the barbarian kingdoms of the West Slavs to embrace Roman Christianity, in large part to acquire a protective legitimacy against the German empire. By 1300 this *Drang nach Osten* had passed the Oder and reached the Vistula; and it had descended the Danube to Vienna. Its furthest advance, the work of crusading knights, came along the Baltic coast from East Prussia to the present Baltic states. In part, this colonization displaced an earlier Slavic population. In greater part, however, its challenge stimulated Bohemia, the vast Polish-Lithuanian Commonwealth, and the sprawling Hungarian kingdom to meet the threat of the farther West by adopting its ways. First came feudal forms of political organization, then urban communes, and by the fourteenth century, universities.[14]

There thus emerged a second Europe, as it has at times been called, east of the Elbe and the Julian Alps.[15] In this semi-frontier zone, everything was poorer and less dynamic than in the Carolingian heartland and England: the three-field system appeared approximately two centuries later; imported feudal institutions were more rudimentary; towns were rarer and smaller; and their gothic was not in limestone but in brick. Moreover, by the late fifteenth century this second, trans-Elbean Europe was becoming a source of grain, minerals, and raw materials for the more developed Atlantic West. This profitable but dependent economic relationship led the local lords to enserf or re-enserf their peasantry, a "second serfdom" that moved society in the opposite direction from the first Europe, and which would last until the early nineteenth century.

From the thirteenth century onward, therefore, it is appropriate to speak of what recent German historiography has called a "West-East cultural gradient," a declivity of development separating an advanced from a backward Europe, and dividing the continent between leader and follower regions. This division, however, does not coincide with the divide between Latin Christendom and the Orthodox East; it exists within Latin Christendom itself. This circumstance would later govern what the same German historiography, in reflecting on the twentieth-century disaster, has called their nation's *Sonderweg*, its "special path," to modernity. Indeed, over the *longue durée* of historic Europe, the most decisive divide on this gradient can be seen to cut through Germany itself at the Elbe. And from that line the declivity, in a succession of further *Sonderwege*, extends eastward to the Urals.

Let us anticipate for a moment the long-term evolution of this second Europe: First, there were the German military marches of Markbrandenburg in the north and the Ostmark of the Danube, which in the seventeenth century became the foundation stones of modern Prussian and Austrian power. Beyond these marcher states, there were the Bohemian, Hungarian, and Polish kingdoms, which at different moments between the fourteenth and the sixteenth centuries lived their golden ages as independent nations. Yet in all three, in contrast to the evolution of the Plantagenet and Capetian realms, the nobility constantly developed in power at the monarchy's expense. So when the seventeenth century brought a decisive test of national strength, one after another the Central European kingdoms were extinguished by Ottoman Turkey, by Habsburg Vienna, and the last of them, Poland, by Hohenzollern Prussia and Romanov Russia together.

For by the time, on the eve of 1500, that Muscovy ended its long absence from Europe by shaking off the last remnants of the "Tatar yoke," it too had become a marcher state about to launch a grand career. It did so, however, with the greatest economic handicap in Europe: its naturally poor soil had been adapted to the three-field system only in the second half of the fifteenth century, or four hundred years later than in France and England. Concurrently, two centuries of warfare with the steppe nomads had permitted the Grand Prince to largely free himself from dependence on the hereditary boyar nobility, and to replace it with a gentry (*sluzhilye liudi; dvorianstvo*) holding its lands on condition of military service. The whole of this structure was now undergirded with peasant serfdom, thereby bringing Muscovy's social structure into line with the second serfdom of the second Europe. And Russian serfdom was destined to endure even farther into the nineteenth century than that of its neighbors. Still, elements of contract did not disappear entirely in this burgeoning Muscovite autocracy. Until the mid-seventeenth century, an "Assembly of All the Land," the Zemskii Sobor, functioned as a kind of embryonic system of estates, at the same time more elaborate representative bodies flourished in the west and center of the continent.

So by the end of the fifteenth century it turned out that there were in fact three Europes. There was the original Europe of the Atlantic West, which was about to spearhead Christendom's second great expansion, this time across the Atlantic and around the world. There was the second Europe of trans-Elbean Germany, Bohemia, Hungary, and Poland. And there was the candidate Europe of Muscovy, still harassed by steppe nomads, but from the time of Ivan IV (the Terrible) onward, seeking to break through to the Baltic and into Poland-Lithuania. And under Peter I, this candidate at last effected its breakthrough in both areas to become one of the five great powers of modern Europe. Thereby, too, trans-Elbean Europe received the configuration it would keep until World War I: three dynastic empires, organized as Old Regimes, astride the three defunct Central European national monarchies.

EUROPE'S CONSERVATIVE FOUNDATION

Throughout this process of trans-Elbean homogenization, however, the center of dynamism of the entire European system remained within the first Europe of the farther West. As of the fifteenth century—the eve of Latin Christendom's overseas expansion and of its own internal splintering—what was the ethos of this world?

Officially, the new Europe subscribed to a thoroughly static vision of life according to which all legitimacy came from above, from God and the timeless natural order. On this earth, therefore, human existence was founded on superordinate authority and a hierarchical structuring of society entailing mankind's division into interdependent, corporate strata. However, as we shall see more clearly in a moment, a sense of individuality was not lacking in this world: the feudal cult of personal honor and right afforded a potent stimulus to individualism. Nevertheless, society was not organized around this value as its supreme principle, as is the modern world. Old Europe rather was what later sociology would call an organic *Gemeinschaft*, or community, not the atomistic *Gesellschaft*, or individualistic society, that characterizes modernity. Man did not make his world; the world rather made him what he was, a member of an "estate"—either of those who pray, or of those who fight, or of those who humbly toil. For everything in this fallen world was ordered to serve the purpose of the God who made it, and to work the redemption of those who served him.

In medieval Europe, therefore, there was no such thing as politics in either the ancient or the modern sense of that term: an organized and legal competition for power. Nor was there a notion of reform through legislative action by the established authorities: according to the reigning dictum of the age, "the law is found, not made." The world was thus viewed as unchanging; and all men were seen as fixed for life in their stations of the social hierarchy, for such was the divine will. In such a world, obviously, revolution had no place. It was, indeed, tantamount to blasphemy. In the frequently quoted words of Saint Paul: "Let every soul be subject unto the higher powers. For there is no power but of God: the powers that be are ordained of God. Whosoever therefore resisteth the power, resisteth the ordinance of God; and they that resist shall receive to themselves damnation."[16]

Our problem here, then, is how in such a static world as was medieval Europe justifications for radical change could emerge and eventually achieve a measure of legitimacy. The answer is to be found in the internal contradictions of the two mainstays of medieval society, feudalism in the secular sphere and the Roman Catholic Church in the spiritual domain. For the conflicting forces latent in these two institutions go far to explain the West's historical uniqueness and its resulting propensity for periodic revolution.

THE FEUDAL DYNAMIC

Beginning with the terrestrial base—feudalism—we again encounter a terminological loose cannon that needs to be bolted down in proper historical place. In common parlance "feudal" now carries the Marxist meaning of a lord-peasant agrarian economy or, in other terms, the manorial system. Marx used "feudal" in this sense because of the legacy of the French Revolution. Seventeen-eighty-nine had abolished what it called "feudal dues," which indeed had their origins in the Middle Ages, but which by the eighteenth century meant simply manorial dues, such as the fees peasants owed a seigneur for the use of his mill, and so on. Marx then gave this limited meaning of feudal the generalizing suffix "-ism" to designate the entire pre-revolutionary political and social system—something that is more accurately described by another post-revolutionary term, Old Regime. By extension—or rather dilution—under the influence of modernization theory Marx's feudalism has come to mean "traditional" as opposed to "modern" society; in other words, agricultural as opposed to industrial society. And in this meaning anything from Saudi Arabia to Manchu China becomes "feudal"—a usage so baggy as to make the term sociologically useless.

The only way to clear up this conceptual confusion is to take the historical path back to the word's origins. As the eighteenth-century gentlemen who abolished feudal dues well knew, feudal comes from fief, and *féodalité* therefore means the lord-vassal relations dominant in medieval Europe—a system, as Tocqueville pointed out, that was in its prime from the eleventh century until the beginnings of royal centralization in the thirteenth, and which took the next five centuries to decline. This is the meaning of feudalism for medievalists, and it is the one that will be used here.

Feudalism in this sense, of course, presupposes the manorial system, and the subordination of the peasant serf to the noble lord. But it is not synonymous with that system. For one or another variant of the manorial system has existed in such diverse societies as the absolutist empire of Diocletian and Constantine, the Russian autocracy of Peter I and Catherine II, and in the latifundia system of Mexico under Porfirio Díaz from which emerged the peasant rebel Zapata. However, feudalism in its proper, medieval sense refers only to the military, judicial, and political relationship of lord to vassal. This relationship, moreover, is a bilateral contract between two free men, a mutual agreement under which the lord grants protection and a fief of land (with its attached peasants) to another mounted warrior in exchange for his knight service under stipulated conditions of time and place. Moreover, if the lord violates his part of the contract, the vassal has a right to revolt, including transferring allegiance to another lord. In the words of one statute: "A man can resist his king or his judge when the latter acts against the law [or his right] and can even help in making war against him. . . . Thereby he does not violate his duty of fealty."[17] Be it also noted that in medieval usage "law" and "right" were designated by the same term, *droit*.

The question, then, is whether feudalism in this sense is unique to Europe. Clearly, similar arrangements have existed elsewhere and in different periods of history, from Byzantium and India to parts of Africa. But the key case is medieval Japan, where masters granted lands and serfs to samurai in exchange for military service very much in the European manner. In Japan, however, the obligation binding vassal to lord was unilateral, with no right of legitimate resistance.[18]

This difference would have momentous political consequences, for feudalism's right of resistance is the source of later Western political rights. To take only the best known example: England's Magna Carta of 1215 was not a bill of rights in the modern sense, as is often supposed; it was a feudal contract between the king and his barons, extorted by the vassals' collective resistance to the suzerain's violation of their rights. It was not a new contract, therefore, but a detailed spelling out of the reciprocal obligations that had always been understood to exist between king and barons. By the same token, it was not a charter for the monarch's other subjects—base peasant *villeins*, or even townsmen—but an elucidation of relationships pertinent only to noble society. A century or two later, similar collective extensions of contractual relations would produce elected representative institutions, the ancestors of modern parliaments—arrangements unknown in antiquity or, until the twentieth century, in Asian societies.

As the political dynamic of feudalism has been expressed by its most authoritative twentieth-century historian, Marc Bloch:

> Vassal homage was a genuine contract and a bilateral one. If the lord failed to fulfill his engagements he lost his rights. Transferred, as was inevitable, to the political sphere—since the principal subjects of the king were at the same time his vassals—this idea was to have a far-reaching influence, all the more so because on this ground it was reinforced by the very ancient notions which held the king responsible in a mystical way for the welfare of his subjects and deserving of punishment in the event of public calamity. These old currents happened to unite on this point with another stream of thought which arose in the Church out of the Gregorian protest against the myth of sacred and supernatural kingship. It was the writers of this clerical group who first expressed,

with a force long unequalled, the notion of a contract binding the sovereign to his people—"like the swineherd to the master who employs him," wrote an Alsatian monk about 1080.[19]

Again making the comparison with Japan, Bloch continues with the observation that the emperor, unlike European kings, was a divine being who "remained outside the structure of vassal engagements" and hence was eternally intangible to his subjects.

Feudalism, then, despite the violence and disorder of the time, as well as of the oppression of the servile poor, brought to medieval Europe a fragmentation of *all* power. It thereby placed strong limits on the ecumenical pretensions of both empire and papacy; eventually it also worked against the centralizing ambitions of the proto-national territorial monarchies. So, by the time its last vestiges were swept away in 1789, its sense of particular rights had contributed in no small measure to the newly proclaimed universal Rights of Man.

THE COMMUNAL DYNAMIC

Similarly, feudal relationships encapsulated the revived urban economy. Slowly emerging in the course of the eleventh century along the trade routes between Northern Italy and Flanders, by 1300 these new towns had become richer than the cities of antiquity. Moreover, they were organized quite differently. The *polis* or *civitas*, at least before the Roman imperium, were not just commercial centers. They were territorial city-states, essentially agricultural at the beginning —as was the case of Sparta—and only later becoming predominantly commercial—as exemplified by Athens. Under the Roman empire, at least in the West, they came increasingly to be administrative centers.

Medieval cities, by contrast, were primarily trading, even industrial centers; moreover, the level of technological and commercial sophistication of such cloth manufacturing and banking centers as Florence or Bruges was quite beyond the level of ancient Athens. To be sure, when these new centers developed around an old Roman civitas, they were also the diocesan seat of a bishop; in this case, the episcopal *cité* was surrounded by a *bourg* of merchants and artisans whose burgers, or bourgeois, would eventually wrest from their ecclesiastical overlord a charter incorporating them as a commune, in one of those class struggles recounted by Guizot.

Such relative independence, however, did not make these centers, even when they ruled the surrounding countryside as in much of Northern Italy, any the less subject to some feudal suzerain, if only one as remote as the emperor or the pope. Similarly, within the city walls, the artisan guilds and merchant associations, the patricians and commoners, were all organized as corporate bodies with collective rights and obligations. So too, the scholars in the bishop's cathedral school were chartered as an *universitas*, still another word for corporation.

In other words, even the "free" enclaves of the new bourgeoisie were in many respects subunits of the ambient feudal world. So the "class struggle" between the burgers and their overlord outside the walls—and within the walls of the commune itself between patricians and commoners, or masters and journeymen—were inevitably framed in the feudal language of corporate rights. Hence in medieval society "liberty" was not used in the singular, to denote an abstract universal; it was always used in the plural, to describe the concrete, contractual "liberties" of the various units of the feudal world. And liberties, or rights, in this sense were also unknown to the democracy of Pericles.

Yet the upstart urban communes, though integrated into the feudal world in one sense, in some basic ways always remained alien. In the long run, as both Guizot and Marx recognized, they were the most dynamic element in the medieval world because the form of wealth they represented was capable of generating economic and political power far beyond that of manorial land-holding. But in the short run the very fact of their wealth created for them, and for the world around them, an acute moral problem. As the Gospels taught, wealth of any kind was suspect; in particular, wealth gained not through productive labor but through the usurious practice of lending for interest was so sinful as to merit damnation. Material goods, and especially their abstract embodiment—money —represented the kingdom of Mammon; and man cannot serve both God and Mammon. Until well into the sixteenth century, therefore, Europe was thus torn between its increasing talent for creating wealth and its enduring conviction that the kingdom of God is not of this world. This conflict, moreover, was at its most acute when Christ's mystical body on earth, the church, was itself caught in the snares of Mammon.

THE RELIGIOUS DYNAMIC

To turn, then, to the development of medieval society's spiritual base—the church—it must be emphasized that its role cannot be grasped primarily in institutional terms. For the church's institutional organization, or ecclesiology, was in the first instance an expression of its theology; and we must take the tenets of this theology with the utmost seriousness if we are to understand its impact on the mundane world.[20]

The reigning modes of social science discourse, however, greatly complicate this task. First, the still important influence of Marxism relegates religion to the superstructure: a mere "ideology," an opiate of the people, serving to hoodwink the masses into resigned acceptance of their exploited state. Nor does culture fare much better at the hands of structural-functionalism: here religion is simply a "non-empirical belief system" providing "value-orientations" to lubricate the meshing structures of the social system.[21]

Taking again a cue from Weber: all religions are not the same, and their doctrinal content makes a great difference in their social impact. There are religions without transcendence, indeed without God, such as Confucianism, Buddhism, and Shintoism.[22] These are perhaps best described as what in the West has been called natural religion. Other religions, such as Hinduism, are archaic polytheisms converging in a universalistic substratum of being that is, however, not transcendent. This theology interacts with the caste system through its belief in the transmigration of souls, a doctrine that makes an individual's present status in life transitory and hence nonessential.[23] Then there are religions, such as those of the Aztecs and Maya of Mesoamerica, that require human sacrifice —clearly, a creed with very particular social consequences. And finally, there are the Near-Eastern monotheisms, Judaism, Christianity, and Islam, which are considered by such different but historically minded philosophers as Hegel and Comte to be the highest form of spirituality because of their commitment to an abstract, transcendent, and almighty God.

Beyond this core belief, however, the three diverge notably in their doctrines, institutions, and cultic practices. To take only the matter of the clergy: rabbis are teachers, the ulema are exegetes of the Koran, and priests are ministrants of sacraments believed to bring individual redemption and eternal salvation to the faithful. In short, priests are sacerdotal intermediaries between God and his people. Another difference is that Christian monotheism is also trinitarian, a trait that has at times led its rivals to consider it a crypto-polytheism. For Christians, however, the triune nature of God is the inescapable consequence of the fundamental dogma of their belief: the Incarnation of the divine *logos* in Jesus as the Son of God. And it is only on this basis that his Crucifixion and the Resurrection could work mankind's redemption. Since God, moreover, is with the church for all time, He exists also as the Holy Spirit, guiding and sustaining the "mystical body" of the believers until the Last Judgment.[24]

To the modern consciousness, this web of doctrines can easily appear abstruse to the point of meaninglessness—if indeed it is not regarded as a superstitious fantasy engendering intolerance and fratricidal strife within the human family. Of course, negative consequences of intransigent monotheism have not been lacking over the centuries. Yet these are not its only consequences, as even a

Michelin Guide tour of Gaul's surviving white robe of churches readily attests. The soaring vaults and the luminous windows of Chartres and the Sainte Chapelle are, in fact, theological declarations in stone and glass; and their message, as derived from the mystical writings of the pseudo-Dionysius by Abbot Suger, is that God is light, the source of being and the end to which mankind shall some day return.[25] Time would indeed show that such a world-view cannot be adequately expressed through a return to the Doric columns of Athena or to the Roman cupolas of Augustus—as is demonstrated by the rationalistic temples of eighteenth-century Paris, the Madeleine and the Pantheon—the latter now appropriately rededicated as a temple of the Republic.

However, in the present context, the most important contributions of Christian theology to European uniqueness are not artistic but ecclesiological. For this theology had secular reverberations which in modern language would be called political and social, but which, given their religious formulation, in fact operated in very unmodern ways. It is thus a mistake to say that the Investiture controversy was merely a struggle for political power or that heresy was really only social protest. Theology is not just an immature form of politics. It treats of matters of faith that concern the unavoidable but rationally unanswerable Big Questions of being and meaning.

The theological base of medieval civilization has perhaps best been formulated by a more wide-ranging sociologist of religion than Weber, his colleague, the Lutheran theologian and social critic Ernst Troeltsch:

> The historical God-Man, who unites in His own Person both natures, the human and the Divine, has founded the Church as a reflection of Himself, as a Divine-human organism. On account of its Divine character this organism must be absolutely uniform, and must dominate the natural realm, just as in the God-Man the Divine Nature dominates the human nature. Thus He stands out in the worship of the Church as the sacramental Christ, who, each time that the Sacrament is celebrated, operates afresh the union of the Divine and the human, making the sacrificing priest the one who effects this unity; thus also He comes to each individual through the vehicle of the Sacrament, through the senses and yet in a supersensual way, in order to place the natural under the direction of the Divine, and to impart the Divine in a marvelous manner to the natural and the material. The sacraments are the extension of the Incarnation, a repetition of the spiritual process through which Divine grace enters into human life.[26]

These doctrines alone, however, could not have generated in the Latin West the spiritual revival and the institutional exaltation of the Church produced by the

Gregorian reform of the mid-eleventh century. After all, these same doctrines were venerated in the Greek East. Yet it was precisely in the mid-eleventh century that Byzantium began its long decline leading to the Turkish conquest of Constantinople in 1453. Indeed, even in the more prosperous days of the Emperor Justinian in the sixth century, the Greek East never displayed a dynamism comparable to the Latin West's after the eleventh century.

The conventional explanation of these contrasting fates has been hinted at in the beginning of this chapter. To spell matters out more fully now, this explanation offers the paradox that in the East the empire was (unfortunately) strong enough to keep the barbarians out, and so saved itself to live a long stagnation; whereas in the West the empire (fortunately) succumbed to barbarian invasion, and so Latin Christendom had to discover a new path back to civilization. Specifically, in the East the church remained in the subordinate position in which Constantine and Justinian had placed it; whereas in the West the church was liberated from secular control, and so its spiritual power could replace the empire as society's paramount force. And this unprecedented primacy of transcendent purpose gave the fragmented West its first impetus toward devising a post-Roman order. Although this explanation is not the whole story, there is a lot to it. The origins of the Western sacerdotal imperium, and its internal contradictions, are as follows.

Under the Carolingians, the spiritual sword of the church was as subordinate to the secular sword of the empire as ever it was in Byzantium, for this "territorial Church," as it is known to scholarship, in fact served as the sole administrative apparatus available to the Frankish emperors. At the same time, since redemption came through the church, lay magnates endowed it with land in order to ensure their salvation. This situation of subordination worsened with the collapse of central authority; after 850, local feudal lords assumed control over church lands and appointments.

Yet one arm of the church, its Benedictine monasteries, retained a relative independence. One of these, Cluny, founded in 910, developed a network of reform abbeys and launched a reaction against feudal subordination of the spiritual to the temporal power. With the support of the Holy Roman emperor, in the mid-eleventh century the Cluniac monks captured the papacy for radical reform of the entire church. So the Gregorian Reform of 1040–1060 made an imperial papacy the effective center of Latin Christiandom, with the mission of christianizing all terrestrial life.

This ambition represented a reversal of previous patterns of church-state relations. Before Constantine, the church stood apart from, but was not hostile to, state power, in accordance with the biblical injunction to "render unto Caesar the things that are Caesar's and to God the things that are God's." After Constantine, the church remained separate from imperial power, which gave it protection while expecting in return subordination in secular matters. The church thus continued to have no mission to christianize the profane world. With the Carolingians, church and society became coterminous, though with the emperor supreme. With Gregory VII the roles were reversed: church and society were still one, but the spiritual power was now paramount. To the monastic clergy and the papacy, this was the only way the church could secure its independence from lay control and hence avoid corruption by the *saeculum*. Gibbon said that ancient Rome conquered the world in self-defense; papal Rome may likewise be said to have conquered feudal Europe in self-defense. Having done so, however, the church acquired the new mission of making that world holy, to effect as it were a social Incarnation of Christianity.

In consequence, the secular, or nonmonastic clergy, was now obliged to be celibate so as to disentangle it from worldly concerns of family, children, and the inheritance of wealth. The pope henceforth would be elected by a college of cardinals in order to avoid interference from the emperor and the Roman nobility. It was ever more strongly emphasized that the central sacrament of the Eucharist was Christ's living presence on earth and the prime conduit of the grace that brings salvation. The clergy therefore increasingly became a sacerdotal caste separate from and superior to the laity. Yet the laity too, in its own sphere, was elevated to a purer level: sexual love among them was now clearly declared to be the sacrament of marriage. And so, the central sacraments of baptism and the Eucharist were inserted in the broader doctrine of the Seven Sacraments, giving human beings support from birth until death. Even war, the professional pursuit of the feudal class, was given moral purpose by directing martial ardor into crusades against the infidels in the Holy Land and for the Reconquista of Iberia, as well as against internal heretics such as the Albigensians, and later the Hussites.

This reform was put through in militant fashion in the second half of the eleventh century by a succession of monks raised to the papacy, of whom the most important was Hildebrand or Gregory VII. The first step in reform was to take the investiture of episcopal insignia away from the emperor and return it to the church, a controversy by and large won by the papacy. The great symbol of this victory was the humiliation of the excommunicated Emperor Henry IV coming barefoot to the castle of Canossa to beg absolution from Gregory VII.

The full reality of papal power was manifested at the beginning of the thirteenth century under the lawyer pope, Innocent III, who regularly intervened in all of Europe's secular affairs. His weapons were the excommunication of individuals from the life-giving sacraments, and in extreme cases the "interdiction" of the sacraments in whole regions. Thus King John was forced to capitulate to the barons at Runnymede in part because Innocent III had placed England under interdict in order to annul the king's illegal interference in the election of a new archbishop of Canterbury.

A second part of the reform was a campaign to raise the level of the secular clergy, both priests and bishops, who often owed their appointments to feudal or imperial patronage. Thus the church fostered a succession of ever more puritanical and rigoristic monastic orders: Cistercians and Augustinian canons in the mid-twelfth century; and, in answer to the challenge of the new towns, the Dominicans and the Franciscans in the early thirteenth century. And so, until around 1270, the reform movement kept ahead of the rising tide of spiritual awakening and the demand for sacerdotal purity that the church's own efforts had instilled in society.

Still, from the very beginning of the Gregorian reform, the drive to root out laxity and corruption had a corrosive effect on the church itself. This began with Gregory's direct appeal to the laity to rise up against unworthy clergy who had bought their offices (the sin of simony) or who lived in luxury or concubinage. Such incitement, to what was in effect revolt, produced the most virulent response in the new towns of northern Italy and France, a dynamic milieu that especially resented the worldliness of a feudalized clergy. It was, therefore, through the Gregorian reform that heretical dissent from the church emerged for the first time since late antiquity.

In effect, Gregorian reformers' efforts to sanctify secular life meant bringing to lay society something approximating a monastic regimen. But this was to demand the impossible of ordinary believers; in the long run, it was demanding too much of themselves. For the austere zeal of the monastic reformers could hardly be maintained from one generation to another. Thus, when zeal abated the church's attempt to christianize the world had the unintended consequence of making the church itself more worldly.

In answer to the twelfth century's succession of monastic reform orders, successive waves of heresy unfolded. Their common characteristic was antisacerdotalism. Its basic principle was that unworthy priests cannot celebrate valid sacraments. The conclusions drawn from this varied from demanding a still more radical version of reform to dispensing with the clergy and the church altogether in favor of small groups of believers communing with God directly through the Gospels (the Patraria of Milan, the Waldensians or Poor Men of Lyons, the Cathars of Albi).

The movement of religious dissent, moreover, soon overlapped with the twelfth-century communal revolts. This symbiosis is most strikingly exemplified in the mid-century by Arnold of Brescia, cathedral canon (that is, a cleric), intellectual versed in the new scholasticism, and townsman. His troubles with ecclesiastical authority eventually led him to be assigned penance in Rome. His program there was described by a contemporary:

> He [Arnold] himself was frequently heard on the [Roman] Capitol and in public gatherings. He had already publicly denounced the cardinals, saying that their college, by its pride, avarice, hypocrisy and manifold shame was not the church of God, but a place of business and den of thieves, which took the place of the scribes and Pharisees amongst Christian peoples. The pope himself was not what he professed to be—an apostolic man and shepherd of souls—but a man of blood who maintained his authority by fire and sword, a tormentor of churches and oppressor of the innocent, who did nothing in the world save gratify his lust and empty other men's coffers to fill his own.[27]

Thus far his denunciation of clerical dereliction was orthodox; indeed, it was quite similar to the contemporary message of Saint Bernard. But Arnold then drew a radical new, political conclusion from that message. The pope, he said, was: "so far from apostolic that he imitated neither the life nor the doctrine of the apostles, wherefore neither obedience nor reverence was due him: and in any case no man could be admitted who wished to impose a yoke of servitude on Rome, the seat of the Empire, fountain of liberty and mistress of the world." [28] In other words, Arnold was urging the communal revolt that had at last broken out in the backward city of Rome to expel the pope and to establish the democratic rule of the people. This he in fact proceeded to do, thereby demonstrating that sedition in the church eventually led to subversion of feudal and hierarchical society as well. Since neither clerical nor lay society, sacerdotium nor imperium, could brook such a challenge, Arnold was defeated by a coalition of the pope, the emperor, and the Roman aristocracy. The Roman commune was suppressed and its leader executed.

THE JOACHIMITE REVOLUTION IN TIME

It was from the purists among the successive orders of reforming monks that the great tradition of millenarian heresy derived. Here the pivotal case is the prophecies of the Cistercian abbot Joachim of Fiore and his theory of the triadic movement of history: the Ages of the Father, the Son, and the Holy Spirit.

The Greco-Roman conception of time had been cyclical, an eternal return— history is not going anywhere. The ancient Hebrews had a linear or progressive conception of time, as measured by God's successive revelations to his people. They also developed an apocalyptic variant of this view, anticipating the arrival of the Messiah and the end of the world. The early Christians took over and adapted both of these concepts. By and large they believed that the end of time was near, and Christianity had appeared to announce it. When the world did not end, Christianity had to adapt to living in it, and the apocalyptic or millenarian version of time was put on the backburner by such theologians as Eusebius of Caesarea, who in fact argued for the providentiality of the Roman Empire, and above all Augustine. For the latter, the Incarnation represents the culmination of God's revelation in history. There is thus no further historical movement, but only the enduring church.

Joachim of Fiore, at the end of the twelfth century, reversed the concept of historical time that had been orthodox since Augustine.[29] The Incarnation was no longer the culmination of God's action in history; it was just the culmination of one stage of revelation and the beginning of a new stage, that of the Spirit. He reinterpreted the Revelation of Saint John to yield the main line of European millenarianism. His view was that the church had grown so corrupt that the end of time was nigh. In fact, throughout the twelfth century the condition of the church had been steadily improving, and the emergence of Joachim's Cistercian order is a major sign of this. But this improvement simply raised the standards of what was acceptable and normal (relative deprivation). Joachim, however, was not a democratic millenarian. The reign of the Holy Spirit was simply to bring a new reform order of monks, and this new reform would be the millennium. He was no revolutionary, or in any sense a heretic. Saint Bernard and Saint Francis and Saint Dominic all thought that a new reform order was necessary.

There is, however, a big difference between Joachim himself and the Joachite tradition after his death, when it indeed became revolutionary. This tradition, begun in 1270 with the Spiritual Franciscans, came to maturity a century later in reaction against the Babylonian Captivity of the papacy at Avignon. In this new form, Joachimism meant that the church and the world had become so wicked that the Last Days prophesized in the Revelation of Saint John were at hand. In the approaching apocalypse, that "saving remnant" of believers, who had remained true to the Bible and to the poverty it commands, would at last come to live the marvelous events prophesied in the Revelation of Saint John.

This tradition would play a major role in European dissent down to and into the German Reformation. It was transmitted to Lessing, Kant, and Schelling. It would endure in Württemberg until the time of Hegel, from whom it was of course transmitted to Marx. It was taken up by Michelet to explain the French Revolution. The first stop on this long itinerary was Czech Bohemia in the early fifteenth century, where for the first time Europe would witness a successful Arnold of Brescia. The following chapter is devoted to those events.

SUMMATION AND A LOOK AHEAD

In its main outlines, the structure behind the medieval ethos of an unchanging, hierarchical world survived until 1789. The ethos itself, however, was progressively eroded after 1300 through a process in which the principles of feudal and Christian Europe undermined the institutions designed to embody them in practice. First, the feudal organization of power, which in the twelfth and thirteenth centuries had fostered society's development, in the crisis-wracked fourteenth and fifteenth centuries became a source of internecine strife: the Hundred Years' War, and its attendant economic "Great Depression," is the prime instance of this crisis. And the result was to throw the balance of political power to the central monarchies, which in the process of policing their still loosely governed realms gave to the estates, or orders, of the feudal hierarchy the constitutional form of elected, representative assemblies. Second, the efforts of the church to christianize the world ultimately had the perverse effect of making the church worldly. The Babylonian Captivity of the Avignonese papacy and the Great Schism are the prime instance of this crisis. And the result was a succession of heresies, from the Cathars to the Hussites, directed toward achieving salvation outside established sacerdotal and sacramental structures.

And so the way was prepared for the Renaissance and then the Reformation of the sixteenth century. Both were intended to renew Christendom, but both ultimately furthered its secularization. The Renaissance did so directly by recovering the non-Christian culture of classical antiquity; the Reformation did so indirectly by unintentionally dividing the single Christendom it sought to purify. By the close of the seventeenth century, it was clear that the religious unity of Christendom could not be restored, thereby casting doubt on religious truth of whatever variety.

Into this breach moved the most momentous innovative force of all, the seventeenth-century scientific revolution. Although not intended by its authors as an anti-religious enterprise, and though it had been partially fostered by the church's scholasticism, it nonetheless offered a source of truth that was radically new: it was incontrovertible as far as human experience ranged; it owed nothing to divine revelation; and it derived everything from natural reason and empirical verification. Here was an alternative culture to that of Christianity and of the classical heritage both, and the warrant therefore for devising a rational science of man and society, by which man could make his *own* world.

This high cultural change coincided with the more mundane force of the seventeenth-century military revolution, which transformed traditional, residually feudal monarchy into centralized absolutism, a system called after 1789 the Old Regime.[30] With a technology and a mobilization of manpower that consumed 80 to 90 percent of any monarch's revenue, royal governments everywhere abolished, or tried to abolish, traditional estates in order to tax the population through their own agents. Concurrently, military absolutism utilized the new science and its accompanying philosophical rationalism to promote a more coherent statecraft, a "policed" or orderly society, and an improved economy. It is this military absolutism, in conjunction with the new science, that gave a single secular culture to the unitary state-system that by the eighteenth century extended from the Atlantic to the Urals.

And so, between the upper millstone of the new science and the nether millstone of royal absolutism, the Age of Enlightenment ground to powder the ethos of old Europe, whether in its Catholic, Protestant, or Orthodox variant. It was only a question of time before the new rationalism would challenge divinely sanctioned royal absolutism and its residual feudal underpinnings. Thus, the way was prepared for the advent, in 1789, of what Tocqueville later called democracy. With 1789 the basic unit of society became the individual as citizen, and equality among citizens became the foundation of politics. Or at least this was so in the first Europe west of the Rhine. In the Sonderwege of the second and third Europe, however, semi-Old Regimes would last until 1917–1918.

Part I

REVOLUTION AS RELIGIOUS HERESY

2

HUSSITE BOHEMIA, 1415–1436

From Heresy to Proto-Revolution

When it was the year one thousand four hundred and ten after the birth of the Son of God, there arose Master John Hus, and he began to preach, and to castigate the people for their sinful life. And the clergymen praised him very highly, and they said that the Spirit of God Himself spoke through the Master's mouth. But then he began to preach also against the sinfulness of the clergy, sparing neither the Pope on his throne nor the lowliest priest, and he preached against their haughtiness and their greed, against simony and concubinage, and he said that priests should not wield worldly power nor worldly estates, and he also preached that in the Holy Communion the Body of Christ and also the Blood of Christ should both be given to the common people. And now the clergy grew furious against him, and they said the Devil himself entered into him and that he was a heretic. And this came to pass in the Kingdom of Bohemia, when Wenceslas, son of the Emperor Charles, was King, and the priest Zbynek was Archbishop in Prague.
—*The Very Pretty Chronicle of John Žižka, Servant of King Wenceslas,* 1436

John Hus was [in Constance] to remind men that the doctrine of brotherhood was of indestructible essence; that, even though adulterated by the Church, it had been . . . preserved by heresy; that even amid the greatest darkness it could always be found somewhere in Europe, off to the side, burning like a lamp stowed away and immortal. . . . Hus continued all those who, in theological terms, had appealed . . . from the Church to the Gospel, from the pope to Jesus [he] continued . . . the massacred Albigensians, the Waldensians threatened with extermination . . . the Englishman Wyclif.

In the constitution of true Christianity, to take communion . . . was to make a profession of equality. By communion, the Christians gathered together in God; they recognized each other as brothers. It was therefore necessary, if the symbol were to correspond to the idea, that communion be accomplished by all in the same manner. . . . By keeping for themselves the exclusive privilege of communion in both kinds, the priests set themselves apart from the rest of the faithful; they made God himself bear witness to the legitimacy of castes; they violated social equality in its most exalted form: religion.
—LOUIS BLANC, *History of the French Revolution,* 1847

> What happened among the Czech rank and file was the millenarian reaction that
> the passing of the [universal] Church [at the Council of Constance] into the hands
> of the enemy was an unmistakable prophetic sign of the impending second coming
> of Christ. Under that great shadow it behooved the friends of God to fuse their
> separate selves in the perfect brotherhood which required the abolition of mine
> and thine and of universal community; and to exterminate with the sword of
> righteousness all who stood in their way. The Czech did not need to invent these
> ideas, since the moral system of medieval Christianity was guaranteed to inspire
> them from time to time.
> —JOHN BOSSY, *Christianity in the West, 1400–1700*

It was the Hussites of early fifteenth-century Bohemia that for the first time crossed the line from religious dissent to political and social upheaval. Why then not call their revolt a full-fledged revolution, without the qualification "proto"? After all, the established church was subverted, the monarchy was suspended in favor of rule by elected estates, and the social hierarchy was half turned on its head. And many books on the subject speak straightforwardly of the "Hussite Revolution."

One of the best of them, however, adds the subtitle "a historical anomaly," as if to say this revolution came into the world out of the proper time for such an event. But this is only partially true.[1] The very fact the revolt occurred demonstrates that medieval society was already capable of anticipating its own dissolution. The Hussite movement is thus best understood as the first round of a protracted European revolutionary process, the initial stage in its long escalation to full self-awareness in the watershed of 1776–1789.

But this was only the first stage; for the Czech "revolutionaries" of 1415–1436 were quite unaware of innovating in any way. All their political and social aims were expressed in religious categories, as these had been defined, both by the church itself and by dissenting heretics, since the Gregorian Reform of the eleventh century. Their goal lay not in any radiant future, but in a *renovatio* of those eternal verities expressed by the doctrine of the two swords in religion and of the three orders in society. Thus the Hussites produced no new concepts, whether religious or political, no corpus of doctrine or treatise comparable in originality to those of such later religious revolutionaries as Luther and Calvin. Similarly, even though they turned Bohemia upside down for twenty years, when the dust settled the realm had not broken out of the medieval Catholic and feudal mold, the way the German Reformation and the Dutch revolt would do in the next century. The Hussite overturn left no legacy or legend to the rest of Europe: for centuries it remained in the consciousness of Christendom largely as a "heresy" that was eventually defeated.

A DIVERSE HISTORIOGRAPHY

The Hussites were first discovered for modernity, not primarily in their own medieval and religious terms, but anachronistically as precursors of nineteenth-century Czech national resistance to the Germans. This was the work above all of František Palacký, who published his *Geschichte von Böhmen* in five volumes between 1836 and 1867, an opus rendered into Czech after 1848, and which also made the point that the Hussites were forerunners of the sixteenth-century Reformation.[2] At the same time the radical wing of the Hussites, the Taborites, were discovered by early socialists (as indicated by the above epigraph from Louis Blanc), the same way that the German Peasant Revolt of 1525 was then being popularized and annexed by Engels. Under the influence of the Saint Simonian Pierre Leroux, in 1842 George Sand even presented a somewhat mystical version of the Hussite cause in her best-selling novel *Consuelo*.[3] In the late nineteenth century this romanticism gave way to the more realistic positivism of Jaroslav Goll and Josef Pekař, whose works, though still emphasizing nationalism, showed a better sense of Hussitism's medieval character.[4]

But the decisive break in the historiography of the Hussite movement came with the imposition of Communism after World War II. The official Marxism of the day of course made it necessary to see Hussite radicalism as an antecedent of Communism, a dubious claim that nonetheless opened the way to exploring the social history of the movement. This in turn led to emphasizing its chiliasm, and hence also its links to medieval heresy generally; the Czechs' national story was thus being integrated into general European history. These new perspectives have found their way into English with the work of František Bartoš.[5] Yet even more prominent as an exponent of the view that the Hussite movement must be understood as an early European revolution is the already mentioned Šmahel. His views are fortunately available in several languages.[6]

By the second decade after the war the Hussite movement was no longer a strictly Czech affair, however. In 1967, to some older work in English,[7] Howard Kaminsky added a major study, *A History of the Hussite Revolution*,[8] which explored in detail the movement's chiliastic phase and its culmination in Tabor, that is between 1415 and 1424. A decade later John Klassen introduced Czech nobility into the picture, again facilitating integration of Hussitism into general European history.[9] Finally, at the century's end the Hussites were given a rousing hurrah by Thomas Fudge in *The Magnificent Ride: The First Reformation in Hussite Bohemia*.[10] Of course, the Czech Republic is now a member of the European Union.

THE PRESENT APPROACH

This European and revolutionary perspective is followed here. Indeed, this chapter argues that in the Hussite movement, for the first time, the basic scenario of European revolution down to 1789 was played out. It should be recalled that this pattern was not presented earlier, on the grounds that pulling explanatory "models" out of thin air at the start of an investigation is artificial; such models can be derived only from the imperatives of explaining concrete cases. Now that the problem of defining the Hussite upheaval is upon us, it is time to set forth our understanding of the basic pattern of revolutionary action. The present chapter builds a preliminary description of the pattern of European revolutions taken individually. Subsequent chapters will then compare that preliminary pattern with later cases in order to discover what is particular to each and what is common to all. By degrees, therefore, the second part of our model of European revolutions will emerge: namely, the overall pattern of their escalation, as each overturn learns from, builds on, or rejects its predecessors.

This chapter begins with a plain narrative of the Hussite story, a classical approach that has been chosen for two reasons. The first is that the fourteenth-century crisis in a "far-off country, of which we know little" (as the British prime minister opined in 1938), is no doubt less familiar than events examined later in this study. A second and more important reason is that a blow-by-blow unfolding is the way history appears to those who are living it at the time. Viewing it as much as possible without foresight, therefore, can help us understand how Europe stumbled into its first, unanticipated approximation of revolution.

Altogether, this revolutionary experience lasted twenty-four years, from Hus's excommunication in 1412 to the defeat of the Hussite radicals, the Taborites, in 1436. But the great crisis of the movement, the moment it became overtly revolutionary, occurred in some fifteen months in 1419–1420, from the first Defenestration of Prague to the city's deliverance by Jan Žižka's Taborites. From that event to his death in 1424 the movement conquered Bohemia and radicalized both its political and ecclesiastical structures. Thus, overall, the active revolution lasted six years, from 1419 to 1424, or roughly the same length of time as the incandescent years of the French Revolution, and almost as long as the nine years of the active Puritan Revolution. Then followed twelve years of militant and largely military government, until a belated Thermidor unseated the radicals in 1436 — a period that more resembles Cromwell's dictatorship than the unstable Directory and Consulate in France.

In short, the scenario of the Hussite proto-revolution, though not a perfect fit with any later case, is still close enough to begin to trace a pattern. Where appropriate, therefore, the following narrative introduces comparisons with well-known episodes from later revolutions in order to limn the contours of European revolutions generally. Once these contours have been established it will be possible, at the end of the chapter, to indulge in more explicit model building.

THE CRISIS OF "OLD REGIME" BOHEMIA

Late medieval Bohemia was the most advanced region in that "second Europe" described in the previous chapter; or, to put it the other way around, it was the avant-garde of the backward, frontier zone of Christendom. As we have seen, it joined Europe only in the second wave of barbarian conversions, together with Hungary, Poland, and Scandinavia, in the class of 1000. After the Carolingian Franks had converted the other Germans, in significant part by conquest, Germany as a whole proceeded to exert similar military pressure on the Slavs and Scandinavians. So their native princes preemptively adopted Christianity and sought a royal title, preferably from the pope rather than the emperor, to protect themselves from conquest and colonization by the Germans. Thus in 973, Prague, which hitherto had been under the jurisdiction of the bishop of Regensburg, became an episcopal see in its own right, though still dependent on the archbishopric of Mainz; and the Přemyslid duke of Bohemia, in 1158, received the title of king under the suzerainty of the empire.

This imperial connection would eventually lead to Bohemia's brief "golden age" in the mid-fourteenth century. Already by the thirteenth century, internal colonization and the three-field system in agriculture had brought Bohemia near to the Western level of rural development. Western-type feudal relationships had been introduced among the nobility. Towns with merchants and artisans with a communal organization had been implanted. All these developments had been fostered by immigration from the more developed German lands—a pattern of Westernization by colonization repeated in Poland and Hungary.

At the beginning of the fourteenth century the crown went by marriage to the House of Luxembourg, which at the time also held the throne of the empire. The new king, and later his son Charles, had been educated at the French court, and both were imbued with a high idea of royal majesty. In the mid-fourteenth century Charles IV, now both king of Bohemia and emperor, undertook to refashion his Czech base on the Western model, thereby elevating it to the highest international rank. Like all strong medieval monarchs, he relied heavily on the church for moral support and administrative talent. In 1344 the bishopric of Prague had already been elevated to an archbishopric, thus liberating it from Mainz. Charles now underlined this promotion by beginning a new Gothic style cathedral in Prague Castle, the Hradčany; he also built a stone bridge over the Vltava more imposing than any in Paris and still admired by visitors to the city. In addition, he laid out a New Town, which was predominantly Czech, alongside the German-dominated Old Town of the city.

His most momentous act, however, was the founding of Prague University in 1348. His motive was in part the practical one of furnishing his kingdom with trained clerics and lawyers, as was the long-standing practice of the French and English monarchies. But he also wished to give his capital international luster, and the new university was the first in Europe east of the Rhine. (The first German university, Vienna, would not be founded until 1365, and the second, Heidelberg, until 1386.) The new university was modeled on Europe's oldest, Paris, with four faculties—liberal arts, theology, law, medicine—divided into four "nations," three of which until the early fifteenth century were in fact German, and only one Czech.

Very quickly this Paris of the east acquired an international reputation as the seat of the empire; at the same time it came to be the highest moral authority in Bohemia. This dual role amplified the power of the local church, which by 1415 was very great indeed. In Prague, two hundred fifty clerics were attached to the Cathedral of Saint Vitus; there were three hundred thirty secular priests in the various parishes of the city, and four hundred regular clergy in twenty-five monasteries; and twelve hundred clerics were studying in the university. All together, one in twenty inhabitants of the city was in orders. The concentration of clergy was of course not as great in the rest of Bohemia, but overall the country was oversupplied with representatives of the First Estate.[11] It is through this abundance of clerics that the Hussite movement would come to Bohemia; and it began when the Czechs at last acquired a majority in that window on the West which was their largely imported university.

Although it would be premature to call the new Bohemia that Charles had built a state, the action of the Hussite proto-revolution did take place within a compact political unit that was effectively subject to the monarch through his feudal intermediaries. Moreover, this center of power, Prague, was for the day an urban metropolis, a city of forty thousand souls, or slightly larger than the population of London, and much larger than any German city. It dominated the kingdom as effectively as Paris, with its one hundred thousand, dominated France. Bohemia, with around one million inhabitants, was thus a smaller scale but well-developed feudal monarchy analogous to Capetian France and Plantagenet England; and the Lands of the Crown of Bohemia taken as a whole, with another million inhabitants in Czech Moravia and German Silesia and Lusatia, were roughly analogous in structure to the contemporary Burgundian Netherlands of the Valois dukes. In all these respects, Bohemia differed markedly from Germany and Italy, where, as we have seen, political power long before 1400 had been divided among a number of local territorial or municipal sovereignties. It was in part because Germany and Italy lacked the focus of a real proto-state that the Paterini, Waldensians, Joachites, spiritual Franciscans, and other heterodox groups had never produced even a proto-revolution. Bohemia thus offered the endemic medieval heretical movement its first real chance at power.

Charles died in 1378, the year the Great Schism began in the church. In Bohemia he was succeeded by his eldest son, Wenceslas IV; but it was his second son, Sigismund, king of Hungary by marriage, who was elected emperor in 1410. Wenceslas soon was confronted with the problems created by his father's success. Resenting the power and wealth of the church, he quarreled with the archbishop, thus giving the great nobles an opportunity to challenge the strong monarchy created by Charles. In 1394, a Union of the Nobility demanded access to the most important royal functions, indeed twice arresting the king. The second time, in 1403, it did so with the aid of Sigismund. Wenceslas had to give way.[12]

Charles' patronage of the church had produced the usual crisis of clerical worldliness. By 1415 the church owned about a third of the land in Bohemia, the common pattern for medieval kingdoms in their formative stage. Again according to pattern, in a second stage the church itself spawned a reform movement. It began under Charles, who invited an Augustinian friar, Conrad Waldhauser, from Austria to raise the level of the native clergy. Soon there appeared Czech reformers, such as Jan Milíč and Matthew of Janov, with a more radical message of returning the church to apostolic simplicity, purity, and poverty. And since the Great Schism had now begun, at least one of the popes could be denounced as the Antichrist without falling into heresy. After the Schism, moreover, Czech clerics went to Oxford rather than Paris, an English connection reinforced when in 1382 Wenceslas' sister Anne married Richard II. Through this channel, the works of John Wyclif had reached Prague by the 1390s, where some of his views were taken up by the university's Czech "nation"; and a young bachelor of the arts faculty, Jan Hus, earned his keep by copying Wyclif's works. Perhaps the aspect of the Oxford master's thought that appealed most to the Czechs was his doctrine of "dominion," which held that the king and lords of the realm should enforce purification of the church by depriving it of its wealth. The problem was, however, that much of Wyclif's writing had already been condemned by Rome as heretical. So in 1403 the German master of theology at the university publicly condemned forty-five Wyclifite "articles."

These disputes did not remain cloistered within the university. In 1391, Bethlehem Chapel had been founded in the Old Town for preaching in Czech, rather than German, and in 1402 Hus began a brilliant career there. Although he spoke more like a revivalist preacher than a university intellectual, his academic culture and knowledge of scripture nonetheless gave his sermons a vividness and authority the common people had not heard before from their clergy. His message was a vehement and eloquent version of longstanding reformist denunciations of clerical worldliness coupled with a call for a return to the "Law of Jesus," by which he meant the authority of the Bible, and to the purity of the primitive church. This message acquired apocalyptic urgency since, like many other medieval reformers across Europe since Joachim, Hus believed that the corruption of the church presaged the end of the world.

From the start Hus had the support of the new archbishop of Prague and, less consistently, of Wenceslas. The German masters of the university, however, denounced Hus's "Wyclifism" to Rome as heretical. The archbishop was frightened into abandoning Hus's cause, but the king continued his support. Wenceslas, moreover, for the first time gave the Czechs a majority on the Old Town's council in 1408; and the next year he gave the Czech nation of the university three votes against one for all the other nations, that is, the Germans (who therefore departed to a new university at Leipzig). Hus was elected rector in 1409.

In 1412, reform first led to crisis when Hus, like Luther a century later, criticized the sale of indulgences. Three students organized a demonstration against such traffic in salvation (from which the king received a share), and the patrician counselors of the Old Town had them executed. Wenceslas, for his part, fearing he would be accused by Europe of supporting heresy, abandoned Hus. The great nobles, however, offered him protection, in part out of commitment to reform and in part to assert their independence of royal power. The leader of this new nobles' league was Čeněk of Vartemberk, the Grand Burgrave and second personage of the realm. In answer, Rome placed Prague under an interdict for as long as the city harbored Hus. The preacher now took refuge under Vartemberk's protection near the South Bohemian village of Sezimovo Ústí — like Luther later at the Wartburg under the patronage of his prince, the Elector of Saxony. In this enforced retreat, Hus began to preach to the peasants in the open countryside.

Though he was now on the verge of open revolt against the church, it should be emphasized that throughout his career Hus remained a moderate. His constant strategy, like Luther's later, was to win over the mighty of this world for the cause of church reform. Indeed, this reliance on secular authority was the essence of his "Wyclifism," rather than the Oxfordian's genuinely heterodox positions on the Eucharist and salvation. During the five or six years after his election as rector, Hus's radical reform movement in fact took the form of a coalition between the university and the Czech aristocracy.

FROM REFORM TO REVOLT

Hus never considered himself separated from the church of Rome. Since the beginning of the Great Schism in 1378 a movement to end it by a general church council had been building across Europe, and in 1414 Emperor Sigismund convened the Council of Constance to reunite Christendom. The central tenet of this conciliar movement was that the supreme authority in the church was not the pope, but rather an elected assembly of prelates and university masters, empowered to choose and depose popes as well as to define doctrine — or in political terms, to transform the church from a papal absolutism into a constitutional monarchy. As such, the conciliar movement was analogous to the elective "estates" of clergy, nobles, and burgers then emerging in Europe's secular monarchies — Parliament in England, the Estates General in France and the Burgundian Netherlands, the Cortès in Spain, and the Diets of Bohemia, Poland, and Hungary.[13] (To this list may be added, a century later, the Russian Zemskii Sobor.)

On Sigismund's initiative, Hus was summoned to Constance in 1414 by what was for the moment the supreme body of Christendom in order to account for his "heresy," and the emperor granted him a safe-conduct. Hus went willingly, for he sincerely believed he could convert the council to his program of divesting the church of all secular power and wealth. Unsurprisingly, however, in 1415 the conciliar constitutionalists who dominated the council condemned his views, and Sigismund had him burned at the stake. The next year Hus's chief witness at Constance, Master Jerome of Prague, met the same fate. In 1418, the council ended the schism by electing a new pontiff, but by then Bohemia had in effect seceded from Christendom.

The effect of Hus's death was to mobilize the Czech reform movement into a proto-political party. In September 1415, the great nobles formed a national league for the defense of Hus and reform. Reform now meant, above all, lay participation in the Eucharist "in both kinds" — the bread and the wine, the Body and the Blood. This practice had been introduced in 1414 by a close disciple of Hus, Jakoubek of Stříbro, when Hus was already in Constance; after his death it became general. Communion in both kinds, of course, had been the practice of the early church; indeed, reservation of the cup to the priest had begun only in the reforming eleventh century. Although inaugurated to simplify the liturgy of the Mass, it had the long-term effect of emphasizing the separation between the sacerdotal priesthood and the body of the faithful. Returning the cup to the laity thus meant narrowing that gap and democratizing the church. The followers of Hus, therefore, came to be known most commonly as Utraquists, from the Latin for "in two kinds," *sub utraque specie*, or Calixtins, from the Latin for chalice, *calix*. "Hussite" originally was a derogatory term used by the rest of Europe to designate the Bohemian heresy.

In answer to this armed confederation on behalf of the Chalice, the Catholic nobles organized an armed counter movement, under the protection of the king, in defense of the Cross. With the two camps about equal in strength, Bohemia henceforth lived under the permanent threat of civil war. At the same time, with the schism ended, the realm faced a united Christendom; and Sigismund, as the guardian of the church's restored unity and the orthodoxy of its doctrine, threatened a crusade against his heretic homeland. Under this accumulation of pressures, by 1418–1419 the royal power had become so paralyzed that it was no longer able to prevent open conflict between the Utraquist and Catholic parties.

FROM REVOLT TO CIVIL WAR

The crisis of the Hussite proto-revolution came in 1419–1420. In Prague, Catholic nobles had displaced Hussite clergy in the Old Town, and Hussites had displaced Catholic clerics in the New Town. In the excitement of the moment, many partisans of the Chalice believed that the anti-Hussite offensive portended the end of the world. The radicalization of New Town Hussitism was driven by Jan Želivský, a priest and millenarian preacher who played to this mood by openly calling Hus's executioner, Sigismund, the Antichrist. On July 30, 1419, Želivský, carrying a monstrance displaying the Eucharistic host, led a crowd of Prague artisans in a well-planned "defenestration" of German patricians from the New Town's city hall (the future military leader of the Hussite radicals, Jan Žižka, also participated). The shock effect of this action invites unavoidable comparison with the taking of the Bastille.

A wave of iconoclasm followed in Prague and the surrounding region; images were smashed and whole monasteries were burned to the ground. Lord Čeněk of Vartemberk and the Hussite nobles were barely able to maintain control of the city. Even the Old Town was dominated by such university clerics as Jakoubek of Stříbro, the initiator of communion in both kinds, and Jan Rokycana, another disciple of Hus, both distinctly more radical than the nobles. The king retrospectively ratified the coup d'état of the defenestration. Under the strain, however, he suffered an apoplectic seizure and died. The queen became regent for the absent heir, Emperor Sigismund, with Vartemberk as her first minister.

The crisis in the capital was magnified by the simultaneous millenarian mobilization of the countryside, where a mood of anxiety had been building for some time. In 1380, the Black Death, which had devastated Western Europe thirty years earlier, at last reached Bohemia. As elsewhere in Europe, the plague bred social instability; "brigands" appeared across the countryside, as in the Great Fear of the summer of 1789 in France. Indeed, the impact of this plague was such that it had altered the demographic balance of the kingdom; for it hit the urban Germans hardest and so fostered Czech migration from the country into the town. There was a smaller outbreak of plague in 1403, and a much more dangerous epidemic in 1414. The regions most affected by these disasters later became the focus of the most ardent millenarianism.

The political events after Hus's death greatly aggravated this latent rural anxiety; so by 1419 a millenarian wave began to move through the unlettered mass of the population. It is not that Czech peasants were particularly oppressed. Indeed, they were all free men, serfdom was unknown, and abundant evidence indicates that they were as prosperous as medieval conditions permitted anywhere. The millenarian mood emerged, rather, from the feeling that the world was coming apart because the church had betrayed its mission, and because public order was breaking down. No one now knew where evil would strike next.

Millenarian excitement was especially strong in Southern Bohemia, near where Hus had once preached. From the beginning of 1419, peasants and artisans gathered to listen to radical priests demonstrating from scripture that present tribulations signaled the end of the world. This led to mass pilgrimages—the first at Easter of 1419—to elevated spots, "mountains," which were given biblical names such as "Horeb" and "Tabor." The latter site, located near Sezimovo Ústí, had emerged because the Catholic league had expelled Utraquist clergy from churches in nearby towns. In answer, in the summer of 1419 these priests gathered their flocks in the open country on a high plateau and, erecting a tent as a chapel, they administered communion in both kinds. Since this open-air, collective atmosphere recalled the biblical image of mountains as propitious to salvation they called this hill "Tabor," after the mountain of Christ's Transfiguration.

Throughout the summer, these gatherings increased in number and size, at times drawing as many as forty thousand people. Soon regional assemblies of the reborn appeared, and word spread that only five cities across Bohemia would escape the Last Judgment. In mid-September one of these assemblies, Plzeň

(Pilsen), called for a gathering of all the kingdom's faithful to bear witness to their commitment by marching from various points on Prague. At the end of the month these converging columns entered the capital in a torchlight procession as all the city's church bells pealed to greet them.

The arrival of this mass movement in Prague in the wake of the defenestration was not wholly welcome to the noble and academic leaders of the Utraquists or to the city's patricians. Yet they also understood that it was only this mighty current of plebeian radicalism, in both the countryside and the cities, that gave them an advantage, or at least a margin of safety, against the forces of the Cross within the country and those of Catholic Europe outside it. In quieter times, this great push from below could have produced an open differentiation of classes, as it almost invariably did elsewhere in Europe—for example in the English peasant revolt that converged on London in 1381. In the face of danger to the true faith, however, the coalition of nobility and university chose to ride the plebeian groundswell. Thus, in what remained a deferential society, the upper-class leadership was able to impose its conception of reform on everybody; this multiclass movement preserved the united front so long as the danger persisted. Drawing some pertinent parallels, Utraquist leaders made the same choice of radical allies as did the seditious and vulnerable Presbyterian Parliament in sponsoring the New Model Army against Charles I. Similarly, in 1793 the bourgeois but regicidal Jacobins, confronted with royalist revolt at home and the First Coalition of monarchs abroad, chose to rely on the turbulent sans-culottes of Paris (the choice also of Lafayette in 1789).

In the first six months of 1420 the latent internal war of the previous year turned into armed conflict between the Cross and the Chalice. The first step in this direction was the transformation of the free-floating millenarianism of the original Tabor into a militarized and institutionalized millenarianism of the fixed and fortified Tabor of Jan Žižka, who combined the zeal of Robespierre with the military gifts of Cromwell.

On the basis of astrological calculations, the peasant and artisan millenarians had expected the end of the world between the eleventh and fourteenth of February 1420. When this did not occur, the Hussite community of Sezimovo Ústí took their town by storm, razed it, and began to build on a nearby hill a permanent Tabor. In their original intention it was to be a perfect community of equal brothers and sisters living solely by the Law of God. Private property was strictly limited and community living was decreed. The use of Latin in the church was eliminated in favor of Czech. The community's articles of faith rejected as a mortal sin the seven liberal arts cultivated by the university, and some books were burned. All traces of Roman and German law were abolished and the Law of God was supposed to govern the life of the community, as that law was interpreted by Utraquist priests. Ornate clerical vestments and images of saints were banished from the church, and for the laity strict puritanism in dress and personal conduct was decreed. Usury was forbidden, and the brothels of Prague were closed. Above all, the church was to be divested of its property.

In the enthusiasm of the first months of the new Tabor's existence, underground heretics who had long existed in Bohemia flocked to the community. There were Waldensians drawn by the prospect of apostolic poverty. There was also a representative of Europe's newest heresy, Wyclifism, the Englishman Peter Payne, who learned Czech and became an important spokesman of the movement. There were Pikards, or Brethren of the Free Spirit, who expected the imminent coming of the Final Days; whether there was direct Joachite influence in this current is secondary to the fact that by now chiliastic expectation had become standard on the extreme fringe of medieval heresy. Finally, there were antinomian Adamites who believed that the world's impending end authorized a return to the innocence of Eden, sexual liberation, and the community of wives.

By the end of the year, however, the necessity of earning a living in this new city on a hill forced an end of social equality and apostolic poverty. The leaders of the community began to collect feudal dues from the surrounding peasant villages to support and arm themselves. For the first priority was now military organization to survive against the Catholic nobles and the menace from Sigismund. The leading role here was played by Jan Žižka, after Hus himself the single most important and symbolic figure of the revolution. Under his leadership the original, spiritual Tabor was transformed into a military-religious confraternity, a community of warrior-saints.

Žižka was a petty noble, by then nearing sixty, who had lost an eye in the course of his years of campaigning across central Europe. By now he had become a deeply puritanical Utraquist and a pitiless foe of all enemies of the Law of God, particularly the monastic clergy. He was also a military commander of genius. In an age when warfare was dominated by a cavalry of armored knights, Žižka devised a means for his plebeian peasants and artisans to defeat their former lords. This was the war wagon of peasant carts drawn up in a circle with boards to fill in the intervening gaps. As a defense, its ability to wear down the attacks of armored knights made it impervious to cavalry; for offense, it offered stunning mobility against mounted adversaries. To this Žižka added rudimentary field artillery to serve against the noble knights; the word "howitzer" is Czech, and such mobile guns first emerged in this period. These devices for utilizing an ideologically motivated plebeian force gave the partisans of the Chalice an advantage that their noble leaders could not match. In all these respects, the parallel with Cromwell's New Model Army is striking.

The Taborite forces were first put to the test in the summer of 1420, and they proved decisive. The pope had by then proclaimed a crusade against the Hussites, and Sigismund moved to claim his capital and his crown. By and large, the Utraquist nobility, wishing to control the succession themselves, refused to recognize Sigismund's hereditary right. Still, the moderates among them had been thoroughly frightened by the armed Taborite plebs, and they began to divide. Thus, Vartemberk, as the royal troops closed in on Prague, in May issued a defiant manifesto against the king; in June he turned coat and let Sigismund's troops occupy Hradčany Castle. (Similarly, Edward Hyde, later Lord Clarendon, after helping rouse Parliament against Charles I, later went over to his side; and General Lafayette, after making Louis XVI a prisoner of the Revolution, subsequently betrayed his command to the Austrian army.) After this treason, Sigismund dominated Prague from two major fortresses and on three sides, and so had himself solemnly crowned king of Bohemia in Hradčany Cathedral. The Hussite cause was saved only in extremis by Žižka and his Taborites. Proceeding from the south by forced marches, they broke the royal vise around the capital in one battle. Following this "miracle," the thirty-thousand-man crusading army disintegrated.

Liberated Prague thus became the leader of a national Hussite movement. This movement was now a confederation of three tendencies: the moderate nobles and university clerics, the extremist Taborites, and the Prague burgers who constituted what may be called the pivotal center. But all three shared the messianic belief that Bohemia constituted the one true church, a beacon that would someday illume all Christendom. The sentiment of Bohemia's special vocation indeed went back to Charles IV, who had wished to make his kingdom the bastion of orthodox Catholicism; this mission had been sharpened by the spread of education he had fostered and by two decades of reformist preaching. After Hus's death, the Czechs believed that they had been granted a special grace enabling them to understand the true meaning of God's Law. They saw themselves as a chosen people, a nation of the elect with a calling to redeem all of sinful Europe. As a part of this messianism, they developed a mystique of the Czech language, as contrasted to both German and Latin. Three translations were made of the Bible —which is two more than existed in English at the time. In fact, the Czechs now defined themselves collectively by their language, the *český yazyk*, called *lingua bohemica* for the benefit of the rest of Europe and regarded as a sacred tongue.

In this exalted mood, the Hussite coalition proclaimed its faith to the world in the Four Articles of Prague. A first draft, representing a restatement of principles previously worked out in the university's Czech "nation," had emerged following the defenestration, in September 1419, in an address from the Prague Diet to Sigismund. During his siege of the city it was recast in more intransigent language, hand-copied many times over (Gutenberg was still three decades in the future), and released to the world. Although it is addressed entirely to the particular issues of the time, without any of the generalized import of later bills of rights, it is nonetheless an incipient declaration of such rights in religious terms, just as Magna Carta was in feudal terms.[14]

The first article proclaimed that "the Word of God" should be preached "freely" throughout the kingdom: in other words, the vernacular sermon, based on Scripture, was placed on the same level as the Eucharist in the liturgy of the Mass; even lay preaching was to be allowed. The second article proclaimed that communion in two kinds should be given "freely" to the laity since Christ had "ordered" it: in other words, the whole sacrament, and not just half as with the Romans, was necessary for salvation. These two matters of conscience together represented the original, religious message of the movement, as it had developed up to the time of Hus's death.

The next two demands, however, crossed the line into politics. Article three proclaimed the usual late medieval condemnation of ecclesiastical worldliness, concluding that the clergy should be deprived of its "unlawful" temporal power and "earthly possessions"; that is to say, the church must be dispossessed of its property and extruded from any exercise of secular authority. But the final article was the most radical of the four. It decreed that "all mortal sins" and "other disorders offending against the Law of God shall be . . . prohibited and punished . . . by those who have the authority to do so." In other words, the church should be forcibly purged and revolutionized by the temporal authorities, that is, the Hussite nobility, the urban communes, and such armed confraternities of true believers as the Taborites.

These last two articles, of course, went far beyond anything that the thoroughly nonviolent Hus had taught; and the convictions that they articulated had emerged only in the course of the movement's struggle during its peaceful phase. Since, however, that phase had amounted to three years of deadlock, it was now clear that only force could break the impasse; indeed, that force was necessary for the survival of reform. Thus did Utraquism discover a quite unanticipated revolutionary vocation—as would be the case for all subsequent European revolutions down to the nineteenth century.

Accordingly, the biblical rhetoric of the movement began to change. At its beginnings, references to scripture had been primarily to the New Testament Gospel of love and fraternity. Now that the movement had to defend itself in armed conflict, justification was found in Old Testament accounts of warrior kings smiting the enemies of the Lord on the field of battle. A similar change of scriptural focus can be found in the rhetoric of Puritanism, as Cromwell's saints became warriors for the glory of the Lord against prelacy and popery, or in that of the Huguenots in the previous century. It is only with the American Revolution that classical references took precedence over the Bible; and it is with the French Revolution that the rhetoric of activism abandoned the Bible completely for the glories of ancient Rome—first the republic, then the empire.

Once the Hussites had discovered their true revolutionary vocation, they set about implementing it systematically. Within a year after the defense of Prague and the Four Articles, Žižka's Taborites had conquered most of Bohemia from the royal forces. Indeed, some of Sigismund's most prominent supporters, including even Vartemberk, returned to the Chalice; soon the archbishop of Prague declared for it, too. In June 1421, therefore, the city of Prague, the archbishop, and the great lords (in that novel order of precedence) summoned a Diet of all the Bohemian lands to meet at Čáslav. This proto-constituent assembly voided Sigismund's coronation, declared him deposed, and elected a regency council to administer the realm until they could find a foreign prince to accept the crown—just as the Dutch would do in 1581. During this interregnum, the collegial regent would consist of eight burgers, seven petty nobles, and only five great lords—a major "democratization" as compared with the composition of the then hundred-odd-year-old English Parliament.

The Bohemian estates, however, never took the final step of declaring a republic. Although republics, such as Venice and Florence, had of course long existed in Europe, it was as yet unthinkable to turn a divinely ordained monarchy into one. At the same time, the estates never found a prince they could work with. In fact, the monarchy was suspended for the rest of the revolution and Bohemia was governed as a republic, though that name was never used. The next step in the dismantling of sacred monarchy occurred when the northern part of the Netherlands, after "abjuring" their lawful prince, Philip II, without finding a successor, became by default the Dutch Republic. It was not until the Commonwealth of Puritan England that a deliberate, ideological choice was made against monarchy and for popular government.

In the wake of the Diet of Čáslav, the two dominant powers in the Hussite coalition, Prague and Tabor, consolidated their forces internally by suppressing their radical fringes. This result was achieved relatively simply in the more substantial and long-established of the two partners, Prague. In 1421, Želivský, exploiting the tension of crisis, had forced the amalgamation of the Old and the New Towns into a single commune, in which the more democratic New Town was dominant and over which he was virtual dictator. In 1422, when the situation had eased, he was summoned by the moderate burgers of the Old Town to the city hall and there summarily executed. But soon this patrician counter-coup was undone, and a coalition of "moderate-radical" burgers and university masters took control under the leadership of Jakoubek of Stříbro. They would retain power in the capital until the end of the revolution.

In Tabor, stabilization was both more difficult to achieve and more limited. At the end of 1420, Tabor expelled the ultra-millenarian Pikards; their leader, the priest Martin Houska, a university product and one of the few Hussites to deny the real presence, was arraigned by Žižka personally and burned at the stake. The even more aberrant Adamists were simply driven out of the community and hunted down in the woods. Then, to ensure continued religious order, the Taborite priests elected their own bishop, Nicolas of Pelhřimov. Tabor thus became a kind of counter-church to mainstream Utraquism of the capital, which throughout the revolution retained the structures, the sacraments, the liturgy, the Latin, and largely the theology of Rome.

Hence, this temporary stabilization of Tabor proved fragile. Žižka was ferocious in his treatment of the orthodox priests, the royalist nobles, and especially the monastic clergy that his troops captured in their campaigns. These brutal methods aroused the opposition of Bishop Pelhřimov and the Taborite clergy. In 1423, therefore, Žižka withdrew to the kindred Orebite confraternity of eastern Bohemia, which was now called "Little Tabor." This new community became the basis for a highly organized military-religious army—in effect a professional corps of some twelve thousand full-time warriors—dedicated to the "Law of God." Although by this time Žižka had lost his second eye in battle, his zeal and military ability remained so great that it was in his last two sightless years that he scored his greatest victories. In fact, his power became such that at the Diet of 1423 Prague and the moderate Hussites voted with the Catholic nobility to depose him, and even took up arms. This anticipation of a Hussite Thermidor failed in extremis; the next year the Czech Cromwell died in battle.

With Žižka's departure from the scene, the most radical and, so to speak, "creative" phase of the revolution was over. His army, however, now called the "Orphans" in a gesture of posthumous fidelity, continued its career for another decade of routinized Taborism. During this time it repulsed four more crusades of foreign, mostly German and Hungarian, mercenaries in Sigismund's service. The Taborites' new leader was the warrior-priest Prokop the Bald (also called the Great); and under his leadership the Hussites now sought to impose their faith on the non-Czech lands of the Bohemian crown. Eventually Prokop's forces made conquests outside the Bohemian lands, indeed ranging as far afield as the Baltic

Sea and Hungary; at the same time, these professional soldiers lived by plundering the conquered territories. Again the comparison with the New Model Army is in order: with it Cromwell for the first time imposed London's authority on the whole of the British Isles; and his army, too, lived off the land outside England. Likewise in France, the revolutionary explosion ended in military conquest, expansion, and plunder, this time on a Napoleonic, continental scale.

Yet despite these successes, and the Taborite military's long hegemony within the Hussite movement, there never ceased to be a strong element of dual power opposing Prague and the university, on the one hand, and the plebeian armies that defended them, on the other. And in this instability lay the causes of the revolution's end in 1436.

THERMIDORIAN CONSOLIDATION

The revolution was brought to a conclusion by its very success in battle. In 1431 the last Catholic crusade, whose troops lacked the Hussites' fierce motivation, was repulsed. The same year, the second reformist council convened in Basel. Its leaders still considered it superior to the pope, so to bolster their claim they sought an international success by ending the Hussite schism through negotiation rather than military action. The Hussites at first insisted that the Catholics recognize the Four Articles as valid for all Bohemia, including the Catholic population, something of course the council could not concede. Still, the very fact of negotiations produced a split in Hussite ranks. The Orphans and other Taborites wanted war to full victory, in part for the faith and in part because war was now their full-time occupation and sole means of support. Since the exhausted country wanted peace, however, the moderate Hussites and the Praguers joined forces with the Catholic nobility; and in 1434 this coalition decimated the radicals at the battle of Lipany. Prokop the Bald himself perished on the field of battle, and the Taborites' strongholds were then demolished.

Moderate Hussites—Hus's old disciples, Stříbro for the university and Rokycana for the Prague commune—now controlled Bohemia. To end the war they made a compromise, called the Compactata, with the Council of Basel (1436). Under its terms, Bohemia was allowed semi-autonomous status within Christendom: communion in the two kinds was accepted for Hussite communities, and in Bohemia alone. This agreement, however, did not signify religious toleration in the modern sense, since it applied to only one dissenting group and to a given region. It was thus like the Edict of Nantes that Henry IV accorded French Huguenots in 1598. Concurrently, the Bohemian estates at last recognized Sigismund as monarch in the land of his birth. Although he died the following year (1437) and an elected Hussite king, George of Poděbrady, reigned until 1471, the Utraquist church remained moderate, and the revolution was in effect over.

OUTCOME

What were its concrete results? Socially, the overturn brought a major reduction of the power and property of the church, particularly of the monasteries, as would be the case elsewhere during the Protestant Reformation. The great gainers from this transfer of wealth were—as would again be the case a century later—the great nobles, the urban burgers, and the lesser nobility, in that order, and among the Catholics as much as among the Utraquists. Politically, the monarchy was permanently weakened, soon becoming de facto elective. The clergy was eliminated from the Diet while the royal cities increased their representation, thus ending the traditional structure of national representation though not the system of orders as such. The Diet's new composition was nobles, knights, and burgers—a constitutional arrangement more weighted toward the lower orders than any in Europe at the time. As for the peasants, after serving as the revolution's foot soldiers, they gained nothing; indeed they were eventually enserfed in Europe's "second serfdom" in East-Central Europe during the sixteenth century.

Does all this make of the Hussite proto-revolution the foundational moment of the modern Czech nation, in the way that later revolutions would do farther west? It more or less looked that way until the end of the fifteenth century. In fact, however, two decades of war had so depressed the economy that Bohemia, a European leader in the mid-fourteenth century, by 1500 had again become peripheral. Hence in 1526 it fell into the hands of Europe's most powerful dynasty, the Habsburgs, in whose possession it would remain for four centuries. During that time the new line of kings made the monarchy hereditary once again, and reduced the estates to impotence. The Hussite church survived until the Reformation, when it was in effect absorbed into Lutheranism. Then, after an anti-Habsburg revolt was crushed in the battle of the White Mountain in 1620, Bohemia was re-Catholicized by the Counter-Reformation and the country's elite was re-Germanized by the Habsburg monarchy.

In effect, all that survived of the Hussite movement was the Moravian Brethren, which went back to a one-time Taborite, Petr Chelčický (ca. 1390-ca. 1460). At first close to the radical millenarians, he was eventually repelled by their resort to violence and so founded a pacifist and ascetic community, the Brethren of

Unity—mutatis mutandis, moral heirs of the Spiritual Franciscans and precursors of the sixteenth-century Dutch Mennonites and the Quakers in the Puritan Revolution.

Still, the Hussite revolt remained in Czech national consciousness as a legend. In the nineteenth century, when middle-class and intelligentsia Czech nationalism began to reassert itself against the new German elite, Hus and Žižka became the great symbols of reborn national identity. In this vicarious and mythic way the Hussite revolution at last, if somewhat artificially, become the Czechs' defining national moment.[15]

THE BASIC PATTERN OF EUROPEAN REVOLUTION

The claim has already been made that in the Hussite proto-revolution the basic scenario of subsequent European revolutions down to 1789 was played out. Its stages have been suggested in the preceding narrative; they may now be stated in more general terms, as a series of escalating stages.

The Czech movement began when a segment of the country's traditional elite, the clergy and the nobility, demanded substantial reform, though not the total change, of existing religious practices, a demand that inevitably entailed such important political and social changes as the secularization of much of the church's wealth. Part of this elite, however, and the monarchy as well, vacillated; their hesitation brought the urban patriciate into the reform movement, thus completing the mobilization of what would later be called "civil society." Since Rome, the king, and a segment of the higher nobility resisted Utraquist reform, radical clerics mobilized the urban plebs to seize power in the capital. This led to the defenestration of 1419 carried out by the petty merchants and artisans of Prague. The ensuing collapse of central authority awakened another actor, the peasantry, thus leading to the first, *millenarian* Taborite assemblies.

What is noteworthy about this pattern of action is, first, that it was a movement of *all* strata of society, and that they entered into action in rapid succession. As a rule, single revolts of burgers or artisans invariably fail, as we have seen in the case of the various Italian and Flemish urban uprisings of the fourteenth century. A second defining trait of the Hussite pattern of action is that the initial general mobilization polarized society between a camp of conservative fear and one of radical expectation, of plot and counter-plot. Thus both sides perceived the developing internal war as a political Armageddon, that is, a struggle that can end only in total victory for one party and annihilation for the other.

In the fever of such all-out conflict, the party of hope is naturally more strongly motivated than the party of fear. And within the former camp the ideological radicals have the strongest motivation of all. This camp, therefore, comes to be dominated by its most millenarian wing, since its zeal fostered the most militant organization. The extreme radicals thus won the crucial battles spearheading the movement as a whole, as occurred in the second, *military* Tabor of Žižka. At the same time, however, these radicals increasingly frightened their more pragmatic allies. The victorious revolution thus remained an uneasy coalition or a regime of "dual power" aligning the Prague City Council and the university on one hand against Tabor and the Orphans on the other. Nonetheless this uneasy coalition roundly defeated the royalist Catholics at home and rebuffed Rome and Emperor Sigismund abroad.

However, after the victory, the consequent removal of the common enemy, war-weariness, and flagging millenarian zeal broke up the coalition. So the moderate Utraquists now allied with the diminished conservatives to purge the extremists, thus ending millenarian fever. This occurred when the defeated royalist Catholics after 1424 joined forces with Jan Stříbro to produce the Thermidor of Lipany. With this outcome the Hussite revolt went through the full gamut of changes of which the European revolutionary process is capable. The Hussite revolution thus offers the maximal European revolutionary formula.

What light does this structure of action shed on methodological issues? Brinton (see Appendix II) was obviously right in a general way about the succession of revolutionary phases from moderation to extremism and back. And this reflects the fact that the basis of his model, the French Revolution, represents the culmination of trends going back to the Middle Ages (as Tocqueville saw very well). By the same token, 1789 was the first revolution that made the explosive potential of these trends fully apparent, thus creating the modern concept of revolution, a circumstance that justifies rejecting that concept backward in European history.

But the Hussite case makes it possible to add other components to this tried and true French model. First, for revolution to occur, ideological and social protest must be given a political focus by the framework of a state with a large, cosmopolitan capital. (Theda Skocpol's "bringing the state back in" is much too feeble a statement of this primordial condition.) As we have seen, the late Middle Ages offer cases of social protest much more potent than that raised by the Prague artisans. Such were the fourteenth-century revolts of the Ciompi in Florence, van Ardevelde in Flanders, or Etienne Marcel in Paris at a moment when the French state was temporarily in collapse; yet none of these amounted to a revolution of any kind. Similarly, in itself the Bohemian peasant revolt was no more powerful as an expression of social discontent than the French jacquerie of 1343 or the English peasant revolt of 1381. Yet it yielded the mighty Taborite revolutionary force because this discontent was linked with the aristocratic and urban struggle for state power, and because both social forces were driven by the exhilaration of religious *renovatio*. In other words, both the state and "enthusiasm" are necessary to transform social protest or "contention" into anything that can plausibly be called revolution.

Second, the enduring changes achieved by the Hussite revolution were made in the first, moderate stage of the movement. These are: the confiscation of church lands, the stringent limitation of the monarchy by the towns and the nobility, and the important religious change (for the time) of according the Cup to the laity. All the radical social leveling, as well as the territorial conquests, achieved at the militant peak of the revolution by Taborite confraternities, was undone by the Thermidor of Lipany. The same pattern holds true for the English and French revolutions: as we will see, for the first, the enduring changes were made in 1640–1641 (limited or constitutional monarchy) and for the second, they came in 1789–1791 (the limited government of the Declaration of the Rights of Man). The English radical Commonwealth and the French Jacobin dictatorship were both soon annulled, to remain only as legends for future revolutions, the first in America and the second in Russia. So the question then arises, why did the fever rage on into bloody and destructive internal wars in all three cases? This question can be fully examined only when we come to the latter two instances.

Still, it is possible to state now that part of the answer lies in what may be called the "revolutionary alliance system." The Hussite revolution could achieve the maximal European revolutionary scenario only because the upper strata of the kingdom were not afraid to ally with lower, and more radical, strata against a common and institutionally superior enemy, in this case, the emperor and pope who were seeking to undo the Utraquist church. To translate the situation into modern terms, the Utraquist leaders, in an emergency of national survival, declared a policy of "no enemies to the left." But this is always a dangerous policy for any establishment since the leftward movement can easily spin out of control. The Hussite pattern of alliances thus goes against the normal order of politics for any elite, the first principle of which is to keep control of the situation, to hold on to the initiative in formulating policy.

Another part of the answer is that the fever raged on longer than was politically necessary because religion had made politics a matter of eternal salvation or damnation. Enthusiasts, therefore, rarely fade away; they have to be stopped. Consequently, the revolution's millenarian dynamic, as well as the leveling programs it promoted, must be sacrificed in order to consolidate the revolution's initial gains. In other words, the activist "overkill" of a millenarian impulse is necessary to fuel the initial revolutionary breakthrough; and then a thermidorian retreat is necessary to preserve the concrete results that the breakthrough accomplished.

And this paradox, which is common to all European revolutions, poses a tantalizing question. What would happen in a case where there was no Thermidor, and where the millenarian aspiration became the practical program of a permanent Tabor? This prospect, of course, points to the culminating case of the European radical tradition: the revolution to end all revolutions, Red October. This too can be examined fully only in due course.

All of the foregoing, finally, raise the question of how far pre-political, religious aspirations are related to the restructuring of society in more democratic fashion. To put the matter another way, how far is it possible to go in viewing religious dissent as an anticipation of modern political and/or social democracy? Is Louis Blanc's outright affirmation that religious heresy was the precursor of 1789 defensible? And if this is rejected as excessively reductionist, how valid is Troeltsch's more complex and nuanced picture of Europe's transition from a hierarchical church-type polity to its more egalitarian sect-type successors and on to a modernity that is still informed with its religious heritage?

A possible answer to this question will be many chapters in coming; for, whether in Hussite Bohemia or later, religious orientation has never corresponded neatly to social class or status. The Hussite faithful ranged from great lords to humble peasants, and so did their orthodox Catholic adversaries. Still, the problem of the relationship between religion and revolution cannot be avoided, since from the time of Arnold of Brescia and Saint Bernard to Jules Michelet and Louis Blanc, commentators have recognized that heresy in the church was always tantamount to sedition in society.

And so, the problem of the relationship between the two forms of revolt leads to a more general question: how independent a variable is culture, including transposed religion, in understanding modern, officially secular society? In other words, how distinctive a branch of culture is religion? Is it fundamentally different from, or just an immature form of, rationalistic political ideologies and social theories? Or does it live on into modernity in rationalistic guise? All these problems will recur in examining the Reformation, where they indeed come into clearer focus than in our first, proto-revolutionary Hussite case.

3

LUTHERAN GERMANY, 1517–1555

The Reformation as Semi-Revolution

All Christians are truly of the "spiritual estate," and there is among them no difference at all but that of office. . . . We are all one body, yet every member has its own work, whereby it serves every other, all because we have one baptism, one Gospel, one faith, and are all alike Christians; for baptism, Gospel, and faith alone makes us "spiritual" and a Christian people. . . . Since, then, the temporal authorities are baptized with the same baptism and have the same faith and Gospel as we, we must grant that they are priests and bishops, and count their office one which has a proper and a useful place in the Christian community. For whoever comes out of the water of baptism can boast that he is already consecrated a priest, bishop, and pope, though it is not seemly that everyone should exercise the office.
—MARTIN LUTHER, *An Open Letter to the Christian Nobility of the German Nation Concerning the Reform of the Christian Estate,* 1520

As Muenzer's philosophy of religion touched upon atheism, so his political programme touched upon communism, and there is more than one communist sect of modern times which, on the eve of the February Revolution [of 1848 in Paris], did not possess a theoretical equipment as rich as that of Muenzer of the Sixteenth Century. His programme, less a compilation of the demands of then existing plebeians than a genius's anticipation of the conditions for the emancipation of the proletarian element that had just begun to develop among the plebeians, demanded the immediate establishment of the kingdom of God, of the prophesied millennium on earth. This was to be accomplished by the return of the church to its origins and the abolition of all institutions that were in conflict with what Muenzer conceived as original Christianity, which, in fact, was the idea of a very modern church. By the kingdom of God, Muenzer understood nothing else than a state of society without class differences, without private property, and without superimposed state powers opposed to the members of society.
—FRIEDRICH ENGELS, *The Peasant War in Germany,* 1850

That the Reformation was "revolutionary" in the extended sense of that word has never been in doubt, for it permanently divided the hitherto unitary world of Latin Christendom into two antagonistic blocks. In this sense, together with the French Revolution three centuries later, it constitutes one of the two great caesurae in the history of that Europe which took form around the year 1000.[1]

But the Reformation was revolutionary in another, more specific and institutional sense, in that it was a revolt against the superior element in the world of the two swords, the First Estate. And in that world any change in religious doctrine or ecclesiastical organization automatically entailed a change in polity and society. Moreover, in what is only a seeming paradox this revolt was initiated by members of the clergy itself: almost to a man, the earliest reformers were priests or monks. Yet, even though these clerics aimed to dismantle the existing First Estate, they by no means intended to diminish the centrality of religion in society. They sought rather to purify the church so as to bring the world into closer conformity with God's law.

As for the long-term meaning of this revolutionary break, an enduring if now somewhat outmoded convention has been to couple it with the Renaissance as the beginning of the "modern" era, a perspective that makes it the harbinger of freedom of conscience, critical thought, and bourgeois individualism. But this surely leaves too little for the epochal turn of 1789 to accomplish; for a genuinely modern conception of modernity, and the one already offered here, would hold that it must be both secular and democratic, and that these values are organically related to an urban and industrial, or at least a market, society. Moreover, the currently prevailing consensus of historiography emphasizes the Reformation's medieval roots as much as its forward-looking character. It was, after all, in the first instance a movement of *religious* reform, indeed with links to a tradition of dissent going back to the eleventh century.

Given this Janus-like physiognomy, in what sense may the Reformation be considered a revolution in terms of the problematic of this book, that is, as a stage in the long-term escalation of the European tradition of radical overturn? How much does it repeat, or deviate from, the basic pattern recurrent in that tradition? How far does it propel the overall process toward still greater radicalism and self-awareness?

These questions will be examined in this chapter and the two following with respect to three cases: the explosive but soon arrested revolutionary process of Lutheran Germany; the ultimate defeat of the powerful revolutionary challenge of the Huguenots in France, a "control" by the negative, as it were, of the other two cases; and the half-successful revolution of the Calvinist Netherlands, half-successful in that it triumphed only in the northern portion of the Burgundian-Habsburg domain. Let us not forget that the outcome of the Reformation was an unintended one. Like the Hussites, those sixteenth-century reformers who after 1529 came to be called "Protestants" sought not to create a separate church, but to purify all Christendom, which to them no less than to Rome must by God's will be one and universal. And if they had to settle for an incomplete reform, this was in part because their very efforts helped rejuvenate the old church that they were challenging. For all these reasons, then, the Reformation is best considered a semi-revolution.

The Lutheran Reformation was a semi-revolution also in that, unlike the Hussite movement, it did not run the full revolutionary course to millenarian dictatorship accompanied by political and social overturn. Although every class, from great nobles to humble peasants, participated in the upheaval at some time, they did not move against the old order simultaneously or as a united front as they had in Bohemia. Rather, the maximal revolutionary scenario was approximated only temporarily and in isolated instances, such as Thomas Müntzer's commune in Mülhausen during the predominantly peasant revolt of 1525 or the later plebeian revolt in the episcopal city of Münster in 1534. In other reformed cities, such as Zwingli's Zurich and Bucer's Strasbourg, when extremism did appear it was successfully contained. But most frequently, it was the territorial princes who determined the outcome of the reforming drive; and they always did so well short of a millenarian outbreak. The central problem of this chapter, then, is to examine the initial sources of that drive in Germany and the reasons why it was cut short before reaching full revolutionary potential.

Even so, the end of the revolutionary process in Germany—marked at the latest by the Peace of Augsburg in 1555—did not signify the end of the Reformation as revolution. The same religious forces that erupted in 1517 in Saxony and slightly later in Switzerland flared up in closely spaced explosions across Europe so that, by the century's end, most countries had been touched to some degree. These successive explosions occurred in part as a response to the German and Swiss examples; but they emerged even more by spontaneous combustion in the regions concerned, touching rural as often as urban areas and finding adherents from the top to the bottom of society. The Reformation was thus both a pan-European radical movement and a series of local upheavals. Clearly, the movement marked a crisis of the entire European system. So vast a process, however, cannot be fruitfully examined as a single whole. It must be approached through its subunits, of which the first and most important is Lutheran Germany.

THE HISTORIOGRAPHY

The historiography of the German Reformation is one of the oldest and most voluminous bodies of continuous scholarship in existence, yet very little of it deals, at least explicitly, with revolution. Its overwhelming focus has been religious, beginning with Luther, the man, and following his movement's development to the Peace of Augsburg in 1555. Indeed, it was in that year that the secretary of the Schmalkaldic League of Protestant princes, Johannes Sleidan, published his *Commentaries on Religion and the State in the Reign of Emperor Charles V*, a work that would influence discussion of the subject until the early nineteenth century.[2] Still, it was confessional history, part of a debate in which Johannes Cochlaeus's *Commentaries on the Acts and Writings of Luther* of 1549 had been the first Catholic blast. And so ideologically driven debate continued as the now separately organized churches faced off in the seventeenth century, and as the eighteenth-century secularists of the Enlightenment sought to fit earlier "superstition" into an overall history of progress.

It was the historiographical revolution of the early nineteenth century that gave us the coordinates for the modern perception of the Reformation, and indeed of the sixteenth century's "modernity" generally. This began in a surge of Romantic nationalism with the Wartburg Festival in 1817, the tercentenary of Luther's Ninety-five Theses, and first received academic form in the work of Leopold von Ranke. At roughly the same time as Macaulay in England, Michelet in France, and Palacký in Bohemia were giving shape to their national revolutionary dramas, Ranke staked out the European sixteenth century as the age of the Renaissance and Reformation, first with his *History of the Popes* (1834–1839) and then with *German History in the Age of Reformation* (1839–1848), a work which gave modern expression to the religion-and-state perspective of Sleidan. This achievement, however, did not deconfessionalize the subject, since Ranke believed in the German Lutheran cause as much as Macaulay, Michelet, and Palacký did in their respective national-revolutionary causes, but it did situate the subject in a documentary and developmental perspective that is still with us.

Yet hardly had Ranke consolidated this picture than Friedrich Engels came forth with another, modern form of confessionalism. In 1850, in *The Peasant War in Germany*, he on the one hand indicted Luther's Reformation as a bourgeois betrayal of the people's revolution of 1525, while on the other he canonized Thomas Müntzer as a forerunner of Marx and presented his movement as an adumbration of communism. And Engels explicitly drew the parallel with the German bourgeoisie's recent betrayal of the people in 1848. Though absent from the official universities, this social interpretation of the Reformation was greatly enriched later in the century by Karl Kautsky, who extended Engels's type of analysis backward to the Taborites and forward to the Münster Anabaptists of 1534–1535.[3] In fact, Kautsky's approach was more than a social interpretation; it offered a general sociology of Christianity. This was fully expressed in 1908 in his *Foundations of Christianity*, a work drawing on the Left-Hegelian critique of religion as an alienated projection of human aspirations, a movement out of which Marx himself came and which would lead also to the later nineteenth-century "Higher Criticism" of the Bible. This mixture of social interpretation and the "sociologizing" of religion, though often crudely reductionist, would bear important fruit for Reformation studies after the mid-twentieth century. At that point, moreover, this tradition was greatly reinforced by the existence of the German Democratic Republic, whose historians worked within the framework of codified Soviet Marxism in whose canons the Reformation was an "early bourgeois revolution."

In the meantime, confessional church history continued to dominate the subject. In 1905 Father Heinrich Denifle attacked the pieties of German national Lutheranism with a ferocious study of the reformer that, for all its invective, successfully made the point that Reformation scholarship's celebration of Luther's originality was founded on a woeful ignorance of the medieval background out of which he came. So the search was on for the roots of Luther's views in late medieval piety, philosophy, and theology, a movement that, like social history, would bear its full fruits only after the middle of the twentieth century. Related to this broadening of the Reformation's temporal horizon was a deepening of perspective within the sixteenth century to include the Anabaptists and other sects that had been persecuted by the mainline confessions at the time and largely excluded from their historiography thereafter. This subject, initially the province of their heirs in multi-denominational America, was pulled together into a monumental synthesis in 1962 by George H. Williams under the rubric *The Radical Reformation*.[4] In a radical democratic age the radicalism of the sects had wide appeal; henceforth the "magisterial" mainline confessions had to share the historiographical stage with these rebels.

In fact, it is only then that we achieved a fully de-confessionalized, indeed ecumenical, view of the Reformation and of the Counter-Reformation, Ranke's old term now abandoned for the more diplomatic label "Catholic Reformation." This new ecumenical spirit also extended to an increasingly de-Marxized social history (especially once the German Democratic Republic had disappeared in 1989), which along with cultural history was now included in the historiographical mix. The result was Peter Blickle's history of the Peasants' War first published in 1975 under the title *The German Revolution of 1525*. By this time, too, the Reformation had been largely denationalized, as witness the career of the Dutch author of *The Harvest of Medieval Theology*, Heiko Oberman,[5] who after many years of teaching at Tubingen finished his days as Regents Professor of History at the University of Arizona. It is from this perspective that the German Reformation as a form of revolution is approached here.

THE FRAMEWORK

The first thing to note about the German case is that, unlike Bohemia earlier or England and France later, the Holy Roman Empire of the German nation was most definitely not a state, or even near to being one. Nineteenth-century German historians, who like their colleagues across Europe viewed the nation-state as the natural norm of any people's development, considered its absence to be a historical anomaly, almost an injustice of fate; and twentieth-century historians saw it as the beginning of Germany's tragic deviation, its Sonderweg, within the pattern of modern European civilization. At the time, however, the fragmentation of German political institutions was much nearer to the prevailing European norm than were the national monarchies of France, England, and Spain, themselves still far from fully formed. True, even in the sixteenth century both the emperor and some patriotic intellectuals, such as Ulrich von Hutten, dreamed of central national monarchy on the Western model. By and large, however, German national sentiment—and it was already strong—was turned in other directions: it was anti-Roman on the one hand and local in its political allegiances on the other. Indeed, a similar failure to rise to the level of nineteenth-century nationalistic expectations was also manifested in ostensibly more centralized realms: such great lords as the Bourbons and the Guises were only slightly less docile subjects of their Valois kings than were the Bavarian Wittlesbach or the Saxon Wettin loyal subordinates of their Habsburg emperors. A variant of the feudal spirit was still very much alive in this allegedly inaugural century of the modern world. Everywhere, moreover, the state was in the first instance a dynastic institution rather than a national one.

In Germany the sword of empire was held throughout the sixteenth century by the Habsburg dynasty; and this dynasty, in the person of Emperor Charles V, thought in truly imperial, pan-European terms more than German ones because of its extensive dominions elsewhere. The process which brought the Habsburgs to international eminence began in the fourteenth century when a younger son of the Valois king of France received the duchy of Burgundy as a virtually autonomous appanage and then, in 1384, married the heiress of the county of Flanders in the Low Countries. This formed the nucleus of a greater Burgundian realm which by 1430 included the Duchy of Brabant, the County of Holland, and a slice of what is now northern France.[6] This new entity was in a sense a revival of the old "middle kingdom" of Lotharingia that emerged from the break up of the Carolingian Empire in 843.

When the last and most ambitious duke of Burgundy was killed in battle against the French king in 1477, for protection his heiress married the son of the Habsburg Emperor Maximilian of Germany (at the same time forfeiting Burgundy proper, thus making her domain essentially Netherlandish). Her son then married Juana la loca, the heiress of Ferdinand and Isabella, whose own union had earlier joined Castile and Aragon to create Spain, which was just about to acquire the lion's share of the New World. And the heir to all this was Juana's son Charles V, born and raised in Flanders, who in 1517 inherited Spain (together with its Italian dependency, the kingdom of Naples, to which he soon added the duchy of Milan) before being elected, in 1519, to the traditional Austrian Habsburg office of Holy Roman Emperor. It also so happened that his tenure of the highest office in Christendom coincided with the apogee of Ottoman power in the Mediterranean and the Balkans. Thus throughout the century the Habsburgs in both Spain and Austria held the front lines of Christendom's defense against Islam, just as it was the first bulwark of orthodoxy against heresy within Europe.

In contemplating the Habsburgs' drive for world empire, amazed contemporaries quipped: *bella gerant allii, tu felix Austria nube* (others may wage war, you, happy Austria, marry). And the dynasty's stunning rise was indeed the most rapid and colossal accumulation of power in European history—indeed, the biggest thing on earth at the time. This empire, however, was not simply the product of chance or matrimonial lottery. In the world of dynastic states marriages amounted to alliances, and the marriages converging on Charles V's empire were so many barriers around the centrally located power of France, which Maximilian may indeed have wished to dismember entirely. In any event, the alliance inaugurated a series of Habsburg-Valois wars which dominated European politics to the mid-sixteenth century. These wars, together with the struggle against the Turks, would complicate the development of the Reformation at every stage.

In geographic extent the core lands of the empire included, in addition to what is now the German Federal Republic, the Burgundian Netherlands (Belgium and Holland), Alsace and Lorraine in present-day France, Austria, Bohemia, and the Oder Valley from Silesia to the Baltic, and technically at least Switzerland. In addition to these sprawling domains it held formal sway over Italy north of the Papal States, although after the collapse of the Hohenstauffen empire in the thirteenth century this sovereignty was largely nominal. In fact, when the imperial effort was revived in the fourteenth century by the House of Luxembourg it concentrated on the German lands north of the Alps, with a base in Bohemia. Later the House of Habsburg pursued a similar policy from its bases in Austria and the Netherlands. Even so, in both cases the emperor's effective power rested on the non-Germanic periphery of the system. It is in this reduced but still heterogeneous empire that the Reformation broke out.

Central authority was further weakened by the empire's constitution. Though there were some central institutions, notably judicial, there was nothing like a central administration, which made the empire in fact a loose confederation of nearly sovereign principalities and self-governing cities. The emperor was chosen by a college of seven electors, four lay and three ecclesiastical; the imperial dignity became hereditary de facto in the House of Habsburg only in the course of the sixteenth century. In the empire's German heartland there existed three fissiparous types of political authority. Rhineland and southern Germany was home to great ecclesiastical principalities, bishoprics, and abbacies, such as Cologne, Trier, Mainz, and Würtzburg. The same region boasted numerous and wealthy Free Imperial cities, such as Frankfurt, Strasbourg, and Augsburg. And these existed alongside an archaic congeries of independent knights' domains. Just about everywhere, but especially in the center and in the north and east, the territorial princes were well on their way to becoming sovereigns of mini-states such as Saxony, Brandenburg, and Bavaria, and whose power threatened both the knights and the free cities. And within these cities there was a social hierarchy of hereditary patricians, big merchants, guild craftsmen, and a sizable "lumpen" mass.

Beginning in the last decades of the fifteenth century the German core of the empire experienced its first notable economic expansion. Commerce and manufacturing were thriving along the Rhine and in the south; silver and other mining were highly developed in the central regions of Thuringia and Saxony, and grain for export to the Atlantic west was the staple of the east. By 1500 the total population was around nineteen million. Cities, or more exactly towns, were numerous, the official account being three thousand, but only fifty of these were important enough to enjoy the status of Free Imperial cities. The largest was Augsburg, with around fifty thousand inhabitants; Cologne had declined from sixty thousand in the thirteenth century to forty thousand, while Nuremberg, Magdeburg, and Strasbourg had around thirty thousand each. The vast majority of towns, however, had fewer than a thousand inhabitants. Yet despite the modest scale of this urbanization as compared with Northern Italy or the Netherlands, Augsburg's Fuggers were among the leading bankers of Europe, Nuremberg was a major center of manufacture, and the Rhine valley pioneered the European print revolution. In short, like Hussite Bohemia, Reformation Germany was on the upswing; indeed, Germany would not enjoy such a preeminence in Europe again until the late nineteenth century.

Yet despite these achievements, Germany lacked a single central focus. There was no capital city. As already mentioned, the Luxembourg and Habsburg emperors had their seat on the periphery in Prague or Vienna; their chief interest was in areas where they themselves were territorial sovereigns, such as Austria, Hungary, and the Netherlands. As titular Roman kings, moreover, their horizon was international more than German. Nor did the paramount national institution, the Imperial Diet, or Reichstag, have a fixed anchor; it roved from city to city and reflected in the conflicting interests of its component "estates" the disparate regional and social elements of the Reich as a whole.

Germany thus fell well short of being even a proto-national state. In consequence, although the Reformation upheaval of 1517–1525 turned out to be the most widespread, violent, and intense crisis that Europe would witness until the French Revolution, it lacked the institutional focus to give it the ultimate power of a full-fledged revolution.

Germany lacked cohesion in still another sense: not only was it without clear-cut boundaries, whether in the west, the east, or the south, but the country was unevenly developed within these mobile limits. Germany west of the Rhine and south of the Danube had been part of the Roman Empire, an experience that left vestiges of sedentary civilization of which the Mediterranean vine is only the most visible example. Germany east of the Rhine and north of the Danube had been brought into the orbit of Mediterranean Christian civilization only under the Carolingians, though quite soon, in the tenth century, it became the seat of a second imperial revival as the Holy Roman Empire of the German nation. These two zones together comprised what is often called "old" Germany, and most of the country's cities were located in it. Then, beyond the Elbe River and extending along the Baltic to East Prussia was "new" Germany, a zone of colonization won by conquest from the Slavic populations beginning in the twelfth century; sparsely settled and poor, it largely lacked cities and so became the most propitious for political organization by the territorial princes.

The Reformation began on the frontier between "old" and "new" Germany— the "dirty outskirts of the west," as Luther himself put it[7]—the same fault line between developed and backward Europe where, just to the South over the Ertzgebirge Mountains, Hussitism had emerged a century earlier.

THE LUTHER AFFAIR

The new movement began, moreover, as what at first looked like a mere "monks' quarrel" in that academic world of the First Estate that had also produced Hus. The sixteenth century is one of many whose originality has been explained by the "rise of the bourgeoisie," and the Reformation would indeed have its first mass success in the cities of the empire. Yet, if the number of towns over five thousand in Germany had increased from around forty to some eighty in the previous fifty years, the number of universities in Europe had increased from thirty to seventy, for in this allegedly modern century "reality still wore a tonsure."[8] Next to last in date of these establishments was Luther's Wittenberg, founded in 1506 by the elector of Saxony to give luster to his rustic capital. Although Luther probably never nailed his Ninety-five Theses to the door of Wittenberg's castle church, and although he certainly never intended to challenge the existing European order, however his theses were made public, the quarrel they ignited was indeed a powder keg under Christendom.

The acute phase of the veritable revolution that ensued lasted eight years, from the beginning of 1518 to the late summer of 1525 (the Reformation as a broad phenomenon would of course continue for decades more). The first phase of this revolution, between 1518 and 1521, centered on the conflict of Luther the man with the ecclesiastical authority of Rome and the secular authority of the empire. After his condemnation at Worms in 1521, Luther's message was taken up by the cities of southern Germany and Switzerland to become the focus of an active movement of urban or "communal" reformation. And this second phase, in turn, shaded off into the great Peasants' War or communal revolt of 1524–1525. After this explosive climax, leadership of the Lutheran movement passed to the victors of 1525, the territorial princes, and the new church began to assume organized form in both the cities and the princely domains.

After the Diet of Augsburg in 1530 failed, unsurprisingly, to end the religious conflict, the new "confessional" map of the empire began to emerge: the "Protestants," as they had been called after the Diet of Speyer in 1529, were divided between the Lutherans of central and northern Germany and the Sacrementarians of Zwingli's Switzerland and part of the south. The next year, with the formation of the Lutheran Schmalkaldic League of princes and cities, the revolution shaded off into an open political, and soon also military, confrontation between what were now the old and the new churches. What is often regarded as the most revolutionary episode of the entire Reformation, the Münster "New Jerusalem" of 1534–1535, was essentially an aftershock of the main German revolution, that indeed may be described as a fortuitous event created by temporary and local circumstances.

So how did a theological quarrel lead to such mighty consequences? When Luther published his famous theses, in Latin, they were addressed to the university community with the purpose of initiating an academic debate with other theologians on the validity of indulgences. Indulgences, however, were so central to the religious practices of the day, and religion was so central to the European order, that the theses were immediately translated into German and disseminated widely.

Briefly put, indulgences rested on the idea of a "treasury of merits" accumulated by the saints on which the church could draw to release souls from Purgatory. Concretely, this could be achieved when the living performed meritorious acts warranting so many days of "indulgence" for their beloved departed; and late medieval society, obsessed with mortality since the plague of 1345 had killed around a third of Western Europe's population, an anxiety reinforced by the Hundred Years' War and its attendant "great depression," was a world where the departed were almost as omnipresent as the living in people's consciousness.[9] Thus the prime symbols of the age were the charnel house and the dance macabre, with the consequence that private masses for the dead were ever more richly endowed and the demand for indulgences grew constantly. Accordingly, when such a high cleric as the archbishop of Mainz needed funds to obtain a dispensation from Rome in order to hold more than one see, or when Pope Leo X needed monies to continue rebuilding Saint Peter's, indulgences came to be simply sold. Such a sale was then going on just across the frontier from Wittenberg in ducal Saxony. In this connection it must be noted that the sale of indulgences could become a scandal only in the German situation. For the absence of a strong central state greatly facilitated the direct exercise of authority by Rome in a way that was no longer possible in the more consolidated monarchies of England, France, and Spain. It is significant that there never was an indulgence controversy in any of those countries.

Luther's response to this scandal, however, was motivated by nothing so simple as indignation against abuses; rather, it arose from a deep spiritual crisis that had been building throughout his cloistered years, a crisis which now came to its culmination and public expression. For Luther, then age thirty-four, was an unusually good monk, scrupulously following the church's penitential rituals and sacramental practices. Yet for all his efforts he could never overcome his feeling of worthlessness before God or assuage his anxiety regarding salvation. Indeed, such an acute crisis was probably possible only in a monastic milieu and the theological faculties of universities. Release came for Luther when, as professor of Holy Scripture, in lecturing on Saint Paul's Epistle to the Romans, he made the discovery that man is "justified," or made "righteous," solely by the gift of "faith" from God. It is impossible for man to secure salvation by his own efforts either through participation in the sacraments or the performance of "good works" in daily life. Release from sin and hope for redemption come only as the free gift of

God's grace to totally undeserving mortals. This for Luther was "Christian free-dom," liberation of the sinner both from his sin and from the legalistic practices of the church. The first bases of Luther's teaching thus were: *sola fide* ("by faith alone") and *sola gratia* ("by grace alone"). Moreover, the free gift of God's grace came to man from the Word, the logos that was Christ Himself, as this was ex-pressed in Holy Scripture; and this yielded a third pillar of his theology: *sola scrip-tura* ("by Scripture alone"). With this triad of tenets Luther had laid the founda-tions of a theology at complete variance with the time-honored practices of the church, a theology, moreover, that accorded almost everything to God and vir-tually nothing to weak, fallen man. Although initially Luther did not realize that his position made the existing ecclesiastical order superfluous, indeed downright harmful, the reception of his theses among the public and the reaction of the church soon brought out the revolutionary implications of his position. But then, all European revolutions until the nineteenth century began unintentionally: reformers aimed first at certain limited, concrete goals and then belatedly discov-ered that these could be realized only by turning the existing world upside down.

Luther's core tenets of *sola fide* and *sola scriptura* are austere doctrines little likely, on the surface at least, to appeal to a broad public and still less to become the slogans of a mass movement. That they did so was due, first, to the way the authorities handled the "Luther Affair." The public response to his attack on indulgences had been so strong that their chief local beneficiary and Luther's ultimate superior, the archbishop of Mainz, referred the matter to Rome for dis-ciplinary action. Rome, usually slow to act in such matters, this time was expe-ditious: in 1518 Luther was reprimanded by his own Augustinian order and an important cardinal was dispatched to Germany to obtain his recantation, actions which only aggravated the crisis. Luther refused to be silenced, and indeed re-plied with new printed rejoinders. Then, the death of Emperor Maximilian early in 1519 and the election of his grandson Charles diverted the attention of the au-thorities, both secular and ecclesiastical, from the Wittenberg monk, while the public continued to devour his pamphlets. So when the guardians of orthodoxy, the Dominicans, belatedly sought to refute the upstart in a disputation at Leipzig in the summer of 1519 between him and their champion, Dr. Johann Eck, popu-lar interest reached a new peak of intensity. The debate also radicalized Luther. The central subject was papal authority, and Eck provoked Luther into deny-ing it outright, and that of a church council as well. And when Eck accused his adversary of repeating Hus's heresies, Luther openly acknowledged the kinship. The Wittenberger had now publicly burned his bridges to Mother Church.

Who were Luther's supporters at this moment of crisis? The very first were other disaffected clerics, many of whom had been in some degree prepared to receive his message by the dominance of the nominalist *via moderna* in the universities of the day. As contrasted with the *via antiqua* of Thomism, which emphasized the ability of natural reason to know God and his universe, the skeptical heirs of Ockham so diminished the power of natural reason that believers were compelled to fall back on faith alone to know God, who by the same token was made infinitely more remote from man. All of this was an excellent preparation for the doctrine of *sola fide*.[10] Luther himself had been trained in the *via moderna*, though by the time of his public ministry he had rejected it, along with all scholasticism, as an impediment to understanding the Word.

Almost equally attracted to Luther's message were adepts of Erasmus' Christian humanism, with its appeal to biblical authority for reform of the church, its hostility to superstitious popular practices, and its call for a more spiritualized "philosophy of Christ." The humanists had been energized by their recent victory over their scholastic foes in the Reuchlin Affair, a struggle for the use of original languages in biblical scholarship. For these humanists the Luther Affair at first seemed like a new Reuchlin Affair which they could turn into another triumph of Erasmian humanism over scholasticism and superstition. They were of course mistaken, and when the differences between the two types of reform became apparent, the older humanists sided with their leader Erasmus and the younger ones tended to choose Luther. Reuchlin's nephew and Wittenberg's professor of Greek, Philip Melancthon, would quickly become Luther's closest aid.

But why did Luther's somewhat abstruse message catch on so quickly outside the world of professional intellectuals? To his surprise his earliest writings were immediately printed in hundreds and then thousands of copies for that 10 percent of the population which was literate; his ideas were then repeated for the illiterate majority in innumerable sermons across central and southern Germany. This enormous popular interest arose not because the burghers and peasants who now evoked his name fully shared, or even understood, his acute anguish about salvation. Instead, the explosion occurred because Luther's assault on the doctrines and privileges of the First Estate overlapped with the concerns of congeries of different groups in society.

This broad public was concerned, with varying degrees of anxiety, about its fate after death. Their disquiet, however, was oriented less to the subtleties of high theology than to a more diffuse dissatisfaction with a spirituality of indulgences, votive masses, pilgrimages, and holy relics. Over the preceding century and a half a specifically lay piety had developed greatly in an increasingly urban Europe. Going back to the thirteenth century, there were lay communities of women, the Beguines, and somewhat later of men, the Beghards, whose members were not in orders but who lived together and devoted themselves to pious works in the world; similar in nature was the tertiary order of the Franciscans. Closer in time of origin to the Reformation were the confraternities and religious schools of the Brethren of the Common Life. Called the *devotio moderna*, their radically anti-rationalistic spirituality emphasized humanity's utterly fallen nature and the consequent need for God's passively accepted grace. The ethical and introspective nature of their program found its classical expression in Thomas à Kempis's *Imitation of Christ*.[11] Luther's protest thus fell on a well-prepared and fertile soil of lay piety. This preparation, however, was not just spiritual. The laity also had secular concerns, economic occupations, political aspirations, and social grievances. And these concerns tapped into a smoldering anticlericalism that coexisted throughout the Middle Ages alongside an increasingly widespread lay piety. The worldly wealth and power of the church were inevitably resented by ambitious secular lords and growing urban communities. Luther's simplified theology of salvation, among other merits, entailed a simplified, and less costly, ecclesiastical structure.[12]

After the Leipzig Disputation Luther was a major public figure and militant support for him began to appear in society. At the end of 1519 the humanist knight and writer Ulrich von Hutten, together with his colleague Franz von Sickingen, already dreaming of a national crusade against Rome, publicly identified themselves with Luther's cause and offered him their protection.[13] Luther was now emboldened to give a fuller statement of his emerging position. This appeared in the three great treatises of 1520.

The first, written in German, was *The Letter to the German Nobility*. In it Luther proclaimed the replacement of a separate First Estate by the "priesthood of all believers"; henceforth, the only difference between believers was to be one of office or function. The secular authorities, therefore, the emperor and the princes were invited to force reform on the church, an appeal that also conveyed a strong dose of national anti-Romanism. The second, written in Latin though immediately translated, was *The Babylonian Captivity of the Church*; it attacked the sacramental system of the church as the mainstay of a blasphemous "works righteousness" and accepted only baptism, the Eucharist, and, in modified form, penance as scriptural. And the third, written in Latin with a covering letter to the pope but of course also translated, was *On Christian Liberty*. More abstractly theological than its two predecessors, this treatise celebrated the freedom of the reborn Christian from sin through the gift of God's grace and from the servitude to works imposed by the old church. With his three treatises, Luther became the first author in history to sell more than a hundred thousand copies of anything.[14]

The impact he had was thus enormous. Still, the question remains of how much of his message filtered down to the common man. In many cases probably not much more than the *Schlachtwörter:* Christian liberty, the priesthood of all believers, and Scripture alone. But these three were quite enough to knock apart the whole medieval order.

The gauntlet had thus been thrown down to the papacy, and to the existing theological and institutional structure of Christendom. Denouncing the pope as Antichrist, moreover, was no mere metaphor. Like Hus and other radical reformers back to the spiritual Franciscans and Joachim of Fiore, Luther was convinced that the corruption of Christ's church was such that the last days were probably at hand.

For these incendiary pamphlets Luther was threatened with excommunication in the bull *Exsurge Domine.* In October 1520, in a public gesture of defiance he burned the codex of canon law and, for the unlettered public, he threw a copy of the bull into the fire. He was duly excommunicated. With matters at this pass, the church's ultimate protector, the secular sword of imperial authority was obliged to intervene. Luther was therefore summoned to appear before his twenty-one-year-old sovereign and the assembled estates of the empire at a Diet in Worms. Remembering the fate of Hus at Constance, the Elector of Saxony obtained from Charles a safe conduct for a figure who was now the chief glory of his duchy.

Luther's journey to Worms was a triumphal progress. The public debate he sought, however, was not granted him. Instead, in a famous encounter with the emperor he was simply ordered to recant, which he refused to do. In consequence, the Diet voted the Edict of Worms, adding to his excommunication the formal ban of the empire. Since he was now a double fugitive, on his return journey to Wittenberg the Elector of Saxony "abducted" him to the safety of Wartburg castle. There he would remain, translating the New Testament into German, for the next year.

THE URBAN REFORMATION

Until this time the Reformation had been an intellectual movement and an ecclesiastical-judicial struggle around Luther the man; the term "Lutheran," which first appeared in 1519, meant simply his partisans. Before the Diet of Worms Luther had reformed nothing, and afterward it was Lutheran intellectuals rather than Luther himself who seized the initiative to actively reform church practices in accordance with what they took to be his doctrines. In the next four years this movement unfolded in a headlong surge across central and southern Germany, culminating in the great crisis of 1525.[15]

It has long been a cliché of commentary on the Reformation that Lutheranism owed its success to the support of the territorial princes. In fact, before 1525 only one prince, Elector Frederick of Saxony, supported Luther—protection that was of course vital to launching the movement. Yet Frederick, a great collector of relics and very traditional Christian, hardly understood Luther's message; he supported the reformer rather as the star theologian of his university. The first prince to embrace Luther's cause was landgrave Philip of Hesse, who reformed his lands in 1526; there would be no other princely recruits until after 1530.[16] In the decisive formative years 1521–1525, then, the Reformation as a movement was almost entirely an urban event.[17] In this respect Wittenberg, a small peripheral city, for all its moral authority could not be a major model. The center of gravity of the urban Reformation, rather, was southwestern Germany and the Swiss cantons.[18]

Although there were of course differences from one city to another, there is nonetheless a rough general pattern.[19] This pattern is that of what may be called a moderate communal revolution of the late medieval type with the crucial added element of religious and not just of political transformation. Most of the urban centers involved were Free Imperial cities, that is corporate communities with no other overlord than the emperor. These cities had first achieved independence in the twelfth-thirteenth century communal revolts against an episcopal or feudal overlord, a phenomenon first given major historical importance by Guizot.[20] Then, as we have seen with the Flemish towns,[21] in the fourteenth-fifteenth centuries the artisan guilds wrested part of the governing power from the dominant merchants in a second revolt. This brought not genuine democratization, but only a broadening of the ruling oligarchy.[22] In all these cities, already before the Reformation the magistrates had acquired a large measure of control over church appointments and property. It was therefore enough for an evangelical preacher to receive a pulpit to generate popular pressure for an overall reformation of the city's parishes. Two or three years of such pressure was usually enough to bring the patricians of the city council to appoint only evangelicals, to remove images, and eventually to ban the Mass. And in this sense the early German Reformation was a genuine popular movement. In most of southern Germany this process had been completed by 1525 or shortly thereafter. In Nuremberg the transition to Lutheranism had been effected smoothly by the oligarchy without great popular pressure. In Strasbourg the transition had been a protracted and conflicted one with the result that numerous independent radicals were drawn to the town. In Augsburg the presence of the Habsburgs' bankers, the Fuggers, made the city council cautious, with the result that both faiths were tolerated for a significant time. In Basel the Reformation, led by Erasmus's one-time associate Oecolampadius, was almost as Erasmian as Lutheran. Memmingen provided a different mix, and one that is emblematic of the whole revolution inadvertently unleashed by Luther. A radical associate of Zwingli, Christoph Schappeler, in 1522–1523 urged the "common man" to pressure the city council to impose a reformation; the next year, his associate, the town clerk Sebastian Lotzer, synthesized the demands of the local peasants to produce the Twelve Articles of the Peasants' War.[23] The resulting document thus reflects all the currents—religious, civic, plebian—that fueled the revolution overall.

One of the earliest of these urban Reformations was launched in 1519 in Zurich by Ulrich Zwingli.[24] A priest in the city's main church, Zwingli was less anguished spiritually than Luther. Indeed, he had begun his spiritual questing with Erasmus' Christian humanism, and only later became committed to a Pauline and Augustinian theology of grace. He was also motivated by Swiss nationalism, as expressed in his protestations against the hire of Swiss mercenaries by foreign powers, France and the papacy. His mature doctrine, then, combined austere reliance on God's unmediated grace, radical hostility to the Mass, and literal-minded biblicism. This theology was joined with a strong sense of communal solidarity and a practical concern for civic ethics in the manner of Erasmus. In his own words: "The Christian man is nothing but a faithful and good citizen and the Christian city nothing other than the Christian church."[25] Although Zwingli began his reforming activity in Zurich's Great Minster as early as 1519, he moved forward only slowly, by argument and debate, in order to bring the magistrates to his cause. The Zurich, and in general the Swiss Reformation, thus proceeded through a number of staged "disputations" between the old and the new faiths. With the ground thus prepared, the city council formally introduced reform in 1523. Zurich indeed may be regarded as the archetypal urban reformation.

Such a reformation, moreover, changed much more than creed and liturgy; it constituted a major institutional overturn as well. In pre-modern Europe when theology changed, ecclesiology had to change, too; and when ecclesiology changed, society as a whole was deeply affected. The Reformation, whether in the cities or the territorial principalities, destroyed the parallel governmental structure of the church. Monastic orders, that international network undergirding papal power, were the first to go; their considerable properties and endowments went in part to the secular authorities and in part to such organizations as hospitals and the charitable "common chests" now established in the cities. This change affected some 10 to 30 percent of the wealth in the areas involved. At the same time the elaborate system of church courts, which had jurisdiction not only over heresy and morals but all matters pertaining to marriage, inheritance, and such social services as the age afforded, was dismantled and its functions transferred to lay authorities. Offenses by the clergy were no longer tried in separate ecclesiastical courts but in civil courts. In the cities, pastors no longer constituted a caste apart, but instead became ordinary citizens. The census rolls, *l'état civil*, were now kept by the municipality. Canon law, insofar as it survived, was subordinated to civil law. It was not for nothing that Luther had dramatized his final break with Rome by burning the *Codex juris canonicis*. The Lutheran clergy, finally, no longer sat in the territorial estates, although clerics of course remained in the Imperial Diet and in the estates of Catholic regions.

Altogether, these changes represented a significant laicization of society. But was it also secularization? The answer must be: *in potentia* yes, *in actu* no. In the long run the Reformation, by dividing Christianity, made all the separate parts more vulnerable, though this did not become apparent until the end of the seventeenth century. In the short run, too, the Reformation greatly enhanced lay power over the church, as in the paradigmatic case of Zurich, where the city magistrates in effect became the government of the church. Still, this secularization was more apparent than real, since Zwingli and his successor Bullinger so effectively managed the city council that reformed Zurich has plausibly been called a theocracy; Bucer clearly would have liked a similar regime in Strasbourg. In the short run, then, Reformation society remained overwhelmingly "godly." All the same, the institutional dependence of the reformed church on the secular magistrates made continued godliness precarious. It was Calvin who finally solved this problem by giving the reformed church structures that made it institutionally independent. Only on that basis could the new church become enduringly preponderant in society—which was after all the common theocratic dream of the reformers.

SCHWÄRMEREI

Even as Luther's and Zwingli's magisterial Reformation became implanted in the cities it developed a radical "left" wing, and the two currents would continue to develop *pari passu* down to the great explosion of 1525 and the Münster commune of 1534. Indeed, the two began together in Luther's immediate circle in Wittenberg during his absence in the Wartburg. Luther's displacement of the theological center of gravity from the sacraments to *sola fide* and *sola scriptura* obviously required a new ecclesiology, but before Worms he himself had done nothing to work it out. By 1521, however, as a result of his successful defiance of both pope and emperor, the existing ecclesiastical structure was beginning to crumble across southern Germany. One sign of this was the arrival that year in Wittenberg of three plebeian "prophets" from the mining town of Zwickau, where there had been Hussite influence from across the Erzgebirge. Claiming direct inspiration from the Holy Spirit, these prophets denounced infant baptism, called for the elimination of the clergy, and predicted the imminent end of the world. Simultaneously, Luther's fellow theologian Andreas Karlstadt, with the approval of the city council, began to say the Mass in German, forbade church images, and demonstratively condemned clerical celibacy by getting married himself. Popular enthusiasm for these changes led to an outbreak of iconoclasm, the first violence of the Reformation. Put off by this outbreak, Luther on return-ing to Wittenberg in March 1522 immediately undid the recent innovations and preached that henceforth all change should be gradual. Karlstadt was transferred to a rural parish where he took a turn toward populism. Calling himself "brother Andy," he exchanged clerical for ordinary dress, partially Germanized the liturgy, and emphasized the people's social grievances in his preaching. He radicalized doctrinally, too, refusing to baptize infants and publicly arguing against Luther's defense of the real presence in the Eucharist.[26] Like all reformers with a limited agenda, the tumult Luther's defiance had raised caused him to be overrun on his left by enthusiasts with more sweeping agendas.

An even greater threat to Luther's Reformation was posed by Thomas Münt-zer. Until 1523 Müntzer had presented himself as Luther's follower. The latter's intervention to slow reforms at Wittenberg turned Müntzer against him. Asso-ciated early on with Karlstadt, Müntzer soon accused Luther of betraying the renovation of Christendom that he himself had set in motion. Eventually, Münt-zer lashed out in print against "the soft-living lump of flesh of Wittenberg" and "Doctor Liar." Conversely, for Luther Müntzer had become an agent of Satan, quite as bad as the papal Antichrist. In his eyes these radical visionaries were "Schwärmer"—"fanatics" or "enthusiasts," in the literal sense of being filled with a divine fury—and their visions were in fact delusions. And the Schwärmer were indeed the Reformation's *enragés*. Thus, from the very beginning of the Lutheran movement it was challenged by its radical doppelganger. In the two short years after the three foundational treatises of 1520, the Reformation had brought forth the full gamut of its radical potentialities.

Although Müntzer's brief career was certainly spectacular, the real question is: was he important? And what indeed was the real nature of his protest? Ever since Engels's 1850 book Müntzer has been the emblematic figure for the Refor-mation as incipient social revolution.[27] But Engels's high patronage should not lead us to expect from him anything significant in the way of social criticism. Müntzer's path to revolution was entirely theological, and even his theology is hard to reconstruct because of the fragmentary nature of the sources.

We first hear of Müntzer, probably at age thirty-one, in 1520 in Zwickau, where he had received a pulpit on Luther's recommendation (he had once studied in Wittenberg) and where he was close to that city's "prophets." His visionary ser-mons and attacks on more moderate clergy soon incited disorders, and in 1522 he fled to Bohemia in the hope of reviving the embers of Hussite millenarianism. In Prague he first formulated a spiritualist theology resting on direct inspiration from God, a position that caused the Utraquist clergy to expel him from the country. He spent the next year wandering around Germany before settling, in the spring of 1523, in the Saxon mining town of Allstedt, a legally incorporated territorial "city" of nine hundred inhabitants. He remained there sixteen months; this was the period of his greatest success. His first feat was the creation of a year-round German liturgy at a time when Luther had not yet begun this task for Wittenberg. This liturgy was so popular that it drew crowds to Allstedt from the surrounding region, particularly the miners of Mansfeld, who then were exposed to his passionately anticlerical sermons.

By this point Müntzer had developed a doctrine quite distinct from that preached at Wittenberg. The three points of Müntzer's doctrine were as follows: (1) The Spirit was superior to the Word, that God's direct speaking to the soul was a more certain witness of the truth than the plain scriptural text: the letter killed but the spirit quickened. (2) This meant that the scriptural words on the page were the outer covering of an inner word which had to be discerned. (3) It also meant that God, who was not, in Müntzer's favorite phrase, a dumb God, had other ways of communicating with mankind, as by the continuing inspiration of his prophets, by visions, and by the witness of all creation. John Bossy has observed, "In Müntzer's amazing sermon to the Saxon princes on the second chapter of the Book of Daniel the burden of this teaching was to identify the official reformers . . . as letter-mongering scribes and to assert the independent access of the 'common man,' including the illiterate man, to the spirit of Christ."[28]

At one point Müntzer hoped to enlist the Saxon authorities to employ force to purge the church. In a sermon to Frederick the Wise's brother and co-prince Müntzer compared himself to the prophet Daniel converting Nebuchadnezzar to God's cause. After this appeal predictably failed, his millenarian rage was directed equally against princes and clergy. Since Luther had now written "against the rebellious spirit in Allstedt," Müntzer threw him into the category of traitorous clergy as well. With the whole of existing society thus condemned, for Müntzer the simple people, the great suffering mass of humanity, came to be God's special instrument; their mission was to destroy, in one great apocalypse, the whole existing order of things. Citing Jeremiah, Müntzer claimed his words were "like a hammer that splinters the rock" of fallen Christendom. In preparation for action Müntzer organized a paramilitary "league of the elect" among the Allstedters. All that came of this, however, was the demolition of a small chapel outside the city walls. Still, the princes were sufficiently alarmed to frighten Müntzer. In early 1524, he abruptly fled by night over the town wall, leaving behind his new wife and baby and his books.

This time he betook himself to Mühlhausen, then a city larger than both Dresden and Leipzig. At the time it was in the throes of a particularly turbulent reformation led by a runaway Cistercian monk, Heinrich Pfeiffer. Müntzer joined the evangelical party against the city council, and the two preachers together created another paramilitary body, the Eternal League. But the reformers quickly lost this round of the struggle, and Müntzer spent the next winter among peasants in the Black Forest, who were then moving toward open revolt. The following spring, however, he returned for the second, victorious round of the Mühlhausen Reformation.[29] The city council was overthrown and a new "Eternal Council" elected. The paramilitary League was revived with its "rainbow flag" symbolizing humanity's rebirth after the biblical Flood. Later, Müntzer claimed that the League's program was *omnia sunt communia*, that all things were to be held in common, though no concrete steps were ever taken to implement this alleged ideal in either Allstedt or Mühlhausen.

At this point the great Peasants' War rolled up from the south into Thuringia. Müntzer, filled with apocalyptic exaltation, appealed to the Allstedters to join with the Mühlhausen League to "hammer away cling-clang on the anvils of Nimrod." In the expectation that "the people will go free and God alone will be their Lord," he led his host of some three hundred men to join several thousand other peasants and miners encamped at the nearby town of Frankenhausen. In other words, Müntzer joined his millenarian league to an already existing popular movement which was not millenarian but quite concrete and specific in its demands.

The princes soon arrived on the scene, and on the day of battle, May 15, the sun was providentially surrounded with an unusual corona. Müntzer, on horseback, proclaimed to the peasant troops that this was their rainbow omen of victory. The ensuing battle was in fact a slaughter, claiming some seven thousand peasant lives. Soon thereafter Müntzer was captured and tortured; after confessing his subversive intentions, he recanted and was executed. Müntzer's Mühlhausen commune—if indeed it may be called that—had lasted two months.

If this story is to be read as an anticipation of modern socialism, the name that comes most readily to mind is not Marx but Bakunin, whose watchword (1842) was "the desire to destroy is a creative desire." Better still would be to forget about linking Müntzer to modern radicalism. There is nothing in his meager apocalyptic writings or in his ephemeral "leagues" at Altstedt and Mülhausen that looks forward to Owen, Fourier, or Marx. Altogether, Müntzer's itinerant life was a pathetic rather than a heroic story.

Wherever he went he immediately generated such disorder that he had to flee somewhere else. His theology radicalized as his flight lengthened. From the time of the Reformation to the 1840s Müntzer was usually demonized just as he had been in Luther's writing. He was first rehabilitated in the 1840s by Vormärz radicals in search of a German revolutionary tradition, a perspective elaborated by Engels and Kautsky. After World War II the Communist German Democratic Republic promoted him to the rank of great forerunner. The combined result of the demonizing and canonizing approaches to Müntzer has both exaggerated and deformed his historical significance. He was a secondary figure in his day, a parasite on, not a leader of, the Peasants' War. The "Müntzer Affair" is more a problem created by the historiography than by the historical record itself. And this is not the only case of a problem created by retrospective analysis. We will encounter several more such historiographical creations right down to the presentation of October 1917 as a profound social revolution rather than a Bolshevik coup d'état.

Shortly after Saxony produced the Reformation's first radical spin-off, Switzerland produced the second. Quickly labeled Anabaptism by its adversaries, this new schism, like the first, was caused by the cautious reliance of the magisterial reformers on the support of the lay authorities. Zwingli, after all, had reformed the Zurich church only by stages and always through agreement with the city's patrician oligarchy. The loosening of existing structures, however, inevitably encouraged more impatient evangelicals to speak up. Thus in 1523, the very year Zurich was officially proclaimed to be "reformed," a group headed by the well-born and learned layman Conrad Grebel inevitably raised the question of infant baptism. The New Testament data were that the qualifications for baptism were repentance and belief in Christ, its consequences the descent of the Holy Ghost, the forgiveness of sins, and community of goods among the baptized. No infant, they argued, could have faith in or understand the Word. Baptism therefore must be reserved for committed adults. However, infant baptism was the foundation of any church that was coterminous with society, and rejecting it therefore dissolved the civic bond that held the Christian-municipal community of Zurich together. Hence neither Zwingli nor the city council could accept adult baptism, which under conditions of the day meant rebaptism. This, in their view, meant secession from society and a retreat into sectarian divisiveness. Grebel and his supporters answered that only adult baptism was mentioned in Scripture and that it alone could found a church of the truly elect. A disputation was therefore arranged between Zwingli and Grebel in 1525, and Zwingli was of course declared the winner. Grebel and his followers then rebaptized themselves publicly. For this defiance they were banished from Zurich and rebaptism was declared a capital offense punishable by drowning. Having thus failed to capture the Zurich church, the Swiss rebaptizers dispersed northward down the German Rhineland into the Netherlands and eastward into Austria and Moravia. Everywhere the movement spread it produced a variety of local sects with a wide spectrum of doctrinal beliefs (eventually absorbing the heritage of Müntzer and Karlstadt). Nowhere, however, were its adherents numerous, let alone majoritarian, probably less than 1 percent of the population at any given time.[30] Adult baptism is in truth a formula for a sect, not a church.

Generally speaking, the Anabaptists' program took the magisterial theology of the priesthood of all believers to its logical conclusion: full abolition of the sacramental and sacerdotal church in favor of democratic congregations of committed believers who had been rebaptized as adults.[31] Thus the radicals moved beyond the Word of Scripture to the inspiration of the Holy Spirit; accordingly, they sought to implement reform outside of existing secular structures. By the same token, the movement had no single structure, nor did it seek to make itself coterminous with society. It was a sect, a grouping of the elect, self-consciously setting itself outside of existing society. It was because of this refusal of existing society that the Anabaptists also refused to swear any oaths. It was also usually millenarian in the most literal sense of the term, expecting the imminent end of the world and the Second Coming of Christ. As a sect of the elect, moreover, it did not believe in predestination but in the freedom of the individual to choose and to join the sect. In this respect it is debatable whether the Anabaptists were part of the Reformation at all but instead the reemergence of older, medieval heresies.

Original Swiss Anabaptism emerged in 1525 during the Peasants' War and it spread to south Germany during the repression that followed, in 1526–1527. Awed by this experience, these first Anabaptists were pacifists. Yet, since their movement was predicated on radical refusal of the existing world, a potential for violence against its wickedness was almost unavoidably present. Indeed, a potential for violence was inherent in the Reformation's dynamic generally. When reformers, no matter how pacifically intended, attempt to fundamentally alter society's moral pillar, the church, force is always a temptation for their more impatient followers. This potential first became actual with Karlstadt and the Zwickau prophets. Its specifically Anabaptist variant would reach its culmination in the Münster commune.

THE REVOLUTION OF THE "COMMON MAN"

It was in this mixed and increasingly radical atmosphere that during 1524–1525 the Reformation spread from the cities and small towns to the countryside and the peasantry. Or more exactly there occurred a symbiosis of urban and peasant radicalism; in both town and country, moreover, religious reformation also came to mean the communal bonding of the population. By now the revolution triggered by Luther was widely perceived to be above all a revolution of the "common man," *der gemeine Mann,* by which was meant both the ordinary man of the lower classes and the "communal" or "communitarian" member of a corporate town or parish.[32] Such democratization, of course, was quite like what had occurred in Bohemia in 1419–1420. This religious-communitarian surge produced the zenith of the German Reformation as a semi-revolution. Representatives of all corporate categories, from the top to the bottom of the estate structure, were now involved; for a moment they seemed to offer a united front against the old church.

The prelude to this expected general insurrection was a revolt of the imperial knights von Hutten and von Sickingen. In 1523, these quixotic representatives of a declining estate attacked one of the great ecclesiastical princes, the Elector Archbishop of Trier. Since Luther's theology had undermined the First Estate's position in the empire, the pair intended to secularize the archbishopric in favor of southwest Germany's multitude of knights. They also wished to set a precedent for dismantling the other numerous and extensive ecclesiastical principalities. This military adventure failed dismally, however; the archaic figure of the free imperial knight was no match for the emperor's new mercenary troops.

But the principal insurrection was the Peasants' War of 1525. This was indeed the largest and most radical social movement to occur anywhere in Europe before the French Revolution. Ranke no less than Engels asserted its centrality in German history and recognized its authentically revolutionary character. Beginning in the fall of 1524 near Lake Constance, the next year the rebellion spread rapidly through Swabia and southern Germany, then north to Thuringia and Saxony, east to Austria and the Tyrol, and west to Alsace. There had been major peasant revolts in the south German-Upper Rhine region before: in various times since 1490 the standard of the *Bundschuh,* the heavy peasant boot, had been raised; as recently as 1514 the "Poor Conrad" revolt had shaken Württemberg. And these revolts had also invoked the religious justification of "godly law." Given this background, even without Luther's Reformation, further rural unrest was to be expected in the same area. But the religious fermentation unleashed by Luther gave the new peasant revolt an unprecedented extent and power.

Nevertheless, this mighty movement, after a single tumultuous springtime, was put down in bloodshed. Its failure, moreover, finally broke the momentum of revolutionary change unleashed by Luther in 1517. The Reformation, of course, continued to produce radical changes in Germany and beyond its borders. But these came in a series of lesser flare-ups; the continuous, impetuous torrent of change was over. Doomed as well was the idea of a united priesthood of all believers. The common man was no longer invited by the Reformation's pastors, magistrates, and princes, its intellectual and political leaders, to join with them in purifying the church and advancing the Word of God. Henceforth, reformation would come only from above.

Although the early sixteenth century was a time of economic growth it was also marked by rising prices, and this led both lay and ecclesiastical lords to tighten the pressure of manorial dues on their peasants. This pressure had been increasing, and the peasants' lots worsening, throughout the previous century, but especially in the decades before 1525.[33] Indeed, serfdom, which had largely been done away with in the thirteenth century, was beginning to return in southwestern Germany, a prelude to the great "second serfdom" which would triumph east of the Elbe later in the century. The state-building activity of the territorial princes was of course one cause of this increased fiscal pressure, though the burden on monastic peasants was even greater. Accordingly, princes and abbots were the chief targets of the revolt. Where the peasants were manorial subjects of towns, their hostility was less intense. Indeed, the towns furnished a model of organized, communal self-help as the wave of municipal reformations swept through the free imperial cities of the region during 1522–1523. In fact, there was considerable symbiosis between these cities and the countryside. In addition, the peasants had the example of successful republican revolt in nearby Switzerland; and they could turn for leadership to the many mercenary *Landsknechte* living among them.

Prodded by these multiple stimuli, by the beginning of the century the peasants were developing something of a political consciousness. As the territorial princes consolidated their legislative and administrative powers by replacing customary law with Roman law, the peasants attempted to respond by creating territorial assemblies, *Landschaften*, partly allied with the old territorial estates against the lords' *Herrschaften*. The peasants' political consciousness thus was cast as a struggle of outmoded customary law against modern, universal Roman law. At this juncture, Luther's challenge to the existing church order with the call for a priesthood of all believers under the divine law of Christ's Word gave the peasants a new weapon against lordly law: the Divine Law of the Gospel.[34] And so the concrete social and economic grievances of the peasantry after 1524 came to be fused with the Christian liberty preached by Luther and the other reformers. In a society where the ultimate principle of legitimacy was theological, the peasants' grievances now claimed the highest benediction. Almost as important in the Reformation's impact on the revolution of the common man was the example that Luther had given in successfully defying both Pope and Emperor, the highest authorities in Christendom. Once this example had been given, everything was up for grabs in the world of the two swords.

Thus, in the summer of 1524 the peasants of the south and center organized armed bands to resist the encroachment of manorial dues and to protest the weight of their fiscal obligations to the church, particularly the tithe and feudal dues owed to monasteries. The extreme fragmentation of authority in southern Germany greatly facilitated this action. For six months the Swabian League of nobles and cities under imperial command negotiated with the peasants (most of its troops were away in Italy fighting in the Habsburg's war against the Valois), and during this time the peasant protests remained peaceful. Lacking central direction, different bands of peasants produced various statements of their demands, usually with the help of urban leaders, especially radical clerics, associated with the ongoing and often turbulent municipal reformations.

The most famous of these documents was the Twelve Articles of the Peasants which, as we have seen, began to circulate from the southern city of Memmingen in February 1525. Phrased in language that was probably more moderate than the peasants' real feelings, it was a reformist rather than a revolutionary statement. Its main points were, first, the right of each community to choose its own pastor, a demand by then quite general in Germany. Other articles accepted the obligation of paying the "great tithe" on grain while rejecting other, "minor tithes." Serfdom, moreover, was denounced as "contrary to the gospel and Christian freedom," an article which was both a specific demand and an assertion of the peasants' right to a more equitable place in society as a moral and religious principle. Other articles claimed the right to fish and hunt and to cut wood in the common forests. Excessive manorial dues and corvée labor were protested. Still other articles attacked the extension of formal, Roman law at the expense of the "old written law" based on immemorial custom. Indeed, in some other lists of grievances peasants called for reviving the central authority of the empire both as a protection against the princes and the knights and as a means of strengthening the German nation. In the twelfth article, finally, the peasants declared their willingness to withdraw any articles contrary to the Word of God. Moreover, they promised not to use force except as a last resort, and called on the Elector of Saxony and on the great prophet of Christian freedom, Luther, to arbitrate their demands with the imperial authorities.

The revolt further sharpened peasant political consciousness. This is in part a reflection of the fact that, although the troops of the 1525 revolution were overwhelmingly peasant, there was also considerable participation of urban artisans and, in some regions, miners, groups that brought greater sophistication to the cause of the common man. Consequently, the revolt threw up a number of what might be called constitutional projects, or at least suggestions. Most of these were variations on the theme of the territorial *Landschaft* assemblies, which are now given a "corporative-associative" form. That is, the new political order was to be based on voluntary groupings of guild-like social *corps* of peasants, artisans, miners or any other species of common man below the first two estates and the magisterial oligarchies of the cities. Thus in Württemberg, Salzburg, Tyrol and elsewhere, different kinds of assembly were proposed depending on local conditions, but in all of them the clerical and the noble estates were eliminated, leaving only the corporative people under the now much reduced authority of the local prince. The revolt of the common, therefore, in modern historiography comes to be a kind of *frühdemokratische Revolution*.

At first the peasant bands indeed eschewed violence; but with upward of three hundred thousand armed men roving the countryside by the end of April, 1525, some bands inevitably turned to plundering and destroying monasteries and attacking noble property. When the revolt reached Thuringia, Luther himself went out into the countryside urging the peasants to interpret Christian freedom "spiritually, not carnally," and returned frightened by the peasants' anger. For its part, the government of Archduke Ferdinand, Charles V's brother, now only pretended to negotiate to gain time for mobilizing its troops. Conversely, the fragmentation of political authority in Germany afforded the peasants no central target of attack: there was no Bastille to storm or national Diet to pressure into enacting their demands. Nor could the various peasant bands stay mobilized for long; after two weeks on the road they had to return home to tend to their fields. So as April turned into May the aimless movement of the "common man," of the "Karsthans," spun out of control. Everywhere, as earlier in Bohemia, a particular hatred was displayed toward anything connected with learning and books. In some places the revolt attracted the last members of the revolutionary knighthood, such as Götz von Berlichingen. In other places, it gathered support from artisans of small towns. And of course it attracted radical clerics and millenarian prophets of whom Thomas Müntzer was the most notable example. Still, overwhelming force was on the side of the princes', not the peoples', sword. By the end of June the revolt had been suppressed virtually everywhere, at a total cost of some hundred thousand lives.

Could things have been otherwise? Blickle and other sympathetic modern historians intimate that they might have been. Several imperial cities, notably Erfurt and Memmingen, had managed to coexist with the peasant bands. One can therefore imagine a peasant and urban-communal victory leading to something like the Swiss formula. But republican-federalist Switzerland had survived largely because the Alps furnished it a natural sanctuary. In the open spaces of the empire the pan-European logic of modern state-building was completely against this early democratic revolution. And this the princes understood very well. Indeed, their consistent refusal to negotiate somewhat resembles Adolfe Thiers's *politique du pire* with the Paris Commune. Faced with the magnitude of the 1525 insurrection, the princes chose to crush the peasants totally so as to end once and for all the threat of the rural *Bundschuh*. And, just as Thiers did in fact end the Parisian insurrectionary tradition, the princes' strategy worked. With a few minor concessions afterward, the German peasants were not heard from again until the nineteenth century.

THE MÜNSTER COMMUNE

Although the first great surge of the Reformation-as-revolution ended in 1525, the national, indeed European, reforming movement ignited by Luther was by no means over. Within Germany itself, the dispersal of political power would continue to channel this movement into a series of local reformations. After 1525 the territorial princes led the way with state-imposed reforms from above, especially in the poorer lands of "new" Germany east of the Elbe; the Scandinavian kingdoms and the crusading orders along the Baltic coast offer similar cases. Yet by now such conversions had become a rather routine revolution. Similarly, the Reformation in the free imperial cities of the north was by and large kept within the magisterial bounds. But in one case, the episcopal city of Münster, the inevitable radical sequel of reform quickly reached an unprecedented peak of intensity.

With the Münster Commune of 1534–1535 Germany at last produced a real if locally circumscribed Tabor. Indeed, during the commune's sixteen months of existence the city lived through the maximal revolutionary cycle pioneered by Hussite Bohemia.[35] And it did so because the "revolutionary alliance system," which broke down in 1525 in the south, now realized its complete radical potential and gave all power to the people, or more exactly to their *enragés* leaders. Here was Müntzer's dream at last acted out in a full apocalypse.

The lurid result came about because of the conjunction of the standard German communal reformation, which came late to the north, with an eschatological variant of Anabaptism, the Melchiorite movement centered in nearby Holland. Münster, a self-governing city of fifteen thousand, began its reformation in 1531 under the leadership of a dynamic priest turned Lutheran, Bernhard Rothmann, who had the support of the guilds. By 1533 this reformation was recognized by treaty with the nonresident bishop and protected by the de facto religious

truce instituted by the Augsburg recess of 1530. Rothmann, however, was radicalizing with the times: under the influence of Zwinglians expelled from nearby
Wassenberg he adopted the symbolic interpretation of the Eucharist, which was
not protected by the Augsburg truce. The Münster reformation was now illegal; the bishop threatened; the Lutheran-cum-Catholic patricians tried to expel
Rothmann; he mobilized the guilds and forced the city council to back down.
Münster was now a haven of toleration, and a magnet for more radical enthusiasts, namely Anabaptists.[36]

When the pacifist Swiss Anabaptists were suppressed in 1525 the movement
spread eastward to Moravia, where its adherents became agricultural communi-
tarians called the Hutterites, and northward to the Rhineland, where Melchior
Hoffmann, a former furrier and lay preacher once influenced by Karlstadt, added
millenarian prophecy to the core creed of believer baptism. In 1529 he arrived
in Strasbourg, then completing an eight-year-long transition to reform whose
hesitations made the city a haven of toleration, much as Münster became in
1533; religious radicals of all stripes, including even the Spanish unitarian Miguel
Servetus, flocked to the city. This fermentation convinced Hoffmann that Strasbourg would be the holy city of the last days and the Second Coming. Claiming the enunciatory role given Elijah in Revelation, he so prophesied to his followers, intimating that 1533 might be the date.[37] He then moved down the Rhine
to the Netherlands, where his preaching brought him a sizable cult following
among artisans and the poor at a particularly difficult time economically. When
he returned to Strasbourg in 1533 he discovered that Bucer, like Luther in 1522
and Zwingli in 1525, was putting the lid on all *Schwärmerei* in Strasbourg; Hoffmann was imprisoned for what turned out to be life. The Netherlands "Melchiorites," however, led by the baker Jan Matthijs, still expected the millennium
imminently, and in 1533 made a botched attempt to seize power in Amsterdam.
Then Matthijs heard of Münster's wonderful revolution, and so sent "apostles"
to persuade Rothmann to accept adult baptism. These Melchiorites' eschatological expectations, moreover, were transferred from Strasbourg to Münster. The
city was now doubly outside the imperial pale, and the bishop declared a legally
sanctioned military "feud" against it. Moreover, the Lower German and Dutch
Schwärmer had not learned the lesson of caution administered by the disaster of
1525, for that great revolt and its repression had never touched the north.

In February 1534, some city council moderates admitted a few episcopal troops
to the city, thus leading the city's hitherto pacifist Anabaptists to take up arms
to defend Rothmann and the guilds. Faced with this defiance, the council backtracked on the grounds that it had more to fear from the bishop, who threatened
its civic independence, than from the Anabaptists and the guilds. Plied with

beer, the bishop's men obeyed the council's order to withdraw; Rothmann and his chosen flock were saved. This "miracle" signaled to Melchiorites everywhere that Münster was now the holy city for the Second Coming. When municipal elections fell due a few days later, the Anabaptists won handily. The essential point in all this is that the Münster Anabaptists came to power legally, and with the substantial support in the establishment; the new council elected a wealthy draper Bernard Knipperdollinck, himself no mean visionary, to be one of the *Bürgermeister*. Exceptionally for Germany, the revolutionary alliance system had created Tabor in a single city. The Münster miracle was now complete: the Melchiorites were no longer outcast dissenters but the *Obrigkeit* itself. Surely, it was God's will that the city was to be the New Jerusalem.

Soon Matthijs himself arrived along with Jan Breuker of Leyden, a tailor, and other Dutch Anabaptists. Matthijs, claiming to be Enoch to the imprisoned Hoffmann's Elijah, began a six weeks' rule as extra-constitutional charismatic leader. Rothmann became his spokesman, turning out apologias and appeals for support from other sectarians. At first Matthijs wanted to slay all the ungodly in the city, but Knipperdollinck persuaded him to let some two thousand Lutherans and Catholics depart; some twenty-five hundred Anabaptists from nearby territories immediately replaced them. The émigrés' property was confiscated, all wealth was declared to be common property, the city took control of the food supply, money was abolished in favor of barter (although confiscated wealth was kept by the city for dealings with the outside world). The constitution was not formally abolished, however, Matthijs appointed twelve elders who in fact administered everything. This "communist" order was in part a response to siege conditions, but it also expressed the recurrent sectarian dream of a society like the primitive church as portrayed in the Acts of the Apostles. Thomas More's *Utopia* twenty years earlier offered a similar vision.

Matthijs's rule came abruptly to an end in April when he sallied forth against the besiegers, as he claimed, to produce a "miraculous" victory. Or did he commit suicide because his prophecies failed to come true?[38] Jan of Leiden immediately assumed the succession. By now, however, eschatological enthusiasm was beginning to wane. Efforts to bring hundreds of new supporters from Holland were thwarted by the Habsburg authorities. An Easter coup by the Amsterdam Melchiorites ended in their massacre. And the siege grew tighter.

Leiden's response was to institutionalize Melchiorite charisma by turning it into permanent theater on cathedral square. After repulsing an attack by the bishop in August, a fellow prophet proclaimed Leiden king after the manner of David. The king surrounded himself with a court, imitated the empire's ceremonial trappings, and promoted the twelve elders to the rank of duke. He claimed his kingship would one day extend over the world, and assigned his dukes vast foreign territories. More pragmatically, he buttressed his power by keeping patrician Knipperdollinck as vice-regent. But Leiden's most notorious innovation was instituting forced polygamy. Had not King David and the patriarchs enjoyed that practice? And were there not more women than men in Münster, while the city needed to breed 144,000 saints (according to Revelation 7:4) to precipitate the end-time. This measure produced a revolt among the citizenry's apparently numerous skeptics. Leiden put the rebels down with fifty executions. He killed one of his own disobedient wives and trampled on her body in the city square. And indeed, terror was essential to his rule. So a desperate mixture of social distress, military mobilization, and visionary millenarianism permitted the commune to survive until June 1535 when the city was stormed by a Protestant-Catholic coalition and the inhabitants massacred. Rothmann was killed during the battle. Leiden and Knipperdollinck were tortured and publicly executed. Their remains were hung in an iron cage suspended from a church belfry. The empty cage is still there today.

As a practical matter the Münster Commune's only impact on the Reformation's development was to give spectacular confirmation to its magisterial leaders' hatred of *Schwärmerei*. Nor did the commune offer any lessons for modern social radicalism. It is of considerable interest, however, for the light it sheds on the basic mechanisms of the European revolutionary process. First, it makes clear that in a religion-driven revolution, theology is not a mere cloak for political or social grievances; theology, rather, determines political alignments and overrides social considerations. Acceptance or rejection of the real presence divides moderates from radicals in all reformed ecclesiastical polities. Likewise infant versus adult baptism divided ultra-radicals from the rest of the ecclesiastical political spectrum, just as violent versus pacific believer baptism divided the ultra-radicals into tolerable, and often meritorious, sectarians and hopelessly asocial, anarchist outlaws. And disputes over the sacraments, especially the Eucharist, would play a central role in revolutionary politics down to 1688.

Second, Münster confirms what might be called the "law," first demonstrated by Hussitism, that the degree of radicalism any upheaval can generate depends on the inclusiveness of the revolutionary alliance system. In the case of Münster the system became all-inclusive, thus permitting the usual German urban communal reformation to implement the most extreme social measures while at the same time keeping the old hierarchical corporate structures basically intact. Münster's "communism," after all, as a practical matter did not go very far; the godly kept their property and belongings, with the reservation that doors be left open with half-height grills to keep out pigs and chickens. This inclusiveness of course was unable to stave off disaster because a mini-revolution in a single city could not survive in a society that overall was non-revolutionary. By contrast, in the case of Tabor the same formula created a military machine capable of conquering state power because the society overall was revolutionary. In so doing, however, Tabor shed its early communism and became just a military machine. And in the perverse logic of utopia, both communes, Tabor and Münster, suggest parallels with the besieged modern millenarianisms of the Jacobins and the Bolsheviks, analogies that will be pursued in due course.

One outcome of the Münster episode was the taming of Anabaptism. The excesses of Leiden's commune had served to discredit violence and revolution, and indeed risked discrediting sectarian religion as such. Eventually, therefore, in the Netherlands Menno Simons reorganized the surviving Anabaptist groups into congregations devoted to pacifism and a moral life of apostolic purity. The post-revolutionary culmination of Anabaptism in Mennonism repeats the transformation of one wing of the Taborites into the Czech Brethren, just as it anticipates the transformation of militant Independency in England into Quakerism. Here, clearly, is a significant regularity in millenarian revolutionary movements.

But that is not the only heritage of Anabaptism. For the myth of Müntzer's Mülhausen and of the Münster commune would live on as symbols of the Reformation's "betrayal" of its own evangelical promise. And in this respect it offers a rough analogy with the Levellers and the Diggers in England and Babeuf in France, those two post-Thermidorian explosions of desperate radicalism whose myths endured as reproaches to the shortcomings of radical Calvinism and Jacobinism, respectively. Although neither produced any results, both adumbrated similar, and far bolder, revolutionary adventures in the future. Even so, Münster remains an anomaly within the Reformation.

A REVOLUTION WITHOUT THERMIDOR?

But what of that mainstream movement? When, if ever, did it reach a Thermidor? In ordinary language, Thermidor means the end of the forward surge of revolutionary change, together with the burnout of enthusiastic "fever." The year 1525 certainly marked an abatement of these forces, though they would periodically return throughout the century, not just at Münster but elsewhere in Europe. So how did the initial German and Lutheran Reformation-as-revolution come to a conclusion?

In the wake of 1525 the Lutheran movement began to settle into stable doctrinal and organizational form. The first step was to establish a clear separation between the churches of Wittenberg and Zurich. The chief subject of discord between the two was, once again, Christianity's central rite, the Eucharist. Although Luther rejected the Roman doctrine of transubstantiation, he held firm to the principle of the real presence; the Eucharist, together with baptism, thus remained genuine sacraments, and hence necessary for salvation. Zwingli and his followers, now called "sacramentarians," on the other hand believed that the Lord's Supper was merely a commemorative action, involving no "substantial" transformation of the bread and wine and hence not a sacrament in the usual sense. In 1529 the two leaders met at a colloquy at Marburg and failed to close the gap between them. Henceforth the two movements went their separate ways amidst increasing acrimony. Thus began the process of fragmentation within Protestantism, and indeed within Germany as a whole, known as "confessional-ization." Zwinglianism thereafter was confined to Switzerland and some cities on the upper Rhine, and ultimately wound up close to Calvinism. Most of the south German cities, however, eventually followed Luther. That they did so was due to the new political configuration in the empire.

In 1530 Charles V returned to Germany after almost ten years' absence tending to his affairs in Spain and Italy, as well as parrying the Mediterranean menace of the Turks. After the Diet of Worms had condemned Luther, the program of his followers was a "free" church council, meaning one not summoned by the pope, which would also meet on German soil. The emperor too wanted a council in Germany, though, in accordance with the two-swords ideology, he wanted the pope to summon it. The papacy, however, dragged its feet because it feared that a council in Germany under imperial auspices would either concede too much to the Lutherans or limit papal authority, as had indeed occurred at Constance and Basel. As a result of this deadlock the religious division in Germany was hardening into schism, and to head this off Charles sought to resolve the religious issue through a debate of the theologians on both sides at the special Diet in Augsburg in 1530. For this purpose Luther and his chief aide Philip Melancthon for the first time systematically formulated the beliefs of the Wittenberg church, and Zwingli did the same for the Zurich community. Although the schism was not healed, Melancthon's Augsburg Confession became the official creed of what was now becoming a separate Lutheran church, and Zwingli's document became the basis of a rival creed, the Helvetic Confession.

The following year the process of confessionalization advanced still further when the Protestant princes and most south German cities formed a defensive alliance, the Schmalkaldic League. Since the Lutheran princes constituted the league's real force, they imposed the Augsburg Confession on all members, thereby moving the south German cities from Zwingli's orbit into Luther's.[39]

Zwingli's death in battle that same year also weighed in the decision. With these events the foundational phase of the Reformation was over.

Luther by then had progressively abandoned many of his more radical positions of 1519–1521. We have already seen his insistence on a fairly traditional interpretation of the Eucharist, as well as of ceremonies, vestments, painting, and music. He backtracked even further as regards church organization. In 1526, right after the Peasants' War, the Saxon Elector organized the first "visitation" of his territory to supervise the workings of the new church. Soon this lay supervision was given institutional form in a "consistory," a board of divines and laymen appointed by the Elector. As the Reformation settled into a routine after 1530, this formula was applied in the various princely states. This outcome fitted logically with Luther's view of the opposition between the spiritual and the secular kingdoms. The former was constituted by the visible church and its vital core, the *corpus christianum*, or the minority of the truly saved; the latter was the realm of violence and evil which could be kept in check only by the firm hand of princely authority. All that the church required of that authority was to ensure that "the pure Word was preached and the sacraments properly administered."[40]

In 1544 peace with France at last made it possible for Charles V to act decisively in Germany; the following year he won a spectacular victory over the Schmalkaldic League at Mühlberg. Believing that Protestantism's progress had now been halted for good, and still waiting for a general council, he imposed what he thought was a compromise solution, the Interim. It was in fact more Roman than Lutheran, and so satisfied no one. In 1547, however, the emperor's chief princely ally changed sides, and the emperor was driven from central Germany to the Austrian Tyrol. Europe's first religious war thus ended in a draw, a fact formally recognized by the Peace of Augsburg in 1555. This institutionalized the confessional division of Germany on the basis of the principle later known as *cuius regio, eius religio* (he who owns the land determines the religion). Dissenters from this formula only had the right to emigrate, the *ius emigrandi*.

Although this settlement formally preserved the empire's unity, since the Reformation still lived by the principle that church and society were one, the religious division sanctioned by the Peace of Augsburg in fact also divided the polity. The year 1555 thus marked the victory of the territorial princes over the Habsburgs' centralizing efforts; Charles V's lifelong effort to preserve the world of the two swords had been defeated. He therefore surrendered the imperial office and his Austrian lands to his brother Ferdinand, and departed for the Netherlands to abdicate all his other dominions to his son Philip.

These events of course did not mark the end of Protestantism's revolutionary progress. The movement would flare up again several times in the second half of the century, and indeed would rumble on into the middle of the next century, both in the continental Thirty Years War and in the English Puritan Revolution. The Reformation-as-revolution thus has no Thermidor, or indeed any clear terminal date. As a serial revolution it simply continued until, at the end of the seventeenth century, religion began to be eclipsed by secular enlightenment as the prime motor force in European culture. Still, within this *longue durée* any given Reformation episode does have an end, and 1555 marks that terminus for the initial Lutheran revolution, both the great forward surge of 1517–1525 and the long consolidation of confessionalism between 1525 and 1555.

AUTOPSY OF AN ARRESTED REVOLUTION

In considering the Reformation-as-revolution, the great question is why that revolution stopped in mid-course, in 1525. Or to put the same problem in terms of a comparison: whereas in Bohemia *all* social strata—clerics, lords, knights, burgers, artisans, and peasants—had come together in the Utraquist revolution, why is it that in Germany these same strata divided *in media res*, thus abruptly ending Lutheranism's revolutionary phase?

Friedrich Engels, in his *Peasant War in Germany*, was among the first to wrestle with this problem. Writing in 1850, he viewed the events of 1525 through the prism of another failed German revolution, that of 1848. Thus, the Reformation become an "early bourgeois revolution" and it failed, from Engels's perspective, because after the movement necessarily turned violent, the "liberal moderates" led by Luther betrayed the proto-proletarian plebs led by Müntzer—a scenario he saw repeated with different actors in 1848. Engels's view of 1848 (though not of 1525) is also similar to the twentieth-century Bielefeld school's judgment that Germany pursued a deviant Sonderweg, or special path, to modernity because of the "failed democratic revolution" of 1848.[41] But if Germany experienced two failed revolutions, does this mean that some special conservative curse has weighed all along on its national destiny?[42] Be that as it may, the question remains why, in both cases of revolutionary failure, German moderates could not make the pact with the plebeian devil made by their analogues in fifteenth-century Bohemia, and later elsewhere?

Many causes contributed to this outcome. The most obvious of these is that the scale of plebeian violence in 1525 provoked a coalition of all the other elements of society to put it down. It is obvious that the emperor's brother and regent Ferdinand, the princes, some of the free cities, and both the new and the old churches had a preponderance of force and institutional legitimacy over the roving peasant bands. Comparison with Hussite Bohemia, however, reveals a wider range of causes.

First come chance and personality. Thomas Müntzer was no Jan Želivský, for all his unbridled enthusiasm a man with genuine leadership capacity and organizational abilities. Similarly, the class of German knights produced no Jan Žižka to give the German Schwärmer an adequate secular sword of their own: Franz von Sickingen and Götz von Berlichingen were only petty condottieri. Another contrast is that the German movement's charismatic prophet, Luther, unlike Hus, was still alive; supported by the majority of ecclesiastical reformers, he ostentatiously withdrew from the revolt its moral legitimation, the sanction of God's Word. In his pamphlet *Against the Robbing and Murderous Peasants' Bands*, in violent language he reasserted the Pauline injunction that all men are "subjected to the powers that be," thereby wholeheartedly endorsing military repression by the princes. In an age when the Law of God was the supreme law for man, this "ideological" or cultural factor counted mightily.

Second come the structural factors, beginning with Luther's new theology. The Reformer was so vehement in his condemnation of the peasants because he correctly sensed that their movement was in fact gravitating toward Müntzer's program of justification by destruction; and for him this millenarian travesty of the Word was just as diabolical as the Roman Antichrist. In short, for Luther what was at stake in combating the peasants was nothing less than the future of God's work in this world. By his repudiation of the peasants in 1525 Luther drew a line beyond which his Reformation would not go without falling into heresy itself. And that line ran between a church coterminous with society itself—that is, old Christendom in new form—and a sectarian fragmentation of the one church founded on spurious inspiration of the Holy Spirit. This view of the indissoluble unity of church and society was of course also that of the princes and the urban magistrates. Although the peasants subscribed to a cooperative-associative view of the good society, in fact their radical deconstruction of the church came near to its complete localization and sectarian separatism.

As a result of all these factors, there would be no German Tabor, but only such disastrous plebeian flare-ups as Mülhausen in 1525 or especially Münster in 1536. Nor would there be anything like the patrician-plebeian alliance of Prague and Tabor. And on this score Engels has a point. Although he completely failed to understand Münzter, because he could not take his religious motivation seriously, Engels did clearly grasp the political alliance system governing the revolutionary process. The Reformation-as-revolution was cut short because its alliance system could not be extended to include the most radical and democratic element. Any revolutionary movement that goes the limit of its radical potential requires a plebeian alliance that is against the natural order of politics.[43] Monasteries were burning in the summer of 1419 in Bohemia, but this did not reconcile the great lords and Prague with Emperor Sigismund. Cromwell's New Model Army was rife with Leveller and Independent democracy, but this did not prevent four years of collaboration with an upper-class Presbyterian Parliament. Chateaus were burning in August 1789 in France, but this did not slow the reforming effort of the Constituent Assembly or throw it into the arms of Louis XVI, nor were Jacobin lawyers afraid to mobilize Parisian *sans-culottes* against all enemies of the Republic. A key explanation of the German failure, then, is that whereas the leaders of Czech, English, and French civil society felt they had more to fear from the armed strength of the old sovereign than from plebeian turbulence, German princes and urban magistrates had far more to fear from the unleashed common man than from their imperial overlord. So the Reformation-revolution against the First Estate never went beyond that basic objective because the holders of the secular sword fought to maintain and expand their traditional position.

Yet had the spiritual sword been wholly eliminated? After all, Lutheran Germany remained a world where church and community were still coterminous. The spiritual sword had certainly been blunted, and the secular sword, at the territorial if not at the imperial level, was much more powerful than before, guaranteed as it was a right of interference in church affairs far beyond what Rome had had to accept before 1517. All this was a mighty demotion and a loss of worldly power for the church. Even so, the Lutheran pastor was not just another liberal professional, although as an university-educated man he was that too. He had a calling, a *Beruf*, one that was more solemn than the ordinary secular calling which in the Lutheran perspective all believers were expected to exercise. His office, his *Amt*, was to preach God's salvatory Word, and this set him apart from, and above, the ordinary Christian. Even in this reduced state, therefore, the Protestant pastorate remained a kind of clerical caste reminiscent of the old First Order. In this respect, too, the Reformation-revolution lacks a decisive ending.

Who then were the overall winners and losers in the German reformation-as-revolution? In the initial revolutionary surge the winners of the Revolution were the urban patriciate in the south and the territorial prince everywhere, but especially in the center and the north. Concomitantly, the main loser in this phase was the "common man." In the period of consolidation, however, when religious matters were settled by war, the cities, for all their defensive walled strength, could not compete with the princes, and so increasingly lost out to them. But in both phases the greatest loser was the church. Although major ecclesiastical principalities such as Cologne and Würzburg managed to survive at the cost of some concessions to princely hegemony, everywhere the spiritual sword was greatly diminished. Overall, then, the emperor, the church, the cities, and of course the common man were the losers and the territorial princes the great gainers.

In sum, the German Reformation represents the first occurrence in the recurring European revolutionary process of what may be called *revolutio interrupta*. It therefore represents the first instance of a major variant on the basic pattern of full European revolution that had been inaugurated in Hussite Bohemia. As we shall see, this variant would turn out to be essentially the appanage of central Europe, most notably in 1849.

4

HUGUENOT FRANCE, 1559–1598

Give me wood, and I will send you arrows.
—JOHN CALVIN to the churches of France

Paris is worth a Mass.
—HENRY OF NAVARRE

After the mid-sixteenth century the radical Augustinian theology of Calvinism and its revolutionary presbyterian ecclesiology would be the driving force of Protestantism throughout Europe, spreading out from Calvin's own Geneva eastward to Poland and Hungary, northward to the Low Countries, Scotland, England, and in the next century to British North America. In Lutheran Germany itself, this "second Reformation" acquired important bases such as the Palatinate, even going on to become the religion of the ruling house in what would eventually be the most important state, Prussia.[1]

But this "Reformed" church, as it usually called itself, scored its first, and for a time most notable, success in Calvin's homeland, France. Between 1555 and 1562 his doctrine penetrated all social classes, from great nobles and intellectuals to artisans and peasants. What is more, between 1559 and 1562 this religious challenge combined with the constitutional crisis of a centralizing monarchy to yield the basic mix that in the Netherlands in 1566 and England in 1640 produced an actual revolution. This religious dissent, moreover, at its acme embraced around 10 percent of the population,[2] the same critical mass that in other revolutionary situations, notably the Dutch Revolt, was sufficient for a minority take-over of society. Yet despite this dynamism, Calvinism lost out decisively in France, its revolutionary potential dissipated in thirty years of civil war. The great question, then, is: why such a paradoxical failure from strength?

And what does this failure tell us about the dynamic of European revolution generally?

Such questions, however, have hardly been central to the historiography of what are usually called the French Religious Wars. As with the Reformation and Hussites, the historiography began with the central concern of religion, in the present case a quest for confessional identity by the minority of modern French Protestants. This effort produced two multivolume classics in the works of Pierre Imbart de la Tour and Emile Doumergue, to which all subsequent writing has been indebted.[3] A second major impetus to research was French patriotic concern with state formation, to which the wars were a deplorable impediment. This is the orientation of the relevant volumes of Ernest Lavisse's classic *Histoire de France*,[4] still the most detailed narrative of the period. But the major turning point in interpretation came with the Annales school. It was the journal's cofounder, Lucien Febvre, who launched the modern, nonconfessional investigation of sixteenth-century religion by viewing it in its social and cultural aspects.[5] A later member of the school, Emmanuel Le Roy Ladurie, rejuvenated the traditional concern with state formation by interweaving it with social, economic, and demographic history.[6] Febvre's emphasis on the centrality of religion has been continued and deepened in several volumes by Denis Crouzet, for whom the protagonists on both sides of the struggle viewed themselves quite literally as "the warriors of God," the Huguenots as soldiers of a new divine covenant and the Catholics as crusaders defending a holy land against an infidel assault.[7]

Only rarely have the Wars of Religion been approached as a species of revolution. To be sure, the striking adumbrations of 1789 presented by the Parisian revolt of 1588 have routinely, if superficially, been discussed. But the obvious parallels with the contemporary Netherlands' Revolt and with England after 1640 have not received the attention they deserve. The most notable effort to remedy this neglect was inspired by the post-World War II surge of staseology. Its author was Perez Zagorin, whose 1980 study exploits the rich national and confessional historiographies of sixteenth- and seventeenth-century Europe to make illuminating comparisons among various kinds of revolts and rebellions.[8] In each case his generalizations ("model" is too strong a word) fit the historical facts like a glove. Although Quentin Skinner in his great history of modern political thought treats the Huguenots as a revolutionary movement,[9] social science staseology paid the idea almost no attention. It is Zagorin's example that is followed in the present section, though the emphasis here is less on contemporaneous comparisons than on sequential ones.

THE FRAMEWORK

Mid-sixteenth-century Valois France had a population of around 19 million, which made it the most populous state in Europe, with the largest city, Paris, at about three hundred thousand. The kingdom was also the largest geographically, and its monarchy, together with that of England and Spain, was one of the strongest. And like its two neighbors, it was then in the first intensive stage of modern state building.

This process was made all the more urgent when Charles V was elected emperor in 1519, thereby surrounding the Valois on all sides with Habsburg power. The result was a series of wars between the two lasting until 1559, a conflict that brought France few gains but that at least directed the nobility's considerable martial energies outward. Peace, therefore, risked sparking internal trouble since royal absolutism still had a good ways to go before the nobility was tamed into subordination.

Another obstacle to consolidating royal absolutism was the kingdom's sheer size and the institutional diversity of its numerous provinces, vast domains that were also bases of aristocratic power. A comparative glance at neighboring England may illustrate the problems this created for the monarchy. In size the English kingdom amounted to three or four duchies of Normandy, thus making it easier to control from a single center than the Capetians' sprawling realm. Moreover, England had been a unitary realm from the time of Alfred the Great, a characteristic reinforced by the centralized Norman variant of feudalism; it did not have to be put together province by province as the French kingdom did. In this respect, France resembled the much younger dual monarchy of Spain—though in Spain the central unit, Castille, had been rather effectively centralized when Charles V suppressed the 1520 urban revolt of the Communeros, thus making the Cortes a harmless body. On the other hand, France possessed an advantage neither of its neighbors enjoyed, namely the mystique of its eminently Christian mission going back to Charlemagne and Saint Louis and those *gestae Dei per Francos* that were the Crusades.

For all these reasons, in France the progress of royal absolutism—or, what is the same thing, state formation—turned out to be not a linear but a two-steps-forward-one-step-backward process. If the reigns of Louis XI and Francis I marked two forward paces, the Religious Wars were the first great step backward.

A SECOND REFORMATION

Crisis came to France, however, not as a direct constitutional challenge from the nobility or the provinces, but as the result of the fermentation from below of the religious Reformation. Pamphlets of Luther appeared in Paris as early as 1519, where they found a ready audience among humanist intellectuals already prepared for reform by the writings of Erasmus and Jacques Lefèvre d'Etaples. Although these new ideas were officially condemned in the 1520s, Francis I did not initiate active persecution until after 1534, when "placards" ridiculing the Eucharist in crude terms were posted in Paris by a French disciple of Luther's more radical rival, Zwingli. As a result, numerous French "evangelicals" sought refuge in south German and Swiss cities, notably Strasbourg and Geneva. Calvinism would be born from the encounter between these evangelicals and the urban Reformation of Switzerland and the upper Rhine.

While in exile in Basel in 1536 Calvin wrote the first version of his *Institutes*, a lucid and structured summary of reformed doctrine which he dedicated to Francis I in the hope of winning the king to the new belief. After heading the French church in Strasbourg for three years, in 1541 Calvin settled permanently in Geneva, then a second-rank dependency of Berne and a city of only ten thousand. Over the next fifteen years, he struggled successfully to transform the republic into a model Reformed community that was in effect a theocracy. By the time of his death in 1564, this model community had become the center of a veritable Calvinist International.

Calvin was not a prime innovator in Reformation doctrine. Though differing on significant points from both Luther and Zwingli, he essentially systematized and sharpened the basic Reformation commitment to justification by faith alone and to a church founded on Scripture. In theology, this meant an extreme and ruthlessly logical Augustinianism in which man's innate corruption and God's transcendent majesty became an explicit doctrine of double predestination — damnation for the many and salvation for the few. This clear division between the reprobate and the elect, however, did not have the depressing psychological effect that modern democratic sensitivities might lead us to suspect. For justification was followed by sanctification, that is, righteous and godly conduct in the life of the chosen. The result of the doctrine of double predestination, therefore, was less to induce in the believer anxiety about his prospects for salvation than to instill in him the conviction that he was Almighty God's agent on earth. Hence, the militant activism that characterized all the Reformed churches, in marked contrast to the greater *Innerlichkeit* and relative quietism of Lutheranism.

On the central subject of the Eucharist, or as it was now called, the Lord's Supper, Calvin took a middle position between Luther and Zwingli. Luther believed in a "substantial" real presence, which he called consubstantiation, whereas Zwingli considered the sacrament to be merely symbolic. Calvin's middle ground was a spiritual real presence; Christ made himself truly present to believers, but only in spirit, not in any "substantial" form. One consequence of this was that in a properly Reformed church only the elect should be admitted to the Lord's Supper. Another consequence was the vehement hostility to the Roman mass as a sacrifice, a hostility that far surpassed that of the Lutherans or Zwinglians. The Eucharistic wafer was ridiculed as a "baked God" and the service of the Lord's Supper by contrast was reduced to a stark simplicity. This attitude was matched by Calvinist hostility to images, vestments, ceremonies, and any signs of religious pomp or spectacle. All this was abominated as idolatry, and as the prophets of the Old Testament smashed heathen Baals so Calvinist pastors encouraged iconoclasm. Lutherans and Zwingli had of course purified their churches of papist superstition, but this had been largely carried out by order of the civil magistrates. With the French Huguenots it was more often done directly by believers led by their pastors.

Calvin's ecclesiology clearly owes a debt to its genesis in the world of south German and Swiss urban republics. There the Reformation had been carried out by the civil magistrates, and in most places, notably Zurich, the result had been their administrative control of the new church. Calvin's position was again a middle ground, at the same time reflecting this patrician constitutionalism and seeking to moderate its impact. His aim, therefore, was to make the church independent of lay authority without corrupting it by giving it direct political power, the great vice in Reformed eyes of the Roman church. Concretely, this meant a church ruled by a consistory composed of ministers and lay elders, or "presbyters," elected by the civil magistrates. These elders were nominated by the clergy and then confirmed by both the magistrates and, at least formally, by the congregation as a whole. In turn, the consistory vetted the appointments of new ministers or preachers. The consistory had the power of disciplining the church members, and the civil magistrates were expected to carry out its decisions. In other words, the civil magistrates had a voice but not a determining role in governing the church, and the church had *the* leading moral role in governing society as a whole. The system was thus a kind of anticlerical theocracy. It removed the church from secular affairs in order to make it supreme over them. The Genevan church was thus oligarchic or urban-aristocratic, like the Republic itself.

After 1555 these well-articulated structures were adapted to the far vaster theater of the Valois state. The kingdom thus passed from a fluid evangelicalism under Francis I to a mature, highly disciplined Calvinism under Henry II. There would be no Anabaptism or anarchic millenarian flare-ups in Huguenot France.

THE HUGUENOT FLOOD TIDE, 1555–1662

Nonetheless, Calvinism itself came to France impetuously and in something of a millenarian surge. By 1555 Calvin, his Reformed church now firmly established in Geneva, seems to have decided that the further pursuit of God's work required the active "planting" of independent churches in France. There, moreover, the time of waiting for the monarchy's conversion had clearly passed, for since 1547 the new king had been wholeheartedly devoted to persecution. Was not the constitutional norm of the age "une foi, une loi, un roi"? Hence Calvin received ever more urgent solicitations for leadership from unorganized and clandestine groups of the faithful in France. Matters moved toward open crisis in 1559 when the king ended the Valois' long contest with the Habsburgs with the disadvantageous peace of Cateau-Cambresis, the better to turn inward toward the rising tide of heresy.

Calvin was no doubt emboldened to pursue his new interventionist policy by the success of Reformed missionaries, such as his old mentor Strasbourg's Bucer and Zurich's Vermigli, in at last introducing a doctrinal Reformation in England between 1547 and 1553 under Edward VI. Even more auspicious an example was the Scottish Reformation of 1558–1559, which had been directly launched by the Geneva Company of Pastors. There, a wave of propaganda pamphlets printed in Geneva followed by a tour of preaching by John Knox moved the new church's governors, the Lords of the Congregation, to take up arms against the queen-regent, a sister of one of Henry II's chief lieutenants, the duke of Guise. This activist internationalism is in marked contrast to Lutheranism's basically national horizon in Germany and Scandinavia.

Geneva was now organized to undertake the huge task of "planting" Reformed churches throughout France. By 1555 this recently insignificant city had become the third-largest publisher, after Paris and Lyon, of French-language books. The Geneva Academy was established in 1559 by the municipal council, with Calvin's second, Beza, as its first rector; its chief purpose was to train missionary pastors for France. These pastors were not only learned; recruited largely from the upper classes, often the nobility, they were accustomed to a role of leadership. Geneva thus became the "fountainhead" of the Huguenot cause, was "the prime source of ecclesiastical leaders and the outpouring of printed propaganda; it was the staging base of conspiracies, a negotiating point for loans, and producer and distributor of armaments."[10] By 1559 the new church was strong enough to convene its first national synod right under the king's nose, in Paris.

Calvinism's great chance came that same year when France was plunged into crisis by Henry II's accidental death. His heir, Francis II, although at age sixteen technically no longer a minor, was in too weak a position to be anything more than a pawn in the factional struggle for power that royal minorities invariably generated in early modern Europe. The first winners in this struggle were the duke of Guise and his brother, the cardinal of Lorraine, uncles of the king through his wife, Mary of Scotland. Their ultra-Catholicism frightened the now rapidly growing Huguenot community into a counter-mobilization. This was led by the Bourbon prince of Condé, who as blood cousin of the king felt that he, not the upstart Guises, should be de facto regent. The Bourbons were seconded by members of the third great noble clan, the Montmorencys, traditionally the first barons of France, who often furnished the constable of the realm. The most outstanding member of this group was Gaspard de Coligny, Admiral of France.

Indeed, it was at this time that the higher nobility converted in large numbers to Calvinism. The doctrine's earliest recruits, in the decade before 1555, had been from the lesser bourgeoisie, skilled artisans such as weavers and printers, and the lesser nobility. With the conversion of numerous great nobles the Reformed church acquired a powerful institutional and military presence throughout the kingdom. This fact became alarmingly apparent in March 1560 when some Huguenot lesser nobles attempted to capture the king in the Conspiracy of Amboise. Condé was waiting in the wings, and though Calvin opposed the plot, it seems Beza gave it clandestine support since Condé's rank as prince of the blood gave it constitutional cover. In response to the crisis, in August the Queen Mother, Catherine de Medicis, prevailed on the king to convoke the Estates General for the first time since 1484.

Before it could meet, however, Francis II died in December after a mere eighteen months' reign. Since his brother, Charles IX, was only ten, Catherine became regent. With the Estates now in session, her chancellor of justice, Michel de L'Hospital, came forward with a policy of toleration and conciliation. The Guises fell from favor and Catherine turned toward the Bourbons and the Montmorencys. But just as the repression attempted earlier by the Guises had only encouraged Calvinism's growth, so Catherine's policy of toleration now only increased Calvinism's self-confidence and militancy.

By the end of the year there were around one thousand Reformed churches in the kingdom, and a second national synod was held the following March. In August there was a new meeting of the Estates General. After a hiatus of seventy-six years, this institution would be a regular recourse throughout the Wars of Religion, meeting again at crisis points in 1576, 1588, and 1593. Even so, it remained a weak instrument, in part because provincial estates channeled the population's loyalties more easily but especially because of the institutional preponderance of the monarchy. The focus of factional struggle thus continued to be the court itself.

Accordingly, the principal effort at conciliation was a face-to-face meeting of Protestant and Catholic divines at the Colloquy of Poissy arranged by Catherine in September. Her hope was to find a via media permitting the two faiths to co-exist within the same national church, somewhat like the policy that Elizabeth of England was then successfully pursuing. In this compromise, the Catholics would reform abuses and simplify ecclesiastical ceremonies while the Protestants would relax doctrinal intransigence. Unfortunately this is a solution for people to whom religion is a secondary concern, and neither Calvin nor the cardinal of Lorraine were at all willing to consider it. The same policy had been tried, and failed, with Charles V's Interim in 1545.

Beza himself came from Geneva for the colloquy and preached openly in Paris under the protection of Condé's soldiers. The Genevan influence was now so strong at court that the Guises felt it prudent to leave for their lands in Lorraine. A first wave of iconoclasm against papist "idolatry" shook the emerging Huguenot strongholds in the south.

By the end of 1561 there were around twenty-five hundred Reformed churches in France. In January of the next year, by the Edict of Saint Germain, Catherine granted Huguenots freedom of conscience and of organized worship outside of walled cities and in the private homes of noblemen everywhere. Despite the geographic restriction, this was an unheard-of concession at the time.[11] The Peace of Augsburg of 1555 had not accepted toleration as a principle; rather, it had partitioned Germany into Catholic and Protestant regions, neither or which would tolerate the religion of the other. To be sure, de facto toleration of Protestants then existed in Bohemia and Poland, but this was a matter of custom not of law. Catherine's January Edict was the first time a European state had formally recognized the coexistence of two churches on its territory. This principle would not be fully accepted in France until the Edict of Nantes in 1598, and even then it turned out to be revocable. It would not be approximated in Holland until the 1630s and then only de facto, and it was distinctly more generous than the English "Clarendon Code" of 1661–1665 and even than the Toleration Act of 1689.

That the January Edict was quite premature in France in 1562 soon became apparent. In fact, the decree quickly polarized the country. On the one hand, the Huguenots, emboldened by royal recognition, created churches wherever they had the strength to do so, in walled towns no less than in noble seigneuries. Indeed, although they officially continued to demand only toleration, they now felt strong enough to envisage the bolder goal of converting the entire church. On the other hand, as the Huguenot flood tide rose throughout 1562 it inevitably provoked a militant reaction. The suddenness of Huguenot expansion, and in particular the iconoclastic "fury" that often accompanied it, were perceived by the majority of the population as an aggression, an impious assault on the kingdom's immemorial and sacred ways. This counter-fury broke out into the open with the massacre of Vassy in March.

The occasion was provided by the duke of Guise's departure from Lorraine, of course with an armed escort, to make a comeback at court. En route, he encountered a Huguenot congregation holding services in a barn on his own lands. A fight broke out, and twenty-three worshipers were killed. News of the massacre quickly provoked a wave of indignation throughout the kingdom's Calvinist network. This turned into fear as Guise entered Paris to the acclaim of the population. He then made himself ascendant at court by the simple expedient of physically removing the regent and the boy king from Fountainbleau to the capital: this was a reverse, and successful, version of the Conspiracy of Amboise. Condé, in answer, then mobilized his forces at Orleans while Guise did the same in Paris. And the war was on.

THE PATTERN OF REVOLUTIONARY WAR

This first war lasted a year. The Huguenots were suppressed in Paris but they captured Lyon and a string of cities in the south. By the end of the fighting, Condé had been taken prisoner by the royal forces and Guise had been assassinated by a Huguenot noble while besieging Orleans. The war thus ended in stalemate, a fact recognized by a royal edict essentially reestablishing the status quo ante of geographically limited toleration.

And so the stalemate continued over thirty more years for a total of eight wars. To put the matter in Charles Tilly's terms, although after 1562 a "revolutionary situation" clearly existed in France, there was no "revolutionary outcome," that is, an actual change of regime or major constitutional transformation. Still less was there a social change, but social change of the sort attempted in 1525 in Germany was never one of the "claims" advanced in the original revolutionary situation. The pattern of this deadlocked revolution, then, is an initial explosion, one quite as big as 1520 in Germany, followed by serial civil war but without a decisive victory for either side.

Yet stalemate is not all that is bizarre about this inconclusive revolution. For the deadlock gradually evolved into an alternating revolution, driven first by the Calvinist "left" then by the Catholic "right," to use anachronistic but in the present instance helpful terms. In other words, the radical action of the Calvinist challengers was eventually replicated by the Catholic resistance. And even though this "counter-revolution" was in many ways more extreme than the Huguenot original, it had even less impact on the kingdom's constitutional and social structures. So what was the nature of the alternating forces in the deadlock?

Preoccupation with ecclesiastical organization was a major trait differentiating Calvinism from Lutheranism and Anglicanism. In France this produced a presbyterian-synodal organization, the form Calvinism took when its institutions were adapted from the Genevan city-state to the national dimensions of the Valois kingdom. This organizational system, along with a standard confession of faith, was finally approved at the French church's first national synod in 1559. Optimal for political and military effectiveness in the service of doctrinal militancy, this system was called "aristocratic," in Aristotle's sense, by Calvin himself. A modern writer, Robert Kingdon, with only slight anachronism, has called it "democratic centralism."[12]

At the system's base the individual churches or congregations were ruled by consistories of elected ministers and elders. As in Geneva, these consistories were in fact oligarchies formed by cooptation among pastors and local magistrates. All the churches in the system were equal and the national hierarchy emanated from this democratic foundation. The churches thus elected delegates to local colloquies, then to regional synods, and finally to periodic national synods, which formulated doctrine for the whole Huguenot community.

Although basically consolidated by 1562–1563, this system nonetheless faced a democratic challenge mounted by a layman, Jean Morély, who advocated a form of "ecclesiastical discipline," or church government, which would later be called congregationalist.[13] In his formula both ministers and elders were elected by the individual congregation; and Morély was aware that this ecclesiology had democratic implications for the civil polity. The established defenders of Calvin's aristocratic "presbyterianism," however, easily beat back this challenge because of the nearly permanent military emergency and the nobility's natural role in warfare. For the same reasons, the presbyterian-synodal system was adopted by the beleaguered Netherlands Calvinists at their first national synod, in 1571. A less successful variant of this system had emerged in Scotland in 1559, where the consistory was called the "kirk session," but where bishops were incongruously retained. The presbyterian model was made official in the Church of England by Parliament in 1643, though there it basically failed, soon splitting between

Parliamentarian Covenanters and the congregationalist Independents associated with the New Model Army. And in Massachusetts, of course, congregationalism, though without a governing consistory, prevailed from the very beginning because these colonial Independents had no military challenge to contend with.

The Huguenots' ecclesiastical organization dovetailed nicely with the parallel organization of their political community. This was composed of the various municipalities where the Reformed church was in the majority, especially in the south but also for a time in such important centers as Lyon, Orleans, and Rouen. Then there were the seigneuries of the nobility and the estates of certain provinces, such as Languedoc, where the Huguenots were preponderant. All these entities then elected representatives to a national assembly. And on occasion a national synod of the church, such as that of La Rochelle in 1571, would serve as a kind of supreme Huguenot congress. Indeed, that gathering drew foreign participants such as Louis of Nassau, William the Silent's brother, and hence was a kind of congress of the Calvinist International, just as the Dutch synod of Dort would be in 1618. Finally, the organization of the Huguenot ecclesiastical-political community fitted well with the estate organization of the kingdom, in a transposition where a first estate of pastors and a second estate of noble captains led a third estate of urban magistrates.

In short, what we are dealing with in Huguenot France is a political-religious *party*, that is, a movement in which the principle of cohesion is not class, or economic interest, or even a given political program, but commitment to a particular religion.[14] More specifically, the political-religious party is the expression of a minority religion seeking to impose itself against the recently consolidated early-modern monarchy and its official church, whether Catholic or Anglican. Only a highly structured and ideologically zealous organization could give such a minority a chance against the power of the state.

As such, late sixteenth-century political-religious movements mark the emergence of "party" in the modern sense, or at least one of its modern senses. The conventional wisdom regarding the emergence of modern political parties is, of course, that they first appeared in England as Whigs and Tories during the Exclusion crisis under Charles II. Yet even these loose, unstructured, and narrowly elite groupings had a confessional dimension, the former favoring toleration for dissenters and the latter believing in divine-right monarchy and an Anglican religious monopoly. The French Huguenots and later, as we shall see, the Dutch "Beggars" were much more formidable affairs, with a broad popular base and a potent military capacity. Thus, if the Whig-Tory formula may be considered the forerunner of modern political parties competing peacefully for power, the sixteenth-century political-religious party is the forerunner of more militant modern political formations—English Puritans, French Jacobins, and Russian Bolsheviks.[15] But more will be said in later chapters about this complex subject.

For the moment it is enough to describe how the imposing Huguenot organization, in combination with the enthusiasm of the faithful, succeeded in imposing godly rule over significant portions of France. The basic formula was this: once a town with a sizable Calvinist element had been militarily secured by the nobility, Catholic officials were ousted, new pastors purged the churches of "idols," and a permanent Huguenot "republic" was born. This scenario would be repeated by the Sea Beggars in Zeeland and Holland in 1572. Among the principal Huguenot republics thus created were La Rochelle, Montauban, and Nîmes; together with numerous lesser strongholds, notably the Cevennes mountains, they formed a crescent running from Poitou in the west, along the Garonne valley through Languedoc, to Dauphiné in the east. Paris from the beginning was a bastion of Catholicism.

As the Wars of Religion progressed the Huguenots were eliminated in the north and the east and were largely relegated to their crescent in the Midi. What were the reasons for this geographic distribution? The south was in many ways a distinct region, one might even say an incipient separate nationality. It had its own language, the Languedoc, now called Occitan; it used Roman law rather than the customary, or common, law of the region of the Langue d'Oil in the north; and it had been forcibly annexed to the Capetian monarchy in the thirteenth-century Albigensian Wars. Even though these were now a memory far in the past, in the present the region still remained farther from Paris than the rest of the kingdom. It so happened that the northern region of eventual Catholic domination had been integrated into the royal domain longer and more closely than the Midi. The Calvinist south indeed formed a kind of emerging "United Provinces" of the Midi, on the model of the breakaway northern provinces of the Netherlands. Yet, unlike in the relatively new state of the Habsburg Netherlands, the sense of a common identity under the venerable Capetian monarchy was already too strong in France for such a solution. And so the stalemate continued.

FROM HUGUENOT TO CATHOLIC "REVOLUTION"

After the first war of 1562–1563 the Huguenots, now under the leadership of Admiral Coligny, enjoyed a decade of relative success. Indeed, in 1567, on the eve of the second war, they made so bold as to attempt, once again, to capture Catherine and the king at Meaux, in part as a measure of self-defense but in part also in the hope of winning the whole contest with one great blow. Indeed, capturing the monarchy—either by laying hold of the king's person, or by his conversion, or by securing a majority in his council, or finally, as the Valois died off one by one, by inheritance—was throughout the Religious Wars the chief objective of both the Huguenot and the Catholic political-religious parties. Operating through the Estates General to limit the king's power or to wring concessions from him, though occasionally used, was never more than a secondary tactic. Thus the monarchy, even in its weakest position since the Hundred Years' War, remained the focus of political contention, the great prize in the struggle for power over the realm.

After the Huguenots' boldness at Meaux had been rebuffed in the Second War of 1567–1568, Charles IX and Catherine again offered a policy of toleration. Indeed, after Philip II's initial successes against the Netherlands' revolt, fear of his power moved the court toward an actual alliance with the Huguenots. Accordingly, the new leader of the Bourbon clan, the young Henry of Navarre, was betrothed to Catherine's daughter Marguerite. Coligny then pressed for a national union of Catholics and Protestants and intervention in the Netherlands on the side of the rebels. This policy, however, appeared too dangerous to Catherine, especially since Coligny's influence over the twenty-two-year-old king was growing. In August 1572, once the Huguenot nobility had massed in Paris for the marriage of Henry of Navarre, Catherine prevailed on the king to check their power by having Coligny assassinated. The attempt failed; Coligny was only wounded. The Huguenot nobles, blaming the Guises, vehemently demanded justice. Seized with panic in this threatening situation, the court decided to liquidate all the Huguenots' principal leaders, believing that the incident would stop there. Once the action started, however, it immediately got out of hand. In a vast eruption of the counter-fury first displayed at Vassy, the fanatically Catholic Parisians, including many responsible magistrates, seized the occasion to purge the city of Huguenots, whose insolence threatened to bring divine wrath on the city. The total number of victims was around twenty-five hundred. This Saint Bartholomew's Day Massacre, as it was called, then spread to other cities throughout France, for a probable total of five thousand deaths for the whole kingdom.[16] It soon was regarded as the prime atrocity of the age.[17] The Huguenot cause suffered a blow from which it would never really recover.

The horror of the massacre at last inspired the emergence of a third force, the *politiques*, so called because they put the interests of the state and of civil peace ahead of any concern for purity of religion. Montaigne, though not politically active, was a prominent example of their mentality. Henry of Navarre, though for political reasons first a Protestant then a Catholic, was at heart a politique. The great theorist of this third force was Jean Bodin, whose six *Books of the Republic*, published in 1576, defined an absolute concept of state authority, which in the context of monarchy meant royal absolutism.[18] Since no one could be religiously neutral at the time, as a practical matter the politiques were usually in informal alliance with the weaker religious party, the Huguenots. For even after the Saint Bartholomew's Day Massacre the Huguenots still had legal toleration in the geographical areas they controlled.

After 1572, however, they were increasingly on the defensive, and this produced an outpouring of Huguenot resistance literature, dubbed "monarchomach" (king-killer) by contemporary supporters of royal sovereignty. In 1573 Francis Hotman published *Francogallia*, which argued that the monarchy rested on popular sovereignty and consent in a constitutionalism going back to the Frankish conquest, a position similar to that of defenders of the "ancient constitution" in seventeenth-century England. And in fact, since 1567, the Huguenots had been calling for a new meeting of the Estates General. To this literature, in 1574, Beza himself contributed the *Right of Magistrates*, which anticipated the still more strongly worded, anonymous *Vindiciae Contra Tyrannos* of 1579. As if in answer to Bodin's definition of the modern concept of sovereignty, both of these Huguenot pamphlets give the first more or less modern defense of a right of revolutionary resistance. Before this, of course, there had been scholastic defenses of tyrannicide, but monarchomach literature went further to give a fully developed political theory of resistance. This literature did not advocate democratic resistance, however. The resistance envisaged was legitimate only for the "lesser magistrates" of the existing constitution, that is, princes of the blood, the Estates General, the judicial Parlements, or the nobility in general if the Estates were not in session. This literature would have its greatest importance in the Netherlands' Revolt and in England from the Civil War of the 1640s to the Glorious Revolution of 1688.[19]

In 1574 Charles IX's premature death put his next brother on the throne as Henry III. Since over time it became clear that the new king would not have children, his heir was a still younger brother, the duke of Anjou. In 1584 Anjou died, thus making the Protestant Henry of Navarre the new legitimate heir. This biological accident, or course, revived the religious crisis, indeed bringing it to its culmination in the longest and final Religious War, "The War of the Three Henrys." The third Henry was the heir of the duke of Guise who had been assassinated in the first Religious War, and who had himself dispatched Coligny in the Saint Bartholomew's Day Massacre.

Since Henry III's first Estates General in 1576, Guise had headed a Catholic League, or Sainte Union, of nobles pledged to defending the church; it conditioned its support of the monarchy on its recognition of the rights of the Estates and the provinces. Anjou's death gave the League new life and indeed the Catholic League became an even more revolutionary force than the Huguenots had been earlier. The League was in secret alliance with Spain, indeed receiving financing from Philip II, who was then preparing to attack England and whose commander in the Netherlands, the duke of Parma, was at the peak of his success in rolling back Calvinist rebellion. The League's publicists now took up and indeed radicalized the Huguenots' resistance and monarchomach arguments.

Independently of Guise, a mutant of the League had appeared in Paris under the direction of some parish priests, royal officials, and substantial bourgeois. This offshoot was a conspiratorial organization with its own governing council, and plebeian branches in all of the city's sixteen quarters. In the sectional organizations a genuinely radical social movement emerged, expressed not so much through explicit demands for change as through an intense hatred of factious and arrogant nobles and resentment of the judicial parliament. This urban League was imitated in other northern and eastern cities of the realm. This network of Leaguer cities, together with the Sainte Union of nobles headed by Guise, formed a political-religious party, and an example of "democratic centralism," that was in all organizational essentials the mirror image of its Huguenot adversary. The only difference, of course, was ideology in the form of religion. But this difference is capital, for it alone gave political meaning and psychological temper to the organizational forms.

In May 1588 Guise, invited by the Parisian League's governing council, the Sixteen, made a triumphal entry into the capital. When the king tried to use force against him, the city rose up in the Day of Barricades, May 9. The king was forced to flee the city, and the Sixteen transformed itself into a parallel government to challenge the legal municipality. All this, of course, is quite similar to what occurred in Paris in 1789. Indeed, it strongly resembles the organization of Jacobin Paris and its national network of Jacobin clubs in 1793. Also like the Jacobins later, the Sixteen were obsessed with the possibility of treason and drew up lists of "suspects" to be eliminated as events might require. The pulpits of the city's parish churches resounded with fervent, even fanatical, exhortations to resist the tyrant, Henry III, and urging vigilance against his supporters within the city walls. The chief difference between the two cases was the ideology involved, but this difference is capital. In 1588 "the ideology" was Tridentine Catholicism, which meant a reformed version of the traditional ecclesiastical order; in 1793 it was a Rousseau-inspired Republic of Virtue, which meant a bold leap into a secular radiant future.

After the Day of Barricades the king had no choice but to ally himself with

Henry of Navarre, commander of the Huguenot armed forces, and to formally recognize his heretic cousin as his heir. (In other circumstances, this would be the choice of Charles II of England in defending the right of his Catholic brother, the duke of York, to the succession.) In an effort to regain control of the situation, and encouraged by the defeat that summer of Philip II's assault against England, the king convened the Estates General in the neutral city of Blois. The League network easily elected a majority of supporters. Faced with this situation, Henry III resorted to the illusory solution of a swift surgical strike. In the royal chateau where the Estates were meeting his men assassinated Guise and his brother, the cardinal. (Catherine then lay dying elsewhere in the residence.) Henry III and Henry of Navarre then surrounded insurgent Paris, which would continue to fight on obstinately for another year. In their camp outside the city walls the king was assassinated in 1589 by a fanatical monk, Jacques Clement, who had been prepared for the task by agents of Guise's surviving brothers.

Though Navarre was now legally king, most of the country would not accept him because of his religion. So Paris and the League fought on, and in 1590 and 1591 Philip II sent Parma's army south to aid Paris and the League. As for the succession, the Guise brothers first settled on the elderly cardinal of Bourbon (although the elder Guise brother had an eye on the throne for himself). When the cardinal died, the League, at Spanish insistence, threw its support to Philip II's daughter by Elizabeth of Valois, the Infanta Isabella. Since by the salic law only males could inherit the throne, a new Estates General, in 1593 in Paris, was convened to make a Spanish succession possible.

At this point Navarre, realizing that he could not win militarily, abjured his Protestantism. In January 1594 he was crowned at Chartres, and a few months later entered Paris. This was the final blow to the languishing Huguenot revolution. Four years later Henry IV granted the Edict of Nantes, by and large recapitulating the Edict of Saint Germain of 1562. The Huguenots, now down to around a million, or 5 percent of the population, could practice their religion openly in certain designated places, and they continued to hold a number of *places fortes*, such as La Rochelle. In other words, the religious settlement provided for coexistence rather than for toleration in the modern sense. It also left the French state with something less than full sovereignty in the modern sense, or indeed in that of Bodin.

The basic reason for the Huguenots' failure is that for all their strength and zeal, they could never capture the monarchy. Nor was limiting the monarchy with the power of the Estates General an alternative option, as it would be later in the Netherlands and England. For this, the Estates were simply too weak an institution and the power of the monarchy was too crucial to national identity. And the basic reason for the Huguenots' failure to capture the monarchy was that the majority of the population was anti-Protestant, and a significant minority of that majority, at all social levels, was militant enough to deny the Huguenots' power even when it was constitutionally within their grasp.

The real effect of the stalemated revolution of sixteenth-century France was to strengthen the centralizing monarchy's hand, to increase its popular support, and so to launch it on its way to the mature absolutism of the Bourbons. As for the analysis of revolutionary processes, this deadlocked and alternating revolution should provide a lesson in humility about finding any basic pattern of revolution within Europe, let alone worldwide and for all time.

As for France itself, the failed French Reformation left a legacy that would contribute notably to the crisis that produced 1789.

5

THE NETHERLANDS' REVOLT, 1566–1609

It is not necessary to hope in order to undertake, nor to succeed in order to persevere.
—WILLIAM OF ORANGE

The first significant fact to note about the upheaval conventionally called the Dutch Revolt is that it did not begin as such. The emergence, by 1609, of an independent Dutch Republic of seven provinces was the unintended outcome of a much broader revolution within the Seventeen Provinces of the Burgundian-Habsburg Netherlands, a dynastic proto-monarchy covering present-day Holland, Belgium, and a slice of northern France. Indeed, the revolution at first had its focus in what is now Belgium, and its principal leader, William of Orange, until his death in 1584, continued to see the movement in pan-Netherlands terms. To further complicate the task of analysis, the revolt was driven as much by international forces as by its own internal dynamic — in marked contrast to the self-contained English upheaval a century later and the initial, decisive phase of the Bohemian one a century earlier, or even to the immediately preceding German Reformation before armed struggle began in the 1540s. The reason for these complications, of course, was the international character of the Habsburg dynasty ruling in Brussels.

Accordingly, the historiography relevant to the revolt is a complex and diffuse affair. It is not focused on revolution, as is the historiography of 1789 or 1776, but on a variety of themes. The first focus is the genealogy of Protestant liberty against Catholic despotism, a story that begins with Luther's "here I stand" defiance of Charles V at the Diet of Worms. This tradition was of course an international enterprise, and its great classic is *The Rise of the Dutch Republic* published in 1856 by the American John Motley.[1] The Dutch Revolt was also a standard episode in the Enlightenment canon of liberty. The Goethe of Sturm und Drang in 1775, during the American Revolution, put it in his play *Egmont*, just as he had put a libertarian Reformation into his *Goetz von Berlichingen*. Schiller, after trying his hand at another staple of liberal iconography, the Swiss *William Tell*, wrote it up as royal melodrama in his *Don Carlos*; and Verdi turned Schiller's version into a soaring opera as *Don Carlo*.

A more viable if internationally less conspicuous historiographical focus is on the revolt as the source of modern Dutch national identity; and it is here that the most serious work has been done. Yet since Dutch is not an international language, this body of scholarship has only occasionally been projected into our general historical consciousness, most notably in Pieter Geyl's *The Revolt of the Netherlands, 1555–1609*, first published in 1932.[2] To complicate matters further, since the revolt produced not one but two modern nations, it has also been presented in comparably serious fashion as *Histoire de Belgique* by the great medievalist Henri Pirenne.[3] Marx and Engels, of course, offhandedly classified it as a "bourgeois revolution," though without attempting any serious analysis; and in the mid-twentieth century this perspective, too, produced a tradition of radical scholarship.[4]

It was only after World War II, under the combined pressure of Marxism and the high tide of staseology, that the Netherlands' revolt at last came to be treated as a revolution, though not necessarily "bourgeois." Even so, there is no consensus regarding this revolution's geographic location, duration, or pattern of development. Likewise, the structure of action of the revolt is so irregular as to defy easy schematization or comparative analysis. Although roughly the same political, social, and ideological factors are present as in the earlier Bohemian and German cases as well as in the later English one, the pattern of action through which these factors played out is idiosyncratic to the point of aberrance. Thus we have the revolt plausibly presented both as a radical and as a conservative revolution, and as a popular and as an elite movement.[5] Moreover, since the revolt's most significant outcome was, in fact, the emergence of the Dutch Republic as the seventeenth-century economic powerhouse and a world power, the discussion constantly tends to return to the old focus on "the Dutch Revolt."[6]

Nonetheless, some pattern can be found in the broader concept of a Netherlands' revolt. This pattern is a stop-and-go revolution, which moreover keeps changing the focus of its action to where it finally settles in the seven northern provinces grouped around Holland. The first revolt erupted in 1566 and, though common to the whole Netherlands, was centered in the south, in Flanders and Brabant—only to be repressed everywhere by Spain the following year. The second revolt began in 1572 and triumphed only in the Dutch maritime provinces of Holland and Zeeland. The third revolt began with the (temporary) collapse of

Spanish military power in 1576 and spread once again to the whole Netherlands until its internal divisions, after 1578, made possible a Spanish comeback in the south. Thereafter, the northern provinces continued what was now essentially a Dutch Revolt, which after 1581 in fact became an international war between Spain and the new republic. This picture of a revolution in three episodes is best brought out by Geoffrey Parker's *The Dutch Revolt*, first published in 1977 at the high tide of staseology.[7] It is this stop-and-go schema that will be followed here.

THE FRAMEWORK

Despite its relatively small size, the Netherlands in 1566, together with Northern Italy, was economically the most advanced, the wealthiest, the most densely populated, and the most urban part of Europe. Roughly two-thirds the size of England and Wales, it had approximately the same population: three million (the future area of the Dutch republic in 1500 had a population of slightly under one million). A perhaps more relevant comparison for present purposes is with Spain, where the crowns of Castile and Aragon together had a total of around six and a half million. The largest Netherlands city, and Europe's principal commercial and financial entrepot, Antwerp, had eighty thousand people (Amsterdam then had a bit over thirty thousand). At the time only Paris with three hundred thousand and London with close to two hundred thousand were larger.

The Netherlands was a key component of the Habsburg international system, for like Spain itself, and quite unlike the empire, it was Charles V's directly ruled, patrimonial land. Accordingly, in the Netherlands the emperor undertook what he could never aspire to in Germany, that is, to turn his Burgundian heritage into something like a unitary monarchy on the French or English model.[8]

This meant, first, conquering or otherwise annexing the northeastern provinces beyond the Zuider Zee. Even so, all of the now seventeen provinces retained their traditional rights and privileges as exemplified, for example, in Brabant's Joyeuse Entrée, charters which every new sovereign had to swear to uphold. Habsburg policy thus meant giving the country a number of central administrative and fiscal institutions alongside the rarely summoned States General and the elite Order of the Golden Fleece. Eventually, in 1548, the Netherlands, technically part of the empire, was organized as a separate Burgundian Circle setting it off from Germany proper as, in effect, a new state. By the same token, Charles' policy brought heavier taxation to help finance his wars with France; and this in turn meant vigorously repressing any outbreaks of municipal sedition, a traditional phenomenon in urban Flanders, expressed most notably at Ghent in 1540. Finally, it meant systematic repression, after 1520, of religious heresy, something that Charles was quite unable to accomplish in Germany. As a corollary to this policy, he planned to give the Netherlands three new arch-bishoprics and fifteen bishoprics (the existing archaic hierarchy of only four bishops was woefully inadequate for the country's population). The sovereign himself would appoint to the new sees. In short, Charles was doing in his domains what all the other sovereigns of the day were doing, or trying to do, in theirs. His reasons were likewise theirs: to build strength for international competition. As Charles once punned in French (his first language): "Je mettrai Paris dans mon gant," the word for "glove" being pronounced the same way as Charles's birth city, Ghent.

By the time of his abdication in 1555, however, this process of state-building was far less advanced than in contemporary France, England, or Castile. Not only did each of the seventeen provinces have its own constitutional bundle of rights, but they had been brought together in a single unit too recently to have acquired a strong common identity, while at the same time they were divided linguistically between Dutch and French along a line running from Dunkirk to Limburg, and passing just south of Brussels. True, there was increasing talk of a Low Country *patrie*, especially among the noble elite, but provincial particularism, as it turned out, was in fact a stronger force.

The Netherlands' revolt was thus a revolution provoked by the ascending phase of European state-formation. At a less mature stage of the same process this had been the case of the Hussites a century earlier. At a more mature stage of the process, it would again be the case of the Puritans a century later.

THE FIRST REVOLT

The Netherlands moved toward crisis when sovereignty passed from Charles to his son, Philip II, who unlike his father had been born and brought up in Spain. Though he had ruled directly in Brussels for four years after 1555 (while concluding the final war with the Valois), he never learned French or ceased to perceive local problems through a Spanish prism. His policy was to continue his father's work of consolidation, particularly in the suppression of heresy and the creation of the new bishoprics. When he returned to Spain in 1559 (as it turned out, for good), to pursue this policy he left behind his half-sister, Duchess Margaret of Parma, as regent but put real power in the hands of a family loyalist, Cardinal Antoine Granvelle, thus bypassing the Netherlands' grandees whom Charles V had favored. He also left behind 3,000 Spanish troops, whereas there had been none in peacetime before.

These dispositions understandably alienated such great nobles as the Prince of Orange and Count Egmont, traditional members of the Council of State; in their eyes Philip's policy seemed to forebode turning the Low Countries into a mere dependency of Spain, like Milan or Naples. In particular, these magnates objected to Philip's religious policies on the grounds that they violated the country's traditional franchises by transferring heresy cases from the provincial courts to the jurisdiction of a special new inquisition. In protest they boycotted the Council of State, and Philip gave way: by the spring of 1564 he had withdrawn the Spanish troops and, more important still, had recalled Granvelle. It is this apparent defeat of royal absolutism by the grandee opposition that touched off a general crisis of the system.

By 1564 the Netherlands had become a cauldron of resentments built up by what was now a half-century of Habsburg state-building and, increasingly, religious repression. The Reformation had reached the Low Countries in 1520–1522, that is, almost as early as its first flare-up in Germany and Switzerland. The difference with Germany, of course, and it was a major one, is that unlike in the territorial principality of Saxony or the free cities of the empire and Switzerland, Charles' secular sword not only refused to espouse the reform but was actively wielded to repress it. In consequence, the Netherlands' Reformation developed from below, clandestinely yet nonetheless vigorously, over the next four decades.[9]

The movement went through three rough phases. First, in the 1520s, a rather fluid Lutheranism overlapped with Christian humanism, initially among the clergy but soon touching the artisan class. By the 1530s a virulent, essentially lower-class, Anabaptism had also appeared. In 1535 its adherents made a failed attempt to seize power in Amsterdam. Thousands of others were driven away by persecution to Northwestern Germany, a circumstance that had much to do with the spectacular Münster revolt of 1536. Its two principal leaders, Matthijs and Jan of Leiden, after all, were Dutch. After the Münster catastrophe, however, militant Dutch Anabaptism, like the Czech adherents of Zalečky earlier or the English Quakers later, settled down to a sectarianism committed to pacifism and benevolent works. The crucial figure in this transformation was Menno Simmons, founder of the Mennonites. The third and most important phase of the Netherlands' Reformation was the rise, after 1540, of a militant but disciplined and structured Calvinism. Coming originally from France through the Walloon provinces, it soon spread throughout the country, though everywhere it had to operate clandestinely, "under the cross," in small conventicles. The most zealous Calvinists immigrated to the Dutch "stranger churches" in London and Emden in Germany, and it is there that by 1571 the church was organized on

Genevan lines with a formal creed and separate presbyterian-synodal structure of local consistories and regional synods.

It is the conjunction of this militant religiosity with the constitutional aims of the nobility that produced the revolt of 1566. In addition, as Marxist historians have pointed out, times were hard economically, especially for the lower classes. In 1564–1566 there had been a severe winter and a bad harvest, as in 1788–1789 in France; but this "hunger year" was an aggravating circumstance, not a primary cause of the revolution.[10] There are far more hunger years in European history than there are what contemporaries perceived as a "wonderyear."

THE WONDERYEAR — 1566

The outbreak of revolt in 1566 appeared as an *annus mirabilis* because of the extraordinary rapidity and radicalism with which events unfolded. In truth, it is one of the great revolutionary years in European history, a shock quite comparable to 1419 in Bohemia or 1520 in Germany, and indeed to 1640 in England if not quite to 1789 in France. In fact, the Netherlands' revolution reached maximum intensity in its inaugural episode.

It is thus an episode that must be approached month by month. The concession of Granvelle's recall in 1564 seemed to signal to the grandees in the Council of State that they could now implement their program; in effect, royal power began to erode throughout the country. In December, therefore, the grandees approached the king about moderating the prosecution of heresy, in February 1565 dispatching Egmont to Madrid to plead their case. Naively, Egmont believed that he had persuaded Philip, who in fact had accepted only further theological consultation, and on his return so informed his colleagues. In May, a committee of theologians chosen by the council recommended moderation. Philip's actual policy, however, continued as before, and in November all illusions were shattered by the arrival of his famous "Letters from the Segovia Woods" reiterating the firm stand he had taken against heresy in 1559. The nobles were now faced with the dilemma: either submit or disobey. As a practical matter, however, the country's expectations of change were now so strong that if the Council did not resist, it would lose its authority to lead.

Throughout the fall grandees and minor nobles, the latter often Calvinist, had been discussing plans for resistance. Now some lesser nobles, led by John Marnix, drafted a "Compromise of the Nobility," that is, a confederation or covenant against the inquisition. Altogether some 400 nobles signed. The grandees, given their position in the government, could not do so, though Orange in January 1566 resigned his stadholderships, or governorships, because he was unwilling to enforce the king's new orders. The lesser nobles, in consultation with the grandees, then decided to present their program as a "request" to the regent. On April 5, in an act of thinly veiled sedition, Baron Brederode with some three hundred armed confederates ostentatiously rode into Brussels and forced their way into her palace to deliver the document. The confederates, contemptuously dismissed by one court official as *gueux*, or beggars, took up the label in proud defiance. The regent, her powerlessness thus demonstrated, had no choice but to capitulate; a few days later she issued a "Moderation" mitigating application of the heresy laws. Although this appealed to the majority in the country, the grandees, to defend their constitutional prerogative, still pressed for more power for the Council of State; in late April they dispatched new spokesmen to Spain.

With the government thus divided at the top, the lower orders of society entered the fray in far more radical manner. Calvinists "under the cross" now emerged publicly and in May began "hedge-preaching" in the open countryside. Disciplined exiles began returning from London and Germany. By summer hundreds and later thousands of people were participating in *presches* (preachings) of the Gospel and psalm singing in fields near important towns. On June 30 some thirty thousand people assembled outside Antwerp. The grandees and Brederode's confederates had quite lost control over the movement they had initiated. The atmosphere in Flanders and Brabant was now reminiscent of the millenarian Bohemian summer of 1419 or of Mülhausen under Thomas Müntzer in the summer of 1525.

Beginning on August 10 this mass "enthusiasm" led to the largest outburst of image breaking to occur during the entire Reformation. This "iconoclastic fury" moved from city to city throughout August. Although spontaneous in some places, in the revolt's heartland of the south Netherlands, it was "the work of a very small band of determined men . . . between fifty and a hundred strong, many of them newly returned from exile abroad," and determined not to leave again. Some were "recruited and paid by the Calvinist consistories off Antwerp and the other great towns"; it was, after all, a time of economic depression.[11] Although the fury was very much a minority "plot," it is also noteworthy that there were very few persons ready to defend the churches.

At the end of the summer, the Regent conferred with the grandees, and on August 25 granted an "accord" conceding freedom of Protestant worship where it was already a fait accompli — in effect, the solution adopted in Germany with the Peace of Augsburg in 1555. But image breaking continued through September, as Orange and the grandees applied the accord more liberally than the regent had intended. Now, however, the grandees were in the impossible situation of being distrusted by both the regent and the Calvinists. They were also aware that the disorders had gone so far that Philip would have to react severely, and indeed to hold them personally accountable. In fact, on October 29 the king ordered an army to the Netherlands under his most hard-line advisor, the duke of Alva.

By December, however, the revolt began to collapse from within. The reason for this reversal was that the precocious minority extremism of the summer had generated an equally precocious reaction among the moderate majority of the population. In consequence, the regent now felt strong enough to besiege two of the most openly Calvinist cities, Tournai and Valenciennes. By the turn of the year, she was able to raise a respectable number of troops. Grandees such as Egmont began to return to her service. And by April-May, the revolt had collapsed everywhere. The prince of Orange fled to his lands in Germany. The regent was again in control of the situation and the open practice of Calvinism was again suppressed.

The headlong radicalization of the Wonderyear and the correspondingly swift reversal of the next six months created a situation that would give the Netherlands revolution a unique pattern in European history. In the summer of 1567, Alva arrived in the Netherlands with ten thousand Spanish troops (ten thousand troops were already mobilized locally) and instituted a policy of reprisals against all those who had participated in the disorders. And repression, when it is massive enough, does work. This meant that henceforth the revolt had to be primarily a military operation to overthrow the Spanish regime in Brussels. Leadership, therefore, devolved onto exiles abroad, a recruitment that automatically favored radicals, in particular the more militant Calvinists. This international dimension, in turn, meant that the fate of the rebellion would depend on finding bases in England, France, and the empire, all of whom had to worry about their relations with the strongest power of the day, Spain. Finally, since Spain had to contend with Turkish power in the Mediterranean, this factor affected how relentlessly Philip could focus fiscal and military resources on the Netherlands.

Alva's iron rule lasted four years. In the beginning, at least, it successfully reestablished royal control, but with new personnel, for this was a government of Spaniards, not of native elites. Alva created a special tribunal, the Council of the Troubles, to punish participants in the disorders of 1566. Counts Egmont and Hornes were publicly executed. Altogether, twelve thousand people were tried, and one thousand executed by what was now colloquially known as the "Council of Blood." Some sixty thousand people fled abroad, an exodus that temporarily eliminated the extremists.

Alva was less successful, however, in conciliating the moderate majority. Given the heavy demands of the Turkish war on Philip's treasury, the Netherlands operation was supposed to be financed by local taxation. The States General, however, alleging their ancient privileges, steadfastly refused to grant Alva the monies he requested. He therefore unconstitutionally imposed a "Tenth Penny," or 10 percent, tax. And this, as much as his persecution of heresy, alienated the population and prepared the way for renewed radicalization. For the moment, however, active internal opposition had been crushed. In 1568, Orange, now clearly the chief leader of the opposition, attempted an invasion from Germany with mercenary troops and failed miserably, thereby demonstrating the weakness of Beggar support among the majority of the population.

THE SEA BEGGARS

What finally revived the revolt was the Sea Beggars: that is, privateers based in foreign ports who had been granted letters of marque by Orange in his capacity as a sovereign prince of the empire. In 1572 Queen Elizabeth, for diplomatic reasons, expelled a Beggar group from London, and on April 1, they landed at the small port of Brill in South Holland in search of supplies and, finding no Spanish forces in the neighborhood, decided to hold the town. They were able to carry out this fortuitous coup because Philip had just withdrawn troops from the region in preparation for an action against England that was later called off. These Beggars were ordinary seamen from Holland and Zeeland officered by members of the lesser nobility and accompanied by Calvinist preachers.

Using Brill as a base, in the summer of 1572 the Sea Beggars took over most of the towns in Holland and Zeeland. The procedure was this. Since the Beggars, though tough, were small in numbers, they usually could not take these towns by storm. Instead, they had to negotiate the transfer of authority from Philip to Orange with the magistrates, or "regents," of each town. The terms of the transfer were usually preservation of the political and social status quo as modified only by religious freedom for both the Catholic majority and the Calvinist minority, which was also Orange's policy. In practice, however, Calvinist preachers usually took over the main church and outlawed the Mass, thus giving the Reformed church the status of an establishment. In July 1572, the Beggars convened the States of Holland and invited Orange to resume the statholdership of the province, as well as of neighboring Zeeland, Friesland, and Utrecht.

Just as the Sea Beggars were securing the two coastal provinces, Orange's brother Louis invaded in May from France with Huguenot troops and captured Mons, while in July Orange himself invaded again from Germany. It seemed that at last Spanish power was tottering. Then, in August the wheel of fortune turned the other way, as the Saint Bartholomew's Day Massacre in Paris ended the possibility of large-scale Huguenot aid. Alva then easily defeated Orange, who this time took refuge not abroad but in Holland, where he at last had a base within the Netherlands itself.

Thus by 1573 the Netherlands revolution had at last become a Dutch Revolt. Orange, after having tried *via media* with Lutheranism, now converted to Calvinism because that was where his hard-core supporters were. In fact, he was a "politique," that is, someone who put civil peace and the welfare of the state ahead of any religious commitment and so favored toleration. The new order was everywhere installed by a coercive minority action. Though this was contrary to Orange's policy of "religious peace" and toleration, he had no choice. The old ruling magistrates were expelled and replaced by new ones, often exiles of 1566–1567. Calvinist preachers took over churches and the Mass was outlawed, even though in most places there was only a minority of Reformed. Only about one tenth of the population belonged to Reformed congregations, and of these only a minority were communicants. Amsterdam did not "go over" to the revolution until 1578.

Outside of Holland and Zeeland, however, Alva remained firmly in control. He now had around eighty-five thousand troops, and used them for a new and more severe repression. In what amounted to a form of terror, the inhabitants of Naarden, Mechelin, and Zutphen were massacred. This was the period of the famous siege and the heroic resistance of Leiden, when the Dutch cut the dykes to wash the Spaniards away and bring in supplies by boat. The historian Geyl is quite right to emphasize the "variable" of geography in the Netherlands revolution. The two mighty rivers, the Rhine and the Maas, and a network of lakes made Holland and Zeeland the indispensable redoubt for the revolt's survival.

APOGEE AND RETRENCHMENT

In 1576, the revolt once again became a Netherlands revolution. Again this happened because of the international situation: Philip's wars in both the Netherlands and the Mediterranean forced him to declare bankruptcy in September 1575. The resulting arrears in troops' pay led to mutinies, culminating in the "Spanish fury" at Antwerp in November 1576. In the midst of these disorders Alva's successor as governor-general died, and Spanish power collapsed everywhere. The States General, convened on its own initiative, assumed governmental functions beginning in September 1576, while at the same time professing loyalty to the king. In November a treaty between the loyalist and rebel provinces, The Pacification of Ghent, was signed that provided for the cessation of hostilities between the two groups. It called for the departure of all Spanish troops from the country, and recognized the religious status quo. The new Orangist regime in Holland and Zeeland thus did not lose its distinctiveness or its separate military force.

There then ensued a struggle between Orange at one extreme and the new governor-general, Philip's half-brother, Don Juan of Austria, at the other, for the allegiance of the States. Without adequate military force, Don Juan could enter Brussels only by accepting, at least outwardly, the Pacification of Ghent. Orange refused to join the States General and accept Don Juan because he was convinced that satisfactory agreement with Philip II was impossible. On July 24, 1577, Don Juan lost patience and tried to use military force against the States. Orange counterattacked by appealing to lower-class radicalism in the cities of Brabant and Flanders.

In effect, in late 1576 a new revolution on the model of 1566 then erupted across the south. In Brussels the guilds formed a Committee of Eighteen that invaded the States of Brabant, and then pressured the States General to force recognition of Orange as Statholder of the province (October 18, 1577). Orange entered Brussels in triumph on September 23, returning to his family's palace ten years after he had been forced to flee it. In Ghent matters took a still more radical turn. There the Committee of Eighteen formed by the guilds purged the Catholic moderates governing Flanders, suppressed the Mass, and welcomed the returning exiles of 1566. From Ghent this revolutionary movement spread to the other Flemish cities somewhat like the Sea Beggars had taken over Holland in 1572. Sometimes called the Dutch Revolt's "radical revolution," and often compared to its English and French successors, this movement produced a string of Calvinist urban republics in Bruges, Ypres, Oudenaarde, and other cities.[12] This was much more than Orange wanted, because such radicalism could only frighten the moderates into seeking protection from Spanish power. Yet at the moment he had no choice but to support his most militant supporters. In the meantime, the "patriot" cause seemed to triumph in the whole Netherlands. Orange, by the beginning of 1578, "had achieved the status he had coveted at least since 1564: he was effectively the head of government. He had succeeded to the position once occupied by Cardinal Granvelle."[13]

But again, as in 1566, popular Calvinist extremism caused the third revolt to fall short of uniting the whole Netherlands.[14] The radical advance continued, as in May 1578, the Calvinists took over Amsterdam in a coup. In reaction, pressure from the nobility and patricians of the south forced Orange to react against his radical allies; in August 1579, he forcibly disarmed the Ghent Eighteen. Nonetheless, the damage had been done. The Catholic leaders in the States General, in particular the nobles and clergy, now thoroughly distrusted Orange and his

Calvinist supporters. By summer the States were resisting Orange's "religious peace" since it would have legalized Calvinist gains in the south. The Catholics, no less than the Calvinists, were unwilling to accept heresy in the regions they controlled.

To protect Catholic interests, the States invited a brother of the king of France, the duke of Anjou, to become "Defender of the Liberties of the Low Countries." This moved Queen Elizabeth to fund a German Calvinist force to protect Brabant. At the same time, the States were having difficulty paying their Catholic troops, and these began to mutiny. Called the Malcontents, these troops then went to war against Calvinist Ghent.

At this point, in October 1578 Don Juan died. He was succeeded by Philip's nephew, Alexander Farnese, duke of Parma. Philip at last had a governor-general of talent who, moreover, understood, quite unlike Alva, that the key to Spanish success lay in winning over the moderate centrist majority.

The duke of Parma was aided in this effort by the fact that the religious differences between Catholics and Calvinists were magnified by the force of provincial particularism. The virtual independence of Ghent and Flanders provoked a similar particularistic stance in French-speaking Artois and Hainaut. In January these provinces formed the Union of Arras, which in May 1579 made its peace with Parma and Philip. This in turn led Calvinist Holland and Zeeland to federate with the five other northern provinces, and to Calvinize them, in the Union of Utrecht. Calvinist Flanders and Brabant were affiliated with this union.

The government of the States General was now effectively a rump, a kind of congress of the northern provinces and the Calvinist republics of Flanders and Brabant. In July 1581, this now radical body voted to "abjure" Philip II as their sovereign—in effect the Dutch declaration of independence. But they did not declare themselves a republic. Rather, like the Bohemians in 1421, they still thought in monarchical terms, and so voted to make Anjou hereditary "prince and lord of the Netherlands." Later, when this solution went sour, they made an offer to Elizabeth, who turned them down but offered them instead the loan of her favorite, the earl of Leicester. When he, too, proved a disappointment the seven provinces became a de facto republic by default, with the princes of Orange as de facto semi-monarchs.

By the beginning of independence, however, Philip II's finances had improved. Parma absorbed the Malcontents into his forces, and began the reconquest of Flanders and Brabant. Orange and the States General first withdrew to Antwerp in July 1583, and the next month to Middelburg in Zeeland. The next year Orange was assassinated by an agent of Philip II. And, although Orange's son and successor, Maurice of Nassau, was an able commander, by 1589 the revolt had nonetheless been pushed back almost to the region it had controlled in 1572–1574, and Parma was still advancing.

The revolt was saved by two factors. First, the internal organization and the military forces of the seven United Provinces were much stronger than Holland and Zeeland had been in 1574. Second, the international situation once again favored the Dutch cause. In 1588, the year of the Armada, Parma's crack troops were diverted to the Channel for possible transit to England. Then, in the early 1590s, they were diverted to France in an effort to prevent the triumph of a Huguenot king in Paris.

So the Netherlands revolution ended in a draw. The patriots and Calvinism triumphed in the north, but Spanish power and the Counter-Reformation church prevailed in the south. Some one hundred thousand irreconcilable Calvinists migrated from Flanders and Brabant to the Dutch Republic, and a smaller number of Catholic notables departed for the south. In 1609 Spain and the United Provinces signed the Twelve Year Truce. Although hostilities resumed in 1621, the truce in fact made the republic an independent state in the European system.

If indeed it was a state. For the United Provinces constituted a very loose federation of the seven provinces. Sovereignty resided in the provincial states, not in the United Provinces as a whole. The States General had little power since the provinces had to be unanimous to make policy. In these respects, the Dutch "constitution" resembled that of the United States under the Articles of Confederation; it even bore a certain resemblance to the ultra-libertarian constitution of the Polish-Lithuanian Commonwealth. In fact, however, Holland, as the wealthiest province and its military base, dominated the federation, thus giving it a strong presence on the international scene.

Within each state the constitution remained pretty much what it had been before 1566. That is, the provincial states were dominated by the towns, and each town was dominated by its magistrate class, the regents, which was not the same as the merchant class. Thus the Dutch Revolt was no more a social than a constitutional revolution, nor was it at all democratic. In fact, it was narrowly oligarchic. Though ennoblement did not exist in the republic, nobles, beginning with the House of Orange, still remained. And their style rubbed off in the aristocratization of the regents.

Consequently, there was almost no republican theorizing or ideology. The republic's chief political theorists, Grotius and Lipsius, wrote in Latin for an international audience and were concerned primarily with natural law in general and its application to international affairs. In all these respects, the political outcome of the revolution may be described as conservative.

This is less true, however, of the religious outcome. Throughout the revolt, organized Calvinism had been the dynamic, driving force, whether in 1566, in 1572, or in the failed "radical revolution" of 1576–1577. And it is only thanks to this force that the Orangist political constitutionalists were ultimately able to prevail in half the Netherlands. Nonetheless, the Calvinists remained a minority (a third of the population or less), and after the victory they failed to dominate society. Each sovereign state determined its own religious settlement, and in all the states the Reformed became the "public church" supported by the state.[15] Even so, not all of society belonged to it, and those who did were divided between full communicants and what might be called "auditors" or fellow travelers. The difference between the two groups was given by the right of participation in the Lord's Supper, which was conferred only by submission to the discipline of the Calvinist consistory. The Regents resisted extending this system to the whole of society and preferred to keep all policing power in its own hands. Thus, although orthodox Calvinism triumphed within the church at the national Synod of Dordrecht, and the less severe Arminian Remonstrants were silenced, Protestant Holland was no Geneva or Massachusetts or even Scotland. It was, for the age, the most tolerant and secular society in Europe.

And this outcome is due in large part to the fact that the oligarchic republic was also a commercial republic, even though the merchant class did not govern directly. Commerce and industry, fishing and textiles, the carrying trade and eventually banking were the republic's lifeblood and the support of its military power. All these activities require international openness and tolerance of diversity. Hence the Republic harbored the Catholic Descartes and the heretical Jew Spinoza and the radical rationalism of both, just as it gave refuge to both the Pilgrim Fathers and the Whig philosopher John Locke. This of course did not amount to what would now be called pluralism, but it was the nearest thing to it that Europe at the time afforded. And this was perhaps the most radical aspect of the revolution, the sixteenth-century Reformation's nearest approach to modernity.

RELIGIOUS REVOLUTIONS COMPARED

Unlike the Lutheran semi-revolution the Netherlands revolution did not begin with religion but with politics. To be sure, extreme religious radicalism was present at the outset. This Netherlands radicalism, indeed, was reflected in the exceptional magnitude of Münster. But it was repressed, first by the Habsburg government, then by the noble *politique* leadership (Orange) of the War of Independence. Thus, there is no millenarian moment in the Netherlands revolution. Calvinism, although the dominant religion, comes in late, is not hegemonic, and

—unlike in Geneva, Scotland, or Massachusetts—has to play second fiddle to the lay republic. The constitutional question becomes progressively larger, and the religious one smaller, as we move from the Hussites to the Beggars. Thus, for purposes of the typology being developed in this book, the Netherlands revolution, although moderate and non-millenarian as a revolution, produces the precociously radical result of a republican, federal *state*. In this it is like the United States much more than like either England or France.

As a preliminary, and in order to emphasize that the whole range of elements discussed earlier are necessary for a Great Revolution, let us make the comparison of the Dutch Revolt of the late sixteenth century with the seemingly similar but in fact quite different case of England in the following century.

In the Low Countries under Philip II there was certainly as much, and most probably more, commercial, industrial, and urban development than in England under the early Stuarts. In the Low Countries likewise there was probably more zealous and militant Calvinism than in the England of Laud. Finally, in the Low Countries there was obviously a much stronger king, with a far mightier army, than had ever held sway at Westminster. Yet in the Netherlands, though there occurred one of the bitterest wars of the century, there was no revolution in the sense of the fanaticization of politics and the structural unraveling of civil society such as was experienced after 1640 in England. For in the Low Countries there was no national focus to give concentrated constitutional-ideological force to the rebellion. Rather, the revolt took the form of a military confederation, first of thirteen provinces, then of seven, against the monarch in his diverse capacities as count of Flanders or Holland, or duke of Brabant, etc. The struggle thus became essentially a military, national-territorial war of liberation, analogous to that of the American colonies against England. But it was not a constitutional-ideological, internal overturn, analogous to the struggle of the English Parliament against its king for sovereignty within a single, unified governmental system.

Part II

CLASSIC ATLANTIC REVOLUTIONS

6

ENGLAND, 1640–1660–1688

From Religious to Political Revolution

No bishop, no king.
—JAMES I, 1604

The dissolution of this Government caused the War, not the War the dissolution of this Government.
—JAMES HARRINGTON, *Oceana*, 1656

The Commons of England in Parliament assembled do declare that the people are, under God, the original of all just power: And also declare that the Commons of England in Parliament assembled, being chosen by and representing the people, have the supreme power in this nation.
—RESOLUTION OF THE COMMONS, January 4, 1649

The poorest he that is in England hath a life to live, as the greatest he; and therefore . . . everyman that is to live under a government ought first by his own consent to put himself under that government; and I do think that the poorest man in England is not at all bound in a strict sense to that government that he hath not had a voice to put himself under.
—PUTNEY DEBATES, 1647

More just it is that a less number compel a greater to retain their liberty, than that a greater number compel a less to be their fellow slaves.
—JOHN MILTON, 1644

Presbyterianism is not a proper religion for gentlemen.
—CHARLES II

The first undeniably modern revolution was also the last European upheaval to be made in the name of backward-looking ideals. And this particularity is as germane to the revolution's outcome and meaning as is the radical structure of action it shared with the Hussite and French upheavals. Making a revolution in the name of allegedly conservative principles, in both politics and religion, is not at all the same as making one in the name of overtly radical and secular ones.

Such ostensible conservatism, it has already been noted, characterized all aspects of pre-modern European life. Until the emergence of the idea of progress at the end of the seventeenth century, all change in Europe, no matter how momentous, was viewed as a rebirth or a re-formation: a *renascita* or renaissance in arts and letters, a *reformatio* or a *restoratio* in religion. We have also seen how this perception molded upheavals of Hussite Bohemia and the Lutheran and Calvinist Reformations. Its moderating effect has, further, been glimpsed in the anomaly of British historical usage where recognition of the turbulent and bloody events of 1640–1660 as a full-fledged revolution was delayed for almost two centuries, while at the same time that epochal designation was reserved for the elite and reluctant coup d'état of 1688–1689. How did this anomaly play out in the three centuries of historiography since then?

A GENTLEMANLY DEBATE

In the seventeenth century itself, at least after the king's execution, articulate opinion was overwhelmingly negative: for one Milton who embraced the Commonwealth there were ten John Lockes for whom it was "that great Bedlam which was England." To the revolution's first historian, Clarendon, the events of the mid-century were "The Great Rebellion," and their political meaning was defined as "Civil War" and "Interregnum."[1] Then the victors of 1688 buried the mid-century sedition under what would later be called the Whig interpretation of history. First framed by a contemporary, Bishop Gilbert Burnet, the contours of this perspective are given by the six volumes of his memoirs: only a third of the first is devoted to the "troubles" before 1660, while all the rest detail the "tyranny" of Charles II and James II and the liberal "glories" of 1688–1689.[2] In the next century, David Hume, though he castigated the Puritans' destructive "enthusiasm," paradoxically recognized that without their assault on absolutism, the balanced freedom of 1688 could not have emerged. At the century's end, however, Edmund Burke, terrified that the example of the French Revolution might revive the smoldering embers of English enthusiasm, once again buried 1640–1660 under 1688 (his famous *Reflections* are in fact less an analysis of French events than a justification of the British constitution).

The inaugural work of the modern historiography of British revolution, Macaulay's *History of England*, took up the emphases of Bishop Burnet, but in a spirit of satisfaction that the Whig wager on the Reform of 1832 had spared England anything like 1848 in France. It was only at the close of the triumphant era of Victorian England stability that S. R. Gardiner could at last safely disinter the story of Puritan enthusiasm, and indeed underline its importance to the ultimate triumph of Whig values and national greatness.[3] Even so, as late as 1938, when Macaulay's nephew and moral heir, G. M. Trevelyan, published a book called *The English Revolution*, he meant 1688–1689, not 1640–1660, which he had treated elsewhere under the bland rubric *England Under the Stuarts*.[4]

Yet this perspective was now an anachronism, for the turn-of-the-century emergence of socialism as a mass movement had already begun to bear historiographical fruit. The first notable example came from a member of the Fabian Society and Anglo-Catholic, R. H. Tawney. In 1926, his *Religion and the Rise of Capitalism* used Max Weber's thesis on the Protestant ethic to argue that Puritanism was indeed the matrix of British capitalism, which he hoped would soon be replaced by an ethical socialism drawing inspiration from pre-Puritan Christianity.[5] As was only to be expected, this soft socialism was soon overrun on its left by the harder variety defined by October 1917.

Thus in 1940, Christopher Hill, Marxist and indeed member of the Communist Party UK, published the first book called simply *The English Revolution*, without any adjectival qualifications. By this he meant primarily 1640–1660, and for him this newfound epochal divide was England's "bourgeois revolution,"[6] while the Puritan sectarians were adumbrations of the modern proletariat—a pair of ideas that of course go back to Engels in the 1890s.[7] In short, under the influence of the Russian example, Hill did for English Levellers, Diggers, and Ranters what Lefebvre had done slightly earlier for eighteenth-century French peasants.[8] Even Trevelyan had to join the new trend by writing a social history of England, a subject he defined as "history with the politics left out."[9] And so scholarship of the bicephalous English Revolution played out over the twentieth century in such close step with contemporary politics that one is tempted to correct Trevelyan's maxim with the verdict of Soviet historian Mikhail Pokrovsky, that "history is politics projected onto the past."[10]

This class-struggle perspective on the revolution culminated after World War II, in what was now triumphantly socialist Britain, in the once-famous "storm over the gentry." In 1941, Tawney radicalized his position in an article entitled "The Rise of the Gentry, 1558–1640," which portrayed these country gentlemen as a rural bourgeoisie readying to challenge the old "feudal" order, a thesis complemented in 1948 by Lawrence Stone's argument for a simultaneous decline of the aristocracy.[11] The matter became a storm in 1953 when Hugh Trevor-Roper turned both Marx and Weber on their heads in an article proclaiming "The Decline of the Gentry." His thesis was that Cromwell's Independents were impoverished squires moved by hatred for the centralizing and expensive monarchy, coupled with nostalgia for a simpler England that had allegedly existed under Elizabeth I. Then, in 1958, in an article entitled "Storm over the Gentry," both sides in the debate were demolished by a crusty Whig from across the Atlantic, Jack Hexter. Tawney and Trevor-Roper alike, he showed, had based their generalizations on evidence so scant as to be meaningless: in fact, part of the gentry was rising and part of it was declining, but there existed no correlation between either trend and actual political alignments.[12] In retrospect, this dispute over a nonproblem, involving as it did some of the period's most distinguished historians, appears as an almost comical *Wechselwirkung* of the present on the past: Clarendon and Burnet were distinctly closer to the mark.

Yet the concept of an English Revolution stubbornly dominated Stuart history for another twenty years. Its most accomplished exponent was Lawrence Stone, now transplanted to America and subject (profitably for once) to the influence of social science "staseology."[13] And, of course, social and economic conditions continued to be investigated on an impressive scale, to the great enrichment of our knowledge. But the "bourgeois revolution" gradually faded away, even Hill himself abandoning the strict definition of the "gentry" as rural capitalists to speak instead of 1640–1660 only creating the general conditions that later made capitalist development possible.[14]

Eventually, of course, mid-century *marxisant* social history succumbed to a backlash of political and ideological "revisionism." Nor was this change due only to the evidentiary shipwreck of the bourgeois revolution; it surely owed something to the fading, after 1970, of British socialism's luster at home and that of "really-existing socialism" abroad. The sense of British historical particularity was clearly highlighted when the tercentenary of 1688–1689 coincided by a matter of months with both the bicentenary of 1789 and Communism's collapse in Eastern Europe.

The new historiography was inaugurated as early as 1971 by Conrad Russell's *The Crisis of Parliaments: English History, 1509–1660*, whose low-key title had clearly been chosen to avoid the term "revolution."[15] However, this did not signify a return to the Whig interpretation, for the "revisionists" were against all teleological views of British history, national no less than Marxist. In the revisionist view, all that remained of the seventeenth-century drama was a series of crises in which Parliament, or more exactly *a* parliament, was not so much an institution as an event. It was only through the vicissitudes of these crises up until the century's end that it was decided whether Parliament would survive to become the pivot of the British constitution. For the controversial decades 1640–1660, therefore, what required explaining was not the outbreak of a revolution, but the origins of the Civil War. Or at the most, "revolution" was reserved for the transparently radical moment around the king's execution in the late 1640s.[16] Thus, revisionism has continued to the present day in what Russell calls "nominalist" fashion alternating between anti-revisionist thrusts and neo-revisionist refinements.

So what will "English Revolution" be taken to mean here? Obviously, both the radical focus on 1640–1660 and the Whig focus on 1688–1689 are partially valid. The former was in truth the most startling and intense moment of the century; nor could 1688 have occurred without it. At the same time, the settlement of the crisis opened in 1640 did not come with the Restoration in 1660; it came only with the modest aftershock of 1688, which is therefore properly considered the foundational moment of modern British politics and its attendant national myth. Since 1688 is undeniably the century's operative legacy, therefore, "English Revolution" will be taken here to mean the whole crisis of 1640–1660–1688.

In this perspective, 1640–1660 was indeed a long parenthesis, a disruption of the national development, as the Whig interpretation contends. Yet, just as Hill and the Marxists went too far in making that moment a bourgeois revolution, so too revisionism has gone too far by reducing 1640–1660 to a mere "crisis of Parliaments" and hence making the outbreak of Civil War the major conundrum to be explained. To one not embroiled in the debate, Lawrence Stone in 1970 offers the right middle ground: "The outbreak of war itself is relatively easy to explain; what is hard to puzzle out [is] why most of the established institutions of state and Church—crown, court, central administration and episcopacy—collapsed so ignominiously two years before"[17]—a list of casualties to which Parliament itself was later added. This is just about the maximum one can do in dismantling a "traditional" European order. Moreover, it is the first European upheaval since the Hussites two centuries earlier to go to comparable extremes. Likewise, the English drama is the first European upheaval to which participants in all subsequent revolutions self-consciously related their own actions. Surely, these are credentials enough to qualify as revolution.

Yet Stone's formulation must be amended by a final puzzle: why did the cataclysmic changes he recognizes leave so little residue in British history? As we shall see later, the Commonwealth's principal effective heirs were America's Founding Fathers. At home there was only a half-submerged though not insignificant tradition of nonconformist radicalism. Its most prominent representative is perhaps Burke's opponent, Thomas Paine—who had to seek his revolution across the

Atlantic or over the Channel. To this roll call we may add such mid-twentieth-century social historians as Hill and E. P. Thompson—who sought theirs in a Muscovite mirage abroad. At home they consoled themselves with seventeenth-century sectarians and pre-1832 industrial workers, proto-proletariats that missed becoming locomotives of history however much their discovery did to stimulate the development of historiography.[18]

And what was the long-term revolution of 1640–1688 about? Here the Whig tradition, for all its simplistic teleology and overdrawn Manicheanism, got to the nub of the matter. The revolution in all its stages was, first, about the constitutional issue of Parliament's relationship to the king, or as Macaulay put it, about the transition from "medieval mixed monarchy to modern mixed monarchy." Concomitantly (though not to say secondarily), it was about what constituted true Christian doctrine and proper ecclesiastical organization, issues that eventually opened vistas onto modern toleration. What the deeper causes of the revolution were is another matter, but no one can dispute that these two issues were what contemporaries thought they were fighting about.

THE FRAMEWORK

If there has been uncertainty about the status of England's "Great Rebellion" as a revolution, there can be no doubt about that of the early Stuart monarchy as a state. But what kind of state? The usual label for the European state of the time is "New Monarchy," the standard examples being the Spain of Ferdinand and Isabella, the France of Louis XI, and the England of Henry VII. As regards the latter, the question is whether the Tudors' New Monarchy is properly called an absolutism. The Tudors themselves certainly thought it was: Henry VIII after his break with Rome referred to his kingdom as an "empire" and Elizabeth referred to herself as an "absolute prince." Even so, a large body of later opinion, for whom the British foundational myth is an amalgam of national affirmations from Henry VIII's 1529 démarche to the final defeat of the Stuarts' absolutist pretensions in 1688, has refused to apply the "continental" scarlet letter to their predecessors. In fact, however, the regime the Stuarts inherited from the Tudors was as absolute as that of any other dynastic polity of the day. The divergence develops only in the seventeenth century, as New Monarchy almost everywhere shaded off into real absolutism, the most perfected example of which was of course the state of Louis XIV (or Lewis XIV as Macaulay called him), against whom the culminating touches of the British national myth came to be defined.[19]

These problems may perhaps be elucidated by a glance at their *longue durée*. European state building came in three stages. First, there was the consolidated feudal monarchy of the twelfth and thirteenth centuries in which the pyramid of vassalage at last became a more or less effective command structure, though without producing anything resembling direct royal rule over the country. Next there was the New Monarchy of the late fifteenth century and the whole sixteenth century, which came near to direct rule by eliminating or taming the great magnates. Finally, in the first half of the seventeenth century came a further wave of state-building, in large part due to the contemporary "military" revolution that at last produced a state in direct control of the national territory and which can therefore be called unequivocally modern. These developments, moreover, were accompanied by the development of the idea of a supreme locus of authority, or sovereignty, in the polity, a view formulated by Jean Bodin in 1576 and the principle of "reason of state" (*ragion di stato*), first formulated by Giovanni Botero in 1589, which made the welfare of the sovereign power an end in itself, freed from traditional moral constraints. It is in the context of this third stage that early Stuart policy must be understood. Charles I was in effect trying to imitate his brother-in-law Louis XIII of France. Unfortunately for him, however, he lacked the fiscal and military resources of his model. In the deepest sense, therefore, what the English Revolution was about was a refusal to accept the absolutist model of state formation and to construct the unavoidable transformation of the traditional polity under parliamentary rather than royal leadership.

Still, this transformation did not mean that the new English state was no longer an Old Regime in the broad meaning of that term as a "traditional" or Gemeinschaft order. That Old Regime, moreover, largely survived the seventeenth century, and indeed 1789–1815 as well, succumbing to modernity only between the Catholic Emancipation of 1828 and the Reform Bill of 1832.[20] And vestiges of the Old Regime still remain, in the monarchy, the House of Lords, and a "Church as by law established."

Thus, England was very much a society of the two swords and the three orders, even though the latter were sliced differently from the paradigmatic French model. The king was the first estate all by himself; the second estate, represented in the House of Lords, was composed of the peers and the Bishops of the realm; the third estate, represented in the House of Commons, was composed of the untitled gentry and the patrician elements of the towns. The church as a whole was not a separate estate, though the bishops and lower clergy did meet together, but separately from Parliament, in a national ecclesiastical assembly called Convocation. Nor was England unique in deviating from the paradigmatic French norm. In Sweden, for example, the peasantry formed a fourth estate, and elsewhere still other anomalies could be found. The main point, however, is that everywhere a legal, corporate hierarchy existed.[21]

But what of other, more important facets of English exceptionalism, a phenomenon that has often been overworked but is still real enough. First, England's famously insular situation greatly simplifies the problem of defense, not only by making invasion logistically difficult, but also by reducing the cost of defense and hence the pressure that war-making exerts on all state institutions.[22]

England, moreover, was a "tight little island," as an old cliché has it. It had been a unitary kingdom from the time of Alfred the Great in the ninth century, and its largely aquatic frontiers have not budged in more than one thousand years. By contrast, its traditional rival, France, was put together as a political unit over a span of a century and a half through accretions to the royal domain; and even then stable northern and eastern frontiers were not achieved until Louis XIV. Likewise, at the other end of the continent, Muscovite princes put together a tsardom by a similar secular process of "gathering of the Russian lands." And everything between acquired a stable national unity only in the nineteenth century.

England, furthermore, was blessed by the manner of its introduction to the institutional matrix of all European states, feudalism. Instead of having to create such a system of relative order out of the near anarchy of the year 1000, as had occurred across the Channel, feudalism was introduced into the kingdom at one fell swoop, by the Norman Conquest of 1066. And Norman feudalism was the most efficient in all Europe, the only one in which the king was truly, not just theoretically, the apex of the feudal pyramid.[23] Only the Norman kingdom of southern Italy and Sicily offered a comparably effective feudal proto-state; and the base for Frederick II of Hohenstaufen's exceptional but ephemeral imperial power in the early thirteenth century, whereas the English kingdom of William I and Henry II, like Charles IV's Bohemia, was the maximal size—roughly two duchies of Normandy—for effective feudal monarchy. This monarchy, therefore, collapsed only twice in its history, in the Wars of the Roses and in the Interregnum of the seventeenth century. A final benediction on the scepter isle was that its unitary state could be governed relatively cheaply, since its county officials, sheriffs, and justices of the peace, were at the same time local notables and unpaid voluntary agents of the king.

Economically England was much less precocious. Until almost 1500 it was principally an exporter of raw materials, chiefly wool for the textile industries of Flanders and Florence. In the course of the sixteenth century, with the aid of imported Flemish workers, it acquired its own woolen textile manufacture. At the same time its ships became active in carrying trade across northern Europe as far east as Archangelsk in Russia, and by the early seventeenth century, with the aid of German miners, the extraction of coal became a large scale industrial enterprise. In fact, sixteenth-century England, which would later become the pilot for the industrial development of more backward nations, in its own industrial debut profited from what is known as "the advantages of backwardness" vis-à-vis its more developed neighbors across the Channel. Thus, by the accession of the Stuarts, England was already launched on the road that would eventually lead to European economic leadership.

Politically, in the sixteenth century England developed a pattern of change by relatively slow, incremental stages, with few brusque or radical breaks. Thus it experienced the mildest possible form of religious Reformation in an age when so crucial a change almost invariably led to violence. The Henrician reform of 1529–1539 was an act of state; it was not launched by zealous clerics as in Germany, Switzerland, and France, nor was it accompanied by mass popular enthusiasm. The same was true of the Elizabethan religious settlement of the 1560s. At the same time, the minority of zealous reformers, the Puritans, remained within the official church until 1640, hoping that their action would one day bring the Reformation to "completion," unlike in France or the Low Countries, where the Calvinists seceded to form a parallel church.[24] And for those who could not wait, there was the possibility of emigrating to Massachusetts Bay, which received roughly twenty thousand emigrants in the course of the 1630s. Moreover, the example of the sixteenth-century French and Netherlands wars of religion helped keep English Reform moderate.

At the same time, the state apparatus was strengthened through the creation of the various "prerogative courts," Star Chamber for secular affairs, and Court of High Commission for religious matters, and other bodies outside the common law courts. Concurrently, Parliament, although historically and in law only an extension of the king's curia, or court, over the century became de facto part of the central government, though still thoroughly obedient to his wishes. The main reason for this of course was the need of both Henry VIII and Elizabeth for public support in putting through their ecclesiastical revolution. And the county gentry and the Crown together were the beneficiaries of the dissolution of the monasteries and the sale of their properties. Due to the frequency of Parliaments, moreover, there was increasing continuity of personnel and the possibility of developing institutional procedures and a sense of corporate identity. As the Tudor system of government was summed up by Conrad Russell: "The essence of this system [was] the sharing of effective power between the Crown and the dominant elements among the propertied classes. The symbolic expressions of this partnership [were] Parliament and the notion of the rule of law, though in practice the two came to the same thing since the highest law-making authority was Parliament."[25]

And there were the relatively modest demographics: a population of roughly five million in England and Wales, with another million or so in both Scotland and Ireland, and a capital city, London, that in the mid-century was just overtaking Paris as the largest European city with a population of 450,000, or 10 percent of the total population of the country.

THE PROLOGUE

So why did the exceptionally successful state machinery created by the Tudors stagger into crisis and collapse under their successors? In fact, the system was already an anachronism when the Stuarts inherited it, which was precisely the moment the seventeenth-century phase of "hard" European state-building began. The principal stimulus to this was what has been called the early modern "military revolution." Between the early sixteenth century and the mid-seventeenth century, the contest between the Spanish Habsburgs and France in Italy and the Low Countries transformed European warfare. First gunpowder magnified offensive power; then, dense fortification multiplied defensive strength—only to be answered by sophisticated artillery and massed infantry, organized into standing armies. During the Thirty Years' War, the revolution spread east to Germany and north to Sweden, reaching the British Isles only in the course of the seventeenth-century Civil War.[26]

All of this, of course, was expensive, and as a consequence, after a flowering of two centuries in most of Europe, in the early seventeenth century, monarchies began phasing out elective estates in favor of more docile and stable permanent bureaucracies. Under James I the drive toward this new-style absolutism was more rhetorical than substantive. He loudly proclaimed the divine right of kings and he stood firmly against Puritan pressure for "completing the Reformation," which in practice meant Presbyterian, that is elective, church government, a system he had known in Scotland and which he correctly understood was incompatible with his idea of strong monarchy. As regards practical policy, he failed in his ambition to unite England and Scotland into a kingdom of Great Britain with a single Parliament. For the rest, he got out of his predecessor's long war with Spain and refused to get into the Thirty Years' War after 1618 even though it appeared to most of his subjects as a struggle for the survival of Protestantism against the Counter-Reformation, and although his own son-in-law was a principal, and losing, protagonist on the Protestant side. Hence, England was not present at the founding event of modern European diplomacy, the Treaty of Westphalia in 1648. The only advantage of this policy was that it kept expenses down, and so avoided conflict with Parliament over new taxes, although there was periodic acrimony over monopolies, and of course religion.

Matters moved toward crisis when Charles I acceded to the throne in 1625. First, he blundered into simultaneous wars with both Spain and France, which of course greatly increased expenses. At the same time, he carried out his most vigorous efforts at state-building, not at the center of his power, England, but in the peripheral monarchy of Ireland. There, under Lord Lieutenant Thomas Wentworth, Charles's would-be Richelieu, the restive population was brought firmly under Dublin's control, Parliament was subdued, and a standing army was established to repress Catholic dissidence—a policy Wentworth appropriately called "thorough." Another aspect of this policy was carried out in England by Charles's new archbishop of Canterbury, William Laud. "Thorough" here meant imposing religious uniformity within the church, standard absolutist policy at the time, but particularly risky in the English case since it meant an active campaign against long-established Puritan positions, which of course was construed as persecution. Laud's policies were all the more obnoxious to a sizable proportion of the population since they entailed rejecting the central dogma of Protestantism, predestination, in favor of the Arminian doctrine of free will, a "heresy" in Calvinist eyes, and liturgical innovations of a High Church nature, such as moving the altar to the east end of the nave and separating it off with a communion rail—practices which smacked of "popery." Moreover, the queen, Henrietta Maria, was a Catholic, and kept a papist chapel in the palace, all of which led to suspicions that the king and Laud were acting for a "popish plot."

Charles was at a disadvantage in both these policies, because of the constraints that the traditional tax system and constitutional structures placed on his ability to act. The king was supposed "to live of his own," that is from traditional revenues and the income from the royal domain. In addition, he had subsidies voted by Parliament at every royal accession. All exceptional expenses, however, such as a foreign war, had to be funded by a special grant from Parliament; and England had no standing army. Nor did the king have a permanent land tax such as *la taille* in France, or the possibility of raising funds through the French system of "venality of offices." As a result of these constraints, the Tudors could conduct only a modest, essentially defensive foreign policy, and James I could hardly do more.

At Charles I's accession Parliament refused the usual grant of the custom's revenue, which he went ahead and collected anyway. In 1627, to finance his losing war, he levied a forced loan from his subjects under threat of legal prosecution. By 1628–1629, Parliament refused to grant any money without redress of grievances. Amidst great disorder he was forced to accept Parliament's Petition of Rights, which detailed what they took to be their rights under the "ancient constitution." Parliament was immediately dissolved, its more vocal leaders imprisoned by royal command, and Charles vowed to summon no more Parliaments.

And so for eleven years of personal government Charles attempted to rule alone, just as the regent of his brother-in-law Louis XIII had ruled without the Estate General after 1614. This meant he had to get along by reinterpreting various ancient imposts to yield what were in fact new revenues. The most important of these was ship money, a tax once paid only by port towns but now extended to the whole kingdom with the argument that since the entire island profited from the navy, inland cities should have to pay for it. too. One John Hampton refused to pay and so was imprisoned, and the courts upheld his conviction in 1637. This case was a major constitutional one, since with time, ship money could have become a permanent direct tax like *la taille* in France, thus obviating any further need of Parliament. The prerogative courts increasingly infringed on the traditional domain of the common law courts. Politically this meant that the parliamentary, common-law opposition to rule by royal "prerogative" did not argue in terms of effecting rational improvements on the existing state of affairs, but in terms of a return to the timeless legitimacy of the "ancient constitution" (a notion founded largely on misreadings of Magna Carta and other medieval statutes), a "constitution" allegedly violated by the recent "innovations" of runaway royal tyranny.[27] Could Charles have gotten away with "thorough" indefinitely? Quite possibly, yes, but on one very stringent condition: that he avoid all military entanglements requiring any new taxes.

THE OPENING OF THE CRISIS

The actual crisis was triggered by a religious issue. In 1638 Charles, in pursuit of religious uniformity throughout all the king's domains, attempted to introduce the Anglican Book of Common Prayer into Presbyterian Scotland. The result was a national insurrection, expressed through a Solemn League and Covenant of the Presbyterian party, and a collapse of royal authority throughout Scotland. When Charles led a rag-tag English militia to recover his northern kingdom he had to settle for an ignominious truce at Berwick. In the midst of the crisis Wentworth was recalled from Ireland and made earl of Strafford. In the spring of 1640 Charles was forced to convene a new Parliament to raise funds. This body refused to vote a levy until its grievances had been addressed and reform was undertaken. The king refused and dissolved what would be known to history as the Short Parliament.

By the summer of 1640 near-anarchy prevailed in England. Riots broke out in London, and Laud's palace was attacked. The population stopped paying the ship money tax. Sensing the king's weakness, the Scots Covenanters invaded northern England, defeated a royal force, and demanded £850 (a prodigious sum at the time) a day until a formal settlement of their grievances was reached. In this predicament Charles had no choice but to summon another Parliament, and this time to negotiate.

The obvious parallel with the convening of what would become the Long Parliament of November 1640 is with that of the French Estates General in May 1789. Both were convened because the monarchy needed a vote of taxes incurred because of war. And in both cases the ancient medieval estates immediately assumed modern constituent functions before they would bail the Crown out of its financial difficulties. The Estates General did this overtly, in so many words. The Long Parliament did it under the pretense of exercising its immemorial rights under the ancient constitution, but did it de facto nonetheless.

The ensuing twenty years of crisis and turmoil may be "emplotted," in main outline, as a simple triad: Parliament and Presbyterianism against the king (1640–1645); the army and Independency against Parliament (1646–1649); Cromwell and the army alone (1649–1660). Alternatively, we may distinguish four phases, each marking a deepening and radicalizing of the revolutionary dynamic. The first phase, in 1640–1641, pitted Parliament against king in a political struggle conducted with near unanimity to achieve a program of fundamental but legally achieved constitutional reform. The second, during 1642–1646, saw Parliament split between Anglican moderates and Presbyterian radicals and the latter's military struggle, together with their New Model Army, against the king. The third, in 1647–1649, saw the Presbyterian Parliament crushed by a second war between the army and Charles now aligned with the Scots, a struggle culminating in the purge of Parliament, the king's execution, and the establishment of a republic. At the same time the Independent "left" suppressed the Leveller "far left." The final phase, extending from 1649 to 1660, brought the Commonwealth's failure, the conquest of Ireland and Scotland, Parliament's suppression, and the dictatorship of Cromwell and the army.

The Long Parliament met in an atmosphere of euphoria and national unity for change. It is this support that emboldened Parliament to assume what were in effect constituent functions. And, like the Estates General in 1789, it was prepared to resort to illegal means and physical coercion to achieve its ends. First, it consciously used the Scots Covenanters to pressure the king into concessions. Second, it had liberal resort to the London mob, the "trained bands" or municipal militia and the London apprentices. There was, moreover, organized leadership behind these activities. On the "left" there was John Pym's "junto," composed of former members of earlier parliaments with Puritan connections such as John Hampden who had often met together in the Providence Island Company (a "conspiracy" analogous to the Club Breton in 1789). This group was in illegal if not downright treasonous connivance with both the Scots and the London crowd. Then there was a second "caucus" (the word "party" is too strong for any parliamentary groupings at the time) around Edward Hyde and Lucius Cary, Lord Falkland, who were more moderate in politics and Anglican in religion. To be sure, the Tower was not stormed as was the Bastille, but there was most definitely an urban revolutionary movement with an armed guard exercising direct physical pressure on the king at every crucial juncture in the next two years.

In this coercive atmosphere, the Long Parliament carried out a veritable constitutional revolution. This revolution began, however, not with any declaration of general principles, as in the subsequent American and French cases, but in the more "naïve" political form of an attack on the king's "evil counselors," a form of protest that obviated accusation of the monarch himself. Thus their first act, on November 11, was to impeach the king's chief minister, Strafford, and soon thereafter Laud, both of whom were sent to the Tower. When it proved to be impossible to make a legal case for treason against Strafford, in the spring of 1641 Parliament condemned him to death by a legislative act called bill of attainder. Charles signed this act under duress as the palace of Whitehall was besieged by a mob of apprentices. The king was overcome with a mixture of remorse over the betrayal of a devoted servant and humiliation at such a forced capitulation. Other important ministers were also impeached, and in 1644 Laud was tried and executed. For the first year of the Long Parliament's existence, Charles had no partisans, and so the would-be "thorough" work of his reign was completely undone.

At the same time censorship collapsed, and the country was soon awash with political and religious pamphlets denouncing one or another evil and advancing a corresponding innovation. As was only to be expected, ecclesiastical discipline collapsed, and altar rails were ripped out of churches. Puritan Presbyterianism gained ground with the active aid of Parliament's Scottish allies, and "gathered" churches of congregational Independents started to appear, as did Baptists and still more radical sectarians. Altogether, the country was seized with a frenzy of politicization in combination with religious enthusiasm. Millenarian expectations of a national rebirth, of the emergence of a New Man and a New World, were in the air. The new MPs "arrived at Westminster with talk of a Reform Church, Godly Commonwealth, Magna Carta, the Ancient Constitution, and the Country."[28] Accordingly, after the revolt of the papist Irish in December 1641, Parliament established the last Wednesday of each month as a national day of public fast on which the honorable members would listen to a sermon by a Puritan preacher of their choosing in St. Margaret's Church. Thus did the revolution feed on its own agitprop. At the same time, the revolution produced its first émigrés. Thomas Hobbes took the road to Paris because he foresaw, he said, "a disorder coming on," for England "was boiling hot with questions concerning the right of dominion and the obedience due from the subjects, the true fore-runners of an approaching war."[29] In short, 1640–1641 marked a great outburst of what Brinton called revolutionary "fever."

In this perfervid atmosphere of collective intoxication Parliament proceeded to the task of constitutional restructuring. In the spring of 1641 it passed the Tri-ennial Act, providing for regular parliaments every three years without the ini-tiative of the Crown. This was immediately followed by a bill to prevent the dis-solution or proroguing of the existing Parliament without its own consent. Both measures were signed by Charles along with Strafford's attainder. In July came the abolition of the prerogative courts of High Commission and Star Chamber. In all these things, of course, Parliament had clearly gone beyond the ancient constitution and was just as clearly infringing on the royal prerogative as em-bodied in that constitution. Between 1629 and 1640 the king, while remaining within the letter of the ancient constitution, had innovated by going beyond the spirit of its recent application. Thus the Long Parliament's actions in its first ses-sion, while in form a redress of grievances, in fact represented basic innovation. In other words, at the end of this first session, the king was permanently boxed in by the existing Parliament-turned-constituent assembly while at the same time he was deprived of his prerogative powers. In effect, these changes made Parliament an official and permanent part of the constitution. That this was their intention is demonstrated by still another innovation: on proroguing in September, each house appointed a committee to sit during the vacation, with Pym chairman of the house committee.

The changes at the first session, moreover, are roughly the terms of the settle-ment at the Restoration in 1660, as well as the restoration of that settlement in 1688–1689. So why did this constitutional settlement not end the revolution? Why does the revolution continue in overt form another twenty years and in a latent state almost to the end of the century?

The most frequent explanation that one heard at the time and that one finds in the historiography almost ever since is the unwillingness of the king to accept and abide by the new order, and his persisting perfidy in all his subsequent deal-ings with Parliament. And the case is argued as if this reaction was basically a function of his personal character. Another sovereign, it is suggested, could easily have accepted and lived with the new order. True, Charles was ever after obdu-rate and devious. But this is not a personal failing; it is ex officio to divine-right monarchy. In this perspective, he had been un-kinged by capitulation to coer-cion in the spring of 1641. Neither of his sons, Charles II and James II, ever really accepted the new order. Louis XVI had the same reaction of refusal of the coercion that had forced him to accept the Declaration of the Rights of Man in the fall of 1789 and the Civil Constitution of the Clergy in 1791. And he, too, was overcome with remorse at having betrayed his coronation oath in these capitulations. With Nicholas II, we find the same reactions: he could never accept the October Manifesto of 1905 and the creation of the Legislative Duma, because he, too, believed that he had betrayed his coronation oath in signing the October Manifesto. (Then there is the pathetic case of the Count of Chambord, alias Henry V, who as late as 1875 would not give up the white flag of the Bourbons to become a constitutional king.) However unreasonable, all these sovereigns were merely fulfilling the obligations of their divinely ordained role in refusing to compromise with sedition. This is why they had to be coerced by further revolution.

And so the revolution continued, as the new order came apart over two issues: First, could the king be trusted to abide by agreements exacted under duress? Second, should the reordering of the realm be pushed beyond politics to the "purification" of the church? Over these two issues the hitherto unanimous Parliament and nation divided. On the one hand, there were the Anglican "moderates," such as Hyde and Falkland, who believed that since Charles had accepted the new order of 1641 he should now be supported. And Charles seized on this division already at the end of the first session by giving office to the leaders of the moderate caucus, Hyde and Falkland. Furthermore, they feared that reforming the church on a Presbyterian model could only have an "overturning" effect on the whole of society. And this issue too had appeared at the end of the first session when the radicals introduced a bill for the abolition of episcopacy, the Root and Branch Bill. For in their view, the revolution was over and Parliament now should cooperate with the king. Pym's junto, however, more wisely believed that Charles would not accept the new order and thus that continued revolutionary pressure from radicals and Scots was necessary. At this point, as if to justify their suspicions, Charles went off to Scotland for the summer to see if he could find support there to help with his English troubles. And in August Parliament paid off the Scots army. Parliament and civil society, therefore, polarized, thus giving the king the political base necessary to attempt a comeback—the outcome of which could only be civil war. And at this point the full logic of coercion and of ideological intoxication began to become apparent.

THE FIRST RADICALIZATION

When Parliament reconvened in October 1641, Charles's third kingdom, Ireland, erupted in its own revolution, and English events lurched toward armed conflict. The Irish, filled with resentment at Wentworth's "thorough," and now fearing to fall under the domination of a Puritan Parliament, were emboldened to revolt because they perceived that the English government had collapsed at its center. In October the Irish Catholics, gentry and peasants alike, rose up in the name of the king against Strafford's successor as lord lieutenant, and in the course of the revolt massacred part of the population of the Ulster Presbyterian "plantation" that had been created under James. News of the massacre horrified English Protestant opinion, bringing to a paranoid pitch its permanent suspicion of a vast "popish" conspiracy against English liberties. Charles and his queen were suspected of being behind the revolt in the hope of using an Irish Catholic army against his English subjects. This belief in a vast alien conspiracy against liberty would become a permanent feature of the revolutionary syndrome. In the American Revolution, the colonists believed the policies of George III were the expression of a British conspiracy against traditional liberties, and in the French Revolution, where the "patriots" saw themselves beset by a conspiracy of aristocrats and nonjuring priests in collusion with Pitt and Cobourg.

As a practical matter, the Irish revolt posed once again the problem of raising and financing an army and, what is more, entrusting it to Charles. Would he use it only against the Irish who in fact claimed to support the king, or would he turn it first against Parliament? As hostility toward the king over this issue escalated to near panic, Pym's junto voted to present him with a Grand Remonstrance detailing, in hysterical tones, all the grievances of his reign back to the beginning. As a sign of the growing schism in Parliament this incendiary document passed by only eleven votes (159 against 148). This division moved Charles to counterattack, and in January he tried to impeach Pym, Hampden, and three other MPs. When Commons refused to order the arrest, Charles went personally with several hundred soldiers to the House to do it himself. But, as he discovered, "the birds had flown." They had taken refuge in London, where the whole Commons soon followed, where they formed a committee at the Guildhall under the protection of the London population. As a result, radical parliamentarians gained control of London's City Common Council, purging it of unreliable elements, as well as of its militia, the "trained bands." Thereafter, the capital was a bastion of the parliamentary cause, and its vast wealth, with appropriate interest of course, was available to finance its armies. (The English currency was basically stable from the time of Elizabeth to the devaluation of the 1930s, and there would be no crisis of inflation as in the French Revolution.)

After this defeat, which had unmistakably revealed his intentions not to accept the constitutional revolution of the previous spring, Charles left the capital for York. In answer, the victorious Commons sent him bills excluding bishops from the House of Lords, a clear violation of the ancient constitution, and giving command of the militia to Parliament (the militia ordinance), a clear usurpation of the central royal prerogative. Since Charles had taken the Great Seal with him, Parliament henceforth arrogated to itself the right to issue "ordinances" on its own, in other words to legislate, tax, and conduct all state business without the king. So the country settled into stalemate. In June Parliament presented to the king Nineteen Propositions codifying these changes, which Charles of course refused to accept. In July Parliament created a Committee of Public Safety to act as a provisional executive in the place of the king, and put the earl of Essex in charge of an army. The next month Charles raised the royal standard at Nottingham, and the conflict became military.

THE SECOND RADICALIZATION

War is always a radicalizing experience, civil war especially so. It militarizes politics and so makes all political and ideological differences sharper. Thus both the constitutional and religious issues dividing English society became progressively more acute as the war continued.

Since the king was firmly convinced of his divine right to rule, and to be obeyed, his tactic was to negotiate, and if necessary compromise, only to gain time for his opponents to divide, as they had already done once at the end of 1641. Hence his unavoidable and permanent duplicity, for until the end he was convinced that he would ultimately win. Parliament, for its part, had a much harder time devising a strategy. On the one hand, until very late its aim was not to defeat the king too thoroughly but to coerce him just enough to get him to agree with one or another version of their Nineteen Propositions. On the other hand, they were half aware that he might well not negotiate in good faith for a compromise because of the very nature of kingship.

There were three parties on the war issue: the peace-as-soon-as-possible party, the limited war party, the all-out victory party. Given the king's nature, time was on the side of the last group.

The country divided only slowly and reluctantly. There is no clear pattern to the division either socially or geographically. Roughly the south and east were parliamentarian and the north and west were royalist, a division that also corresponds approximately to the more developed as opposed to the more backward parts of the country. Even so, although London was solidly "roundhead," England's second city, Bristol, was "cavalier." And East Anglia, though largely rural, was heavily Puritan, in part because of proximity to and the influence of the Calvinist Netherlands. And representatives from all the social classes, from great peers to simple artisans, are found in both camps, although "the meaner sort" played a more vocal and visible role on the parliamentary side. In short, the real principle of division was ideological: political and religious.

Militarily, at the start the king's side had the advantage in part because he had more military professionals in his camp, such as Prince Rupert who had won his spurs in the Thirty Years' War. Parliament, after its early military failures, had to create a professional corps of its own. Its most effective fighting force of course was the militia of the Eastern Association, composed of artisans and peasants under Cromwell's command, the famous Ironsides. In 1644 these were amalgamated with other armies raised by Parliament to form the New Model Army. What was new about it was that the Self-Denying Ordinance removed all members of Parliament except Cromwell from military command, thereby turning the war over to more professional personnel. The new entity had some fifty thousand troops, under Sir Thomas Fairfax, with Cromwell in command of the cavalry.

Politically, parliament had the support of the Scots as formalized in a Committee of the Two Kingdoms. And since religion was always intertwined with politics, this alliance was accompanied by the creation of the Westminster Assembly, composed of Presbyterian Divines from the two countries. In 1643 this produced the Solemn League and Covenant between Parliament and the Scots, pledging to reform the religions of England, Scotland, and Ireland "according to the word of God and the examples of the best reformed churches." This meant making the British Isles uniformly Presbyterian and committing Parliament to the abolition of episcopacy but without opening the door to Independency, or the congregational organization of church government. Thus there would still be a single national church and a single orthodoxy. This of course was unacceptable to the growing number of Congregationalist Independents, particularly in the army, a position shared by Cromwell. In consequence, Presbyterianism was not introduced de facto throughout England, and religious pluralism in fact continued to spread.

Again, politically, Parliament had to become a real government. Taxation increased several times over what it had been under Charles. This was burdensome to the whole population, especially the lower classes, and the 1640s were overall a time of economic disruption and depression. After the abolition of episcopacy, church lands were confiscated and sold. Crown lands were also sold or auctioned off, as well as the estates of certain royalist peers.

By means of these expedients, by 1646 parliament, by its victory at Naseby on June 14, had won the war against Charles. His capital, Oxford, capitulated, and the king surrendered himself to the Scots. Parliament submitted to him a new set of proposals to end the crisis by accepting the Presbyterian Covenant and giving

Parliament control of the army for twenty years. Charles, seeing that a breach between parliamentary Presbyterians and army Independents was obviously in the making, refused Parliament's terms. So the Scots turned him over to Parliament in return for back pay of some £400,000, which the financial leaders of the City supplied to the Presbyterian Parliament.

THE THIRD RADICALIZATION

And indeed, the break between Parliament and army occurred the next year. After six years of turmoil, the country was yearning for stability, and very weary of heavy taxation for war. Parliament's plan for a settlement was to establish a uniform Presbyterian order in England and present this to Charles as a fait accompli which he would have to accept to regain his throne. Accordingly, the bishops' lands were confiscated and sold, while at the same time, in a move against the Independents, laymen were prohibited from preaching. Parliament then made the mistake of deciding to disband the army immediately except for units necessary to subdue Ireland. Money for the Irish campaign could only come from the City, and it was pressing Parliament to reduce expenses by disbandment. The veterans, however, refused to accept this program until they had received full arrears of pay. In March, therefore, the army took an oath not to disband until their arrears were paid and until freedom of conscience, a main tenet of Independency, had been secured. To defend these positions the rank and file began to organize what one can only call a soldiers' soviet. Each regiment elected two "agitators" (a word that at the time simply meant "agent" or deputy). Eventually, these agitators joined with junior officers to form a Council of the Army to keep the pressure on Parliament.

At the beginning of June, the army lost patience and in effect mutinied by swearing a "Solemn Engagement" not to disband until their grievances had been met. No doubt the most important of these grievances was money; but religion for many was also a real concern; and finally honor was at stake. As the army declared on June 14, "we were not a mere mercenary army hired to serve any arbitrary power of a state." At this point, Cromwell and his chief aide and son-in-law, Ireton, fearful that the Presbyterian majority in Parliament would strike a deal with the Scots and Charles against the army and Independency, left London to join the army encampment some twenty miles north of the City. These senior officers then had to join the insurgent Council of the Army both to champion its grievances and to keep the mutiny from going too far. In the midst of the confusion, a junior officer, Cornet Joyce, with five hundred men from the army seized Charles's person. The army then demanded the impeachment of eleven leading Parliamentary Presbyterians.

By July the situation had degenerated into the worst anarchy since the summer of 1640. Again there was a tax strike. Soldiers disbanded from earlier militias when the New Model was created in 1645 now swarmed London demanding *their* arrears. Together with the ever-turbulent London apprentices, these "reformadoes" invaded Parliament to demand that their grievances be redressed before those of the New Model. The speakers of both houses and about one hundred members fled to the army. On August 3 the army occupied London, restored the two speakers of Parliament, and ousted the eleven Presbyterian leaders. The semi-mutinous army was now in control of the situation. The army's terms were presented to Charles in August. Called the Heads (i.e., chapters) of the Proposals, these were more radical than any previous program for a settlement: they demanded the dissolution of the existing Parliament and the election of a new one on a reformed, broader franchise.

In the midst of the crisis, the army radicalized ideologically. Already strongly Independent in religion, they now became overtly democratic in politics. This occurred under the influence of John Lilburne and a group of radicals derisively called Levellers by their opponents, a group that had emerged in the summer from the Independent congregations of London under threat from the new Presbyterian ascendancy.[30] In October, in the parish church of Putney, where the army was now encamped, recently elected agitators, radical younger officers, and Leveller spokesmen debated the draft Leveller constitution called Agreement of the People. The program that it proposed was popular sovereignty and parliamentary supremacy, and its cornerstone was universal (manhood) suffrage.[31] They argued their case not on the basis of historical precedent, but of natural rights and natural reason. Cromwell and Ireton, in alarm, countered that only people with a "stake" in society, that is with property, should be allowed to vote for any new Parliament. Thus was defined the outer limits of even Independent radicalism. And from this time on, the army command took active steps to control, and eventually suppress, the Leveller movement.

At the same time, the army command entered into negotiations with the king. The result was the same frustrating inconclusiveness the Presbyterian parliamentarians had encountered earlier: Charles still expected his enemies to divide thereby convincing the nation that his rule was indispensable. And indeed, royalist sentiment was on the rise and hostility to both army and Parliament was increasing. And sure enough, the king's enemies did divide. Parliament and the Scots were apprehensive that the army would strike a deal with Charles at the expense of Presbyterianism. And the army was apprehensive that Parliament and the Scots would do the same at the expense of Independency. The upshot of this triangular game of reciprocal suspicion was that the Independents and the moderate Presbyterians in Parliament proposed a final compromise deal to Charles, "the four bills," putting Parliament in command of the army for twenty years and Parliament's tenure at its own pleasure. The king refused, because he had gotten a better bargain from the Scots, that is, his command of the militia in exchange for a uniform Presbyterianism in the two kingdoms. In answer, at the beginning of 1648, Parliament at last renounced its allegiance to the king.

This unleashed a second, shorter, and conclusive civil war. On one side, an invading Scottish Presbyterian army in conjunction with a number of regional royalist revolts in England sought to restore Charles. On the other side, the army, which had again seized his person, sought to repress the revolts and repulse the Scots, and in six summer weeks they succeeded decisively in both tasks. The losers were the English Presbyterians in the middle. For having wavered during the conflict they were purged from Parliament in December when Colonel Pride stopped about half the membership from entering the Commons, leaving only a "rump" of Independents.

Cromwell and the army had now lost all patience with Charles and so proceeded to bring him to trial for having "made war against his people." The Rump was therefore pressured to create a special High Court of Justice. After a summary trial, the king was condemned to death and beheaded on January 30, 1649. This was not an ideologically motivated act, or the intended prelude to a new order. It was a political expedient imposed by the harsh fact that there was no other way of dealing with an obdurate monarch. Thus, without any of the actors in the revolution intending it, England stumbled into a republic as the surviving fifty Independent members of the Long Parliament voted to abolish monarchy and the Lords and to proclaim England a Commonwealth.

Why did the great radicalization of 1647–1648, and the victory of Independency over Presbyterianism, occur? Because once parliamentary Presbyterianism had used coercion against the king and the existing constitution, they had shown the way to army Independency to do the same thing to them. As Gardiner put the matter long ago, "In 1647 as in 1642 force had been called forth to resist misgovernment, and the habit of using force would never cease till the sword had been broken in the hands of those who wielded it."[32] This proposition is indeed the fundamental law of all real revolutions, and the chief reason that a revolutionary process is so difficult to end.

RADICALIZATION AS CUL DE SAC

In a sense the Commonwealth is the radical culmination of the English Revolution: in form, at least, it marked the creation of a new world, a republic based on popular sovereignty, and a new man, the sainted warrior of the New Model

Army. And indeed, in many quarters the king's execution was viewed as the prelude to the last days and the Second Coming. Accordingly, the early 1650s became the high point of English sectarianism with a proliferation of new movements. The Levellers were now in decline, but in their wake in 1649 there appeared Gerard Winstanley's Diggers, who advocated the suppression of private property and common ownership of the land. Although Winstanley is an attractive figure, radical historians have made too much of this movement as a precursor of modern socialism; by comparison with the radical Taborites or Thomas Müntzer, it was a tame affair and had little impact at the time.[33]

Simultaneously, there was an outburst of millenarian thinking, and a proliferation of new sects. The most notable, and certainly the most durable, of these was George Fox's "inner light" Quakers. Theologically, they represent the ultimate in the deconstruction of traditional Christianity: there is no church, no clergy, and virtually no doctrine. Socially, at their radical beginning they had clear affinities with the activist Levellers, but once the revolution was over they retreated into their own separate "society of friends" committed to pacifism, self-discipline, money-making, and civic beneficence — much like the former Taborite Petr Chelčický and his Moravian Brethren. Almost as important at the time were the anarchist Fifth Monarchy Men who believed that once the Antichrist, Charles, had been destroyed, the Saints should immediately establish the Fifth, and final, Kingdom of the Just as prophesized in the book of Daniel.[34] Practically speaking, this meant insurrection against the existing, imperfect Commonwealth, and so the movement was duly put down by the army, only to make a last desperate attempt against Charles II immediately after the Restoration. In effect, this movement is the last, despairing gasp of the millenarian current that had run throughout the 1640s and that now ran amuck against the betrayal of the Saints in power. Here the appropriate analogy in the future is with Gracchus Babeuf's "Conspiracy of the Equals," the enraged sans-culotte reaction to the "betrayal" of the post-Thermidor Jacobins.[35]

At the same time, the Commonwealth produced, at last, a bit of republican theorizing. Providing for a successor to the Long Parliament, which had now been in power for so many years as to have lost most of its legitimacy, had been on the agenda since the Levellers' Agreement of the People of 1647. The most notable example of new reflection is James Harrington's *Commonwealth of Oceana*, published in 1656. His program was secular and, though not really democratic since it provided for a propertied suffrage, was in many respects forward-looking. Its principal novelty was to found the political right to participation in the republic on property rather than historical precedent or heredity. And, although the Saints then in power were completely uninterested in implementing it, it had considerable influence on later republican theorizing, above all in Britain's North American colonies.[36]

Just as important for the future of republican thought were the Saints' confused attempts to create a new political order. At first, the minority Rump continued to govern, trying in desultory fashion to provide for the election of a new Parliament (a matter on the agenda since the Levellers' Agreement of the People), as well as to reform a cumbrous and expensive legal system, where Law French was still used in the courts. In 1653 Cromwell lost patience with the Rump and on his own initiative simply disbanded this last remnant of the Long Parliament.[37] He then tried a nominated assembly of Saints, nicknamed Barebone's Parliament for one of its more "godly" members, Praise-God Barebone. When this failed, too, he had the body name him Protector of the Commonwealth under a written constitution (generally considered the first such document in history), the Instrument of Government. There was a new Parliament, this time elected, but it did not work either and was dissolved. Cromwell was offered and refused the crown; so he fell back on governing with a regime of major generals. Anglican clergy was forbidden to preach, and Catholic priests were expelled from the realm. Censorship was reestablished, and "puritanical" blue laws were imposed on the country. In short, the revolution's culminating moment, the Commonwealth, had ended in a cul-de-sac.

All that its various constitutional experiments represented was that the Saints had no feasible practical program. Indeed, their improvisations revealed that the only such program was a restoration of monarchy. This is all the more true in that the regime was now a detested minority while royalist sentiment had been growing ever since the execution of the king. At the same time that millenarian sects were multiplying in the 1650s, a collection of Charles' last sayings, illegally published as the *Eikon Basilike*, was becoming a bestseller. And this situation is quite unlike the French Revolution after Thermidor, when the work of the revolution's most radical phase was indeed capable of preservation and institutionalization.

How to explain this anticlimactic ending of an upheaval that had gone the limit of what it was possible to do in overturning a society of the two swords and the three orders? The explanation cannot be found in class structures, economic conditions, or demographic pressures. The most convincing explanation lies in the mentality of all the major actors in the drama. The king, the Parliamentarians, whether Presbyterian or Independent, and Cromwell and the officers of the New Model Army all thought in terms of restoring the proper balance of the national constitution, with its king, Lords, and Commons, and a comprehensive national church. Only the marginal groupings of Levellers, Diggers, and the millenarian sectaries thought of going beyond those traditional coordinates, and they were not strong enough to tip the balance toward a radical new departure. It is thus "consciousness" that determined "being" in bringing the English Revolution into the blind alley of the Commonwealth and the Protectorate.

And what of the inevitable comparison with the gold standard of modern revolution, 1789–1799? In a sense, the Commonwealth is the English Revolution's Thermidor and the Protectorate is the revolution's Empire: the conquest of Ireland and Scotland, the British Isles for the first time ruled from London as a single unitary state, the Navigation Acts, the Dutch War, and Jamaica. In fact, these analogies do not go very far, because the overriding reality was institutional impasse.

But, given the strength and maturity of English civil society, matters could not end in so minoritarian, sectarian, and coercive a solution. After Cromwell's death, therefore, the moderates, among both the victors and the vanquished, patched up the more viable national consensus of the Restoration of 1660. Ecclesiastically (and, by implication, also socially) all elective, Presbyterian or Congregationalist, arrangements were abolished, and the divine authority of the Anglican bishops was fully restored; at the same time, all "nonconformists" were put "five miles" out to pasture and deprived of full civil rights. Politically, the solution was more moderate: all legislation voted by Parliament and signed by Charles I was automatically valid, which in theory legitimized the constitutional revolution of 1640–41.

TO THE AFTERSHOCK OF 1688

But the revolutionary process begun in 1640 did not end with the Restoration of 1660, because the new king, Charles II, still would not accept the monarchy's reduced role. Hence, the new crisis of the 1680s culminated in the secondary shock of 1688–1689.

On the surface, at least, the Restoration settlement was a thoroughly reasonable compromise, except for one thing: by the very fact that it was a compromise, it begged the question of who ultimately was sovereign—the "sacred" king or the "natural" nation. The basic constitutional conflict thus could not fail to break out anew; for neither Charles II, in his last years, nor James II, at any time, ever acted as though they viewed royal authority differently from their father, or from their first cousin, Louis XIV (the propensity to "forget nothing, and to learn nothing" is no monopoly of the Bourbons; it is the common characteristic of all true Old Regime sovereigns, from the Stuarts right down to Wilhelm II and Nicholas II).

Thus, by 1688, civil society-in-Parliament was confronted with the same dilemma as in 1640: how to handle a king who would be absolute. But Parlia-

ment *had* remembered and *had* learned; and the burden of its lesson was that
alliance with the urban crowd in overt revolution against the king was as dangerous to civil liberty as was royal absolutism itself (this, in brief, is the message
of Locke's *Two Treatises*).[38] The answer, tactically, then was to circumvent the
"rascal multitude" of the capital, with its wild "Irish nights" of rioting against
the royal troops, by calling in a plausibly legitimate prince with a foreign army
of Dutch and French Huguenot regulars to drive out James — hardly a dignified
solution in national terms, but socially a very safe one. And constitutionally the
answer was to pretend that James' flight amounted to "abdication," and hence
that no "overturn" had occurred at all. Hence the momentous epithet of "Glorious Revolution," which would translate into modern English approximately as
nonpopular and ostensibly legitimate restoration of ancient liberties.

But even with this stunning feat of unavowed revolutionary statesmanship England was not yet home safe to a modern constitutional order. William III had
first to win the unpopular War of the League of Augsburg to make this precarious settlement work. For the new arrangement stuck mightily in the throats of
innumerable Tories, Jacobites, and Scots; and any foreign disaster to so dubious
a king could easily have reopened the whole constitutional crisis anew. Thus it
was not until after victory had been achieved in 1697 that it was possible for the
new order to be regularized through the Act of Settlement of 1701. For by this
instrument Parliament, in effect, elected the dynasty and defined the conditions
of its tenure. It thereby asserted in definitive yet noncoercive fashion the sovereignty of civil society over its chief executive officer, the king, and through him
over the nation he now merely administered but no longer commanded. And
it might even be argued that the constitutional crisis was not terminated until
1714, when the new, elected dynasty actually "assumed office," without turmoil
or any effective opposition.

The moral of this narrative is the following: even under the most favorable
of circumstances — in secure, insular, and imperfectly absolutist England — the
revolutionary transition from the Old Regime to the new required decades to
achieve stabilization and viable "modern" equilibrium — from the initial shock of
1640, to the abortive restoration of 1660, to the lucky coup of 1688, and in fact to
1701, if not to 1714. And if matters were this rough in *felix Anglia*, what would they
be across the Channel, over the Rhine, or beyond the Nieman? And what would
they be like in an age and a culture when men understood "revolution" not in the
sense of "restoration," but of a deliberate, conscious, and positive "overturning"?
But these considerations bring us to the crucial particularity of the English Revolution: its ideological envelope, and the latter's moderating political impact.

The political dynamic of the English Revolution is that of all European great revolutions—a radicalizing movement from euphoric national unity, to acid ideological polarization, to armed minority dictatorship. The political content of the English upheaval is also a constant in Old Regime Europe: a contest for national sovereignty between a centralizing royal state and the various estates of the old order now turning into a self-conscious civil society. What is peculiar to the English case is that it was a modern revolution made in what was still essentially a pre-modern cultural-ideological context—that is, religious and firmly traditionalistic.

The fact that the Parliamentary-Puritan revolution was cast in terms of a conservative, restorationist ideology singularly blunted awareness of the momentous changes that were in fact occurring. Hence no cult of revolutionary change per se could emerge from what all parties concerned were agreed in assessing as an aberrant and unwanted "civil war." This circumstance, in conjunction with the remarkably smooth coup of 1688, made it possible for Edmund Burke and others ultimately to assimilate the heritage of the English seventeenth century into an eminently conservative canon—with the result that to this day the English do not think and act as though they had ever made a wild, messy revolution, as had the lesser breeds across the Channel.

The ideological particularities of the English seventeenth century had still another moderating consequence. The constitutional issue of sovereignty was expressed directly in political and revolutionary terms through the struggle of king and Parliament. But the social question—the reordering and democratization of civil society—was expressed only indirectly, in religious terms and thus in less overtly revolutionary form. Because of this ideological particularity, furthermore, the two issues were disjoined, thereby making it possible to complete the political revolution without also making a social revolution. In fact, in the seventeenth century only the constitutional issue was resolved, leading to the liberalization of English society but not to its democratization; and after 1688 the country socially was as thoroughly oligarchic as it had been in 1640. For the reestablishment of Anglicanism in 1660, which was left untouched in 1688, meant also putting off the social question *sine die*. At the same time, the practical policy of toleration, first adopted in the wake of 1688, permitted the old dissenting sects to survive and new ones, notably Methodism, to arise, thereby giving to the excluded elements of English society a means of expression, a possibility of hope, and ultimately the ability to exert pressure for social change. Thus religion continued to give a distinctive, moderate cast to the social question in England right down to the formation of the Labor Party in 1905—as Elie Halévy pointed out in order to explain the contrast with the far more radical social politics of France.[39]

One final moderate aspect of the English Revolution must be noted. Given the fact that it was not consciously experienced as a revolution, that it was not deliberately directed toward the creation of a new type of society but toward the restoration of an "ancient" order, and finally that it was made in terms of specifically English legal norms and English ecclesiastical issues, it could not serve as a revolutionary model for the rest of Europe. Unlike the French and Russian Revolutions later, it was not exportable. To be sure, all of Europe was appropriately horrified that an anointed king had been executed by his rebellious subjects, and most foreign governments broke off diplomatic relations with England. Still, no other monarchy seriously feared that the contagion would spread, or that the English example could be imitated elsewhere. To be sure also, after 1688, continental dissidents, notably Voltaire and Montesquieu, were well aware of the liberal character of English constitutional arrangements and proposed them as something of a model for France. But they did this in a spirit of limited reformism, not out any desire to imitate the English revolutionary experience.

7

AMERICA, 1776–1787

Revolution as Great Good Fortune

I always consider the settlement of America with reverence and wonder, as the
opening of a grand scene and design of Providence for the illumination of the
ignorant, and the emancipation of the slavish part of mankind all over the earth.
—JOHN ADAMS, 1765

The cause of America is in a great measure the cause of all mankind.
—THOMAS PAINE, 1776

The great advantage of the Americans is that they have arrived at a state of
democracy without having to endure a democratic revolution and that they are born
equal instead of becoming so.
—ALEXIS DE TOCQUEVILLE, 1835

Can a people "born equal" ever understand people elsewhere that have to become
so? Can it ever understand itself?
—LOUIS HARTZ, 1955

The Americans [as of 1774] were in fact on the verge of a discovery that would
turn the course of history in a new direction, a discovery that is still reverberating
among us and liberating us from our past as it was soon to liberate them, in spite of
themselves, from theirs. This discovery was nothing more or less than the principle
of human equality.
—EDMUND S. MORGAN, 1956

The transition from the English to the American Revolution presents a strange
paradox: whereas the English after 1640 clearly lived through a major institutional upheaval yet have hesitated to this day to call it a revolution, the Americans, who following 1765 experienced only a modest structural overturn, im-

mediately considered it a maximally radical event and have ever since gloried in its results. And so, together with France, British North America godfathered the concept of revolution as the modern world knows it. But in what sense was this colonial rebellion a revolution?

The structure of the action leading to and following from 1776 in no way resembles the scenario played out in England a century earlier and in France a decade later. No Bastilles were stormed and no royal heads rolled. Rather, the main emblematic events were a Tea Party in Boston Harbor and a few musket shots on Lexington Green. And the overturn ended not with a man on horseback riding onto center stage, but with a closed Convention of establishment gentlemen drafting a constitution for a political order that is still in place. These Founders, moreover, were by and large the same leaders who had started the revolt twelve years earlier. This was a revolution, clearly, that did not devour its children. It is such lack of high drama that makes the American Revolution the odd-man-out in the canon of "staseology."

The American Revolution was anomalous in still other respects. To begin with, the sovereign against whom the colonies were rebelling was not present on the scene but three thousand miles over the waters, thus making the revolution in large measure a territorial War of Independence. Second, within the colonies themselves there were few entrenched hierarchical institutions to overthrow, thus obviating those serial upheavals within the rebellion that in England had radically transferred power from king to Parliament to army. Rather, in America events escalated through a series of tax protests, and over not very high taxes at that (the tax burden in America was only a quarter of that in Britain). Finally, the American rebellion occurred in provinces with a level of per capita income higher than that of any old world country, thus drastically reducing pressure for social change.

A number of contemporaries, moreover, especially adversaries of the rebellion, were well aware of the disproportion between the modest grievances and the explosive reaction of the colonists. "Never in history," said one American Tory, had there been so much rebellion with so "little cause." It was, wrote another, "the most wanton and unnatural rebellion that ever existed. . . . The annals of no country can produce an Instance of so virulent a Rebellion, or such implacable madness and Fury, originating from such trivial causes, as those alleged by these unhappy People."[1] What, then, was "revolutionary" about 1776?

Chiefly, it was the creation of a democratic republic on an unprecedented continental scale, a feat moreover presented as the beginning of a New World and a New Man, and a beacon for the rest of humanity. Second, this republic had been born amidst an escalating millenarian "fever" quite comparable to that driving earlier revolutionary episodes in Europe. This ideological surge mounted rapidly between its emergence in the Stamp Act crisis of 1765 and the outbreak of armed conflict and the Declaration of Independence, in 1774–1776; it continued steadily on the "patriot" side during eight years of war; and it returned, in more sober form, to inspire the establishment of a new constitution in 1787–1788. It is this eschatological republicanism that the Founders had in mind when they put the words *novus ordo seclorum* on the national seal and changed the conservative, 1688 meaning of "revolution" to the modern one of epochal overturn.

On a more concrete level, however, there *is* a pattern of action in Old Regime Europe to which the American events roughly correspond, and that is the sixteenth-century Netherlands revolt. Recall that then, too, the royal sovereign's base was in another country. Since in the Netherlands itself he was merely "duke" or "count" of separate provinces held together only by the weak and ineffective States General, the sovereign undertook to make his heritage into something like a genuine monarchy able to tax and police the population, as well as to enforce religious uniformity. This provoked resistance from his nobles and commons, and eventually popular revolt. In answer the king resorted to armed repression, which only radicalized the situation; he then tried concessions and these, too, failed. He therefore resumed repression, while the rebellious provinces sought aid from France and England. The issue was only settled by a long war leading to the formation of a federal republic in the seven northern provinces (offset by the success of repression in the south). Give or take a number of not insignificant details, and with due allowance for the ideological changes created by the lapse of almost two centuries, this is roughly the structure of action in British North America in the twenty-four years following 1765. In other words, like all European revolutions the American rebellion started as a reaction against royal state-building and ended with a form of representative constitutional government.

The connection with Old Europe, however, runs much deeper than this mechanism of contention. Ideologically, the Americans began their struggle in the long afterglow of 1688—that is, as an attempt to defend their historic rights as Englishmen. But they ended it, both literally and figuratively, on the eve of 1789—that is, with a citizens' republic that the French were then readying to radicalize and universalize further still.[2] Thus, the American Revolution, though anomalous in political form, in moral content was quite in the mainstream of the overall European revolutionary process.

Still, in the New World this process was significantly modified, and the success of the bold Republican "experiment" was made possible, by what was unique to the American situation. First of all, America lacked what had hitherto defined European civilization: an Old Regime. Not only was there no resident king; more important still, there was no estates system or other forms of hereditary privilege. Nor was there was a single ecclesiastical establishment, or any tradition of the sacrality of power.[3] There were only vestigial remnants of an aristocratic order, such as quitrent, primogeniture, and entail in some colonies; and there were only weakly established local churches in nine of them. Each colony had a well-developed representative assembly, in which the lower house was paramount, and which in many cases antedated the installation of a royal governor; and the suffrage, though based on property, in most places was broad enough to include a majority of the adult male population. The colonies were 80 percent peopled by Congregationalist and Presbyterian Calvinists—the descendants of the defeated left wing of the English Revolution. Even the Anglicans were "low," and without a resident bishop. Given these circumstances the seeds of 1688 fell on exceptionally favorable ground. In fact, as we shall see, 1688 was largely out of date before the first shot was fired on Lexington Green.

The second great factor of American exceptionalism was geography. Not only were the thirteen colonies separated from the seat of British power by three thousand miles of ocean, they were on the edge of a thinly populated continent providing almost endless space for social mobility and sources of new wealth. To be sure, the continent was not "empty," as has often been assumed. As of 1770, some 150,000 Indians lived east of the Mississippi. But they were still hunter-gatherers only minimally engaged in agriculture; and such radical underpopulation and underdevelopment for an area so vast foreordained their defeat at the hands of advancing American agriculturalists.

Given these two great anomalies, to create a new people it was necessary chiefly to fight a national-territorial war of liberation. This entailed, it is true, considerable violence, a number of social excesses, and a surge of millenarian afflatus. But it yielded nothing so shattering as an Old World revolution, and it lacked the structure of progressive and increasingly minoritarian radicalization of a European drama. A final, and unique, feature was that national constitutional government was successfully established on the first try. Thus between 1776 and 1788 the Commonwealth first dreamt by the "saints," and which had aborted in England, was at last established in the New World, but in a more moderate, secular, and especially more stable form. Altogether it was the English Revolution's most successful, if vicarious, creation, more remarkable perhaps, and certainly more modern, than the liberal yet narrowly oligarchic order that by 1688 had resulted in the mother country.

NATIONAL SATISFACTION AND ITS CRITICS

This difference is reflected in the historiography of the two revolutions. In both countries the basic consensus of satisfaction with their respective foundational events has always been countered by a current of radical criticism directed at the establishments that those events ultimately produced. These countercurrents, however, are quite different. In aristocratic England, they stemmed from dissenter radicalism and culminated in imported Marxism. In democratic America, they derived from muckraking populism and could never really adapt to Marxist grand theory.[4] After all, the only possible American analogue of Marx's "feudalism" was the antebellum South; and although this lead has been tried by an occasional historian and such sociologists as Barrington Moore, it was patently too artificial to get very far.[5] In consequence, no one has ever attempted to shoehorn 1776 into the mold of a "bourgeois revolution"—another example of American exceptionalism.

The story of 1776 begins in the mid-nineteenth century on a familiar Whiggish note with George Bancroft's *History of the United States*.[6] To this contemporary of Macaulay and Michelet, the American Revolution appeared essentially as it had to the people who made it: it was an eminently justified and heroic refusal of foreign, monarchical tyranny; and the republic that resulted was indeed a beacon to mankind. By the century's end, however, academic scholarship in the new German manner modified this narrowly national perspective by introducing the colonies' British imperial context, an approach that involved taking account of contemporary British politics.[7] From the work of this "imperial school" it became apparent that George III was no tyrant determined to undo 1688 in both Britain and America; that the errors of his policy were the product more of bungling than of malice; and that the British, after the victory of 1763, indeed had a legitimate case in attempting to give their now sprawling empire some central organization, and hence to make the colonists pay their share for defense. At the same time, in Britain itself emerging rivalry with the Kaiser's Germany was producing a sense of "English-speaking" solidarity with liberty-loving America, a change of mood reflected in George Otto Trevelyan's *The American Revolution* published beginning in 1899.[8] Some writing of the imperial school, however, went too far in suggesting that the revolution might have been unnecessary, even an avoidable mistake. A corrective reaction to such unpatriotic excesses quickly ensued, though the imperial context remained a permanent part of the picture.

The real challenge to national orthodoxy came from the debunking historiography of the turn of the century. In contemporary Europe this challenge had been mounted by socialism, usually Marxist; in America it came from the Progressive movement, and was expressed in more homespun, nontheoretical terms. In Europe the enemy of this social radicalism was called "capitalism" and the victim/challenger was the "proletariat"; in America the enemy was prosaically "big business" and the victim/challenger was simply the "little man." The difference was more than rhetorical; it was also a measure of the magnitude of social change the radicals envisioned.

The new school was launched by two works, the one in 1901 by Charles H. Lincoln on Pennsylvania and the other in 1909 by Carl L. Becker on New York, unearthing lower-class rebelliousness in both cases. The revolution they now portrayed was a struggle of Western frontiersmen, often Scots-Irish Presbyterians, in league with urban artisans and "mechanics" against the seaboard oligarchies of Philadelphia and New York City; and the lower classes' aim was to break into power by acquiring the franchise.[9] As Becker famously put the matter, the American Revolution was not only about "home rule"; it was just as much about "who should rule at home." Behind all the patriotic rhetoric, therefore, these revisionists saw a class struggle "just like in 1789" or any other European upheaval. Moreover—as Arthur Schlesinger, Sr., authoritatively explained in 1918 —the American Revolution was not a struggle over constitutional principles, as national orthodoxy had it, but over economic interests in which big seaboard merchants were pitted against the colonialist mercantile system of Britain.[10]

The most sensational statement of this new orthodoxy had come a bit earlier, however, in 1913, with Charles A. Beard's *An Economic Interpretation of the Constitution of the United States.*[11] In this immensely influential work he in effect unmasked the Constitutional Convention as a conservative business conspiracy to emasculate the legacy of 1776—a kind of cynical Thermidor rather than the culmination of revolutionary principles that the orthodox imagined. Specifically, Beard sought to show that the framers were not so much landed property holders as investors in manufactures and trade, and especially in public securities, who would benefit handsomely from the establishment of a strong federal authority. The book engendered endless controversy and detailed checking of the author's evidence. The result was to discredit his thesis about public securities, while at the same time confirming that economic interests were very much part of the revolutionary struggle. Accordingly, through the economic boom of the 1920s and the Great Depression of the 1930s social historians pursued research emphasizing the popular radicalism driving the Committees of Correspondence as well as the democratic intellectual life that the age fostered.[12] And as Progressivism gave way to the New Deal the decentralized Articles of Confederation, hitherto condemned by orthodox reverence for the Constitution, were rehabilitated by Merrill Jensen between 1940 and 1950.[13]

As the postwar era advanced, however, the pendulum inevitably swung back to politics and constitution-making, and thus also to ideas and ideologies.[14] The path-breaking work, published in 1953, was *The Stamp Act Crisis: Prologue to Revolution* by Edmund S. and Helen M. Morgan, a magisterial demonstration that the colonists from the beginning rejected Parliament's authority to impose not just internal taxes but any kind of levy for purposes of raising revenue. The constitutional principle of "no taxation without representation" was thus rehabilitated as the revolution's real motivation, unwaveringly adhered to moreover from 1765 onward.

This perspective was developed and deepened in 1967 in Bernard Bailyn's *The Ideological Origins of the American Revolution.* Drawing on recent work showing that the heritage of the seventeenth-century Puritan republic had continued into the eighteenth century as a radical critique of the "corrupt" governing Whigs,[15] Bailyn demonstrated that this "Commonwealthman" ideology, even more than the Enlightenment, furnished the staple of protest literature in America from 1765 onward. It was this ideology that lay behind the manifest events at the time, the well-known succession of crises from the Stamp Act to the Boston Tea Party. Specifically, the British government's restrictive measures of those years appeared to the colonists as clear "evidence of nothing less than the deliberate conspiracy launched surreptitiously by plotters both in England and in America."[16] And so the search for the role of ideas in the revolution was on. Perry Miller had already explored the Puritan mentality in his books on *The New England Mind* of 1939 and 1953,[17] and expanded on this in an important article, "From the Covenant to the Revival."[18] Alan Heimert now emphasized the religious origins of the revolution.[19]

The upshot of this accumulated concentration on ideas as the revolution's driving force was to downplay the role of radical socioeconomic forces showcased by the Progressive school and to give us instead a conservative revolution. As Bailyn summarized the new perspective: what "endowed the Revolution with its peculiar force and made of it a transforming event" was not the "overthrow of the existing order" but the "radical idealization and rationalization of the previous century and a half of American experience."[20]

Matters, of course, could not rest with this uninspiring, conservative assessment of the Revolution's meaning. And indeed, the Wisconsin school of Merrill Jensen and his followers continue to develop the tradition of social radicalism. Moreover, as the bicentennial approached, still younger historians took to criticizing the Revolution's compromise with slavery, its failure to give women the vote, and its genocidal treatment of native Americans. But this, too, produced a reaction as Gordon Wood came forward with *The Radicalism of the American Revolution,* meaning by that the essentially egalitarian institutional heritage of colonial America as this had been amplified through popular action in the course of the Revolutionary struggle.[21] Yet whatever the dosage of conservatism and radicalism we find in 1776–1786, we must still conclude with Tocqueville that this least revolutionary of modern upheavals in form, in democratic content was fully up to the most advanced eighteenth-century standards.

THE FRAMEWORK

The stage on which this new upheaval played out was quite unlike that of any previous revolution in the European cultural orbit: British North America was, in every sense of the word, a New World. Geographically, it was continental even though only a fringe of the actual continent had as yet been settled by colonists. As of 1776 they numbered two and a half million, or about one quarter the population of Great Britain itself. Five hundred thousand of the American population were black slaves. The largest city in the colonies, Philadelphia, had forty thousand inhabitants (New York had only twenty-five thousand), whereas London had already reached the million mark. And of course there was no national capital, because there was as yet no national state, or even an American nation.

The colonies thus were overwhelmingly rural and agricultural, though this of course does not mean that they were in any sense pre-modern. The colonies were very much a part of what Adam Smith in 1776 baptized "commercial society"; the inhabitants were highly literate, as one might expect where religion was predominantly evangelical. To be sure, a part of the population had arrived as indentured servants, but that was only a temporary status on the way to economic independence, often on the fast-moving western frontier. The most original factor in the American situation, however, was that its relatively meager population was increasing exponentially.[22] From one million in 1750, it had grown to more than two million by 1770. By the end of the Seven Years' War in 1763 the seaboard had been almost completely settled and frontiersmen were already advancing over the Appalachians. By Independence in 1783 the population had exceeded three million, despite the ravages of war and Tory emigration, and in 1800 it was five million, three hundred thousand. At this rate of growth there would be a new "East" and a new "West" every generation until the Pacific was reached in 1848. Such demographic fluidity and social mobility were unique in the European experience, and the contemporary inhabitants of the colonies were quite aware of this fact.

Moreover, as previously noted, the two million settlers were already the most prosperous per capita as well as the freest of any population in the European orbit. This was in large part due to the manner in which the colonies had been created. New Spain and New France had ultimately been organized by state initiative and the result was a transplanted Old Regime with a manorial system, an aristocracy, an established church, and a vice-regal governor; heretics, moreover, were not allowed to settle there (Louis XIV's Huguenots therefore went to Holland, England, Prussia, and the Carolinas). New England had been founded by a royally chartered commercial company, the Massachusetts Bay Company, which then turned its governing board of stockholders into a provincial assembly that elected its own executive. Virginia, likewise, though more aristocratic and Anglican than was congregationalist New England, had been founded by a private company, and had created its House of Burgesses in a similar manner. Other colonies, notably Maryland and Pennsylvania, had been founded by royally licensed proprietors who nonetheless endowed them with representative assemblies. Even when colonies such as New York had royal charters and royally appointed governors, they, too, received assemblies. And although the governor's appointed executive council almost everywhere served as the upper house, thus embodying the aristocratic principle of British government, the popularly elected lower houses quickly became predominant in the system. In short, everywhere the executive, whatever its origin, had to govern with the consent of the "Commons." The suffrage was of course based on property, but everywhere, even in such "aristocratic" colonies as Virginia and New York, it was relatively low, quite inferior to that prevailing in Britain; and a majority of the adult male population almost everywhere were property holders.

Until quite late, moreover, the colonies were neglected, and hence little interfered with, by the mother country. The first two Stuarts, despite Puritan cries of "despotism," were too weak to have a strong colonial policy, or even to prevent their heretics from settling in their overseas claims. Cromwell's Commonwealth was more interventionist, both in acquiring West Indian "sugar islands" and in imposing on the entire British system Navigation Acts that required the North American colonies to trade only within that system. From the British point of view, the original purpose of the colonies was to serve as sources of raw materials such as tobacco, indigo, and rice or such crudely processed items as salted cod. The colonies were to be a closed market for British manufactured goods; and they were not encouraged to engage in manufacture themselves. The later Stuarts took a more active interest in North America, Charles II chartering two more aristocratic and Anglican colonies south of Virginia. James II, who under his brother had conquered New York from the Dutch, for the first time tried to give dissenter New England greater coherence as a royal province. Sixteen eighty-eight undid this project and the colonies again enjoyed benign neglect, a policy that continued under the first two Hanoverians.

In the eighteenth century there were two primary links between the colonies and the mother country. The first was commerce: by 1763, for example, almost half of British shipping was occupied in trade with the colonies, and a good part of it had actually been built there. The second link was military. Since North America was a principal theater of Britain's worldwide eighteenth-century rivalry with France, the colonies needed British protection against French and Indian pressure from Canada and in the Ohio Valley. George Washington cut his military teeth in an unsuccessful effort to take what is now Pittsburgh from the French in the Seven Years' War of 1756–1763.[23] (In fact, though, with only sixty thousand French in Canada and a few thousand more in Louisiana, demography had already sealed the fate of North America.) The real significance for the future of Britain's sweeping victory of 1763 was that the colonies no longer needed this protection. Overnight, the mother country had become potentially dispensable.

A DECADE OF REVOLUTION

It has already been noted that one of the most striking facts about the beginnings of the American Revolution is how little it took to get things started. Throughout the century, the colonies had lived comfortably within the closed mercantile system established by the British Navigation Acts, yet hardly had peace been signed in 1763 when they became restless. The trigger of their discontent was, as in the Netherlands revolt, an initiative at the center of the imperial system.

For the England against which the colonists revolted was no longer the "tight little island" of 1688; it was now the imperial seat of what has appropriately been called a "fiscal-military state," perhaps the most thoroughly consolidated national unit in Europe.[24] Moreover, the Whigs who had governed it without interruption since 1715, though allegedly the more liberal of the two British parties, had by 1760 become a closed, conservative oligarchy committed to the principle that 1688 had settled Britain's affairs to perfection and for all time.

It was at this juncture that George III, the first really English Hanoverian, came to the throne at age twenty-one. Unlike his predecessors he was determined to rule himself, though not, as was once believed, as a despot. He was quite committed to the legacy of 1688, as it had been adapted since 1717 by the emergence of the office of prime minister — that is, he would govern through Parliament by means of a King's Party of "placemen" (royal officials who also held seats in Parliament) and other forms of clientage, a decision that meant replacing his Whig ministers with new men. His colonial policy was to create a more central administrative structure for an empire now extending from North America to India. To this end, in 1763 his ministry traced a Proclamation Line along the Appalachians to set off the newly acquired interior lands from the seaboard colonies, even though many of the colonies had long-standing claims to those very territories.

A more serious problem was London's decision, for the first time since the colonies' founding, to tax them directly: until then all taxes had been voted by their own representative assemblies. The reason for this was that, though the victory of 1763 had been glorious, it left behind a staggering debt of more than £122 million, the service of which required more than £4 million annually. The tax burden that this debt necessitated, many times higher than anywhere in the colonies, generated discontent throughout the home islands. In consequence, London not unreasonably decided that the colonies should pay a fairer share of taxes for the benefits they received from the British imperial system. And it should be noted that the taxes imposed on the colonies went only for maintaining some ten thousand British troops in North America, not for retiring the national debt at home. For it so happened that the war had left behind, for the first time, a British military force in the colonies—just as Charles V's last war had for the first time left behind a permanent Spanish army in the Netherlands. It is the implementation of British taxation policies, in conjunction with this armed British presence that, between the Stamp Act of 1765 and the outbreak of open conflict in 1775, produced the American Revolution. And it is those same years that were the most revolutionary part of the Revolution era overall.

The properly revolutionary part, or the mounting ideological fever, began with the Stamp Act of 1765. Already the previous year, resentment had been aroused by a Sugar Act designed to raise revenue from the importation of molasses from the West Indies for making rum in New England, a commodity in turn used to fuel the slave trade. The Stamp Act raised a veritable storm of protest that quickly assumed crisis proportions. The stamp tax, a practice long-established in England, required purchase of an official paper for all sorts of legal and commercial transactions; and various prominent colonials were chosen by London to sell the required stamped paper. When the news of these regulations reached North America, the result was an immediate and massive protest in the name of "no taxation without representation." This would henceforth be the leitmotif of the entire revolution.

For what was involved was not so much the sums, which were modest, but the constitutional principle of popular consent to taxation, which is after all a levy on individual property; and property, as every free-born Englishman knew, is the sole sure guarantee of liberty. The protest was thus framed in thoroughly loyalist terms. In the colonists' view, they were demanding no more than their historic rights as Englishmen, as these had emerged triumphant in the revolution of 1688–1689. All their arguments were taken from the British Whig tradition, holding that the British constitution, mixing as it did the monarchical, aristocratic, and democratic principles in a marvelous balance, was the most perfect in the world.

In pleading these rights, however, the colonists immediately resorted to measures that violated the "King's peace" and indeed bordered on the seditious. Responsible local authorities organized artisans, "mechanics," and other muscular individuals into "patriot" vigilante groups called the Sons of Liberty and encouraged them to run out of town the new Stamp Act agents, and to destroy their odious papers, and sometimes their property. Often these actions degenerated into mob violence, as in the case of the demolition of the house of Massachusetts Lieutenant Governor Thomas Hutchinson. At the end of the year, these spontaneous local protests were capped by the Stamp Act Congress at New York representing nine colonies, a body for which no legal warrant existed. The enthusiasm attending this gathering is in marked contrast to the abject failure of the British-sponsored Albany Congress of 1754 to coordinate defense during the war with the French.

At first London assumed that the colonies were objecting only to "internal" taxation for revenue, a function they claimed for their own representative assemblies, but that they were not hostile to "external" taxation for the regulation of commerce. To this misinformed and not very meaningful distinction Parliament answered that, though the colonies were not directly represented in Parliament — just like such cities as Manchester or Birmingham at home — they were "virtually" represented there, since Parliament by immemorial historic right spoke for all British dominions. The colonists of course rejected this argument on the grounds that although virtual representation might be meaningful within Great Britain, the English constitution when applied to North America meant taxation only by locally chosen representatives. The issue then became a distinction between taxation, as a colonial prerogative, and legislation, as a parliamentary one. Throughout the argument, however, the colonists insisted on their loyalty to the king as sovereign — a misperception on their side because, in the British constitution which they claimed as the basis of their protest, the sovereign was the joint entity king-in-Parliament.

In any event, the matter was resolved not by argument but by direct action on the part of the colonists. Persons foolish enough to accept appointment as Stamp Act agents were threatened by mob violence from plebeian Sons of Liberty, organized by such figures as Samuel Adams. This pressure, together with a campaign of boycott of British trade through nonconsumption and nonimportation led by patrician merchants, astounded the British government. Thus, by the end of the year Stamp Act had in effect been nullified. The next year the British government, realizing it had made a mistake, repealed the offending act. To save face, however, Parliament voted a Declaratory Act affirming that it still retained the (abstract) right to "legislate" for the colonies "in all cases whatsoever," that is, presumably to tax them as well. It was of course the worst possible solution to affirm a principle while not daring to enforce it.

A second surge of protest began with the Townshend Duties of 1767 on glass, lead, painters' colors, and tea. This time the crisis built up more slowly, by stages over several years. But it culminated most drastically in armed conflict in 1775 and separation from Britain in 1776.

With the Townshend duties the British were determined to prevent the sedition of 1765; customs commissioners were therefore dispatched to enforce the new duties, and their salaries were to be paid from the customs intake. In 1768 a ship named *Liberty* was seized in Boston Harbor for alleged nonpayment of duties and a riot ensued. The commissioners requested the protection of troops from Britain. At the same time the Massachusetts Assembly refused to rescind a "circular letter" protesting the duties that had been sent to and approved by the other colonial assemblies. The city's merchants adopted a nonimportation boycott of British goods. Thereupon the royal governor dissolved the assembly, which nonetheless continued its defiance by reconvening as an extralegal "convention." British troops then arrived in Boston but the town refused to provide quarters as they were obliged to do by the Quartering Act of 1765. Inevitably, friction between troops and townsmen produced a clash, the so-called Boston Massacre of March 1770.

Then came another retreat that same year with the repeal of all the Townshend duties except that on tea. This caused the nonimportation policy to collapse, and things again quieted down. In 1772, however, the burning of a customs' coastal vessel provoked the formation of a royal commission of inquest and the rumor spread that the presumed guilty parties would be transported to England for trial, that is, not by a jury of their peers as the common law required. The vice-admiralty courts attached to customs also operated without juries. Simultaneously, Governor Hutchinson of Massachusetts announced that henceforth his salary and those of the superior court would be paid by the crown, thus making them independent of the local assembly and direct agents of the king. At the end of the year this accumulation of incidents and grievances led to the formation of a Boston Committee of Correspondence, sponsored by the town meeting and under the leadership of John Adams, an example soon followed in the other colonies. This intercolonial network introduced in effect a kind of dual power alongside the regular royal administration.

Then London blundered again. In order to help the East India Company out of financial difficulty, in 1773 Parliament authorized it to appoint its own agents in America to sell tea directly to retailers, thus eliminating American wholesale merchants. Even though this meant cheaper tea, the Committees of Correspondence mobilized citizens to turn back ships carrying it, and most of them did so. In Boston the governor refused to let the ships depart without unloading, and so in December "patriots" disguised as Indians boarded the vessels and unloaded the tea into the harbor.

This "Tea Party" exhausted London's patience and ended all search for compromise. Parliament's answer came in the five Coercive Acts of 1774. The port of Boston was closed; town meetings were forbidden and the provincial assembly was subordinated more thoroughly to the crown; royal officials indicted for a capital offense were to be tried in England, far from a hostile colonial jury; a new Quartering Act, strengthening that of 1765, was promulgated. To implement these acts, the commanding British general in North America was made governor of Massachusetts. At the same time, the Quebec Act, though unrelated, appeared as another attack on liberty since it extended the government by prerogative of "papist" Canada south to the Ohio Valley, thereby taking control of Indian lands coveted by the colonists.

These "intolerable" measures at last convinced the colonists that their troubles with Great Britain were the result of a vast conspiracy of corrupt powers in the mother country and such officials as Hutchinson in America to reduce the colonies to slavery, and so destroy British liberty everywhere. Indeed, since, outside of Switzerland and Venice, real liberty existed only in the British world, this plot aimed at extinguishing freedom everywhere. The cause of the colonists, therefore, was the very cause of humanity itself.

Behind this growing belief in the power of an all-pervasive plot against freedom lay an intellectual tradition extending from the Puritan Parliamentarians of the 1640s to the earliest Whigs in the Exclusion crisis under Charles II to the eighteenth-century Commonwealthmen opposed to the governing Whig oligarchy of Robert Walpole under the first two Hanoverians. To be sure, the colonial elite was well versed in the high political theory of John Locke and Montesquieu. But they were emotionally and psychologically more attuned to the republicanism of James Harrington and that martyr of the Rye House Plot, Algernon Sydney, as well as to the radical, minority Whig critics of the early eighteenth century.[25]

The worldview they absorbed from this source was founded on an assessment of human nature quite at variance with the optimism usually attributed to the Enlightenment and which indeed characterized the period immediately preceding the French Revolution. Men, in this radical Whig view, were neither rational nor naturally good; they were governed, rather, by passion, prejudice, vanity, ambition, and a lust for power and wealth (a very Calvinist view). Given these propensities, human government therefore invariably tended toward corruption and despotism, and liberty, in those rare times and places where it had triumphed, as in ancient Greece and Rome and then post-1688 Britain, was permanently in danger of being extinguished. Hence the constant efforts of the seventeenth-century Stuarts to reduce the people to slavery. Even after 1688 dark forces around the king and in Parliament itself—venal placemen, pensioners, and the "monied interests" in general—continued to threaten liberty. With the Coercive Acts of 1774 it became clear to the colonists that since 1765 America had been the victim of a stealthy conspiracy to reduce them to slavery and to undo the results of 1688 in Britain itself. How else to explain maintaining a standing army in North America, the campaign to deprive them of property by arbitrary taxation, to deny trial by jury in all too many instances, and to suspend the government of Massachusetts? How else to explain the campaign of 1774 to establish an Anglican episcopate in dissenter America?[26] And did this not fit with expanding the jurisdiction of "papist" Quebec?

In short, by 1774 the colonists believed that they were in effect reenacting the seventeenth-century parliamentary struggle against Stuart despotism, though with the Stuarts now replaced by Parliament itself. This view of the matter is obviously a great exaggeration of the realities of the situation, in fact a perspective bordering on paranoia. How then to explain it? The Stuarts had in fact been a real threat to parliamentary liberties, and in the Counter-Reformation seventeenth century "popery" had been a real and powerful adversary of Protestantism. But George III was patently no Charles I or James II, and American pluralism and individualism were too deeply entrenched to be easily extirpated. The best explanation is that the exceptional privileges and liberties that the Americans enjoyed made them hypersensitive to any prospect of their diminution. Hence the instantaneous explosion of 1765. Hence also the deep conviction of a plot when matters at last reached a genuinely dangerous pass with the Coercive Acts of 1774.

As the situation now was genuinely critical, the colonists moved to organized a coordinated resistance. On the initiative of the Committees of Correspondence, an intercolonial or continental congress was convened in the fall of 1774. This First Continental Congress accepted a set of Massachusetts's resolutions, presented by Samuel Adams, endorsing active resistance to the Intolerable Acts. It also adopted a nonimportation and nonconsumption agreement. And it rejected once again all of Parliament's claims of legislative authority over the colonies, recognizing only its right to regulate commerce. In short, the Congress demanded a return to the status quo before 1765.

The British government, for its part, now believed that Adams and the Massachusetts radicals were bent on independence. Firmness, therefore, was the only appropriate response. Accordingly, in April 1775 the British forces beleaguered in Boston were ordered to send an armed column to Concord to confiscate munitions stored there by the colony's militia. It is this action that provoked the famous shots on Lexington Green and the beginning of hostilities between redcoats and minutemen. This confrontation in turn provoked the collapse of British government throughout the colonies. One after another royal governors abandoned their posts for the protection of British warships. The colonial assemblies, which formerly required the governor's authorization to meet, now reconvened as ad hoc "congresses" and started acting as sovereign bodies, raising troops and issuing paper money to pay them, paper money then being a novel and, to most observers, reckless device.

Confronted with this situation, the Second Continental Congress, meeting the next month, had no choice but to move from the declaration of general principles to conduct of the war and acting as a provisional central government. They transformed the provincial militia surrounding Boston into a Continental Army and appointed militia colonel George Washington commander. They issued Continental paper money and undertook to negotiate with foreign governments, in particular to secure aid from France. Yet despite such actions of de facto sovereignty they still were not ready to cut all ties with England. Though Parliament's authority was completely rejected they reaffirmed their loyalty to the king and petitioned him to seek repeal of Parliament's tyrannical enactments. And these measures they blamed, in the time-honored manner of neophyte revolutionaries, on the monarch's "evil counselors," his ministers. But the king did not answer the colonists' petition and soon proclaimed them to be in a "state of rebellion," while Parliament voted to send twenty-five thousand more troops. The only way out, then, was independence, and in January 1776 Thomas Paine's pamphlet *Common Sense* crystallized sentiment that not only was George III a tyrant but that monarchy as such was an absurdity, by its very nature incompatible with human dignity. So in July independence was duly declared; and the colonists, without anguish or debate, became convinced republicans.

Seventeen seventy-six saw the apogee of revolutionary fever and fervor. The collapse of British authority had returned the colonies to a modified and partial state of nature. The Continental Congress advised all the states to give themselves new constitutions. Long experienced in politics, and with a wealth of British precedence to draw on, the colonists rapidly constructed a new political order. Provincial "congresses"—in effect the old colonial assemblies—in 1776 and 1777 gave themselves new, and more democratic, provincial assemblies with strong bills of rights. They did this while continuing to act as the current government of the state. This brief period saw the enactment of the radical Pennsylvania constitution, the Virginia bill of rights, and separation of church and state and the beginning of the abolition of slavery in the north. But the big innovation in this recasting of government was the invention in 1780 by Massachusetts of a separate constitutional "convention" that did not govern. This would become the formula for the national constitutional convention, and a device imitated worldwide over the next two centuries.

At the same time the most urgent task was to make independence stick by winning the war. The weakness of the Continental Army and the state militias dictated the necessity, therefore, of just staying in existence until British errors and foreign aid (from France) made victory possible. The intrinsic difficulty of the British position was too few resources for such a big geographic area and a hostile population. The United States could not have won when it did and as it did without French assistance. Even so, it took eight years to win. In the long run, however, geography and demography would have destroyed the British tie.

To recapitulate: The second time a variant of the grand revolutionary process occurred was in Britain's North American colonies. There, however, conditions were such as to modify the European scenario in major fashion. For although America had a cultural, religious, and constitutional heritage that was thoroughly European, it had only vestiges of an institutional Old Regime: there was no resident monarch, no resident bishop, no single established church, no legal class hierarchy, and only a moderate Lockean or Scottish Enlightenment; moreover the New England and Middle Atlantic states were largely founded by the radical wing of the English Revolution in exile. At the same time, there was virtually unlimited and undefended land into which the restless poor of the Atlantic coast could move.

Thus the American revolt had far less to overthrow than in any European case, and so generated none of the acute social conflicts that radicalized European revolutions. There was, of course, slavery, but this had the paradoxically conservative effect of removing the most aggrieved part of the population from the body politic. The American Revolution therefore became essentially a war of independence from an overseas semi-Old Regime, whose parliamentary privileges were for Britons only, and the creation, by 1789, of a unitary national state where none had existed before. In Tocqueville's words, "America enjoyed the fruits of revolution without going through the process." But the fruits were indeed revolutionary, for the resulting egalitarian and secular republic represented a striking negation of all Old Regime structures and values. Indeed, it is because America never had an Old Regime, as Louis Hartz argues, that it later never had a socialist movement.

8

FRANCE, 1789–1799

Revolution as Militant Modernity

Are we going to end the Revolution, or begin it anew . . . ? You have made all men equal before the law; you have consecrated civil and political equality; you have regained for the State all that had been removed from the sovereignty of the people. To go one step further would be a disastrous error. One step further on the path of liberty would be the destruction of the monarchy; one step further on the path of equality, the destruction of property. . . . Today everyone knows that the Revolution should be ended. Those who have lost know that it is impossible to reverse it; those who have made it know that it is completed and for their glory must be consolidated.
—ANTOINE BARNAVE, July 15, 1791

The provisional government of France is revolutionary until peace.
—SAINT JUST, Fall 1793

The Revolution continues Christianity, and contradicts it. It is at the same time Christianity's heir and its adversary.
—JULES MICHELET, 1847

The Revolution brought back to earth faith in the impossible.
—EDGAR QUINET, 1854

If the Reformation had been a revolution against the First Estate, 1789 was in the first instance a revolution against the Second Estate, with the First Estate only thrown in for good measure. Discarding the monarchy, too, was an afterthought, decided upon only when it became clear that the king would not accept social leveling. And so there remained only the Third Estate, which was now indeed the nation, that great modern mass of equal and fraternal citizens.

With 1789, European revolution attained a new and unprecedented order of magnitude. As its first great enemy, Edmund Burke, immediately understood (though as of 1790 he had not seen the half of it): "All circumstances taken together, the French Revolution is the most extraordinary thing that has hitherto happened in the world." Indeed, it marked the end of a thousand years of the regimen of the two swords and the three orders, not only for France but also, indirectly, for all Europe: after 1789 nothing anywhere could ever be the same again. Surveys of European history thus invariably divide at 1789 but only rarely at 1688, and almost never at 1640. The only comparable previous shock to the European system had been 1517 and the beginning of the Reformation, but this upheaval of course is not conventionally considered a "revolution." The only comparable subsequent shock would be October 1917, yet even this event defined itself as the fulfillment of 1789 on the higher and final socialist level of history.

A CONTENTIOUS LEGACY

The historiography of the French Revolution is accordingly the most copious of any event so named, the passion animating it exceeded only by that surrounding Red October. This historiography is also the most pivotal for understanding revolution as such, and it is of vital import for our most influential theory of revolution, indeed our most ambitious theory of history in general, Marxism. Seventeen eighty-nine was the matrix of Marx's concept of "bourgeois revolution," which in turn was the template for a putatively future "proletarian revolution." Hence, what in England had been a "storm over the gentry" (and in America mere shadow-boxing over planter "feudalism"), in France blew up to a veritable tempest over the bourgeois status of 1789. For the stake was not just the course of French history, but the march of mankind in general: If the case cannot be made for 1789 as bourgeois revolution, then no such beast exists; if it does not exist, its putative proletarian projection is a phantom, too.

The course of the Revolution's historiography may be presented through generational cohorts defined as the country debated its present politics in terms of past history.[1]

The class of 1830. The debate began during what was supposed to have been the Revolution's negation, the Restoration of 1815.[2] Hitherto, Revolution history had been the province of émigré royalists—notably the abbé Baruel, who saw it as a Masonic plot. Once royalty, aristocracy, and church were back in power, it was the turn of the heirs of 1789 (though not yet of 1793) to defend the great year's liberal heritage—as a preliminary, of course, to reviving its politics, which they in fact did in 1830. So a future Orleanist prime minister and founding president of the Third Republic, Adolphe Thiers, together with his friend François Mignet, in 1823–1824 staked out the classic liberal distinction between the creative Revolution of 1789–1791 and the aberration of 1792–1794.[3] The great figure of this tradition, though, was the already noted François Guizot, later Louis Philippe's longest-serving prime minister.[4] Now too often remembered only for Marx's attack on him in the opening of the *Communist Manifesto*, as well as for the phrase "enrichissez-vous" addressed in the 1840s to opponents of the existing property suffrage, Guizot was one of the most widely read European historians throughout much of the nineteenth century.[5] His message was Whiggism on a pan-European scale: European civilization was defined as the progress of liberty from the Reformation, to the seventeenth-century English Revolution (unlike Macaulay, he knew that 1640 was its real beginning), to its triumph in the Revolution of 1789–1791. And the earliest origins of 1789 lay in the twelfth-century communal revolts of the "bourgeoisie" against its episcopal or seigneurial overlords, a "class struggle" that brought the Third Estate to full power in 1789. (This was the source of Marx's idea of class struggle as the motor force of history, although he claimed that he "discovered" that principle himself.)

The class of 1848. Once the liberals were in power, younger historians geared up for a more adequate sequel to 1789 than the class-based July Monarchy, and so rehabilitated the republican Revolution of 1792–1795. The most prominent of these democratic lyricists was Jules Michelet, the first volume of whose *French Revolution* appeared in 1847. In full romantic throat, he defended the Revolution's entire work (though not the Terror's excesses) as the rebirth of France and indeed of mankind. It was the world-historical triumph of the "people," of all those oppressed and excluded during the long centuries of medieval superstition and servitude.[6] The same year there appeared more partisan treatments, first by the poet Alphonse de Lamartine, whose heroes were the Revolution's moderate republicans, the Girondins,[7] while the socialist Louis Blanc began a ten-volume celebration of the Republic's Jacobin Mountain.[8] Of course the next year, the pair found themselves together in the Provisional Government of the Second Republic, though not for long—they could not manage the Parisian plebs, whom another early socialist, Marx, was then anointing as the bearer of proletarian class struggle.

The failed replay of 1789 also produced its sobered realists, foremost among them the reluctant democrat Alexis de Tocqueville. In the 1830s he had prepared for what he suspected would be further change in France by looking beyond the liberals' aristocratic English model to the more pertinent example of egalitarian America, for by "democracy" he understood not so much constitutional government as *l'égalité des conditions*, the social leveling launched by the fall of the

Old Regime's *société à ordres*. As a deputy in 1848, he helped draft the Second Republic's constitution, and then became the foreign minister of its first and last president, Louis Bonaparte.

After Bonaparte's coup forced him into retirement, Tocqueville pondered the question of why France and Europe had such difficulty adapting to the democratic age. In 1856 he published *L'Ancien Régime et la Révolution* which argued that the Revolution was the mirror image of the old monarchy: royal absolutism, by depriving the aristocracy of its political functions while leaving its privileges intact, had generated a culture of democratic envy that led the Revolution to put leveling equality before individual liberty. Popular sovereignty therefore turned out to be as absolute as royal sovereignty had been earlier, and the result was Jacobin centralization and then the dictatorship of the two Napoleons.[9]

To explain this perverse outcome, Tocqueville broadened his range of comparisons:[10] to the usual French comparison with England he had already added America, and now, in preparing his book on the Revolution he learned German to study a fourth case, the largely intact Old Regimes across the Rhine. He even looked in on a fifth example, the empire of the tsars, by reading the then famous book of 1847–1852 by Freiherr von Haxthausen on the Russian peasant commune. His reaction deserves to be placed alongside the famous comparison between Russia and America that concludes his *Democracy:* "We find on the one hand a population legally bound to the land as in the tenth century, and on the other the perpetual geographic and social restlessness of the Americans. . . . It gives the impression of an America without enlightenment and liberty. A democratic society to frighten you." [11]

Similarly disillusioned with the French revolutionary tradition was Michelet's fellow republican, Edgar Quinet[12] — though unlike his friend, Quinet felt that 1789 had been less a breakthrough than a noble failure. Like Tocqueville, he blamed this outcome in part on the institutional heritage of the Old Regime, yet unlike him, he held Catholicism to be equally at fault. Though not a Protestant like Guizot, he nonetheless believed that the Reformation's failure in France left the Revolution too many problems to confront simultaneously to solve any of them in a liberal manner. Again he made the comparison with England where the religious problem had been solved in the sixteenth century and the constitutional one in the seventeenth — thus making it easier to confront the advent of democratic equality in the nineteenth.[13] The thesis of revolutionary overload and the Catholic heritage in 1789 is certainly worth pondering.

The class of 1870. With the Third Republic, the Revolution's meaning changed again. Since the Republic had been born amidst the disasters of 1870–1871, the first voice to be heard, that of Hippolyte Taine, was negative.[14] Like the Orleanists earlier, Taine was an Anglophile and hence hostile to the Revolution's Jacobin culmination. Unlike them, however, he was hostile to the Revolution overall and so derived the Terror from the initial "anarchy" of 1789, and indeed from the abstract and leveling *esprit classique* of the Old Regime. His *Origins of Contemporary France*, begun in 1876, was thus a summa of pessimism about modern France. It would periodically resurface in such royalists as Pierre Gaxotte, Jacques Bainville, and Charles Maurras.

The dominant tone after 1870, however, was positive. The year Taine went to press, the new regime fell into the hands of republicans, who of course recognized their pedigree in 1792 as much as in 1789: "la Révolution est un bloc," as Dreyfusard Clemenceau defined it. Bastille Day became the nation's holiday, and "La Marseillaise" its national anthem, in 1880. A subscription was raised for a Statue of Liberty in New York harbor. The monument was presented in 1889 on the dual centenary of the Bastille and the application of the American constitution.

The Republic's commitment to universal suffrage, moreover, meant universal primary education to raise the young in the proper patriotic spirit, a mission that required an appropriate historical corpus. So in 1886, as the Sorbonne was refashioned into a research university on the German model, the first chair in the history of the Revolution was created. In 1901 its titular, François Aulard, answered Taine with a *Histoire politique de la Révolution française* that firmly derived the First Republic from the principles of 1789 and defended the Terror as a government of national defense against foreign attack and internal revolt, a position since known as "la thèse des circonstances." Aulard's hero was the earthy Danton, both democrat and patriot, while the Terror's excesses were fobbed off on the fanatic Robespierre. The distinction has lived on in mainstream republican myth:[15] Paris boasts both a prominent statue to Danton and a nearby rue Danton, whereas the Incorruptible has no monument of any sort, anywhere.

The class of 1900. Yet scarcely had orthodoxy been established when it was overtaken by the emergence of socialism as a mass movement. In the same year as Aulard's political synthesis, Jean Jaurès launched a four-volume socialist history of the Revolution from outside the academy. Until then the great epic had been presented "from above," through the records of the revolutionary assemblies and the deeds of leading figures, even under the pen of Michelet. Jaurès now told the story "from below," through archival materials focusing on the economic problems and political activism of the masses. The message, in a spirit as much of Michelet as of Marx, was that the existing Republic, ultimately, must be a social one.[16]

Yet hardly had this point been made when the subject was overtaken by the

Soviet model of what socialism might in fact *mean;* and in October's reflected light Aulard's one-time pupil, Albert Mathiez, undertook the rehabilitation of Robespierre's hardcore Terror. No longer only a government of national defense, the Committee of Public Safety, by instituting price controls (the Maximum), now became an embryonic dictatorship of the proletariat, alas cut short by the reactionary Thermidorian bourgeoisie. Accordingly, Mathiez vilified Aulard's Danton and eulogized *his* Robespierre in a proxy campaign for socialism against the existing republican establishment. This first quasi-Marxism, though, lacked sociological depth, for Mathiez detailed "la vie chère" during the Terror as if that could account for the Incorruptible's dictatorship of republican "virtue."[17] In any event, Mathiez's dissent from Aulard ended the brief career of what may be called neo-Jacobin "Whiggism." For the next half-century, revolutionary studies belonged to Marx.

The class of 1936. The movement's high tide came with Aulard's successor, Georges Lefebvre.[18] A socialist and Jules Guesde Marxist, his work offers the maximum of what the social interpretation of the Revolution could accomplish. In the early 1920s, following the lead of Russia's rich pre-revolutionary scholarship on the eighteenth-century French peasantry, principally that of J. Loutchitsky (I. V. Luchitskii),[19] an inspiration reinforced by the spectacle of the peasantry's crucial role in 1917, Lefebvre virtually created the modern field of French agrarian history with a monumental study of the peasants of his home department, the Nord, under the Revolution.[20] Methodologically he was also open to Emile Durkheim's sociology and to the Annales School historians, influences apparent in his survey of the peasantry nationwide, *La Grande peur* of 1932— social history in the mode of what would later be called *mentalité.*[21] In 1937, in the wake of the Popular Front, he was elevated to the cathedra of the Sorbonne, and in 1939, the sesquicentennial of 1789, he produced a concise treatment of the fateful year that is a better exercise in class analysis than Marx's own famous pamphlets on 1848.[22] After the war, in 1951, when he had become sympathetic to a CPF now reflecting the light of Stalingrad, he produced a synthesis of the Revolution in all its aspects, political, economic, and social.[23] In particular, it incorporated Ernest Labrousse's meticulous economic investigations showing increased prosperity until 1778, followed by a crisis decade that put the price of bread at its high point for the century exactly on July 14, 1789.[24]

Though Lefebvre considered 1789 overall a "bourgeois revolution," he did not reduce the event to a one-on-one correspondence of politics to class interests, or see it primarily as a way station to October. Like Michelet, he considered that popular sovereignty and the Declaration of the Rights of Man were in themselves an epochal culmination of history. His class analysis of 1789 is accordingly a nuanced one. The movement began as the aristocratic revolution of 1787–1788, proceeded to the bourgeois revolution of May-June 1789, thence to the popular and municipal revolution of July, and finally to the peasant revolution against feudal dues in August—the four stages culminating that same month in the Declaration of the Rights of Man and the abolition of the estates system. And this cascade of change is indeed the way the Revolution destroyed the Old Regime.

The fifteen or so years after World War II were the high point of "the Party's" prestige in France, a time when Paris' premier mandarin, Jean-Paul Sartre, could plausibly declare Marxism to be "the inescapable horizon of our age." In this atmosphere Albert Soboul, Lefebvre's pupil and eventual successor at the Sorbonne, revised Mathiez's work with a more dialectical investigation of the sans-culottes of 1793. Published in 1958, his thesis shows how the foot soldiers of the Revolution were tragically ground to dust by the Revolution's internal contradictions:[25] On one hand, they were the revolutionary class par excellence, advocates of direct democracy and proto-socialist economic controls; on the other, they were only an archaic pre-proletariat of artisans and small shopkeepers in alliance with propertyless salaried workers. Even so, it was their capacity for direct action that had driven the revolutionary assemblies leftward from 1789 to the Jacobin dictatorship of 1793, a role in which they indeed appear as the adumbration of the modern proletariat and the Russian soviets. The tragedy of Thermidor, then, resulted from the incompatibility between this popular movement and the Committee of Public Safety's "bourgeois" commitment to mere representative democracy and economic liberalism. Indeed, the Mountain had only used the sans-culottes to protect itself against "feudal" reaction; and once its own power was secure, Robespierre closed down the popular movement—unwittingly leaving himself without a bodyguard on the showdown of 9 Thermidor.

All was not lost, however: there remained the forward reference to October, a theme increasingly emphasized in successive editions of Soboul's *Précis* of Revolutionary history.[26] With this "Short Course" the social interpretation of the Revolution hardened into political dogma. And Soboul, the Party member, used his tenure to transform a chair created to be the pulpit of the bourgeois Republic into a Communist fief.

The class of 1968. As was only to be expected, a "revisionist" challenge soon followed. The first salvo came from empiricist British historians, for whom, moreover, 1789 was neither national destiny nor present politics. In 1964, the height of Marxism's postwar hegemony (E. P. Thompson had produced his major work the previous year, and Soboul his thesis only a few years earlier), Alfred Cobban published *The Social Interpretation of the French Revolution*.[27] Its premise was that "The supposed social categories of our histories—bourgeois, aristocrats, *sans-culottes*—are all in fact political ones" (indeed they are metaphysical ones as well).[28] So he mined Lefebvre for examples showing that the fabled bourgeoisie and its feudal adversary were hollow abstractions. Unfortunately, however, he could produce no better counter-thesis than—you guessed it!—foisting the Revolution onto a "declining bourgeoisie" of embittered lawyers and royal officials (*officiers*).

The next year the revisionist challenge emerged in more analytical guise in France. It came from two former communists, François Furet and Denis Richet, and took the bold form, for such young historians, of a general synthesis provocatively emphasizing politics and ideology.[29] In 1971, battle was joined directly with Soboul's Sorbonne when Furet, in the Annales School house organ, published his "The Catechism of the French Revolution," said catechism being the eschatological linkage of 1789 and 1917.[30] In 1978, once Aleksandr Solzhenitsyn's *Gulag Archipelago* had fatally damaged the Soviet mystique in France, revisionism received its manifesto in Furet's *Penser la Révolution française*.[31] He now declared that the Revolution, which had divided France directly in the nineteenth century and indirectly, through its projection onto October, in the twentieth, was at last "finished." Since the Soviet reference was no longer a factor in French politics, it was time to get its specter out of scholarship as well.

Furet's heroes were two figures from the nineteenth-century tradition, Tocqueville and Taine's pupil Augustin Cochin, both now "discovered" in France.[32] In fact, both had merely been abandoned to the "anglo-saxons"— Tocqueville obviously, and even Cochin, whom our first "staseologist," Crane Brinton, had followed in his still pertinent 1934 history of the Revolution.[33] Cochin now became relevant in France because he brought the antidote to explaining the Terror by "circumstances": *la thèse du complot*—an unfortunate term since Cochin did not mean an actual conspiracy but political caucusing by an ideologically illuminated minority. Indeed, such organization, in truth, lay behind all the Revolution's *journées*, from the taking of the Bastille to the purge of the Girondins in 1793. "Men make their own history," after all, as history's greatest sociologizer, Marx, qualified his own system to explain the fiasco of 1848.

In Furet's synthesis of Tocqueville and Cochin, the former gave the key to the origins and the consequences of the Revolution and the latter to the actual revolutionary process. This process Furet defines as a "torrent," a "cascade," or a "deluge" of events, driven by a dialectic of ideological outbidding (*surenchère*) between Revolution and counterrevolution. So the years 1789–1791 unfolded in an escalating spiral of "patriot" suspicion and preemptive action against a pervasive "aristocratic plot"—all in the name of "pure democracy" and leveling "equality." Revolutionary politics, therefore, is no longer about specific economic, social, or other issues, but about manipulation of the egalitarian *parole* or discourse.

Of course Furet, too, had a political agenda. In taking the Revolution back from Marx by counterpoising him with Tocqueville and Guizot, he sought to de-ideologize the present-day French political debate. And international conditions were propitious for this task. By the 1970s, Revolutionary history had ceased to be a Gallo-centric affair: the modern mass university had made the field a vast enterprise, with Britons and Americans increasingly prominent alongside the Parisian core.[34]

The class of 1989. At this juncture, in 1981 François Mitterand's presidency took France on its last fling with a Popular Front. His attempted "transition from capitalism to socialism," however, soon fizzled, and the generic socialist myth emerged almost as discredited as the Communist one. The author of the once scandalous book *The Opium of the Intellectuals* (1951), Raymond Aron, was now seen to have been right all along against his one-time classmate, Sartre.[35] And so, just as the Berlin Wall fell, France marked the Revolution's bicentennial. The Socialist government's celebratory commemoration was eclipsed by the critical stocktaking of Furet and his long-time collaborator, Mona Ozouf.[36] For Furet had now revised his own revisionism: in his synthesis of 1965, he had presented 1793 as a *dérapage* (skidding off course) with respect to 1789; in his synthesis for the bicentennial, 1793 derived from the breakthrough year itself. The Revolution was once again a "bloc," but in a more tragic mode than in the days of Clemenceau. Indeed, some historians judged the Revolution and Napoleon to have been an excessively costly form of modernization, arguing, with a glance across the Atlantic, that it had set economic development back a generation and inaugurated France's slow decline as a power.[37]

In any event, revisionism was now the reigning orthodoxy. Yet it was an orthodoxy that did not lend itself to dogma or catechization. It thus did not mean the elimination of social history, but its incorporation into (and usually subordination to) political, intellectual, and cultural history. Accordingly, raw socioeconomic class gave way to more appropriate analyses of eighteenth-century estate structures and royal institutions.[38] Both nobility and bourgeoisie were consequently fragmented into antagonistic internal strata, each often overlapping with a cognate level of the rival "estate." For, strangely enough, detailed investigation of the Old Regime, not in modern class terms, but in its historical specificity as a *société à ordres,* had not really been properly done.[39] So it turned out that bourgeoisie and higher nobles belonged to the same economic class, and the wealth of both was largely landed property, not modern capital; this same core of "notables" would dominate French society after 1799 as surely as it had in 1789.

Moreover, both noble and nonnoble notables shared the same Enlightenment culture, which hence ceased to be the ideology of the "rising bourgeoisie." Royal officials, too, shared this culture, just as they were socially imbricated with the propertied elite.

In short, the Revolution occurred not because of bourgeois pressure against nobles and clergy, but because existing monarchical and estates structures, overall, were no longer compatible with a rapidly evolving society and culture. The Revolution hence was "essentially a political revolution with social consequences and not a social revolution with political consequences."[40] Accordingly, bourgeois revolution and feudalism (understood as a "mode of production") have now largely dropped out of the historian's lexicon. The only problem such terminology now poses is: where did these obfuscating categories come from, and why did they dominate the modern historical consciousness for so long? The answer, obviously, lies in Marxism's seductive powers. But "Why Marx?" is the subject of another chapter.

To make the parallel with the English revolutionary historiography, in France we find a far shorter liberal-republican "Whiggism" and a much longer and deeper Marxism. This correlates nicely with Communism's varying strength in the two countries, as well as with the differing natures of their respective revolutionary myths. (And it correlates just as nicely with the absence of a Marxist phase in the American Revolution's historiography, as well as with a clearly defined national myth almost from 1776 onward.) The historiographical endpoint in England and France, however, is roughly the same: an eclectic nominalism and the absence of any teleological master narrative. In neither country, after all, is the existence of the present "market democracy" in question as it was in both, for varying parts of the population, in the postwar decades.

THE OLD REGIME FRAMEWORK

The English comparison is once again unavoidable. In fact, it was built into the institutional fabric of the two polities, and this from their very beginnings. The Plantagenet and Capetian monarchies, after all, were the two oldest in Europe. Both, moreover, had been molded by the exceptional dynamism of the Norman duchy—the first by conquest, the second by institutional mobilization to meet the Plantagenet challenge.[41] Finally, they had developed over the centuries in rivalry and conflict with one another.

As late as 1614–1629—the last "medieval" Estates General and Charles I's putative final Parliament—the two monarchies in many respects still offered variations on a common set of themes. Wentworth's appointment to head the

Council of the North in 1628 may be judged an unsuccessful analogue to Richelieu's rise to power in 1624. From then on, however, the paths of state formation in the two cases diverge, the one toward a failed absolutism culminating in modern mixed, or constitutional, monarchy, the other toward the most "thorough" of modern absolutisms leading, in the most "thorough" possible counter movement, to a universal suffrage republic.

This dialectic of the French route to modernity was preceded by a similar dialectic within the Old Regime itself. This first zigzag unfolded in two phases: an ascending development of royal absolutism from Richelieu to the death of Louis XIV in 1715; then a descending movement of "thaw" and deconstruction to the implosion of 1789.[42] This pattern was governed by certain historical particularities of the Capetian realm.

As of 1789 it was the largest and most populous country of Europe (Russia, of course, was larger, and by the eighteenth century's end, also as populous, but its peripheral location made it politically marginal). This kingdom covered roughly 545,000 square kilometers, compared with 230,000 for the Island of Great Britain (Ireland must be counted a liability for British strength). Its population was 28 million, while Paris counted between 650,000 and 750,000, compared with 10 million in contemporary Britain and almost one million in its capital. In short, the stage on which the Revolution played out was huge for the time. It was also central, both geographically and culturally, to the European system as a whole, a particularity going back to the Carolingians' alliance with the papacy under the sign of Christendom. Each successor of Saint Louis was thus called *le roi très chrétien*, and the national mythology saw the Crusades as *gesta Dei per Francos*. This special role of *La Grande Nation* continued in secular form in the seventeenth century, as its absolutism was imitated east of the Rhine, and in the eighteenth, with its preeminent role in the Enlightened "republic of letters."

The stage for 1789 was also variegated and complex. Unlike unitary England, the French kingdom was a "mosaic" formed over the centuries as the royal domain conquered, married, or in one or another way annexed a congeries of provinces, each coming under the Crown with its own institutions, customs, and laws—all considered immemorial "liberties," "privileges," and "rights." Provinces such as Brittany, Languedoc, Normandy, or Provence were large enough to be separate kingdoms of the political importance, say, of Scotland or Catalonia; some had in fact been independent entities. In gathering in these regions, moreover, the monarchy discarded almost nothing of their various institutions; it simply superimposed its own central institutions on them, the latest layer being Richelieu's emergency regional governors, the *intendants*, an institution made a regular part of administration by Louis XIV. Only then was the French state basically complete and beyond the challenge mounted, in Louis XIV's childhood, by the parliamentary and noble revolt of the Fronde between 1648 and 1653.

Still, the degree of centralization was hardly up to modern standards. Economically, the realm did not yet constitute a single national market, divided as it was by internal customs barriers and differing weights and measures. It also had different systems of law, customary or common law in the north and Roman law in the south. Only a minority of the population spoke the king's French; the peasant majority, often illiterate, used one or another *patois* of the north's *langue d'oïl* and the south's *langue d'oc*, while foreign languages thrived from Brittany and Alsace to Bearn.

State formation under Richelieu was driven in the first instance by war against encircling Habsburg power in Spain, the Low Countries, the Empire, and Italy —the constraints of *not* being an island. The inevitable corollary to this was increased royal power internally. The Cardinal Minister began by depriving the Huguenots of the "fortified places" left them by Henry IV's Edict of Nantes. He continued by subduing and disarming a nobility that as recently as the Wars of Religions had devastated the realm. And to pay for his ambitious foreign policy, he imposed such onerous taxation on the population that he had repeatedly to repress fiscal revolts among the peasantry. By such near dictatorial methods, upon his death in 1642, he had at last given his master that unchallenged monopoly of coercive force which for Max Weber defined state sovereignty.

Establishing this monopoly had of course infringed numerous corporate liberties and rights, and so generated anti-absolutist resistance. In 1648 (just as the English Revolution reached its climax) this resistance burst forth in the quasi-insurrection of the Fronde against the new Cardinal Minister, Mazarin. The first and principal phase came from the Parlement of Paris, the most important of the king's several "sovereign courts." These magistrates, once wealthy commoners, had in the previous century and a half purchased their charges from a monarchy ever pressed for funds. Their tenure soon became hereditary, thus conferring noble status. Yet, such "venality of office" was in no way incompatible with a high level of learning and a sense of civic responsibility. This "nobility of the robe" thus became the principal channel of anti-absolutist resistance, which now took the pacific form of legal challenges and remonstrances to the king. The second phase of this revolt took the traditional form of the "nobility of the sword's" immemorial "right of armed redress of grievances" against the crown. Resistance to royal power also was articulated in the minority of surviving provincial estates, such as Languedoc and Brittany.

All these "intermediate bodies" between king and people argued from what might be called a French "ancient constitution" allegedly hearkening back to the quasi-mythical assemblies of the Franks on the "field of Mars" (where the Eiffel Tower now stands). Parlement, therefore, claimed to be the guardian of the realm's "fundamental laws," indeed to be the nation's representative in the absence of the Estates General. Its boldest pretension was to exercise legislative co-authority with the crown on the grounds that royal decrees became law only after parliamentary registration by the magistrates. By the time of the Fronde, however, it was far too late to make good such claims. Absolutism had paid off handsomely abroad when the Peace of Westphalia in 1648 consecrated victory in the main war against the Habsburgs. Internally, monarchical consolidation was too well institutionalized to be reversed. By 1653 Mazarin had successfully put down France's last semi-feudal sedition.[43]

After 1661 Louis XIV's personal rule brought these developments to their acme. That very year, he cowed the Paris Parlement into silence by a *lit de justice*, in which he personally ordered the body to register a disputed edict. He withdrew the seat of royal government from the potential turbulence of Paris to the safe splendor of Versailles. He neutralized the higher nobility with the pageant of the court, and gave lesser nobles glorious careers in his 400,000-man army, the largest in Europe. In 1685 he revoked the Edict of Nantes, thereby depriving the Huguenots of the liberties Richelieu had left them, and he eventually proscribed their religion altogether. Concurrently, he harassed the religious dissent of Jansenism within Catholicism, a movement particularly favored by parliamentarians. With the Jansenists' complete suppression at the end of the reign, religious unity was at last complete, at least in law, according to the Old Regime ideal of state sovereignty across Europe. By 1700, the Grand Monarch's regime appeared as the acme of modern statecraft to much of Europe, and the very model of a civilized or "well-policed" polity.[44]

Yet Bourbon absolutism's very success had already created the conditions for its demise. Its international power led to a European coalition against France in the War of the Spanish Succession of 1701–1713, thus checking its expansion for nearly a century. Internally, centralization had gone beyond what a now long-pacified society would accept as the price of its security. Opposition began immediately on the king's death in 1715: his "cousin of Orleans" had the Paris Parlement break the royal will and name him regent, thereby inaugurating absolutism's descending eighteenth-century curve.

This movement was led for most of the century not, as widespread opinion has it, by the *philosophes*, but by the parlements, which now stepped forth a second time as a constitutionalist opposition. They were inspired, moreover, by a politicized version of Jansenism, something that has only recently been recognized.[45]

Original, religious Jansenism had emerged in the 1640s as a radical Augustinian response to the humanism and skepticism of such Renaissance figures as Montaigne, a *"laxisme"* that the "solitaires de Port-Royal" (their abbey near Paris) found also in the accommodating casuistry of the worldly Jesuits. This austere theology led to countercharges that they advocated a crypto-Calvinism within Catholicism, a "heresy" they vehemently denied. In fact, their theology was quite Tridentine and their emphasis on the inner cultivation of the soul was matched by a thoroughly eucharistic piety. What distinguished them, rather, was a quest to purify the church of all worldliness, and in particular to promote the dignity of the rank-and-file clergy as distinct from the hierarchy, who were more often than not drawn from the higher nobility. Jansenist clerics soon acquired a secular base in the judicial parlements—a combination of dissident religion and constitutionalist opposition reminiscent of Puritan parliamentarinism in England, a parallel that French loyalists were quick to draw.

This fact, together with Jansenists' hostility to the Jesuits, unavoidably cast Port-Royal in a political role. Though the Jesuits were on principle ultramontane and papal, as a practical matter they became close allies of the Gallican monarchy, which since Henry IV had employed them to restore religious conformity; they also furnished the Bourbons' confessors. Jansenism accordingly became an anti-absolutist force, in Rome no less than in Paris (contemporaries were aware of the parallel with Puritanism across the Channel). The monarchy, for its part, insisted on the French church's administrative independence of Rome in all temporal matters, yet at the same time needed Rome and the Jesuits to testify to its own sacred character and to unify the French church. Beginning in the 1650s, therefore, the king and the mainstream Gallican clergy prevailed on Rome to condemn various "articles" drawn from the Jansenists' literature, condemnations which their theologians (and such laymen as Pascal) steadfastly maintained were misrepresentations. In 1705 Louis, exasperated by this continuing opposition, ordered the abbey of Port-Royal in the fields razed. In 1713 he extorted from the pope the bull *Unigenitus*, formally declaring Jansenism heretical, a document its objects claimed to be the ultimate misrepresentation.

After 1715, religious Jansenism gave way to an essentially political movement to become the center of a shadow politics during the Old Regime's last century. Since the papacy now supported the monarchy's policy of repression, the Jansenists adopted the tactic of appealing from the pope to a general council of the church, thus becoming known as the "appellants." In order to stifle this opposition, in 1730 the monarchy made the bull *Unigenitus*, or "constitution," part of civil law, and the clergy who supported this action became known as the "constitutionaries." In a number of spectacular cases, the Parlement consistently ruled for appellants against the constitutionaries; and in moments of acute crisis, the monarchy responded by "exiling" the Parlement to some provincial town. Even-tually, in the mid-century, the monarchy decreed that Jansenists could not re-ceive the last sacraments without a *billet de confession* from a "constitutionary" priest, a decision that led to a number of dramatic and scandalous deathbed inci-dents. It was, after all, unprecedented even under the regimen of the two swords for the civil authority to intervene directly in a religious matter. The upshot was to desacralize both the Gallican church and the divine-right monarchy.

On another front, the parlements relentlessly campaigned against the Jesuits, accusing them of systematic infringement of Gallican "liberties." In 1762 the monarchy at last gave way and expelled the Jesuits from the kingdom.[46] This tri-umph, however, soon produced the parlements' own undoing. In 1770, Louis XV and his chancellor, Maupeou, in a surge of reforming energy, replaced those hereditary bodies with a more modern system of salaried but lifetime magis-trates. Yet the nobility of the robe's powerful friends among the other privileged "corps" prevailed on the new king in 1774 to undo Maupeou's reforms and re-store the parlements. This retreat only made the monarchy seem vacillating and retrograde, but without making the parlements appear as a genuine recourse for change.[47]

In fact, Jansenism by 1770 had reached the end of its relevance as an opposi-tion. It had always functioned in the time-honored European mode of promoting reform by advocating return to an idealized past, whether the primitive church as a means for purifying present Catholicism, the ancient Frankish constitution to stimulate current constitutional reform, or an earlier and purer Gallicanism to combat the existing alliance of the papacy and absolutism. By 1770, however, the slow erosion of the sacred Old Regime had gone too far (in part through the Jansenists' own efforts) for such appeals to the past to be capable of meeting the looming problems of the present. In a decade when the American Revolution was putting the idea of a republic back on the political agenda, the seventeenth-century program of turning medieval mixed monarchy into modern mixed mon-archy was no longer an adequate means for transforming a flagging absolutism into an unambiguously constitutional policy. Eighteenth-century judicial Jan-senism thus proved to be the last gasp of the conservative radicalism that had driven European revolution from the Hussites to the Puritans. Henceforth only an ideology that looked forward rather than backward would be adequate to ad-dress the accumulated problems that two centuries of absolutism had engen-dered. So *les lumières*, or the Enlightenment, moved to the fore of the Old Re-gime opposition.

This, of course, is not to repeat the old refrain that the Revolution was "la faute à Voltaire, la faute à Rousseau." Obviously, before 1789 no one imagined, let alone advocated, revolution of any sort. Such an elitist as Voltaire, for example, would hardly have been at home in the revolutionary turmoil, and Rousseau's *Social Contract* went almost unread before 1792.[48] Just how, then, did *les lumières* act on politics? Though empirical research can eventually decide whether the higher nobility and the upper bourgeoisie were converging in economic status as of 1789, it is impossible to specify with comparable certainty the ways in which the Enlightenment conditioned revolutionary politics.[49]

Still, a few basic things are obvious. From the fifth century to the seventeenth, European culture had been dominated by revealed religion; all other intellectual currents, from Aristotelianism in the twelfth century to humanism and Platonism in the fifteenth and sixteenth, had to be subordinated to Christianity. The first intellectual force for which this was not true was the natural science of the seventeenth century. To be sure, the new scientists, from Galileo to Newton, were all religious—indeed quite convinced that their discoveries magnified the glory of the Creator. In fact, however, revelation was irrelevant to the scientific quest, as the new century quickly made apparent.

The result was that for the first time, the balance in European culture was tipped from the religious to the secular, from the sacred to the profane.[50] For the new science soon became the model for analyzing everything in purely secular and terrestrial terms, from politics and society to ethics and morals, and indeed to religion itself. Indeed, it is only in the eighteenth century that the term "religion" acquired its modern meaning of a separate province of human activity alongside philosophy, the body politic, and the commercial and manufacturing activities we now call the economy. Accordingly, successive thinkers throughout the century, even the skeptic Hume, had as their ambition to become the Newton of the moral universe. To be sure, the new secularism was restricted to the literate elite, and at that did not claim all of it. But the future belonged to this minority, which after 1690 quickly succeeded in conquering the old humanist republic of letters.

Concurrently, Europe's sense of time changed from a supernatural to a this-worldly perspective on the future. History's providential course to the Second Coming and the Final Days was replaced by belief in human progress in the here and now.[51] The Renaissance and the classical age of Louis XIV had shown that modern Europe had at last equaled, in fact surpassed, the ancients in letters and the arts; but it was the new science that made progress appear to be an open-ended conquest of nature and of the ills of human society.[52] Accordingly, the European adventure was divided into ancient, medieval, and modern history—two enlightened periods surrounding the long, dark, and religious Middle Ages.

Surely, this revolution in historical perspective was a precondition for the bold attempt after 1789 to build a whole new world on the repudiated ruins of a dark past. Without the ideological envelope of the Enlightenment the Revolution could not have been perceived as a new beginning in which "men make their own history"; or as a conscious creation of constitutional and social structures; or as a culmination of natural and mundane historical process.

On a more concrete level, the Revolution was *preceded* by a large body of explicit reflection on the nature of politics and society, from Montesquieu's *The Spirit of the Laws* to Rousseau's *Social Contract*, to name only the most obvious examples.[53] The English Revolution, by contrast, had been preceded by nothing more explicitly subversive than theological and ecclesiological speculation as well as theorizing about the nature of the *existing* body of law, the "ancient constitution." English political theory emerged only during and *after* the Revolution in the work of Hobbes, Harrington, and Locke. It had, moreover, its chief impact abroad, in America and France.

More precisely, the *philosophes* did have a philosophy in the exact sense of the word, and this was the empiricism of John Locke. The basic tenet of empiricism was that "there is nothing in the mind that was not first in the senses." In other words, our knowledge derives not from a supernatural Creator, but from the purely "natural" processes of our physical, material, being.

This new epistemology, however, could be wielded in a skeptical and moderate spirit or in a radical reformist one. In the British version, as enunciated by Locke and refined by Hume, it was directed against religious "enthusiasm" and so emphasized the *limits* of our understanding and warned against confusing real knowledge with the vast area of mere "opinion."[54] Skeptical British empiricism may thus be considered a position favorable to maintaining the status quo created in 1688.

In France, however, empiricism was construed as "sensationism" which makes ideas the direct *reflection* of sensation—a mantra repeated throughout the century from Voltaire, to D'Alembert, to Condorcet, and usually associated with the watchmaker God of deism. Others, however, such as the radicals Helvetius and D'Holbach pushed sensationism to outright materialism and atheism. Yet all varieties of sensationism emphasized the *extent* and certitude of our knowledge, and so transformed empiricism into an ideology of activism and change. Indeed, sensationism clearly implied that if we can control or engineer the stimuli coming to the mind from the outside world of nature, or more pertinently of society, we can change the inner man. This "environmentalism" at least means that *les lumières* aim to remold mankind through education, and ultimately remaking him through the building of new institutions.

Philosophy, then, was not understanding for its own sake, but understanding in order to change the world: it was doctrine for living. Indeed, this new "philosophy," though nominally hostile to a priori innate ideas, psychologically had much in common with the rationalistic spirit of an allegedly superseded Cartesian, which also sought to comprehend the totality of reality. It may also be noted that the dogmatic quality of French empiricism perhaps might well owe something to the spirit of French Catholicism: almost all the *philosophes* had been educated in Jesuit colleges, and even such an atheist as Diderot had once been a seminarian.

Nevertheless, there are significant nuances within this common epistemology.[55] It was soberly comparativist and moderate with the Anglophile Montesquieu. It became militantly irreligious with Voltaire, who moreover oscillated politically between Anglophilia and enlightened despotism—and all the while quite unmindful that "crushing the infamous thing" (the Catholic Church) could only produce a monumental social upheaval. It became technological, social, and economic (and methodologically rather scientistic) with the Encyclopedia of Diderot. Finally, with the radical democrat Rousseau, sensation was transmuted into sentiment ("I had feelings before I had ideas"). In consequence, Voltaire's good society is founded on natural religion, his "voice of conscience" sounds very much like the Puritan Saints' "inner light," and his General Will has an aura of theology.

As of 1774 these accumulated strains of philosophy coexisted and intermingled without ever producing a dominant Enlightenment doctrine. There was nothing like what Marxism was in the radicalism of the late nineteenth and twentieth centuries. These strains also coexisted, often in the same person, with a devout Gallican Catholicism or a pious Jansenism, and whether among great nobles such as Lally-Tolendal and Lafayette or ordinary clerics such as the abbés Sieyès and Grégoire. Thus, though *les lumières* contributed no doctrine or set of principles to 1789, it did generate a "climate of opinion," a common discourse of public affairs, which all the future actors of 1789 had been imbibing since at least 1770. The sensationist philosophical perspective, progress, the sovereignty of law, the nation as the basis of the polity, natural law, and reason were the very air the literate classes breathed; they would inevitably resort to its precepts once the action began in 1789. Indeed, in the two decades before 1789, enlightened culture descended rapidly to the less literate strata of society through the massive dissemination and popularization of the great corpus created between Montesquieu's *The Spirit of the Laws* in 1748 and the completion of the Encyclopedia in 1771.[56]

This forward-looking way of perceiving the Revolution contributed mightily to its radicalization. First, it helped bring the process of constitutional and social change fully out into the open, and hence made it more swift and thorough. Even more, it made it possible to go beyond the English challenge to divine-right kingship or apostolic episcopal authority merely as false, "Babylonish" sacred ordinations, while keeping the notion of the sacred itself but transferring it to the

Commonwealth of the "saints under God." For the rationalistic envelope of the French upheaval denied the notion of the sacred per se in the political and social world. And once one denies the notion of the sacred—that is, of the inviolable, of that which is by essence beyond human will and power—then there remains no earthly constraint on change, either. One can "overturn" whatever one wants, if only one has the means, the will, and the power. (This violation of the immemorially inviolable was precisely what Burke so feared, and Marx so admired, in the French Revolution, in the way that Right and Left have felt about it ever since.)

Not all was in crisis, however, in the Old Regime's last century. One of the reasons the enlightened opposition could be so optimistic about progress was that the age was in fact a time of visible terrestrial improvement. Ever since the general European internal strife of the 1640–1650s, all the major states had enjoyed civil peace and public order. What is more, France in particular experienced exceptional economic and demographic growth. The seventeenth century, except for Holland, and, at the century's end, England, had been a period of depression, or at least stagnation, in most of Europe. France had been especially hard hit in the last years of Louis XIV. By contrast, the eighteenth century virtually everywhere saw the most rapid economic expansion since the thirteenth century. Indeed, the eighteenth century was the beginning of that sustained economic growth, which is one of the defining characteristics of what we mean by "modernity." In France, this growth was spectacular from 1715 until 1774, when fifteen years of relative crisis ensued. The Revolution thus broke out at a conjuncture of surging long-term prosperity and cultural optimism with temporary social distress.

THE OUTBREAK

The deluge began when the burden of debt the monarchy had incurred during the American War of Independence put it on the verge of bankruptcy; in the now complex economy of the late eighteenth century, default was not an option since it would foreclose future credit. In 1787, therefore, the king was forced to convene an Assembly of Notables, composed of great nobles and prelates, a body that had last met in 1626. Its members, however, refused to accept new taxes without reform, thus leaving the Estates General as the only alternative. The two privileged orders fondly expected to dominate the Estates and so obtain co-sovereignty with the monarchy—Lefebvre's 1787–1788 aristocratic revolution, or what is more usually called the "pre-revolution."[57]

At the end of 1788, the monarchy's accession to this demand brought the de facto collapse of royal authority—as with Charles I's acceptance of a new Parliament in 1640. In the ensuing agitation, spokesmen for the Third Estate, most famously the abbé Sieyès, declared that their order was in fact the "nation," and so demanded that in the forthcoming assembly the Commons (as they now said) should have the same number of deputies as the first two estates combined, and that the assembly should vote by head, not by order. The king conceded double representation, but the Parliament made nonsense of this by ruling that the ancient constitution required the vote by order.

When the Estates General convened in May 1789, therefore, the Third, supported by lesser clergy from the First, illegally forced the fusion of the three into a single body rebaptized the National Assembly. Unlike the Long Parliament in 1640, however, this body explicitly claimed constituent functions and immediately set to work. Thus began the deluge, the torrent, the cascade of events that we call the Revolution. The current ran with increasing acceleration until 1794.

This revolutionary core breaks down in two basic phases that we have already seen: 1789–1791 and 1792–1794; that is, constitutional monarchy and Jacobin Republic. Within these two main phases there were a number of secondary phases as the rush of change and the accompanying ideological intoxication escalated from the moderate constitutional monarchists, Mirabeau and Lafayette, to their more radical successors, Barnave and Lameth, to the moderate republicans, Brissot and Condorcet, to the ultra republicans, Danton and Robespierre (and with several subcurrents within each secondary unit).

Nonetheless, all the crucial decisions of the overall process were made between May and December 1789. The first was the transformation of the Estates into a National Assembly with constituent functions, in which a "patriot" party undertook to speak in terms of the whole "nation." The second was the defeat of the royal counterattack by the storming of the Bastille and the formation of the first Paris Commune and a municipal National Guard as permanent counterpowers to the monarchy. The third was the clean sweep of fundamental Old Regime institutions—feudal dues, noble status, and the estates system as such—on the night of August 4, an avalanche triggered, but not caused, by the Great Fear of late July. (The Old Regime had already been doomed by the king's capitulation in June and the fall of the Bastille in mid-July.) The end of the Old Regime in 1789 was decided in Versailles and in Paris, not in the countryside, and the Revolution's course thereafter was determined in the cities. Once the peasantry had got the main thing it really cared about, the abolition of feudal dues, it dropped out of the revolutionary dynamic, to come back only as the foot soldiers of the Republic's and Bonaparte's crusade across Europe.

In the wake of August 4 the essential constitutional decisions were taken. The Declaration of the Rights of Man and the Citizen was framed and voted before making the constitution. The drive of the *Monarchiens* for a British- and American-style bicameral Parliament and real royal, executive veto power was quickly defeated in favor of a single sovereign representative body. The royal executive was now created by the constitution (even though it paradoxically remained hereditary), not by history and/or God. Finally, in ominous contradiction to the universalistic principles of the Declaration, a property suffrage was established. When the king withheld his signature from the Declaration and the decrees of August 4, he was coerced more massively than in July. On October 5 and 6, a march on Versailles by Paris women, accompanied by Lafayette, took the royal family back to Paris, where they henceforth would in effect be the prisoners of the Revolution.

The final decision of the year was taken almost as an afterthought when, in a December motion by Bishop Talleyrand, the church's property was "placed at the disposition of the nation" to pay the royal debt. Though not intended as an attack on the First Estate, and still less on religion, this provision contained the germ of the Civil Constitution of the Clergy, actually voted early the next year, which by 1793 would split the nation in two. Indeed, the accumulative decisions of 1789 contain the seeds of all the future political divisions within the Revolution, as well as the of its mounting ideological intoxication.

THE REVOLUTION'S COURSE

At first glance, however, the balance sheet of 1789–1791 appears overwhelmingly positive. After all, the replacement of royal absolutism by constitutional government, and hereditary privilege by the equality of all citizens before the law, clearly represents progress. The same is true of the Constituent Assembly's administrative reforms: the replacement of the centuries-old clutter of overlapping and at times contradictory regional jurisdictions by eighty-three uniform departments and appropriate subunits, the abolition of internal tariffs, differing weights and measures, and unequal rates of taxation. Civil disabilities were removed from Protestants and Jews, and the nation's differing legal systems were simplified and standardized (though this process was not completed until the Code Napoleon of 1810). Finally, in a parting gesture, in June 1791 the Assembly voted its most distinctly "bourgeois" measure, the loi Le Chapelier outlawing all artisan guilds and associations as archaic restraints on free trade. But was this measure, though clearly welcome to entrepreneurs of the day, so quintessentially bourgeois? Turgot had done as much in 1774, only to be overruled later by his king, and Catherine the Great of Russia, as early as 1765, had begun promoting laissez-faire principles with the Free Economic Society. Free trade was not just a bourgeois convenience; it was part of the rationalization of life in movement everywhere at the time. Its ultimate symbol was, of course, the metric system, introduced in 1792 though prepared earlier: applicable as it was to the entire universe, this represented the very essence of modernity.

To be sure, this "modernity" was not complete. A property suffrage separated citizens into "active" and "passive" categories; the emancipation of slaves in France's Caribbean colonies was refused; and universal primary instruction, though contemplated, was not introduced. (Equal status for women was not on the reform agenda anywhere at the time.) As if to recognize that democratization must be a continuing, even open-ended process, the seating arrangements in the Assembly had for the first time produced the modern distinction between "left" and "right." Still, the Constituent Assembly's work created conditions that were distinctly more "modern" than existed in any country, including the American Republic.

In fact, in 1790–1791 the overwhelming majority of the population approved the new order. In 1790 the first anniversary of the storming of the Bastille was celebrated by an elaborate "Feast of the Federation." National Guards had sprung up across the country, causing some fear for national unity, so the National Assembly now undertook to "federate" them in the capital. In the presence of the royal family and 200,000 people, Talleyrand celebrated Mass on the altar of the *patrie*, Lafayette read the civic oath, and the king swore to it. Internationally, enthusiasm was just as widespread. Jefferson, who had witnessed most of the great year, ardently defended its results on his return home, and Tom Paine wrote a vehement answer to Burke's sour judgment. The twenty-year-old Wordsworth then felt "Bliss was it in that dawn to be alive, but to be young was very heaven," while the aged Kant felt that humanity had at last "matured."[58]

Indeed, the Revolution seemed to have stabilized so well that it could afford to repress an emerging left opposition. Thus, in July 1791, when republicans staged a tumultuous protest against the monarchy, the commander of the National Guard, Lafayette, raised the red flag of martial law and put them down at the cost of thirty lives. With this the then-dominant Feuillants, or moderate constitutional monarchists, thought that they had "ended the Revolution," a slogan which each successive governing group would adopt in turn. In fact, however, the Revolution was only moving toward high gear. And the red flag, defiantly adopted by the radicals, though little used at the time, was not forgotten and would reappear in 1848.

By 1792, however, the new order created by 1789 had collapsed; and the roots of the collapse lay in the foundational year itself. The first of these flaws was the Civil Constitution of the Clergy, made necessary by the confiscation of church property decided in principle in December 1789. Quite independently of the question of the national debt, there clearly was a problem with the institutional position of the church as of that date. It still possessed some 10 percent of the national wealth, and even though it also still handled most of what now would be called social services, this was clearly a situation that could not endure. The solution adopted, however, was far more drastic and brutal than most of society would support. Finally voted in the spring of 1790, the Civil Constitution provided for the rationalization of the church according to the same principles as governed the new polity. The number and boundaries of the diocese were to be the same as for the eighty-three departments, and both priests and bishops were to be elected by the population at large, including non-Catholics, and the clergy accordingly became the salaried civil servants of the state. Although quite unprecedented in church history, these arrangements were not intended as anti-Christian measures. They were rather the product of monumental insensitivity to the religious dispositions of the nation. The archbishop of Paris, for want of any feasible alternative, advised the king to sign. The pope, for fear of a schism, hesitated to take a position, condemning the law only at the end of the year. In the meantime, implementation had begun, and so schism quickly followed with only a minority of the clergy accepting the "Constitutional Church."

The second flaw was organically related to the first. For the king, like Charles I in 1640, never accepted his new role, and without a willing king, failure of the constitutional monarchy was only a question of time. Already in July 1789 Louis had written his Bourbon "cousin of Spain," protesting that all his future actions must be considered coerced. This silent refusal was deepened when in 1791 he concluded that his signature on the Civil Constitution of the Clergy violated his Christian conscience and his coronation oath. Moreover, after the fall of the Bastille, a growing stream of émigrés seeking foreign support offered a potential base for a royal *revanche*. Suspicions of such treason was confirmed by the royal family's attempt to flee the kingdom in April 1791, stopped only in extremis at Varenne. Although the king was restored to office, the fiction of his "abduction" was too transparent to survive for long.

Beginning in 1789, therefore, royal and noble resistance fueled belief in an "aristocratic plot" against the Revolution, a syndrome that would henceforth drive its constant radicalization. This process was accelerated when the clergy, as civil servants, were obliged to take an oath of loyalty to the new regime and the Civil Constitution. So the majority of "refractory" or "non-juring" priests was added to the list of aristocratic enemies of the people.

These tensions were heightened by the declaration of war against Austria in April 1792. The war had first been advocated by the Girondists seeking to give the

Revolution new dynamism by turning it into a crusade against Old Regime Europe as a whole. War was also desired by the king, who seemed to hope for a defeat that would bring his liberation and the Revolution's collapse. And indeed, when the country was invaded, a demoralized noble officer corps performed poorly. The sense of danger increased when the "hero of two worlds" and Washington's comrade in arms, General Lafayette, abandoned his command and went over to the Austrians. The Revolution now was clearly menaced by an international-cum-internal Old Regime plot.

Under such circumstances, the untrustworthy king had to go, and so the Jacobins—Gironde and future Mountain together—used the sans-culottes to overthrow him. This was engineered through a new, "insurrectionary" Paris Commune on August 10, which placed the king under arrest for treason. And, what is less often noted, the new constitutional "sovereign," the Legislative Assembly, was also undone. On September 12 that body accordingly provided for its own demise by proclaiming France a Republic. Elections, by universal suffrage, were swiftly held for a Convention to draft a new constitution. All these decisions were accompanied by the Revolution's first, "spontaneous" Terror, the "September Massacres"—which were at least allowed to happen by the conspicuous inaction of the provisional government's justice minister, Danton. Under such conditions, only committed republicans dared vote, and the Convention was elected by only 10 percent of the population, far fewer than the proportion that had chosen the Estates General in 1789.

In January 1793, the trial and execution of the king marked the beginning of the split within the Jacobins, between the vacillating Girondists and the intransigent Mountain. The military situation at the front worsened, as England joined Austria and Prussia in the anti-Revolutionary coalition. Even more seriously, internal revolts mushroomed, first in the peasant Vendée and then in the "federalist," or Girondist, strongholds of Lyon and Marseilles. In answer, on May 31-June 2, therefore, the Paris Commune and the sans-culottes surrounded the Convention with cannon and purged it of its Girondist deputies. In the summer of 1793, under the watchword *la patrie en danger*, the *levée en masse* was decreed to raise an army of a million men.

The result, by September, was the establishment of a revolutionary dictatorship of the twelve-member Committee of Public Safety. The forty-eight Paris "sections," and the capital's "revolutionary societies," were in virtually continuous session in white-heat mobilization against the now universal "counterrevolutionary plot." The new Revolutionary Tribunal now functioned relentlessly, and *représentants en mission*, with full powers to act, were dispatched to the provinces to recover recalcitrant regions.

In September also, a Maximum, or price controls, was voted as a concession by the economic liberals of the Mountain to their sans-culottes allies. Indeed, the economic policies of the Revolution had largely been a failure: Confiscated Church property had been used to issue paper *assignats* with which to pay off the national debt, while the property itself was auctioned off too rapidly by a desperate government, therefore going at prices below its real worth. The economy was also disrupted by peasant resistance to redeeming feudal dues, and so in 1793 these were abolished without compensation. At the same time, the expedient of using the assignats as currency generated an accelerating inflation. Times were clearly harder than at the end of the Old Regime.

In these straitened circumstances, Danton and the less militant Jacobins began to fade from power. Concurrently, the thirty-two-year-old Robespierre and his two lieutenants, the twenty-seven-year-old Saint-Just and Couthon became the dominant figures of the Committee of Public Safety. Yet on their left, the Revolution, under pressure from the Commune and its leader Hébert, together with other *Enragés*, moved beyond the Civil Constitution to active dechristianization.

By the end of the year, the political leadership of Robespierre, in galvanizing the Convention and the organizational talents of Lazare Carnot in building and equipping the new mass army, had ended the perilous circumstances of the Republic's heroic year. By December the Coalition had been repulsed on all fronts and the internal revolts put down. Nevertheless, the Terror continued, indeed intensified, through the first six months of 1794. This brings us to the great mystery of the Revolution: why this final surge of delirium?

As an introduction to this crescendo, in a crisis of penury and under sans-culottes pressure, in March the Convention decreed the "nationalization" and redistribution of émigré property. Although later hailed by radical historians as an anticipation of socialism, these "decrees of Ventose" were in fact of a piece with the Maximum of September 1793, that is, an emergency wartime measure. Even so, this was the peak of the lower classes' pressure for state regulation of the economy. And indeed, throughout the Revolution, but especially during the Terror, the possessing classes lived in constant fear of a *loi agraire*, or the imitation of the land redistribution of the Gracchi's *lex agraria* of 133 B.C.—though such a measure was at no time contemplated, let alone attempted.

As if to drive this point home, in March also the spokesmen for popular radicalism, Hébert and the ultras of the Commune were guillotined for treason. As a counterweight to this, in April Danton and the "Indulgents," under suspicion of seeking a deal for peace with the Coalition, followed them to the scaffold. The Revolution, after eliminating Lafayette, Barnave, and the Girondins, was now devouring its last generation of children. From April to July the Revolutionary government and the Terror were the near dictatorship of Robespierre and his two close colleagues (he still had to have a majority in the Convention). Terror had become a kind of cultic purgation of society in the name of republican purity, virtue, and unity. Some twenty thousand were executed in the Terror, nearly fourteen hundred in the last two months of June-July 1794.[59]

Clearly, "circumstances" cannot account for these extraordinary events. Only the "plot thesis" will do, and this on the condition that the activist minority is understood not as any social, economic, or other interest group, but as a community of ideological intoxication. Once again, the framework for this final escalation of revolutionary fever had been put in place in the foundational first year. For the recurrent bouts of panic generated as each forward step of the Revolution constantly generated new conspiratorial enemies—from émigré aristocrats to refractory priests—had produced increasingly stringent laws defining enemies and "suspects."[60]

So what was the Jacobins' ideology? Their ideal was a society of small, individual property holders: no one should have too much wealth, for riches inevitably breed corruption.[61] Moreover, this society was dedicated to a cult of civic virtue, that is, it was to live in a state of permanent mobilization against aristocracy, privilege, and the revanche of the corrupt past. After all, most of the recently emancipated citizens were products of that corruption.

They are thus similar to what the Calvinists had earlier called the reprobate. Virtue therefore meant the inner emancipation of the population from past corruption through constant civic activism. The emancipated, the true citizens, moreover, are a minority. They are, as it were, the elect of the modern age, the only true republicans. The elects' purging of the reprobate, consequently, is not an offense against liberty; it is the only guarantee that liberty will survive and triumph. There is no great text or body of explicit theory underlying this worldview, of the sort that Marxism and Leninism later gave to revolutionary socialism. The nearest thing to such a body of theory is the works of Rousseau, which offer more a set of egalitarian attitudes than an explicit ideology.

This was made explicit by Robespierre's last official act, the celebration of the Feast of the Supreme Being in June 1794. Before thousands of spectators an effigy of Atheism was burned in the Tuileries Gardens; the Incorruptible himself officiated, like some latter-day Savoyard Vicar, at this Mass of republican virtue.

The next month, the ideological spell was broken. Feeling he had become over-mighty, Robespierre's fellow Jacobins overthrew him in a parliamentary coup d'état on 9 Thermidor (July 27). They were able to succeed because, after putting down the Commune and the sans-culottes in the spring, Robespierre was without defense against a loss of parliamentary majority. But the Thermidorians had in no way intended to end the Terror, and still less to abandon the Jacobin program. It was public pressure after the coup that forced them to retreat. Within months the fever had gone out of the Revolution, and for good.

Defense of the Revolution now meant safeguarding the new interests it had created. In the first instance, this entailed perpetuating the power of the Thermidorian Jacobins. Accordingly, they set aside the ultra-democratic Constitution of 1793 and tried to stabilize the Revolution's conquests with a new constitutional device, the Directory of 1795. This oligarchic expedient in fact reversed all the sacrosanct principles of the Republic, for it introduced a stringent property suffrage, two chambers, and a five-man collective executive. The constitution stipulated further that two-thirds of the members of the new legislature should be former members of the Convention. In short, the Directory of 1795–1799 was a minority government of former regicides fending off, successively, royalist resurgence on its right and answering neo-Jacobin resurgence on its left. On three occasions in four years the directors called in army units either to put down the street or to purge duly elected but politically hostile deputies.

Socially, the Directory represents a phase of the Revolution that may be appropriately described as "bourgeois." Its tenure brought the ostentatious display of new wealth deriving from the sale of *biens nationaux* or from war industries, a display all the more provocative for coming at a time of economic distress aggravated by continuing inflation. It is in this atmosphere that there appeared the first clear anticipation of modern socialism and Communism in the Conspiracy of the Equals of Gracchus Babeuf, of which more must be said later.

The main business of the Directory, however, was war. Once the emergency of 1793 had been surmounted, the Republic embarked on a career of relentless conquest that would continue until 1812. What began as an effort to repel the invader, after 1795 became a Jacobin crusade against the kings of Europe. The Directory created sister republics with classical names from Batavian Holland to Cisalpine Lombardy to Parthenopeon Naples, while at the same time establishing France's own "natural" frontier on the Rhine. This expansion did indeed have a strong ideological component: the "Carmagnole," long since forgotten in Paris, continued to be sung by the troops. But glory also brought with it tribute and plunder to keep the fragile government afloat financially. What the directors noted only belatedly was that dependence on the military to keep a majority at home and to garner glory and pelf abroad made it vulnerable to the ambitions of a successful general. The twenty-seven-year-old Bonaparte turned out to be the lucky man. On 18 Brumaire (November 10), one of the directors, Sieyès, organized a parliamentary coup to put him at the head of a dictatorial Consulate as the only way both to end the Revolution and to stabilize it.

THE AFTERSHOCKS

And the ideological phase of the Revolution was indeed over, but the results of the process begun in 1789 had hardly been stabilized. As we have seen, the process that began in England in 1640 did not end until the aftershock of 1688, and its results were not definitively consolidated until 1715. In France, where the initial shock of 1789 had been much more severe than the shock of 1640 in England, the number of aftershocks was correspondingly greater and consolidation was therefore achieved only under the Third Republic in the 1870s—a near century as opposed to half of one.

Moreover, in England the revolutionary outcome could be stabilized with a much lower coefficient of structural change than in France. The leap from medieval mixed monarchy to modern mixed monarchy, and a narrowly oligarchic one at that, is not comparable to the quantum leap from high royal absolutism to a universal suffrage republic. The results of the French Revolution could only be consolidated at that pure form of political modernity. To be sure, the crucial, irreversible changes made by the French Revolution were decided in the first year, just as the crucial changes made by the English Revolution were decided in its first year. To be sure also, the changes made in 1789 contained in germ the universal suffrage Republic of 1792: an already neutered monarchy and the principle of comprehensive citizenship made the universal suffrage Republic a likely, indeed logical, culmination of the new order. This fact, together with the heroic struggles attending the First Republic's birth, made the Jacobin myth inseparable from the revolutionary myth overall, and so determined the point at which the heritage of 1789 itself could at last be stabilized. (The Commonwealth of the Saints, on the other hand, is not a marketable ideal for the modern age.) Jacobinism further meant strict *laïcité*, that is, complete separation of church and state; and if this is taken into account, then the terminal date would be 1905 and the separation of church and state.

Such a comprehensive agenda hence required, not two, but four aftershocks to achieve consolidation. The Revolution's man on horseback, Bonaparte, of course temporarily stabilized the Revolution's results; but he failed to consolidate them because he did not know when to stop riding. Cromwell had been halted by the maritime frontiers of the British Isles (and the range of naval power to conquer Jamaica). Napoleon had no comparable geographic limits to the range of his ambition. So in 1814, defeat deposed him.

France then lived through a replay of its whole prior revolutionary experience. From 1814 to 1830 there was a "hard" Restoration in a simulacrum of the Old Regime.[62] From 1830 to 1848 there was a more enduring version of the constitutional monarchy of 1791. From 1848 to 1851 there was a simulacrum of the First Republic, and from 1851 to 1870 of the Napoleonic Empire. Only after 1870 was it possible to create an enduring republic, in part because the country had now run out of alternatives, in part because this Republic began its career by definitively repressing the Parisian plebs, and in part because the monarchists, who until 1876 had a majority in the country, could not unify behind a single Bourbon pretender. So, for the first time France produced a durable democratic order in nonideological, ad hoc, almost British manner, and with no comprehensive constitutional document. Furthermore, though the new order made a cult of universal suffrage, it also had a quite un-Jacobin upper house.

COMPARISONS WITH 1640–1688

The principal differences between the revolutions in England and France have already been noted. First, 1640 and its consequences were lived and thought as restoration, not innovation, and this constituted a built-in limit on radicalization; by contrast, 1789 and its sequel were experienced as deliberate revolutionary "regeneration," and hence were open-ended in their radicalism. Second, the ideological envelope of the English events was religious and supernatural in orientation; the ideological inspiration of the French events was secular and resolutely this-worldly, circumstances that reinforced the two revolutions' different perspectives on time.

Another radicalizing factor in the French case was the exceptional backlog of things to be overthrown. It has already been mentioned that Calvinism's failure left France with ecclesiastical structures, a level of clerical wealth, and a dogmatic culture not far removed from sixteenth-century conditions, indeed reinforced by the Tridentine Counter-Reformation, and the Jansenist counter-Counter-Reformation had complicated this heritage without lightening its weight. It has also been noted that modern state formation had been the work of royal absolutism and achieved at the expense of all "intermediate bodies." A second round of state formation was thus necessary to give civil society a genuinely modern, that is, participatory role. This could only be the more wrenching since absolutist centralization had not penetrated very deeply into the body politic, in fact leaving intact a network of now archaic and obstructionist local institutions. Moreover, piecemeal reform of such a cumbersome structure had patently failed during absolutism's descending eighteenth-century curve, the fate of the Maupeou parlements and of Turgot being of course the prime examples.

This accumulation of problems and failures by 1789 confronted the country with a veritable logjam of necessary and urgent institutional changes. And when long-building logjams break at last, they unleash a deluge—the torrential radicalization that has already been traced. Surely, the raw hydrodynamics of the Revolution was one of the reasons it swept along so many and cut so deep in the body politic, while at the same time destroying so much and leaving such scars that France took a century to heal.

Another factor of radicalization was the tight fabric of the French "hard" Old Regime, as opposed to its British cousin, and the total absence of such an order across the Atlantic. Although both French and British polities were sacred orders in which monarchy, church, and aristocracy were interlinked and interdependent, this was articulated more starkly in France.[63] There the king was at the same time *évêque du dehors*, or outside bishop, and first gentleman, or chief noble, of the realm. In other words, all three components of the system stood or fell together. Thus, fusing the First and Second Estates with the Third in June 1789 automatically made the monarchy a phantom, and so also transferred the fullness of his sacred sovereignty to the now sovereign and sacred Nation. The English estates system of the seventeenth century, in contrast, started with the loose formula of lords spiritual, lords temporal, and commons; under the Stuarts it became, more simply still, king, lords, and commons. Moreover, since lords and commons together, or Parliament, made revolution against the king—but only to bring him to reason—the system as a whole was not desacralized. And when Parliament itself was abolished under the Commonwealth, in a still religious society, the new order was overwhelmingly rejected and the Restoration came, as it were, by acclamation. The result was a diluted modernity, that is, the reality of society's (or at least its elite's) co-sovereignty with the Crown, and thus the framework for a gradual transition to a fuller modernity when the temper of the country required it.

In consequence, the tempo of action in France was much more rapid than in England. There was considerably more civil (as opposed to military) violence, that is, a Terror. And there was more socioeconomic disruption and/or transformation—confiscation of property, steady inflation, economic crisis, and material want.

This meant that in France the political and social questions were for the first time fused into one, and it was therefore impossible to settle either separately. In order to subordinate the monarchy to society, it was also necessary to destroy the estate system, to fuse all "citizens" into a single nation, on a footing of equality. The French Revolution, consequently, was directed simultaneously against *l'arbitraire* and *le privilège*, against *le despotisme* and *l'aristocratie*. Conversely, the Revolution had to be made simultaneously for liberty *and* equality.

In other words, it had to be both a political and a social revolution at once (for under an eighteenth-century Old Regime, when the majority of the population was illiterate, raising the question of political democracy and universal suffrage was to raise the most momentous social question).

But the French Revolution was even more than this. For if the clergy decided —as the majority of them did—that they could not abjure a sacred king or accept an oath of allegiance (i.e., subordination) to the purely secular authority of the nation, moreover against the express spiritual command of the pope, then they too had to go the way of the "tyrant" and the "aristocrats." Thus the Revolution came to mean the proscription of the church and ultimately the dechristianiza-tion of the nation, together with the replacement of religion, of whatever form, by the cult of reason or an impersonal supreme being.

Thus the outer limits of conceivable change in the two cases were quite dif-ferent. In the English case, the outer limit was the universal suffrage republic of the Levellers. (The proto-socialism of the Diggers has been greatly exagger-ated by twentieth-century radicals searching for ancestors; it played no signifi-cant role at the time.) And this outer limit of the 1650s of course became the culminating program of the French Revolution. In the intermediate American case, the Commonwealth, organically rejected in England, took firm root in its colonies. However, it did so without the French corollary of universal suffrage, which was never an issue in the upheaval of the 1770s. Thus, the unfulfilled outer limit in France was constituted by the most extreme demands of the crisis year, 1793: the "socializing" decrees of Ventose and the dechristianization of the Hébertists in the fall. Indeed, three years later, in reaction against the Thermi-dorian response, Gracchus Babeuf rounded off this proto-socialism with a sketch of the dictatorship of the proletariat.

Even without this intimation of 1917, however, the fruits of 1789 were a full-blown, militant modernity. Sovereignty and sacrality had been compressed into a single entity, with a unitary general will—the Nation or the People, one and indivisible.

ATLANTIC REVOLUTIONS COMPARED

The consolidation of the French republican tradition after 1870 brings us to the end of the series of revolutions that established durable new orders, regimes, and myths that are still present in the world today. All later, twentieth-century revolutions, as has already been noted, are no longer real forces in the world, though the hulks of the regimes they created still clutter the landscape. By con-trast, the legacies of what may be called the Atlantic revolutions have now been fused to create what after 1989 came to be called "market democracy." (In the nineteenth century it went without saying that any democratic polity, indeed any functioning society, had a market. The label "market democracy" was produced by the collapse of Soviet planning in the 1980s, and until then the non-Soviet world was called "the industrial democracies.")

How, then, do these Atlantic revolutions compare in their outcomes? Are they separate and distinct, or perhaps even antithetical: claims are often made that some revolutions are "better" than others,[64] with America, of course, usually getting the highest grade. Or do they add up to an Atlantic revolutionary process overall, a cumulative unfolding of modernity during the century from 1688 to 1789?[65]

Let us begin with the median case, 1776. Despite the American Declaration of Independence's ringing evocation of the divine dispensation of equality, that value was not in fact central to the Revolution's unfolding. The Revolution's great theme, rather, was liberty, as denoted by the Liberty Bell totem enshrined in Philadelphia's Independence Hall and Patrick Henry's bold declaration of 1775, "Give me liberty or give me death!" Such liberty meant, first of all, individual liberty as the historical birthright of Englishmen allegedly guaranteed since Magna Carta, a liberty then menaced by British royal tyranny; and second, it meant national independence from the now equally odious tyranny of Parliament, the two kinds of freedom being summed up in the slogan "no taxation without representation." Equality was not placed on the same level as liberty in the American canon until the Civil War and Lincoln's Gettysburg Address, in which the great president undertook to revise the meaning of the Founders' Declaration;[66] and even then the slogan of "equality" never acquired the same stirring resonance as "liberty."

Equality first acquired top status, in fact preeminence, with the French Revolution, whose founding Declaration began: "les hommes naissent libres et égaux en droits." Indeed, equality was the driving passion of the French Revolution throughout. We have already seen the origins of this crucial difference between the late eighteenth century's "sister revolutions."[67] It was determined not by *who* was rebelling, a merchant and planter elite in America versus sans-culottes and peasants in France, for in fact the leaders and the ideologues of the French Revolution were very much from the elite, even into its extremist phase; and in both cases, the most prominent spokesmen were lawyers or journalists. The explanation lies, rather, in *what* the American and French elites were rebelling against. Elites, after all, are not normally stridently egalitarian.

In the American case, the "patriot" elite was not rebelling against a higher social layer, but against an overseas political authority. The French "patriot" elite,

by contrast, was revolting against a legally privileged social stratum, the hereditary nobility, indeed against the whole starkly hierarchical estate system.[68] Hence,
under the specific conditions of the French Old Regime, the wealthy and educated upper echelons of the Third Estate had every incentive to demand equality
with the kindred higher nobility, for the two shared a common social and cultural status. They were in fact an incipient class of what after the Revolution
would be called *les notables;* and both elite groups were quite different from
the petty nobles and the petty bourgeois in their respective orders. Hence, the
French bourgeois "patriots" did not so much rise up against the nobility as such
as against the invidious *principle* of *noblesse,* the humiliating *legal* distinction between a "well-born" aristocracy and the "base" commoners, *la roture.* Thus the
French Revolution was driven by the paradox of a privileged elite overturning
the existing order in the name of equality and "the people," and mobilizing for
this purpose the more primitive fury of the really excluded, the sans-culottes.

In order to break into the establishment, they had to smash all existing structures and create an entire new order capable of accommodating them in dignity,
indeed in preeminence. In so doing, however, they created a new, equally invidious and humiliating division in society—between the rich and the poor, the
bourgeoisie and "the people," *le bas peuple.* Indeed, this new division would generate the driving *ressentiment* of the New Regime of the nineteenth century.

How do these comparisons relate to the English case? In England, the parliamentary opposition to the Crown and the Puritan opposition to the established Anglican church were not about equality at all. Rather it was about liberty,
though not in the American sense. Rather, the freedom in question referred primarily to institutions, not to individuals. The historic rights of Englishmen, of
course, were considered sacred; but they did not have to be created through revolutionary struggle. They were deemed to be adequately guaranteed by the existing common law allegedly going back to Magna Carta; in the present, they only
had to be freed from the tyranny of the new royal "prerogative," something that
was done in the first session of the Long Parliament. After that, the struggle for
liberty meant the struggle for the liberties—indeed the existence—of Parliament
as a body vis-à-vis the Crown. Nor did the English consider monarchy as such to
be tyrannical, as the French came to believe in the course of their Revolution.
In religious matters likewise, the English Revolution (or as men said at the time,
"the cause") meant the struggle for an elective yet oligarchic organization of the
church (Presbyterianism) or elective and congregational organization (Independency). At the margins, the struggle of both groups meant freedom of individual
conscience, the logical conclusion of which was religious toleration. But toleration was demanded for what in the eighteenth century came to be called "de-

nominations" more than for individuals. These confessional "freedoms," finally, applied only to the minority of the elect, not to humanity in general, the vast majority of whom were held to be reprobate. Thus in the English struggle there is no element of universalism—that is, rights, whether political or religious, that would apply, even only potentially, to all humankind. All rights—liberties, privileges, or franchises—were historical and distinctively English, because they had been fought for and won only by Englishmen. Thus, the English Bill of Rights, voted in 1689, is a bill of the rights of Parliament, not of the king's various subjects.

The Americans, by contrast, when they appended a Bill of Rights to their Constitution, expanded on the general principles of the Declaration of Independence to give rights valid for all citizens as individuals and for whatever voluntary associations, both religious and political, that they might form. Hence, it carried a quotient of universalism far higher than its more archaic British counterpart. Even so, the expanded American rights concerned specific things the state, and the federal state *only*, could or could not do under a particular national constitution.

The process of abstraction and universalizing rights reached its culmination in the French Revolution. Although the Declaration of the Rights of Man and the Citizen was attached to a given national constitution, as in the American case, it was not presented as an appendage. Rather, it was drafted prior to deliberations on the document itself and presented as a preamble annunciating the fundamental principles in terms of which the nation should be governed. The French thus made the concept of right absolute and universal by framing their declaration of rights as the Rights of Man, and thus implicitly valid for all places and all times. The Declaration of 1789, moreover, has appeared as the preamble of almost all of France's subsequent eleven constitutions, and is still there to this day.

Given this mixture of ideological constancy and institutional variability, Anglo-Saxon critics (beginning with Thomas Jefferson's objections to Lafayette in 1789) have replied that it is better to build from the particular and the concrete to the abstract and the universal rather than the other way around. The consensus of world opinion is against such critics, however. In 1948 the United Nations adopted a Universal Declaration of Human Rights, drafted by an international commission chaired by Eleanor Roosevelt, in which the French and the American perspectives were synthesized; and in 2000 the fledgling European Union adopted a Charter of Fundamental Rights under which European citizens, even in constitution-less Britain, can sue their respective governments. In modernity the criterion of universality, it seems, is the norm for human worth and dignity.

The last time this had been stated so comprehensively was in the religious form of the individual immortality of the soul, particularly its Christian version in which God became incarnate to redeem all humanity. To be sure, Christianity existed only in a restricted geographical area, seen moreover as surrounded by pagans and infidels. To be sure also, since the eleventh century (at the latest) it was divided between a Greek and Latin area, and after the sixteenth century the latter was in turn divided between Catholicism and various forms of Protestantism. Nonetheless, the principle of universality or catholicity had been asserted as foundational, and the unity of the species thus proclaimed *in potentia*. Indeed, the Four Articles of Prague may be considered the first fumbling effort to define rights, not in a particularistic feudal charter, but in religious terms, as specific rights of conscience: to hear the Word of God preached in Czech and to receive the sacraments in both kinds.

In other words, the series of European revolutions not only grew more radical from one outbreak to another, but the overall European revolutionary process itself was a cumulative one. Thus, the Hussite proto-revolution, while fought out basically in religious terms, in fact furthered an untheoreticized constitutionalism which adumbrated the next round of completed revolutions, in the Netherlands and England, though this filiation of course was not explicitly recognized. (Recall that the Lutheran Reformation was an incomplete revolution.) Next, the English Revolution, insofar as it was also a radical Reformation, drew on continental Calvinist theology and ecclesiology, including the political resistance theory of the French Wars of Religion. Just as obviously, the Americans took up where the English had left off, with the historic rights of Englishmen as formulated in 1688, and then generalized these in the language of natural law going back to the Stoics and medieval Christianity. Finally, the French, beginning where the Americans had left off, completed the process of universalization: human rights became ahistoric rational principles, founded moreover on pure popular sovereignty, and entailing a social corollary of equality.

So what could possibly come next? It could only be to take off from the eternally unfulfilled promise of equality, together with its even more elusive magnification in "fraternity," and to grasp at them in some ultimate and perfect revolution. The nineteenth century would call this Second Coming of 1789 "socialism." It would turn out to be the great theoretical project of the nineteenth century, and the great practical endeavor of the twentieth.

Part III

THE QUEST FOR
SOCIALIST REVOLUTION

9

From the First Modern Revolution to the First Anticipated Revolution, 1799–1848

The Nineteenth Century at a Glance

After 1789 there could never again be an innocent revolution. The rush of change begun in 1776 and brought to a climax in the years after the fall of the Bastille had for the first time revealed to the world that it was possible to reinvent the human condition. The secret was now out that history happens by revolutions, and the scenario of the modern liberation drama lay open for all the world to read. Henceforth, men could anticipate a more perfect reenactment, they could theorize about its nature and unfolding, and even organize to trigger its outbreak. The century 1815–1914 therefore lived in a culture of permanent revolutionary anticipation.

What is more, the American and French Revolutions had between them defined what the reinvented human condition would look like. Though differing notably in details, both affirmed that it must be a republic founded on liberal, egalitarian, and secular principles. The Americans arrived at this ideal the soft way, by simply turning their backs on the traditional European order: the French could come to it only the hard way, by demolishing a heritage going back, beyond two centuries of royal absolutism, to the world of the two swords and the three orders. But despite these differences, in the eyes of monarchical and aristocratic Europe the two cases correctly appeared as equally alien and subversive.

Even so, of the two models of liberation, the United States and France, it is the latter that was by far the more relevant for the future of the revolutionary idea. The American model was of course always here, off on the horizon, as an example to Europe of what a functioning republic might look like. Yet, this model carried with it no revolutionary tradition and so gave Europe, still largely under an Old Regime, little idea of how to liberate itself. The French example offered the rest of Europe a more pertinent message. Since its Republic had proved ephemeral, radical sentiment focused instead on the revolutionary action that had first produced that Republic and was once again necessary to retrieve it. The new age of anticipatory revolution therefore drew its inspiration essentially from the French tradition.

The long nineteenth-century revolutionary wait falls into two main periods. Broadly speaking, radical expectation was lyrical and Romantic before 1848 and positivist and "scientific" after that date. Before 1848, a new upheaval had constantly seemed imminent, and outbreaks were in fact frequent. And between them there was a continuing revolutionary movement, international in scope and sustained by a network of secret societies. During this period action was centered in Paris, the holy city of revolution to which men flocked from across the continent. For revolution was now a full-time profession for an international group of votaries, as Giuseppe Mazzini, Karl Marx, and Mikhail Bakunin strove to adapt the French model of liberation to the more backward regions of Europe.

Revolutionary practice in these years meant essentially armed insurrection and street barricades, a ritual of emancipation immortalized in Delacroix's 1830 painting of bare-breasted *Liberty Leading the People* and, for 1848, sentimentalized in Victor Hugo's *Les Misérables*. Indeed, these images still define "revolution" in the popular imagination. But these tactics burned themselves out in the failure of 1848 (to be given aesthetic burial in Flaubert's *Sentimental Education*), and their final flare-up, in the Paris Commune of 1871, was by then a hopeless anachronism. So after the disaster the revolutionary movement settled down for a long, more patient struggle.

Revolutionary anticipation was now institutionalized in the First and Second Internationals. Their emblematic moments were periodic multinational congresses, while the exuberant utopianism of the century's early years gave way to the rationalistic materialism of Marxism.[1] At the same time the revolution moved east, by the 1890s becoming a learned and increasingly parliamentary movement centered in recently united Germany, whose industrial preeminence had created Europe's mightiest workers' movement. Revolutionaries of the backward East, from Austria-Hungary, Poland, and Russia, no longer looked to Paris but to Berlin—not of course as a model of insurrection, for German Social Democracy was notoriously action-shy, but for guidance about Marxist theory and practice.

This unabated radical expectation notwithstanding, the nineteenth century was the first since the fifteenth *not* to produce a successful revolution. Most studies of "staseology" therefore omit 1848 from the canon of great revolutions, jumping directly from 1789 to 1917. Marx at the time called 1848 a "farce" as contrasted with the high "tragedy" of 1789. A. J. P. Taylor famously derided it as "a turning point in history when history failed to turn." To dismiss 1848 as pure failure, however, is to sell short an event of real importance.

To begin with, it was crucial for the modern revolutionary myth since it offered the first—and only—case of an all-European revolution. Although the events of 1848 were in the first instance a series of separate national revolutions, they also interacted with and reinforced each other to yield a general European conflagration. In the future, therefore, true revolution was expected to be international, bring salvation to all humanity. Accordingly, European socialism organized itself as an "International" and gave the same name to its hymn.

Ignoring 1848, moreover, is bad comparative method. Failed, stunted, or interrupted cases of historical phenomena are pertinent "controls" for more developed cases, as we have seen in the contrasted fates of the German, French, and Netherlands Reformations. Indeed, so many of the ingredients present in 1848 were also present either in 1789 or 1917 that it is the beginning of interpretative wisdom to ask why, in 1848, they produced such meager results. Or, to put the matter another way: how did conservatives for the first time manage to win a major modern revolution?

The full importance of 1848, finally, became apparent only in subsequent years. In the near term, of course, the failure of liberal revolution in Germany set it off sharply from the contemporary West since the task of national unification then fell to semi-autocratic Prussia. But what if, in the longer term, this post-1848 Sonderweg, or special path, of compromise with Old Regime forces actually prepared Germany for a totalitarian "revolution of the Right"? The question is a real one, but no amount of debate seems able to settle it.

Less debatable is the legacy of 1848 to Russia's revolutionary future. Indeed, the greatest of modern revolutions would have been impossible in the form in which we know it without that quintessential product of 1848, Marxism. For that doctrine, though formed amid early nineteenth-century Romanticism, nonetheless had the logical rigor to become the reigning ideology of later "scientific" socialism—just when Russia was moving toward revolution. If there exists an overall European revolutionary process, as this book seeks to argue, then Marxism, as the mediating agent between 1789 and 1917, is surely one of the crucial links. Although in the realm of events history may not have turned very far in 1848, in the realm of theory it took a great lurch leftward.

But the most salient feature and the true uniqueness of 1848 is that it was three revolutions in one. It was in the first instance, and most basically, a liberal democratic revolution made in the name of the principles of 1789, of which the republic was the most radical form. Second, it was a series of national revolutions almost invariably associated with the cause of the liberal republic. Finally, it was a first, feeble, and ultimately disastrous attempt at a socialist revolution, and at that in only one country, France—a fiasco nonetheless with a great future. Thus the basic question posed by the first half-century of anticipated revolution is the relationship of *both* nationalism and socialism to the revolution's Ur-ideology of liberal democracy, that universal suffrage republic first sketched in the wake of 1789. It is surely noteworthy that the democratic breakthrough of the Great Revolution was made by a party of "patriots" acting in the name of the "nation," a position that could easily elide into nationalism *tout court*. And it is just as significant that the collective virtues of equality and fraternity outweigh the individualistic value of liberty in the Revolution's most famous emblem, a position pregnant with socialism. The present treatment of the nineteenth century, therefore, is centrally concerned with the overlapping and ambiguous forces of that presiding trinity of modernity: liberalism, nationalism, and socialism.

In the first part of the present chapter, socialism is examined as the product of the already mentioned aftershocks of 1789 in France. In the second part of this chapter nationalism is treated in conjunction with the failed liberal revolutions of Germany in the three centers of Frankfurt, Berlin, and Vienna. In the interest of simplifying the inordinately complex pattern of events offered by the pan-European sweep of 1848, the important cases of Italy and Hungary will be mentioned only incidentally. By contrast, Karl Marx, though unimportant in 1848 itself, will receive a chapter of his own in view of his indispensability to twentieth-century Communism.

HISTORIOGRAPHY

Precisely because this array of subjects is so vast, the historiography on 1848 as a whole is quite meager. Since the Revolution of 1848 is at the same time a single, international movement—the first such secular movement in European history—and a series of particular national revolutions, most of the relevant literature is devoted to the individual outbreaks with only incidental reference to the total picture. The more important items of this literature will be mentioned where appropriate.

There are, however, historiographical traditions relevant to 1848 as a whole. The first of these, obviously, is Marxism, the most important historical studies of which—Marx himself on France and Engels on Germany—were written in the heat of battle. Although little noticed at the time, these works were prodigiously influential for the later historiography, and not just of 1848 but of the whole modern era. Similarly relevant to 1848 as a whole are histories of socialism and studies of labor history, much of it written by socialists—to the point where one can almost say that social history is socialist history. As regards liberal historiography of the pan-European movement, as of revolution-in-general, Tocqueville's masterpieces all cluster around 1848, which may indeed be called the springtime of staseology. And beyond these two examples commentary on 1848 merges into modern social science in general. Auguste Comte's ambition to found a "positive" science of society is a product of the buildup to 1848; Herbert Spencer is an analyst of its aftermath. Max Weber at the end of the century is an answer to Marx, and his contemporary Emile Durkheim is a more serious and successful heir of Comte. Although little of this is explicitly concerned with the great convulsion that shook Europe in the mid-century, all of it is devoted to the industrial, democratic, and restless world which that convulsion left behind. More clearly even than 1789, the failed Revolution of 1848 announced the world of mass politics and ceaseless social change that the twentieth century would call modernity.[2]

REVOLUTION AGAINST A RESTORATION

The first defining particularity of 1848 was that it was a revolution not against a long-established order, but against a restoration. This restoration, moreover, was not just national, a regime in France alone, but international, a policy enforced by the Concert of Europe, a term forged after 1815 precisely to indicate the new conservative sense of community. The French Revolution and Napoleonic Empire had, however crudely, unified Europe; Engels, following Mme. de Staël, had called Napoleon "Robespierre on horseback," the conqueror who brought revolution to all of Europe. The Restoration of 1814–1815 thus meant not just the Bourbons' return to France but an all-European return to Old Regime dynastic "legitimacy." There was one important new element, however: although the empire of the tsars had been a European power since Peter the Great, it was now, as the strongest single continental power, a leader of the Concert of Europe.

Yet the Vienna Settlement, as it was called, and the Holy Alliance created to give it religious sanction, was an intrinsically fragile structure. A glance at the other notable European restoration, England in 1660, can help us understand why. The English Restoration had been acceptable to, indeed desired by, most elements of society; and it broke down in the 1680s because the Crown refused to live by the new constitutional rules. The Restoration of 1814–1815, by contrast, was doomed from the start because it was unacceptable to key elements in France, and its collapse there would automatically challenge the Vienna order internationally—an order all the more tenuous since it was held together principally by the military strength of its two most backward members, Austria and Russia. Probably not even the Austrian chancellor Metternich believed that the system he had devised was more than a chancy holding operation. Indeed, as early as 1817 the Restoration was challenged in hitherto quiescent Germany at the nationalist Wartburg Festival commemorating the tercentennial of the beginning of Luther's Reformation.

The European Restoration fell victim to three successive revolutionary waves. The first hit in 1820–1821 with a series of constitutionalist revolts across southern Europe, in Spain, Italy, and Greece. These uprisings were carried out by small conspiracies of intellectuals and army officers. In Spain this elite group was called Los Liberales, a name that did much to put the word "liberal" into Europe-wide circulation. In Italy such liberals acted through hierarchical secret societies called Carbonari, a form of organization going back to the earlier resistance against Napoleon. Carbonarism then spread to France, where its rather extensive conspiracy included such a star as Lafayette, who was also a leader of the parliamentary liberals. In Germany the contemporary Burschenschaften held similar liberal sympathies though they never attempted any political action. By 1825 elitist revolutionary liberalism had even appeared in far-off Russia, where the rebels became known as "Decembrists" after the month of their abortive uprising. Though all the 1820s insurrections ended badly, they nonetheless demonstrated that in the long run the Restoration could not be made to stick.

It at last cracked in the Revolution of 1830. In July the Bourbon monarchy collapsed in France, thereby producing a liberal revolution in Belgium and, in November, a major liberal-national insurrection in Russian Poland. The Belgians made good their independence from Holland, and henceforth served as a model of constitutional monarchy for the rest of Europe. The Poles, however, were crushed by the Russians, thereby becoming a sacred cause for the international revolutionary movement. Conversely, Nicholas I of Russia became the "Gendarme of Europe"; backing up Prussia and Austria, Russia was the mainstay of European reaction. In advanced, democratic quarters of the West, therefore, the further liberalization of Europe automatically meant war against Russia, and perhaps also Austria.

Eighteen forty-eight brought the opposition forces that had been building up since 1830 to a general European explosion. In February and March almost all of Europe except Great Britain and Russia was shaken by a chain reaction of revolutions, as barricade insurgencies forced established monarchies to accept constitutional assemblies in Paris, Vienna, Milan, Prague, and Berlin. Eighteen forty-eight thus generalized to all Europe the pattern of 1830.

Ideologically, too, the Carbonarism of the 1820s set in motion a development that would climax in 1848. From the start the basic demand of all movements of opposition to the Restoration had been "the principles of 1789." Concretely, this generic constitutional liberalism meant representative government, civil equality, and individual rights. This creed came in two antagonistic variants, descended respectively from 1789 and 1793. The first was constitutional monarchy based on a property suffrage that limited political participation to the well-to-do and the educated. The second variant was a republic founded on universal male suffrage. After 1830 this formula also came to be called "democracy," a term which from Plato's time had usually connoted mob rule.

The years 1815–1848 demonstrated, moreover, that the line defining the "pays légal," which enjoyed political participation, could not be held at a property suffrage against the "pays réal," which was unenfranchised. Indeed, as the political fermentation of the July Monarchy built up toward 1848, it became clear that the line of political participation could not be held at a universal suffrage republic. For beyond the formal democracy of the political republic there was, or should be, the full equality and fraternity of the social republic, "social democracy" as the men of 1848 first called it.

This constant escalation of the principles of 1789 is reflected in the evolving terminology of the day. In the 1820s the watchword of men of good will was liberalism, understood in the sense of a constitutional monarchy. In the 1830s the watchword of the avant-garde was republic, understood invariably as requiring universal suffrage or "democracy." Yet an even more perfect form of democracy was offered by a new and still nebulous teaching, socialism. In the 1840s republic still remained preeminent, but nascent socialism was already under pressure from a new avant-garde ideal, communism, along with its emblem, the old symbol of 1791, the red flag. Though in its strict construction this meant the end of private property and the full collectivization of society, in practice people used the word almost interchangeably with "socialism," and that practice will be followed here.

THE PROBLEM OF SOCIALISM

But what, precisely, are we to understand by "socialism?" Over the past two centuries the term has been used to describe such a variety of theories, movements, and regimes that, taken by itself, it is meaningless. It acquires meaning only when situated in a historical context, and since the rest of this book is concerned with socialist revolutions and regimes, all that follows will also be an exercise in bringing socialism down to earth. Therefore, the process of clarifying its meaning may begin here in conjunction with its emergence in history.

The first problem is minor, but so ubiquitous that it cannot be ignored. Many authorities, including eminent socialists like Karl Kautsky, have traced the socialist idea back to such sources as Plato, the Acts of the Apostles, Campanella, or Thomas More. Although this custom started as an effort by modern socialists to give themselves an illustrious genealogy, it also suggests that socialism is a universal idea or an eternal verity, at last crystallized into a concrete movement by the appearance of the industrial proletariat. Almost all the usual items in this genealogy, however, bear only the most superficial resemblance to any actual form of socialism.

Plato, in particular, had nothing to do with it. The essence of socialism is equality, whereas Plato's ideal city, though organized as a commune, is hierarchical and elitist; and although his patrician "guardians" hold no property, the lesser craftsmen of the polis in effect do. The apostolic communism of the first Christians is also a poor analog since it existed only among the small group of the faithful, whereas modern socialism is meant to apply to the whole society. Occasionally the search for ancestors yields historically meaningful results, as when Kautsky, after a bow to Plato's *Republic*, began his history of socialism with the twelfth-century heretic Arnold of Brescia, who, as explained in an earlier chapter,[3] in fact had links with a real social movement. By and large, though, the collectivist utopias of the past were merely speculative *ideas*,[4] and using them to explain socialism's origins is fundamentally ahistorical.

A second misapprehension is much more important, in fact fundamental, in that it reflects the view that most socialists have had of the origins of their movement. This view is that socialism arose as the response of the working class to industrial capitalism. But no sooner is this answer given than it runs into trouble from the first piece of evidence necessary to support it, namely the English industrial revolution. After all, on the basis of this explanation it is only logical to assume that where there is more industry there should also be more socialism. In fact, at the beginnings of socialism things were the other way around: Britain was the homeland of advanced industry, and though socialism existed there in the form of Owenism, it was not comparable to the variegated socialism of France, which however lagged behind in industry. In Britain the working class responded to industrialization with Chartism, a movement for political, not socialist, reform. Crudely put, this difference is due to the differing political histories of the two countries. More must be said about this shortly; for the moment, it is enough to note that there was no one-to-one correlation between industrialization and socialism when the latter first emerged.

Still, as of 1800 France and England were so obviously together in the forefront of the changes leading to modernity, that we must have some way to designate their relationship. So it has long been a commonplace of historical writing to assert that the modern age was inaugurated jointly by the French political revolution and the English Industrial Revolution. But once again what seems obvious can get us into trouble, for this commonsense observation is only a step away from conflating the paired national developments into a single historical process. A notable, and once very influential, example of this is Eric Hobsbawm's concept of "dual revolution," in which French political development and English economic development function as if they were separate facets of a single revolution of modernity.[5] In short, they are made to add up to Marxism's "Bourgeois Revolution" on a Pan-European scale. In fact, Engels himself came close to saying as much outright: in a footnote to a translation of the *Communist Manifesto* he declared, "For the economic development of the bourgeoisie, England is here taken as the typical country; for its political development, France"[6]—an assertion made without any awareness of its implication that British industrialization had produced the French Revolution of 1789.

But what the comparison between English and French developments circa 1800 really shows is that economic and political development moved not in tandem but out of phase one with another. Thus the alluring but deceptive conflation of the "dual revolution" in fact conceals an important historical problem: namely, why is modern history characterized by a disparity between economic and ideological developments, or, if one prefers, between the progress of capitalism and that of socialism? The historical task therefore is to explain this disparity, not to make it go away with such a subterfuge as "dual revolution." For this disparity indicates that the roots of socialism are to be found not so much in economic as in political development. It is this lead that will be followed here. Of course, more will be said on this major matter as we move east, where it becomes increasingly relevant. For the moment, however, we may consider it an established fact that early socialism's chief arena was France and hence explain its emergence by the conditions prevailing there.

These conditions in fact go back to the late Enlightenment and the Revolution. The first stirrings of what may plausibly be called modern socialism come out of Rousseau's attack on inequality. In the mid-eighteenth century the rationalistic, science-oriented Enlightenment came under attack from the sentimental and moralistic Enlightenment associated above all with Rousseau. As sensation gave way to sentiment, and reason to intuition, pity for the weak and compassion for everyone became the foundation for a nascent democratic civic religion in which all men were at the same time brothers and citizens. In this new religion inequality therefore became the great sin against nature and humanity, and thus also the source of all evil in the organization of society. Although Rousseau himself only occasionally related these beliefs to the abolition of private property, that conclusion was a logical one, and some of his disciples, notably Mably and Morelly, did in fact produce communist utopias in print.

But these were still only ideas, and the first impetus to creating a socialist movement came from the revolution itself, or more exactly from its failures. And a revolution with such exalted ideas as that of the First Republic could only fail, or more accurately, disappoint. For the liberty promised by 1789 could be real only for the minority that had the wealth to make it so, and the equality vaunted by the sans-culottes of 1793 was even more vulnerable to economic forces beyond the people's control. These threats to the ideals of the Republic could be warded off so long as the Jacobin Revolution was on the upswing, thus providing the illusion of ultimate success. When, however, Robespierre fell in 1794, the illusion was shattered and the "people" were confronted with the reality that the Revolution had nothing in it for them. For behind the citizen there stood only the bourgeois, and a new system of inequality as oppressive as that of the Old Regime.

And this new awareness produced Babeuf's "Conspiracy of the Equals" under the Directory at a time of real economic distress in Paris, and the first draft of what later would be called communism. The opening sentence of a placard distributed widely in Paris in April 1796 were: "Nature has given to every man the right to the enjoyment of an equal share in all property." But the "Conspiracy" was nipped in the bud with the help of government agents who had infiltrated Babeuf's organization, and its leader and several of his associates were guillotined in May 1797.[7]

Still, modern socialism, once all the egalitarian precedence has been recognized, remains a *movement* that had been in existence only once the term "socialism" itself became current in the 1830s; it is possible to call something "socialist" only when there is some direct continuity with later movements that in fact use that name.

As an initial approximation to giving it substance, let us consider what it is *not*. In this perspective, socialism is in the first instance the *negation* of something called "capitalism"; by the same token it is the *anticipation* of what comes after that negation.

Indeed, it is in this antithetical relationship that the paired terms came into existence. It is "socialism" that appeared first, in 1831, under the pen of Pierre Leroux right after the founding of the property-suffrage "bourgeois monarchy" of Louis Philippe. What it then signified was that the universal-suffrage republic of the mainstream opposition was an inadequate ideal and that a variously defined social republic was required for true human equality. Although the obstacle to socialism was first labeled "capitalism" in 1850 by Louis Blanc (who used it in a neutral, descriptive sense), the term failed to catch on. Marx, for example, never used it, speaking instead of the "bourgeois mode of production," or at times the "capitalist mode of production." The term's real career dates from its adoption in German in 1869 by Rodbertus, who employed it as a kind of smear word to designate the society that he wished to destroy. In this usage it gained momentum in Germany until the end of the century (though less so in the more advanced polities of France and England). Confronted with this mounting pressure from the left, therefore, the monarchist-to-liberal German academic world tried to defuse the antithesis by making capitalism the subject of scholarly investigation. Hence we have Werner Sombart's *Modern Capitalism* in 1902 and Max Weber's *The Protestant Ethic and the Spirit of Capitalism* in 1904.[8] Be it noted, however, that the two had been preceded, in 1899, by Lenin's *The Development of Capitalism in Russia*, which was no agitational pamphlet but a heavily documented investigation that could be legally published in the Tsar's empire. What, then, is involved in the socialism-capitalism dichotomy whose partisans would fight it out for the duration of the twentieth century?

The usual approach is to view it as an antithesis of economic systems. In this perspective, socialism means the public (or collective, or social, or communal) ownership and operation of the means of production and distribution, while capitalism means the private or individual ownership and operation of those same economic instruments. Within this standard dictionary definition of the problem, furthermore, the late Soviet experiment highlighted state planning versus the free market as the crucial distinction.

But other common assumptions about the socialism-capitalism antithesis complicate this picture. If we move beyond economics to history, the two systems are generally assumed to be conflicting modes of industrial society. In this perspective the more capitalism there is, the more socialist pressure there ought to be. Hence, socialism is regarded as the political ideology of the working class, and economic liberalism as the congenital philosophy of "capital" or the "bourgeoisie." Indeed, pushing this rule-of-thumb reductionism to an extreme, the once famous and influential sociologist, Karl Mannheim, used to refer off-handedly to Marxism as "proletarian thought," as if that coupling of terms was self-evident.[9]

With the twentieth century now behind us, however, these historical presuppositions hardly hold up. On the contrary, attempts to "build socialism" have occurred more often than not in backward peasant societies than in advanced industrial ones. Moreover, the fidelity of industrial workers to universalistic socialism has been distinctly spotty, particularistic nationalism being equally, if not more, likely to win their primary allegiance. And since the discovery in the 1920s and 1930s of Marx's early manuscripts we know too much about the metaphysical foundations of his system to mistake it for "proletarian thought."

All of which indicates that socialism is much more than an economic project or the logical product of industrial development. Indeed, enough has already been said to indicate that socialism is a total project, aiming as it does at transcending present society completely and creating a whole new world and a new man. In other words, socialism is not something that exists or has existed in the real world; it is a utopia. Thus, in the capitalism-socialism dichotomy that we usually employ in discussing modern politics, the two terms of the antithesis are not symmetrical ones, with equal ontological status. Nor do they designate comparable yet competing systems of social organization or equally feasible policy options or political alternatives. Rather, they designate the really-existing (and of course messy) present order and a fantasy (and of course ideal) future alternative. Yet for almost two centuries now, and especially in the twentieth century, we have talked as if capitalism and socialism were equally real historical formations between which society could choose.

BACK TO 1830

The French Restoration was fragile on two counts. First, it came about because France had been defeated in war, and the Bourbons, "returning in the baggage-train of the Allies," had been imposed on the country; after an age of Napoleonic glory "legitimate" monarchy was experienced as a humiliation. Second, it was impossible to undo the momentous changes that had occurred between 1789 and 1815, yet incorporating them into the restored monarchy could only undermine the new structure. Consequently, the civil equality of 1789, the Code Napoleon, the Concordat, and the Empire's administrative structure all remained intact, and most of its personnel kept their places. Politically, Louis XVI's brother, Louis XVIII, though he claimed to rule by divine right, nonetheless had to accept a constitutional Charter with a representative assembly and significant freedom of the press, concessions theoretically "granted" (*octroyées*) by the hereditary sovereign but in fact necessary if the Bourbons were to stand a chance of ruling the country. In the space of fifteen years the Restoration regime was torn apart by the contradiction between its dynastic and its revolutionary heritage.

On the one hand the Chamber of Deputies, despite a narrowly restricted property suffrage (some hundred thousand voters in a population of thirty million) produced an opposition committed to the principles of 1789. In the persons of such historians as Thiers and Guizot (already noted here for their writings), these "liberals" wanted an English-type constitutional monarchy with parliament chosen by property suffrage. On the other hand the monarchy, after a quasi-liberal start, increasingly favored its natural clientele, the old aristocracy, returned émigrés, and the church. As the 1820s progressed, this alliance of "throne and altar" became increasingly assertive in favoring the Old Regime heritage, and in response the liberal opposition grew ever more strident. Finally, in July 1830, when a royal dissolution of the Chamber produced a liberal victory in the new elections, the King, invoking the Charter's hitherto unused decree power, attempted what amounted to a coup d'état. The new Chamber was dissolved, the suffrage was restricted still further, and the press laws were tightened. The parliamentary liberals led by Thiers issued a public protest, the Paris working class (alone) responded and the barricades went up. The monarchy had earlier disbanded the national guard as unreliable, and it turned out that the army could not handle street fighting. After three days of skirmishing, the insurrection triumphed without bloodshed. Charles X abdicated in favor of his nine-year-old grandson—a solution, of course, that the liberals would not accept.

The question then came to be, would the new regime be a constitutional monarchy under the younger branch of the Bourbons, the House of Orleans, or a republic based on popular sovereignty? The victors of the July Days, the Paris workers, wanted a republic, but the largely middle-class liberals wanted to turn July into a French 1688, thereby at last consolidating the heritage of 1789 on a moderate note. The liberal leaders, therefore, prevailed on the prestigious Lafayette, who really wanted a Washingtonian republic, to endorse the Duke of Orleans, Louis-Philippe, as the safe middle way out: a tricolor constitutional monarchy with the old Charter only somewhat revised. The decree power was abolished and the suffrage expanded to 250,000 so as to include that bourgeoisie which Guizot had long argued was the class that had forged the nation under the Old Regime and had made the great breakthrough of 1789. Thus was established a regime that proudly called itself the "bourgeois monarchy" under a self-proclaimed "citizen king" whose title was therefore not King of France but King of the French. The pivotal question of French politics then became whether the country could live with this set of incongruous criteria of legitimacy. As we know, 1830 did not turn out to be a 1688. Nor had it even decided whether France could have a new 1789 without a new 1793.

WORKER RESISTANCE AND SOCIALIST AGITATION AFTER 1830

And indeed there were bloody working class strikes and a semi-insurrection in Paris and Lyons in 1832, 1834, and 1839. For the workers were convinced that they had been robbed of their July victory and so continued to demand the Republic and universal suffrage. Their basic tactic was the direct democracy of street action, as in 1793, and their organization was the secret society, as in the time of Babeuf's Conspiracy of the Equals in 1796. This quasi-revolutionary working class pressure affected the entire political system.

First of all it furnished the background for the emergence of socialism as a movement in the 1830s. Even more striking was the socialist literature of the 1840s. There was no hard and fast line separating it from the republican, or even the Bonapartist, tradition, both of which came out of the Revolution. The Revolution had always stood for liberty and equality, and in the 40s a third term "fraternity," which had been a minor note in the 1790s, now became prominent, and the three terms were fused into a new trinity—liberty, equality, fraternity—destined to become the official motto of the anticipated new republic.

Most of the socialism of the two decades preceding 1848 has been classified as "utopian," a derogatory term first applied to it by Marx and Engels but which has long since become canonical.[10] Most of this socialism also was nonrevolutionary. Indeed, its ideal was promoting harmony between the social classes and not class struggle. Positively, what these utopian socialists proposed was one or another scheme for promoting harmony, progress, equality, association, economic security, etc. through the voluntary reorganization of society, that is cooperatives whether of producers or consumers (Owen and Fourier); state aid for workers (Blanc's "organization of labor" and his "social workshops"), in other words remote anticipation of the welfare state; the technocratic improvement of society (the Saint-Simonians); or schemes of free credit to aid workers to found their own enterprises (Proudhon and Owen). Most of these schemes were indeed impractical and few of them, outside of the cooperative movement, ever produced results. Nonetheless they all focused attention on the "social question" and their message was that the universal-suffrage political republic was not enough to make men free, equal and fraternal, and that a social republic promoting some sort of organization of the economy was required. In this manner the principle of 1789 and the republican ideal both shaded off into socialism and hence into the negation of the rule of the bourgeoisie established in 1830. Once again, we see that the origins of modern socialism lie in the political and ideological tradition created by the "bourgeois revolution" of 1789.

And so the situation continued to radicalize. The Restoration had produced an outpouring of liberal political literature. The July monarchy now produced a flood of republican and, increasingly, socialist theory. First of all, Tocqueville's best-selling *Democracy in America* inevitably, and by intention, raised the question of democracy's prospects in Europe. And, as we have seen, the year 1847 produced massive histories of the Revolution idealizing, not just 1789, but the First Republic (though not the Terror) of 1792: this was the work of Michelet, Lamartine, Louis Blanc and others.[11]

THE LAISSEZ-FAIRE REVOLUTION

Socialism was all the more prominent because of the economic crisis of the "Hungry Forties," of which the Irish famine of 1846–1847 was perhaps the most spectacular case. This was indeed an exceptional case of the phenomenon of dearth and depression already noted for 1788–1789 and for 1565–1566 in the Netherlands. One reason, over and above bad weather, that the crisis was so exceptional was in the laissez-faire ideology of the day. Laissez faire was not just a "bourgeois" demand. It was a part of the Enlightenment assault on Old Regime absolutism which had also entailed mercantilism and cameralism, that is, statist policy fostering economic development. For the enlightened a free market was more efficient and productive than state protection. This ideology was developed by Adam Smith and Physiocrats in the advanced states and eagerly embraced by more backward enlightened despotism. The first triumphs were such measures as the Anglo-French Free Trade Treaty of 1788 and the Le Chapelier law of 1791 banning "associations," and the British Anti-Combination Act of 1801. This campaign against Old Regime guilds as conspiracies in restraint of trade were a logical part of the new ideology. And all of this, with the first great modern depression, in 1815 at the end of the Napoleonic War, created the problem of mass unemployment and "pauperism." Another neologism for the paupers was "proletarians." Their plight was at the center of the social question and the great concern of the utopian socialists. Both Robert Owen and Charles Fourier began their criticism of the new market society during the revolutionary and Napoleonic years. The great enemy to both of them was competition. And the remedy for both men was cooperation. In other words, it was not the factory system as such but the anarchy of the market and its accompanying social insecurity that were the economic stimulus to socialism.[12] And this, in combination with the French revolutionary tradition, furnishes the wellsprings of modern socialism. The French bourgeois monarchy offered a particularly egregious example of this new market society. It was all the more vulnerable in that it lacked solid legitimacy in terms of the principles of 1789.

The more middle-class segments of the bourgeoisie formed the liberal opposition in the Chamber of Deputies and the press. Their newspaper, *Le National*, agitated for "reform," that is, a broader suffrage and forbidding state functionaries to serve in parliament. In other words, these liberals did not want a republic or democracy. The newspaper *La Réforme* was bolder, willing to envisage a universal suffrage republic. However, once the July regime was at last fully stabilized, in the 1840s, the King and his most long-lasting chief minister, Guizot, stubbornly resisted reform, even though a modest decrease in the cens would have brought him the bulk of the bourgeoisie, who would naturally support the existing regime. Why this intransigence? Guizot's theories about 1688, the historical role of the bourgeoisie, and the doctrine of rule by "les capacités" are one reason.[13] This restriction of participation in "representative government" to the capacities of wealth and education was standard among liberals of the day. Another reason was that Guizot wanted to stabilize a political situation that had been turbulent since 1830, indeed since 1815. Given French conditions and the spell of 1789, such caution might seem only prudent. In the light of those same conditions, prudence proved to be a losing gamble.

THE FAILURE OF 1848 IN FRANCE

All these revolutions followed roughly the same trajectory. The common characteristic of 1848 everywhere is that it began, not with the summoning of an assembly, but with the initiative of the urban plebs. This precipitate radicalism, however, had the consequence of frightening civil society and thus of quickly turning 1848 everywhere into a conservative triumph. This was the only time the conservatives ever won a major revolution. They moved from the Romantic euphoria of the spring of 1848, to the defeat of these hopes at the end of the year, to a resurgence of democratic strength in early 1849, to the final defeat by the forces of order in 1850–1851. Europe's first anticipated revolution thus yielded a quite unanticipated scenario of defeat. This frustrating turn of events, however, did not put an end to the politics of anticipation. Rather, failure, at least in radical quarters, only reinforced the need to anticipate still another revolutionary return. The Second Coming of 1789 would therefore also have to be a second but successful coming—indeed the revanche—of 1848. The disastrous Paris Commune of 1871 was in large measure just this. And so by 1888, the traditional revolutionary hymn, "La Marseillaise," now expropriated by a "bourgeois" republic, was replaced by a new anthem, the "International," written to verses composed in 1871.

What brought down the July monarchy was middle class pressure for electoral reform in conjunction with popular republicanism now veering to socialist expectation. In February 1848 the middle-class opposition mounted a series of public rallies disguised as banquets. When Guizot refused to permit one such gathering in radical Paris the workers threw up barricades. The bourgeois national guard refused to defend the monarchy, and the King again abdicated in favor of a minor grandson. This time, however, the street refused to be cheated of its victory. The editors of *Le National* and such deputies as the poet Lamartine and the radical republican Ledru-Rollin repaired to the Hotel de Ville to proclaim the Republic. There the insurgent plebs forced the deputies to take Louis Blanc and a worker named Albert into the Provisional Government—the first time ever the socialists tasted political power. This long anticipated but in fact unexpected February Revolution went off more smoothly than anyone could have dreamed. For a brief spring it looked as if France could have 1789 without a 1793.

This easy victory, however, created prospects that were far more radical than what the country desired. The history of the Second Republic, therefore, would be largely one of reversing the conquests of February—the scenario of 1789 run backward as it were. The Great Revolution had taken four years to reach its maximum radicalism. Eighteen-forty-eight began with its maximum radical program, a universal suffrage republic with intimations of socialism. From this high-water mark it could only recede. And the prime cause of this retreat was the red specter of socialism embodied by the Paris crowd.

To ward off this danger Louis Blanc was not given a ministry but only a Commission composed of workers and employers to discuss the social question. This body was sumptuously lodged in the Luxembourg Palace but was completely without power. At the same time the "right to work" was given nominal recognition by the creation of National Workshops for the unemployed. In practice, this meant assigning workers who were often skilled artisans to menial tasks, and the workshops quickly turned into poorly managed outdoor relief. Masses of unemployed, furthermore, were drawn to Paris; the middle classes increasingly resented this expensive enterprise and feared its potential for disorder. However, it is difficult to see how this explosive situation could have been avoided. On the one hand, the workers had brought the republic into being and therefore had to be accommodated, yet on the other hand under the conditions of the day it was impossible to do more than to improvise a mere simulacrum of a welfare state.

And so the country prepared for a great clash between plebeian Paris and conservative, largely peasant France. From the beginning Lamartine had assured the European Powers that the new republic would not embark on a revolutionary crusade in the manner of 1792, thereby disappointing the radicals. Likewise, the provisional government wanted immediate elections for a constituent assembly to stabilize the situation by creating a republican counterweight to the Paris crowd. The crowd, of course, wished to delay elections to preserve its leverage with the government. On March 17 a huge demonstration came near to toppling the government. Further radical pressure, however, only succeeded in delaying the inevitable elections until April 28. And the result, predictably, was a victory for moderate republicans and crypto-monarchists. The provisional government gave way to a five-man directorate, with no socialist among them. In rage and despair, on May 15 the Paris radicals, using the pretext of the plight of oppressed Poland, invaded the National Assembly in a new attempt to seize power. The government now arrested Blanqui and other prominent radical leaders, and at the same time prepared for the now inevitable showdown with Paris. At the end of June the government ordered the removal of the National Workshops to the provinces, and the city's eastern, plebeian half threw up its ritual barricades in what was now a revolt of despair. The government's troops, under the good republican general Cavaignac (his father had been a member of the Convention), was ready and waiting. The ensuing urban war lasted three days and claimed seven thousand victims. Cavaignac became de facto dictator until the Assembly finished writing the constitution.

As a result of these "June Days" the concept of class struggle, first put into circulation by the liberal historians of the Restoration to describe their ancestors' lot under the Old Regime, now acquired a new, more contemporary meaning. Henceforth it would designate the conflict of bourgeois and proletarian within the democratic republic. Thus the first lesson of the inverted revolution of 1848 was that political democracy's most fundamental demand, universal suffrage, could in fact be a conservative institution.

This was stunningly confirmed when on December 10 the revolutionary year culminated in Louis Bonaparte's election as president of the republic. In conformity with French revolutionary tradition the constitution created a unicameral legislature chosen by universal suffrage. Yet, since under the Jacobins this device had prepared the way for dictatorship, the constitution added an American-style presidency, also elected by universal suffrage. The principal candidates were the leader of the "Mountain" Ledru-Rollin (370,000 votes), the classical republican Cavaignac (1,448,000), and Napoleon's nephew Louis Bonaparte (5,434,000).

Marx, in his most brilliant pamphlet *The Eighteenth Brumaire of Louis Bonaparte*, famously explained this victory by the sociological argument that that "sack of potatoes," the peasantry, had been seduced by the nephew because they remembered that the uncle had secured their title to their lands. In fact, the explanation is not social but political and in significant measure just plain contingent. By the end of 1848 what the peasantry, and most of France, wanted was order and an end to the "red" menace of Parisian turbulence. Cavaignac could of course have provided that. But a Bonaparte was even better, for he added to order the promise of national glory after the lusterless decades of Restoration and bourgeois monarchy. Louis Napoleon's victory thus resulted from the political conjuncture and the ideological magic of a name—together with the chance availability of a candidate, for the constituent assembly had not deigned to bar members of former dynasties from politics. Nor did all the peasants vote for him, any more than were all of his electors peasants; many peasants voted for the "red" Ledru-Rollin while many workers voted for Bonaparte.

Given this inauspicious debut, the question was then posed whether the new Republic could be made to work. By 1849 the economic crisis was past and a long era of prosperity began. Fear of social democracy, however, remained strong and on May 13 the "party of order" swept the elections to the Republic's new legislature, with overt monarchists, both Orleanists and Legitimists, outpolling the moderate republicans. Yet at the same time the radical republicans, the "democsocs" as they are now called, also gained strength. Emboldened by this success, on June 13 the Left took massively to the streets to protest the government's intervention against the Roman Republic and in favor of the pope. The "party of order" and the Prince President interpreted this manifestation as an attempted coup (which it could, conceivably, have turned into, as on May 15 of the previous year). So they cracked down firmly on the Left by requiring three years' residence in the same place to vote, thereby eliminating that large body of workers who had to move frequently: universal suffrage remained in form but was in fact restricted. Thus the polarization of society between hard Right and hard Left, so starkly exhibited in the June Days, was given durable political expression as a schism between social democracy and the bourgeois republic.

With the radical Left thus eliminated from the picture the political game of the republic became a contest between the Prince President and the monarchists' party of order, and in this struggle the executive held all the cards. Louis Napoleon first tried the legal route by getting the assembly to amend the constitution to permit him a second consecutive term. When this failed, as commander in chief of the armed forces, he instigated a coup d'état, indeed introducing that term into the modern political vocabulary. In 1851, on December 2, the anniversary of Napoleon I's great victory at Austerlitz, his nephew proclaimed that "the Assembly is dissolved, and universal suffrage is reestablished" and so made himself president for life. A year later, he proclaimed himself emperor. Victor Hugo called him Napoleon the Little and went into exile. Karl Marx called this new Brumaire the final act of the "farce" begun in February 1848, and retired from active politics to write up the laws of history that would ensure a red victory the next time around.[14]

THE PATTERN OF ACTION 1848–1849

The great particularity of 1848 in France, Prussia, Austria, and the various Italian states was that it turned out to be the scenario of 1789–1793 run backward. Events began on the far left of the political spectrum of the day with the universal suffrage republic combined with intimations of socialism and then moved by stages increasingly to the right ending with the restoration and a strengthening of the monarchy, whether legitimate or Bonapartist. Marx was very sensitive to this reversal of revolutionary expectation, thus his comments on how the men of 1789–1804 thought in terms of Roman precedents and how the men of 1848–1852 thought in terms of the precedents of 1789–1804.

Indeed, both Hugo and Marx were right to maintain that a major cause of the revolution's failure lay in the weight of historical memory. All the actors of 1848, in attempting to relive 1789, whether as a return to the republic of 1792 or as a replay of the original drama on the higher level of social democracy, by the very fact of anticipating their assigned roles automatically changed the nature of the new drama they were living. Thus the Parisian plebeians, who were in fact largely the grandchildren of the sans-culottes of 1793, by attempting to lead the revolutionary action, prematurely frightened the moderate republicans and drove their constituents into the ranks of the monarchist party of order. Moreover, in 1848 the Left forgot that, unlike in 1789, there was no credible right-wing menace to keep the left-plebeians and bourgeois, socialists and republicans — united. The monarchist Right, whether Orleanist or Legitimist, was too weak to play this role, and the simultaneous collapse of the Austrian and Prussian Old Regimes removed the specter of international reaction from the picture. In these circumstances, the real forces of reaction could draw on the past in order to camouflage themselves in revolutionary costume. Thus the conservative and monarchist forces of order first proclaimed themselves to be moderate republicans. Thus also Bonaparte could surreptitiously creep up on all the other players relatively unopposed. And he could do this all the more easily in that he could plausibly claim to be the expression of the revolution's democratic essence: universal suffrage. Indeed, on this basis he could claim a measure of affinity with the concerns of the Saint-Simonians and other exponents of the social question. In short, a basic explanation of the revolution's failure is that it was an anticipation, a recourse to old formulas in a situation that was new.

THE ENGLISH CONTROL

At mid-nineteenth century, English and French conditions were closer to each other than at any other moment either before or after. Both had a constitutional monarch and early industry. And yet . . . different political circumstances arose from the timing of revolution in the process of modern state formation of the two countries. The seventeenth-century British oligarchic revolution had created a political mechanism that had made it possible to absorb the shock of industrialization (more exactly marketization) peacefully, while the eighteenth-century French revolution created a radically egalitarian political culture that could not be contained within a liberal but class-based constitutional monarchy. Thus in England free-market industrialization led to Chartism, whereas in France early industrialism led to radical republicanism tinged with welfare-state socialism.

GERMANY, CENTRAL EUROPE, AND NATIONALISM

In Germany 1848 was a much more significant event than in France: it was in fact Germany's 1640 or 1789—but *manqué*; the central problem of 1848 in Central Europe, therefore, is to explain why, for the first time, a Great Revolution failed to produce the classic, constitutional result. A part of the explanation lies in certain particularities of 1848 in the general sequence of European revolutions; another part of the explanation lies in the institutional and cultural particularities of Germany and Central Europe.[15]

To elaborate on the first point, 1848 was Europe's first totally conscious revolutionary experience. As we have seen, the English Revolution was not perceived as a revolution when it began; but consciousness of the true nature of the events emerged quickly in the course of their unfolding, and by 1799 France and all Europe knew fully the scenario of a Grand Revolutionary drama. Thus there could never be another "innocent" revolution again, anywhere in Europe. As a consequence, in February-March 1848 all the potential actors in the drama then beginning knew, or thought they knew, their appointed roles. And this circumstance goes far to explain the already noted precipitate initiative of the urban crowd. In Paris the February Days were quite consciously a reprise of 1830 and of the still greater *journées* of 1789–1793. And in Milan, Vienna, Prague, Budapest, and Berlin the March Days were quite consciously and explicitly a responding echo to the Parisian action of February. But anticipatory consciousness of the nature of an event can—and in 1848 did—distort and deflect the course of that event once it is actually under way. As mentioned earlier, this was so, first, in that the self-conscious and precocious radicalism of the urban crowd early on frightened civil society into a more conservative stance than in previous Great Revolutions. Whereas Pym and Lafayette long thought they could control the urban crowd, the Frankfurt Parliament from the beginning knew it could not, and hence never tried to lead it. This was so, second, because the conservatives, particularly among the nobility, had also learned from 1789; they, too, now knew the scenario, and hence bided their time and stuck by the beleaguered king until civil society began to divide, notably over the social question and urban violence (whereas the English and French nobilities, at the beginning at least, thought that they would be the chief beneficiaries, and the natural leaders of the nation, once power had been wrested from the king).

But the unshakable conservatism of the nobility in 1848 brings us to the question of the institutional and cultural peculiarities of Germany and Central Europe. In this respect, it is worth recalling what was said earlier about the crucial importance of a strong, preexistent national focus in making possible a successful Great Revolution—and the illustration of this point by the contrast between revolutionary England and simply rebellious Holland. For in Central Europe, too, there was no institutionalized national focus, but only the military monarchy of the Hohenzollerns in northern Germany and that of the Habsburgs in Austria and Italy. Yet throughout this area there was—unlike in sixteenth-century Holland—a genuine, modern national consciousness. And it is the conflict between this national consciousness and the institutional framework of supra-national, dynastic, and military monarchy that above all explains the failure of 1848.

For this national consciousness was of a new kind in European history. It has already been pointed out that Western European nationalism—in England and France—was not ethnic, but political: it meant membership or citizenship, in a historic-legal community (whether under the crown or the nation is secondary). The example—and the conquests—of the French Revolution, however, forced all of trans-Rhenan Europe to come to terms with the Western concept of national community, now expressed in the devastatingly dynamic form of the mass mobilization of a revolutionary citizenry in arms. Yet the French political definition of the nation did not fit the institutional realities of Central Europe. As a result, and with the aid of Romanticism, the Germans devised a new concept of nationhood: the ethnic-linguistic *Volk*. And this definition of nationality was viewed as the cultural anticipation of the political-institutional nation, indeed as the spiritual matrix out of which the nation would be created. Then this ethnic-linguistic concept of nationality was taken up by the Italians, Slavs, and Magyars; and it is no accident that (except for the special case of France) 1848 was exclusively a revolution of that part of Europe where the political-institutional nation had yet to be built, yet where ethnic-linguistic nationalism was already fully developed.

But if Central Europe were to be reorganized into ethnic-linguistic political entities, this meant that the machineries of the Hohenzollern and Habsburg monarchies had to be totally destroyed (not simply captured by the nation, as had happened to the English and French monarchies)—Prussia by dissolution into Germany and Austria by dismemberment. But each of these monarchies rested on an establishment of military aristocracy and civil bureaucracy, which thought in dynastic, not in ethnic-linguistic, terms; and these establishments did not want to be destroyed. Hence the Prussian and Austrian aristocracies did not join in the revolution, even in its euphoric initial phase of near unanimity. As a result of this loyalty the Prussian and Austrian monarchs always had a viable army in reserve—something Louis XVI lacked after the Bastille.

The national issue in Central Europe also helped blunt the revolutionary élan of civil society (in addition to their fear of the urban crowd). This was expressed in part by the diversion of revolutionary energies away from limiting the power of the king of Prussia to secondary issues of nationalistic *point d'honneur,* such as Schleswig-Holstein, which only served to turn England and Russia against the German revolution. This was expressed also in the fact that liberal civil society needed an army of the king of Prussia to occupy Schleswig-Holstein against the Danes (and possibly also to intimidate Austria) and hence dared not confront him too boldly. Finally, the prominence of the national issue served to divide German from Slav and Magyar, whereas all three would have had to act together if they were to stand a chance of cracking the Prussian and Austrian establishments.

The result of all these circumstances was what will be called here a *revolutio interrupta.* After the March Days and the initial capitulation of the king, the Frankfurt Assembly and the Berlin Diet acted as though they had won and proceeded with the usual Great Revolutionary act of assuming constituent functions. But the continued turbulence of the urban crowd, and civil society's increasing ambivalence toward it, gave the king an opening. At the end of the year he moved in his army from Potsdam and put down the Berlin populace. Thus the Frankfurt and Berlin assemblies were deprived of any coercive weapon against the king. After this they could vote all the constitutions they wanted; they had no means of enforcing them. Hence the following year the king dispersed both assemblies and rejected the results of their deliberations. Thus the supremacy of the royal executive was preserved, and the king made only the limited concession of a "granted" or "imposed" constitution, under which he remained ultimately sovereign.

Then, after 1862, this solution was made creative and enduring by Bismarck. When the majority liberals in the Prussian Diet attempted to expand their power by refusing the military budget, Bismarck answered with a policy of what may be called "legitimist Bonapartism." For he had learned from the example of Napoleon III that universal suffrage could be turned to conservative uses—and nationalism and a policy of social welfare as well. He therefore held firm on the issue of royal supremacy by continuing the military budget without parliamentary approval. At the same time he gave the German nation a modified form of the rest of what it wanted: national unification, but by Prussian arms; universal suffrage, but without ministerial responsibility, and with a class suffrage in dominant

Prussia; and social welfare so as to tame the urban crowd. At this half-modern price, the essential elements of the Old Regime — monarchy and aristocracy — remained dominant until 1918.

By way of conclusion, let us review what the revolutions of 1848 had in common:

1. They all began, not with the summoning of a representative assembly (Estates General), but with the direct action of the urban plebs.

2. All these barricade revolutions triumphed easily in the spring of 1848. The reason is that they had no serious adversaries. In 1789 the revolution had to be made against a thousand-year-old order of the two swords and two centuries of successful absolutism. In 1848 the adversary was only a recent and shaky restoration. Consequently, the revolutionary alliance system worked against further radicalization. In the spring of 1848 the constitutionalist middle classes accepted the revolution as a fait accompli and then tried to keep it within constitutional bounds. But they were not afraid enough of a possible reaction to continue acting in concert with the plebs. In 1789 the revolution feared a royalist comeback in alliance with monarchical Europe and so the leaders needed sans-culotte militancy. In 1848 all the dynasties except the Russians were neutralized at once; there was no general European war. The reflex "no enemies to the left" therefore did not enter into play.

3. The revolution after the spring of 1848 was accordingly driven by fear of the "reds" and the left. And this of course prepared the way for a new type of reaction, either pseudo-democratic and pseudo-social Bonapartism or aristocratic legitimism willing to employ a similar strategy in combination with the use of force, notably Schwarzenberg and especially Bismarck.

4. From 1815 to 1848 there existed a liberal international. Moderate liberals such as Guizot felt solidarity with ideological kin across frontiers. So too did liberals open to democracy such as J. S. Mill and Tocqueville. So too did radical democrats such as Michelet, Ledru-Rollin, Mazzini, and Kossuth. So obviously did socialists such as Bakunin, Marx, and Weitling. Note especially the role of martyred Poland in mobilizing this liberal radical internationalism. This international saw itself as pitted against the courts of Vienna, Berlin, and St. Petersburg, especially the last. And these internationalists would have welcomed a general war led by France to liberate Europe from the Holy Alliance. This was the syndrome of 1830, but Louis-Philippe opted for a peaceful policy. This was the anticipation of much of the left in 1848, but Lamartine continued the July Monarchy's prudence.

5. In the course of the revolutions of 1848 the emergence of nationalism destroyed the liberal international. In particular the aims of Germans were in conflict with those of Slavs (Poznan and Bohemia), while Magyars clashed with both Slavs and Germans. The nationalism of the old states, Britain and France, caused fewer problems. Italian nationalism was less plagued by overlap with other nationalist claims.

6. The period 1815–1848 was also the Romantic age par excellence. Liberalism, nationalism, and socialism were all expressed in a lyrical Romantic idiom. This is also linked to the age's habit of self-consciously inventing new secular religions, moreover, "religions" that were simultaneously thought of as "scientific." The idea of revolution itself thus came to be considered as both redemptive and scientific.

7. The spectrum of revolutionary programs embraced constitutional monarchy with property suffrage, the universal suffrage republic or radicalism, some form of economic "association" or socialism, and on its left egalitarian collectivism or communism.

8. The revolution's trajectory was similar everywhere: after the fraternal and euphoric spring of 1848 came first an open bourgeois-plebeian clash (summer or early fall) and by the end of the year the open triumph of the party of order though still in constitutionalist form. This moderate reaction then generated a new radical thrust in the spring of 1849. This new challenge then produced a lasting authoritarian solution.

10

Marxism and the Second International, 1848-1914

The philosophers have only *interpreted* the world . . . the point, however, is to *change* it.
—KARL MARX, 1845

Karl Marx was a German philosopher.
—LESZEK KOLAKOWSKI, 1978

The great paradox of the Revolution of 1848 is that although it failed to achieve any of its objectives—whether democratic-republican, national, or socialist—it left an ideological legacy of greater magnetic power than the revolution it had sought to imitate, the successful Revolution of 1789. This legacy, of course, was Marxism. Without it, all subsequent European politics, and in particular the Russian Revolution, would be unimaginable.

Marx first proclaimed his message to the world in the *Communist Manifesto* published on the eve of the February Revolution of 1848 in Paris. At the time, it attracted almost no notice. Greater attention began to be paid to Marx only after 1864 and the foundation of the International Working Men's Association, usually known as the First International, of which he was one of the leaders; and his actual ideas only attracted attention after the first volume of *Capital* in 1867. What really made him famous, however, was the Paris Commune of 1871, which was quite undeservedly blamed by all the governments of Europe on the alleged machinations of the International. As a public phenomenon, therefore, Marx and his doctrine belong to the last third of the nineteenth century. And this is Marx as "the Darwin of social science," as Engels said at his graveside in 1883, the economic Marx of those "internal contradictions" of capitalism that would produce its doom: the labor theory of value, the confiscation of surplus value, the diminishing returns of capital, and so on.

But this is not the Marx that would lead to actual revolution. That Marx, rather, the patron of all twentieth-century revolutions, was the young, philosophical Marx of the 1840s. Indeed, the dialectic of negation and creation, the principle of self-enriching alienation that undergirded the economic laws of the later Marx had its genesis quite precisely in the years between his arrival in Paris in 1843 and the *Manifesto* five years later. This is the Marx that interests us here, for the scheme of history he then developed would serve as the means by which the millenarian anticipation of 1848 was transmitted to the twentieth century. The stages of that scheme of history, together with the sociology underlying it, are outlined in Appendix I. It is necessary to trace here the route by which he arrived at these theories.

GENERIC SOCIALISM

The great breeding ground of anticipatory theories of revolution was the "bourgeois monarchy" of France between 1830 and 1848. It has already been noted that it was the problems of this interlude between two revolutions that led Tocqueville to formulate his political sociology of democracy as the driving force of the modern world.

To develop his insight in slightly different terms, the central issue fueling the politics of his day was indeed social inequality. In the eyes of what was now, for the first time, generally called the "left," this social question, not the class-based liberalism of Prime Minister Guizot, was the real legacy of the Great Revolution. In this view, the political republic of 1792 had manifestly failed to effect humanity's liberation; and the constitutional monarchy of July 1830 had come up even shorter. In consequence, a social republic would be necessary to carry the democratic promise of 1789–1792 to completion. Or, to put matters more concretely, the abolition of the legal inequality of the Old Regime's society of "orders" or estates did not make men equal citizens in fact, but instead laid bare the new injustice of social inequality founded on private property. To achieve true justice and equality, therefore, some redistribution of wealth and property was required. Thus the idea of "socialism" was put forward by the far left as the historical stage beyond liberal constitutionalism, indeed as the culmination of human emancipation.

Although this generic socialism was not necessarily revolutionary, as 1848 approached it became increasingly more radical in the homeland of 1789. And this was so because France was the only European nation with a living revolutionary tradition, backed up moreover by the most radical form of the eighteenth-century Enlightenment. Indeed, as noted in Chapter 9, the first adumbration of revolutionary socialism emerged directly from the Great Revolution itself, in the Conspiracy of the Equals of Gracchus Babeuf of 1796, an insurrectionary tradition transmitted by Philippe-Michel Buonarroti to the generation of the 1830s, and on to Auguste Blanqui and Armand Barbès—and ultimately Karl Marx.

And it should be emphasized that the focus of nascent socialism was France, whereas, according to the common supposition that socialism is a movement of the industrial proletariat, the focus should have been England, more advanced economically than its neighbor. Robert Owen's cooperatives to the contrary notwithstanding, however, there was little socialism in Britain until almost the end of the century. What there was in Britain, rather, was an embryonic labor movement which was launched in the years preceding 1848 in the form of Chartism. This movement was essentially the creation of workers themselves, and its priority was the political struggle for universal suffrage in order to promote social reform through parliamentary representation. Thus the constitutionalist legacy of 1640–1688 softened the radical edge in Britain of the challenge of the Industrial Revolution.

In other words, the difference between France and England in the period of socialism's gestation is not to be explained by social and economic conditions but by political and ideological traditions. This point merits redoubled emphasis, since from Marx onward it has rarely been recognized. In a footnote to a translation of the *Communist Manifesto*, Engels explained that he and Marx had taken England as "typical" of the economic development of the "bourgeoisie," and France as "typical" of its political development. But he did not notice that it is a non sequitur to derive French politics from English economics, an elementary error current to this day.[1] Yet, unless it is recognized that socialism is not the class consciousness of industrial workers, it is impossible to understand its historical role anywhere, and particularly in Russia.

The socialist idea, as distinct from the labor movement, throughout its history has been what it was at its inception under the July Monarchy: ideological prognostication about how best to effect the transition from estate and/or class society to a fully egalitarian one; that is, socialism was the logical culmination of what de Tocqueville called "democracy" in the sense of "l'égalité des conditions," or social leveling. Moreover, this anticipatory theorizing has not been primarily the work of the laboring classes themselves, even though there have been occasional socialist leaders from among them, such as Wilhelm Weitling, Pierre-Joseph Proudhon, and August Bebel. Socialist theory and politics—as distinct from the labor movement—have been the province of intellectuals, as both Karl Kautsky and Vladimir Lenin declared in oft-quoted statements.[2] And the prime example of this phenomenon, of course, is furnished by Marx and Engels themselves, whose anticipatory theory of revolution would displace all others by the end of the century. Since this theory supplied the justification for Red October and all its works, its basic components must be examined here; and this reexamination must be revisionist, since our usual perspectives on Marxism hardly prepare us for its paradoxical role in Russia.

THE GENESIS OF MARXISM

The common perception of Marxism is that it is a social-science theory designed to analyze advanced industrial society. The fact that its author was from then-backward Germany, and that he had dabbled in his youth in Hegel, is incidental; after all, he spent most of his mature life in the British Museum working on the most up-to-date English data. Yet if we look at the emergence of his doctrine historically, a reverse order of causality emerges: Germany and Hegel become primordial, and the advanced Western data become illustrations of a more basic, and a priori, pattern of thought.

It is now generally recognized that the fundamental coordinates of Marx's system were first set forth in the prime product of his Hegelian youth, the *German Ideology* of 1845–1846,[3] written when he was just twenty-six and first published only in 1932. In this work, he transposed philosophical and idealistic theory of the logic of history into a socioeconomic and materialistic version of mankind's dialectical and agonistic ascent to freedom and self-fulfillment.

Briefly, the sociological coordinates of Marx's emerging system are that the "division of labor" generated by man's efforts to wrest a living from nature leads to dehumanizing class inequality, and that the resulting exploitation of man by man would one day produce a revolutionary "consciousness" among the workers, thereby igniting an explosion culminating in egalitarian "communism." The *Manifesto* of 1848 is a transcription of this vision into slogan-like formulas for political agitation; and the *Capital* of 1867 is a "scientific" exposition of the internal contradictions of the "bourgeois mode of production" leading to the communist explosion. This last work later lent itself to reading in a "positivistic" manner, thereby winnowing out the metaphysics of the first drafts of the system, a reading which furnished the basis of the Second International's "orthodox" Marxism.

Yet the system was not first formulated as a theory of capitalism in general; it emerged as the scenario for the coming German revolution. The young Marx repeatedly expressed his "shame" at Germany's "medieval" backwardness, and his hope was that the future revolution would propel Germany to the level of France and England. However, since France had already made its "bourgeois revolution" and was now building up steam for its socialist sequel, Germany need not repeat 1789. Instead, boosted by the anticipated socialist explosion in Paris, it could telescope the bourgeois and proletarian revolutions into one; and it could accomplish this feat because in one domain—rational philosophy—Germany was more advanced than the West. As the twenty-five-year-old Marx, on arriving in Paris in 1843, saw Germany's role in the coming revolution: "In politics, the Germans have *thought* what other nations [i.e., France and England] have *done*. Germany has been their *theoretical consciousness*."[4]

He then sketches a putative revolutionary Sonderweg for Germany.

> Where is there, then, a *real* possibility of emancipation in Germany?
>   *This is our reply.* A class must be formed which has radical chains, a class in civil society which is not a class of civil society, a class which is the dissolution of all classes, a sphere of society which has a universal character because its sufferings are universal, and which does not claim a particular redress because the wrong which is done to it is not a particular wrong but wrong in general. [. . .] This dissolution of society, as a particular class, is the proletariat.

Socialism's basic principle is thus that the last among men shall be first, indeed that *only* the last, by their very degradation, are the class capable of emancipating mankind. Thereby the proletariat is defined as the universal class, the only class whose self-interest is that of humanity as a whole.

Likewise, national backwardness is a form of being "last." It too, therefore, can be a way of being first, thereby becoming the vanguard of mankind's emancipation. "The emancipation of Germany is only possible *in practice* if one adopts the point of view of that theory according to which Man is the highest being for man. Germany will not be able to emancipate itself from the Middle Ages [i.e., the Old Regime] unless it emancipates itself at the same time from the partial victories over the Middle Ages [i.e., French and British property-suffrage constitutionalism]. In Germany no type of enslavement can be abolished unless all enslavement is destroyed. [. . .] The emancipation of Germany will be an emancipation of Man."

The final principle of socialism is that it represents universal reason in social form: "Philosophy is the head of this emancipation and the proletariat is its heart. Philosophy can only be realized by the abolition of the proletariat, and the proletariat can only be abolished by the realization of philosophy." Then comes the French connection: "When all the inner conditions ripen, the day of German resurrection will be proclaimed by the crowing of the Gallic cock."[5]

This document of 1843 is usually described as Marx's "discovery of the proletariat." But the proletariat evoked here is less a social than a metaphysical entity; and indeed Marx knew almost nothing about the actual working class at the time. Later, of course, his proletariat would acquire more social and economic flesh with the labor theory of value, the capitalists' confiscation of surplus value, the law of increasing "immiseration," and so on. Still, Marx's proletariat never ceased to be in the first instance humanity's "universal class," the bearer of a messianic mission as the class to end all classes, predestined to be society's redeemer because it was society's most dehumanized class.

But what is perhaps most striking in this ur-Marxism is that the proletariat is defined as the chosen vessel of philosophy. This philosophy, of course, is Hegelianism, as Marx had transformed it into a historical materialism under the influence of Ludwig Feuerbach's *Essence of Christianity*. It is precisely this Hegelian component of Marx's system that makes it a system. No English economist or French "utopian" socialist was capable of coming up with anything so systematic, and hence compelling, precisely because—Marx was right on this point—they lacked "philosophic consciousness."

The Hegelian component of Marxism is doubly potent since this "consciousness" is not just philosophical but also residually theological. Although many would dispute such a judgment, Hegelianism has been appropriately called a "philosophical religion," offering a transposition of Christian providentialism into would-be rationalistic categories.[6] With Hegel divine reason becomes immanent in history, evolving through humanity's increasingly complex cultural forms toward absolute "self-consciousness," which is also absolute human freedom. Reason advances, however, only at the price of "alienation," a dialectic whereby all forms of being "externalize" or "negate" themselves in "contradictory" forms, thereby creating new forms higher and richer than their incomplete predecessors.

Marx transformed Hegel's metaphysical teleology into a socioeconomic one in which successively higher "modes of production" overcame mankind's dependence on the blind forces of nature; and he secularized the dialectic into the "class struggle," by which the species' advance to higher modes of production required ever more exploitative class relations. Yet social alienation was also self-enriching, since it engendered among the oppressed "consciousness" of society's cruel but creative logic, thereby pointing to emancipation at the "end of prehistory." In this agonistic eschatology the proletariat occupies the most exalted position since, as the most dehumanized class under the highest mode of production, capitalism, it alone can abolish all exploitation, thereby bringing man at last fully into his own.

Thus Marx's system falls into two basic parts, and they are not wholly compatible. First, there is the logic of history necessarily leading mankind upward from slave-holding society, through feudalism, to capitalism, to socialism. This progression is governed by objective historical laws, acting independently of human will. Second, there is the class struggle serving as the motive force of the "law-like" logic of history. This struggle, moreover, is fueled by the "consciousness" of exploitation, an ideological factor which introduces human will into the objective historical process. On a theoretical plane, Marx resolved the potential conflict between objective logic and subjective consciousness in his system by saying that at the moment of historical ripeness the latter was automatically generated by the former, according to the fundamental axiom of historical materialism that "Being determines Consciousness." The great question of Marxist praxis, of course, is whether revolutionary incitement to class struggle will in fact always coincide with the "ripeness" of objective historical conditions.

Marx's system is put under even greater strain by his goal of socialism, or communism as he preferred to say. In general terms this goal was the classless, stateless society—an anarchist program at variance with his predominant emphasis on history's "law-like" pattern. Though such a goal is patently unrealizable, we should not make the common error of dismissing it as an irrelevant aberration. Lenin, for one, took it most seriously in justifying the dictatorship of the proletariat proposed in *State and Revolution*. Indeed, it is the surest sign of the millenarian aspiration underlying Marxism and Leninism both.

But the most crucial internal contradiction of Marxism is the relationship between this utopian goal and the instrumental program advanced for achieving it; and most of this program, unlike the utopia itself, *can* be realized. For Marx the essence of socialism is to be the "negation" of capitalism; concretely, this noncapitalism entails the abolition of private property, profit, the market, and indeed money. All these instruments of exploitation are to be replaced by rational planning. Similarly, the "petty-bourgeois" world of individual peasant agriculture, with its attendant "idiocy of rural life," is to be "negated" by rational collectivization.

The details of this program are spelled out quite explicitly in the *Manifesto*, issued after all in the name of a hypothetical "Communist Party." The goals of these Communists are, first, to seize political power in order to "wrest, by degrees, all capital from the bourgeoisie," and then to "centralize all instruments of production in the hands of the State, i.e., of the proletariat organized as the ruling class." All production, moreover, would be "concentrated in the hands of the vast association of the whole nation" with "industrial armies, especially for agriculture," and a "common plan." In short, "the theory of Communism may be summed up in the single sentence: Abolition of private property." And what is vague in places of the *Manifesto* was clarified in *Capital*, which offers one long excoriation of "commodity production for exchange" (i.e., manufacture for the market) and of the "bloodstained" medium of profit for "capital accumulation"—money. Marx's concrete program for "human emancipation," then, is nothing less than this total noncapitalism.

And it is necessary to insist on this fact, for many commentators have refused to recognize it, holding that Marx, unlike "utopian" socialists, offered no vision of the future but only "scientific" knowledge of history's laws. The reason for this strange blindness, of course, is that once Stalin implemented that very program by mass violence many Westerners backed away from it, either preferring to believe that some other Bolshevik could have built a better socialism or choosing to read his doctrine only as a critique of capitalist society, as in the "Marxism without a proletariat" of the Frankfurt school. The great question of Marxist praxis, then, is this: would the instrumental means of total noncapitalism in fact produce the expected moral and rational results?

At this late date, it is enough to ask this question to see that there are so many contradictions in Marx's system that it is *impossible* for it ever to be realized in full. This fact must be emphasized, for otherwise Marxism's historical fate in Russia and China is incomprehensible. For, given a body of doctrine that is impossible to realize, startling surprises are inevitable whenever an attempt is made to act on it.

The greatest such surprise, of course, was Red October. It is often said that the Bolshevik Revolution developed despotically because Russia "was not yet ripe for socialism," and that Leninist Marxism was therefore "unorthodox"—the implication apparently being that if "orthodox" Marxism had been followed, the revolution would have worked out canonically. But no country is *ever* ripe for socialism—anywhere, anytime—*in Marx's impossible sense.*

The same is true of what most Second International Social Democrats understood by socialism. It is often forgotten that the maximalism of Marx's *Manifesto* (though without explicit mention of violence) became the doctrine of the International's leading parties once the prestigious German Social Democrats wrote it into their Erfurt Program of 1891—the first time a major labor movement came under the leadership of Marxist intellectuals. True, it turned out that most of the International's member parties were not prepared to act on their official doctrine; but they themselves did not know this until 1914–1918.

THE DILEMMAS OF THE SECOND INTERNATIONAL

Nonetheless, Marxism's internal incompatibilities were put under increasing strain by the pressure of Europe's diverse Sonderwege, its differing combinations of Old Regime and industrialization. By the 1870s-1880s industrial society had spread from the Atlantic West across Central Europe; and after 1890 it had indeed arrived in Russia. Concurrently, after the tragic failure of the Paris Commune in 1871, the socialist movement, largely dormant across Europe since 1848, began to revive. (The Paris Commune of 1871 does not mark a real revolutionary flare-up. It was a last gasp, a tragic fluke occasioned by the Franco-Prussian War, and was Jacobin and patriotic much more than proto-socialist. But it did leave a potent myth for "the next time.") In 1889, therefore, on the hundredth anniversary of the French Revolution, a Second International was founded in Paris. And the increasingly numerous workers of the world now had some prospect of seeing the long-hoped-for socialist 1789 at last come to pass.

At the same time, however, universal or near-universal suffrage, even in the pseudo-constitutionalisms of Germany and Austria, permitted socialist parties to enter parliament and work for reforms which, though not "socialist," still benefited workers. These conditions also produced, at last, a solid trade-union movement. And these changes revealed, first, that capitalism was not generating increasing "immiseration" but was instead raising workers' living standards, and, second, that parliamentary reform might well make revolution unnecessary.

The crisis of Second International Marxism was at its most acute in the contradictory conditions of Imperial Germany—now Europe's industrial giant, yet still a semi-Old Regime. In 1898, Eduard Bernstein drew the obvious reformist conclusions from German Social Democracy's actual practice in the decade since Erfurt. He declared that Marx was wrong regarding both immiseration and the development of a revolutionary consciousness among the workers, and so concluded that for socialism "the movement is everything, the goal is nothing."[7]

This position was condemned—accurately—as "revisionist" by the "orthodox" majority of the Social Democrats led by Karl Kautsky. Kautsky, however, did some revising of his own by arguing that parliamentary democracy had become, in effect, the final stage of the logic of history, and that socialism could thus be realized by electoral means. Yet it should be emphasized that by "socialism" Kautsky meant not what it is now understood as "democratic socialism"—a cradle-to-the-grave welfare state—but Marx's maximalist goal of noncapitalism. The orthodox position is thus best called "evolutionary revolution."

It must also be noted that this revolution would come in a fairly distant future—the Social Democrats' "program maximum"—for it should not be forgotten that in Kautsky's time Central Europe (as we have seen) remained stubbornly pseudo-constitutionalist. The immediate task of Social Democracy, therefore—its "program minimum"—was to struggle, not just for improvements in the workers' lot, but for that democracy which the "bourgeoisie" had failed to achieve in

1848—a failure aggravated when, under Bismarck, German liberals abandoned their "natural" constitutionalist vocation in exchange for national unification under the Prussian semi-autocracy. Thus, in the skewed German Sonderweg Marxism's first role was to claim the democratic terrain abandoned by the bourgeoisie, and so to assume leadership of the political struggle against German political backwardness.

It is this ambiguous "evolutionary revolution" that for the next half-century would be known in the West as "orthodox Marxism." Yet it must be noted that "orthodox" Marxists, even with an overwhelming parliamentary majority, have never dared to act on their program maximum. And they were reticent for the good reason that the expropriations necessary to implement socialism as noncapitalism could lead only to resistance and civil war. (A case in point is Salvador Allende of Chile, who believed that once he achieved 51 percent of the vote he could introduce Castro-style socialism without having to fight.) In practice, therefore, the theory of an evolutionary revolution defended by orthodox Social Democrats turned out to be as utopian as Marx's original "big bang" theory of revolution.

The defeat of the Second International's "orthodox" Marxism was brought about by World War I. The war accomplished this, first, by discrediting the revolutionary credentials of Kautsky's Social Democrats. Its outbreak conclusively demonstrated that they were merely reformist, and, at that, only within the bounds of patriotism. And its conclusion, with Germany's defeat, at last brought these "Marxists" to power in the Weimar Republic, though now under the trade-union leader and party bureaucrat Friedrich Ebert, who was hardly even reformist. All the same, the Social Democrats continued to insist that their movement was the sole orthodox one—even though it now suspiciously resembled what Marx had always excoriated as "petty bourgeois democracy." So once the Social Democrats' minimal program of "bourgeois democracy" had been effortlessly achieved by the monarchy's collapse in 1918, their maximal utopia withered away into welfare-state reformism. Still, it took until 1958 for the German Social Democrats to acknowledge this fact and renounce explicitly their Marxist allegiance.

THE BEGINNINGS OF LENINISM

It thus fell to a third, provincial participant in the revisionist controversy, Lenin, to produce a revision of Marxism that remained revolutionary and yet could be acted on in the real world. His deeds are chronicled in the next chapter. His theory, however, must be examined here, in the context of the Second

International debates that gave it birth. Still, it should not be forgotten that there exists an organic link between this theory and his later practice: as the founder of Bolshevism always insisted, "without theory, there can be no revolutionary movement."

The first impetus to Lenin's activity came from a Russian form of revisionism stigmatized by its opponents as "economism." Hardly had Marxism been acclimated in Russia in the 1890s than some comrades took to advising the workers to limit themselves to economic demands, leaving the dangerous political struggle against autocracy to intellectuals—a program that separated the workers from the revolutionary movement which, according to Marx, it was their mission to incarnate. This heresy stimulated another impatient young man, the thirty-year-old Lenin, to formulate his theory of the vanguard party.

In doing so, he in effect agreed with Bernstein that the economic struggle of the workers was not generating a revolutionary consciousness. But unlike Bernstein, he concluded that the goal was everything, and the movement toward it therefore had to be guided. Hence, Lenin's remedy for the deficit of worker consciousness was to refuse to follow the "spontaneity" of the workers into "trade-union" reformism. His solution, rather, was to inform the proletariat "from without" with the "consciousness" of "scientific" revolutionary theory. And Lenin tirelessly insisted: "There can be no revolution without theory." Such a theory, moreover, could come only from the "intelligentsia," organized into a party of professional revolutionaries.

The essence of Lenin's solution to the crisis of fin-de-siècle Marxism was to keep the doctrine revolutionary but at the cost of subordinating the logic of history to ideological "consciousness," or political will. Formally speaking, of course, Lenin had turned Marx upside down, and subordinated "being" to "consciousness." In reality, however, he had adopted the only solution that would make "being" culminate in the total revolution that Marx had supposed life would generate on its own. Lenin's theory of the party thus supplied the missing link in Marx's scenario for revolution by designating a vanguard intelligentsia as the sole agency capable of bringing the socialist revolution into the world of praxis. Set forth in *What Is To Be Done?* in 1902, when Lenin was just thirty-two, this solution to the turn-of-the-century crisis of Marxism led to Lenin's "party of a new type," the Bolsheviks, with which he proposed "to overturn all Russia."[8]

It is obvious that these Leninist revisions of Marxism were a response to Russia's Sonderweg under the Old Regime. Industrialism had developed enough to generate working-class discontent, but not enough to significantly improve the workers' lot. Before 1906 there was no parliament, and before 1917 (that is, too late) no universal suffrage—the two things necessary to give reformism its main chance.

But Russia's sociological particularities are not the only cause of Leninism's emergence. Equally important are the internal incompatibilities of Marxism itself.

Since it is impossible to realize the whole doctrine, its adepts must ultimately choose among its components. Bernstein chose to follow the logic of history to where it in fact leads under industrial society: the welfare state. Such an option, however, ultimately destroys Marxism, for a welfare state hardly requires a revolutionary doctrine. Indeed, the first draft of the welfare state was produced by the radical conservative Bismarck, and later versions came from Fabians and New Deal Democrats. Kautsky, though he chose formal fidelity to Marxism, in fact was simply living the illusion that the logic of history leads democratically to Marx's maximalist goal; so his followers eventually wound up as de facto revisionists. Lenin, finally, chose fidelity to Marx's goal, and made sure he would get there by putting the class struggle of the proletariat under the direction of the Party. And it *is* necessary to be Marxist to make this option for the goal of noncapitalism over all else, and to persevere in it to the bitter end.

It is thus idle to dispute which of these Marxisms is "orthodox" or the truly socialist one, for there is no such thing in the real world as true Marxist socialism. In the real world, there is only the banal but comfortable welfare state or the exhilarating yet terrifying Leninist Party-state. But it should be noted that of the two, only the latter realized Marx's vision of socialism as noncapitalism. And it was able to do so only by inverting Marx's logic of history and building socialism not in an advanced industrial society, but in a backward one.

But this outcome had been Marxism's long-term vocation, unbeknownst to its author, from the beginning. For Marxism, just as it had begun as a theory for overcoming German backwardness in the 1840s, made its entire career essentially in economically and/or politically backward countries.

Before 1914 Marxism took deep root only in Imperial Germany, Austria-Hungary, Congress Poland, and Russia, and to a lesser degree Italy. The strongest socialist parties of the Second International are from this area, as are all the International's major theorists—Kautsky, Rosa Luxemburg, Rudolf Hilferding, Otto Bauer, and of course Lenin and Trotsky. (Farther west, Jean Jaurès, for example, was closer in spirit to Michelet than to Marx.) It was the example of the Russian Revolution, and then the anti-fascism and Popular Fronts of the 1930s, that first acclimated Marxism west of the Rhine, occasionally in mass Communist parties and almost everywhere among intellectuals. After 1917 Communism spread above all to areas of European colonial expansion; after 1945 it was only there, especially in East Asia, that it came to power on its own outside of Russia.

This persisting correlation of Marxism generally, and of Communism in particular, with political and/or economic backwardness ought to be an object of considerable sociological curiosity. But no: the problem is largely ignored, or still worse shrugged off with the observation that since the backward countries were "not ready for socialism" they only denatured Marxism. But, the real problem (and a quasi-Marxist one at that) should be: what is the logic of Marxism that gives it a social base and makes it relevant *only* in backward areas?

The answer, in general terms, is that Marxism makes capitalism alluring on two counts; it is the supremely creative "mode of production" in all history and at the same time the necessary precondition for transcending that exploitative history by achieving socialism. Thus intellectuals in backward areas are drawn to it first to rise to the level of the advanced West; and then to trump the West's ace by becoming socialist.

So it was that the one successful product of the failed Revolution of 1848—Marxism—came to mediate between the French and the Russian Revolutions, the two nodal points of the modern revolutionary tradition. The transcendental German theory for completing the French Revolution landed on earth as the rude praxis of the Russian Revolution; and these three stages of ideological escalation together gave us our basic categories for talking about all revolutions.[9]

It is precisely this circumstance that has confused our perception of the Russian Revolution, for we persist in assessing it as either the fulfillment or the betrayal of Marx's script for a socialist 1848. But the putative scenario for a "higher" German 1789 worked no better in the Russian Sonderweg of 1917 than it had the first time around in the German Sonderweg of 1848. The result was that Lenin's revolution was at one and the same time the fulfillment and the betrayal of Marx's vision: for the application of Marxism's instrumental program proved in practice to be the betrayal of the moral ideal of social justice originally animating the system. Hegel, had he lived to see this outcome, would hardly have been surprised, for such is the Cunning of Reason in history.

Again, it is politics, not the dynamic of the class struggle, that produces the first socialist revolution, politics in the form of the impact of World War I on Europe's least reformed Old Regime, that of Russia.

11

RED OCTOBER

The Revolution to End All Revolutions

The farther east one goes in Europe the weaker, meaner, and more cowardly becomes the bourgeoisie in the political sense, and the greater the cultural and political tasks which fall to the lot of the proletariat.
—P. B. STRUVE, first manifesto of the Russian Social Democratic Party, 1898

> The wind whirls, the snow flies.
> And twelve men march forth . . .
> The bourgeois stands across their way,
> His nose in his fur collar . . .
> The bourgeois stands like a hungry hound . . .
> And the old world, like a mongrel cur,
> Tail between legs, slinks down . . .
> Forward, forward, forward
> You toiling masses!
> Hey, comrade, it's going to be rough,
> Come out and begin to shoot!
> Trak-tak-tak . . .
> The people march on with commanding stride—
> And at their head—with a bloodied flag,
> Behind the screen of whirling snow,
> Untouched by any bullet,
> Walking weightless over the drifts
> In a dust of snowy pearl,
> In a white nimbus of roses—
> At their head marches Jesus Christ.
> —ALEKSANDR BLOK, *The Twelve*, 1918

The teaching of Marx is all powerful because it is true.
—V. I. LENIN, as engraved on the Marx monument in central Moscow

The Russian Revolution has been a presence throughout this book because of the long shadow it cast over our understanding of all previous revolutions. Just as the nineteenth century lived under the hypnotic spell of the French Revolution, so the twentieth century was hypnotized by Lenin's October. And, as the putative terminus ad quem of human progress (of the process of which Hus and Žižka were the terminus a quo), its categories of explanation interjected themselves into, indeed often dominated, the historiography of every revolution since the time of Hus and Žižka.

Understandably, yet also unfortunately, this same spell has dominated the historiography of the regime which October inaugurated. To be sure, partisan Whig and Jacobin historiographies in their day often distorted the meaning of 1640 and 1789, but October has done a much more thorough job than either, since the historiography of the Russian Revolution developed contemporaneously with the protracted revolutionary process to which it gave rise. This leaves us with a picture of the Russian Revolution similar to what we can learn of the Lutheran Reformation from Sleiden and Cochlaeus.[1] Soviet, that is, domestic, historiography had to work under constraints quite unknown in the established historiographies of the West. Essentially, in matters of broad interpretation it was the handmaiden of the state's "historiosophical" ideology and may be considered a subset of official ideology. American and Western historiography on Russia was thus as firmly set apart in modern scholarship as was its subject matter in modern culture and politics. This historiography will come into play in the course of the discussion that follows.[2]

In approaching the Russian Revolution it is first necessary to state what one understands by that term. For some it means ten October days that shook the world.[3] For others it is the year 1917 from February to October, that is, the eight months of the Bolsheviks' advance to power.[4] For still others it is the years 1917–1921, or the period the Bolsheviks required to achieve control of most of the former Russian Empire.[5] And for still others it extends from 1917 to the fulfillment of October's mission with the "building of socialism" in the early 1930s. Finally, for adepts of the broad perspective, it is the entire transition from the Old Regime to the new, from the Revolution of 1905 to Stalin's "revolution from above" and Purges of the 1930s.[6] It is this comprehensive definition that will be employed here.

The events of 1905 were certainly the first phase of the two "revolutions" of 1917, with the same monarchy, the same political parties, and the same chief actors. February definitively sealed the fate of the monarchy; as regards the future, however, 1917 decided very little. October only gave the Bolsheviks a chance at power; it was not certain they would hold it until the crucial struggles of the Civil War in 1918–1919 and the concurrent construction of a Party dictatorship under War Communism. But the full meaning of this "Soviet power" did not become clear until Stalin used it to "build socialism" in the 1930s. Indeed, the complete ramifications of this "socialism" did not emerge until its swift collapse in 1989–1991 revealed that it had always been, basically, a fraud.

The discussion here, therefore, will range over the broad process from 1905 to 1991, while treating the period from October 1917 to 1939 as the Revolution's culmination. For it is those years that produced what was distinctive about the Russian Revolution: the creation of the world's first Marxist regime and first "socialist" society.[7] After 1939 this society had a grand international career, but domestically the zeal of the founding years was transformed into state dogma.

In all these respects, the Russian Revolution presents an anomaly in the series of revolutions we have considered thus far. All the others had a clear beginning, middle, and end, and all spanned no more than a decade or two. In these cases, then, "revolution" refers to an event or a rapid succession of closely related events. In Russia, developments at first took this form with the upheaval of 1904–1907. And it must be stressed that this event was no mere "dress rehearsal" for 1917, as the Bolsheviks (specifically Trotsky) later claimed; rather, it offers one variant of what has been called here a "normal" European revolution against an Old Regime, whether played out in full as in France in 1789 or interrupted in mid-course as in Germany in 1848.

Russia moved toward its new model of revolution in two stages. The first, the Revolution of 1905, was a replay of the pattern of *revolutio interrupta* already observed in Prussia and Austria in 1848—that is, a foreshortening of the classic scenario of European revolution, ending in a *Scheinkonstitutionalismus*, or pseudo-constitutionalism, an outcome made possible since the monarchy retained control of the armed forces and so was able to resist the revolutionary assembly's pretensions to sovereignty.

Russia in 1905–1907 offers a variant of this scenario. Its pseudo-constitutionalism took the form of a Legislative Duma reluctantly conceded by the autocracy in October 1905. The powers of this body, however, were more poorly defined than Bismarck's Reichstag, and public support for it was correspondingly weaker than support for parliamentarianism in Germany. At the same time, Russia's huge, disaffected peasant mass created a social situation far more volatile than Germany's. So when the collapse of this unstable semi-constitutionalism came in 1917, Russia departed from both variants of the previous European pattern to embark on an unprecedented *Sonderweg* of its own.

Russia moved toward this new course in two stages. In February 1917, under the impact of war, the dormant Russian Revolution resumed, and at first it seemed to resolve the constitutional deadlock by a victory of the constitution-alist left. In October, however, the Russian revolutionary process underwent a sea change unique in European history; once the ultra left had seized power, it simply stayed there, and no Thermidor or Bonaparte ever came along to displace it. It is as if the Jacobins had retained control of France until 1863 (the same seventy-four years of Soviet power), and in the interval had leveled existing so-ciety and replaced it with one of their own contriving. Thus, in the Russian case, "revolution" eventually came to mean less an event than a regime, and so be-came (to borrow a phrase from its Mexican near-contemporary) what hitherto had been a contradiction in terms, an "institutional revolution."

The emergence of this revolution-as-regime, however, is no paradox. It de-rives quite logically from Communism's pretension to be the culmination of human progress, the end of history, beyond which there is nothing but counter-revolution and "the restoration of capitalism." A Communist revolution, there-fore, necessarily institutionalizes itself as a regime, because it is by definition the revolution to end all further need for revolution. For with Communism hu-manity has at last "arrived."

This pretension derives from another anomaly of the Bolsheviks' October: theirs was the first revolution in history to be "made" according to an explicit theory of revolution. All previous European revolutions, of course, had been fueled by ideologies; but none had been guided by an ideology of history as revo-lutionary process. And the Bolsheviks could have such a theory only because of the antecedent experience of the rest of Europe.

To recall: although the English most definitely made a revolution between 1640 and 1660, they never admitted it, but wound up instead viewing its out-come, in 1688, as a restoration, thereby largely expunging the radicalism of their deed from the national consciousness. The Americans knew very well that their revolt was a revolution, at least in its outcome if not as a process; but its radi-calism was quickly encapsulated in a stable constitutional system, and so led to no cult of revolution per se. The French made a revolution so radical with re-spect to Europe's millennial past that for the first time revolution as an impla-cable historical force became apparent to all. And it is this example that furnished the modern world the model of revolution as process, a force of nature acting independently of human will. Henceforth radicals believed, and conservatives feared, that revolutions are the way history happens, the "locomotives of history" in Marx's metaphor. From the French Revolution onward the European left was able to anticipate a replay of the scenario of 1789 on a "higher," more progressive level.

THE RUSSIAN OLD REGIME

Concretely, what happened when the accumulated baggage of the European revolutionary tradition was unloaded on Russia? In general terms, of course, Lenin's Bolsheviks at last carried out Marx's scenario for a socialist 1848 by making a national revolution against the Old Regime predicated on a concurrent Western explosion. But the Bolsheviks did this in the context of a different Old Regime from those farther west, and against the background of an indigenous revolutionary tradition.

The Russian Old Regime, the youngest in Europe, was also the most rudimentary and brutal. A simple military autocracy, a government by centralized bureaucracy, a subservient church, a stark two-class society of gentry and peasant serfs (with only a minimal merchant class, less in the middle than off to the side), a feebly developed secular culture—this was the Russia that Peter the Great, by the time of his death in 1725, had made one of the five great powers of Europe. Although not quite "an army with a state," as contemporary Prussia has been called, Imperial Russia was a state whose chief purpose was to field an army, in which gentry officers and serf conscripts had to serve in effect for life, and which was financed by peasant and merchant taxes. By 1762 and the reign of Catherine the Great, however, the gentry had been freed from compulsory state service; and later they and the other principal social categories (except the peasants) received a status resembling estates, while secular Western culture was creatively acclimated among the gentry elite. And so, by the eve of 1789 Russia had become an Old Regime—just as that regime crumbled in the West.

This gap between the phases of Russia's "Europeanization" and those of the Western original meant that it could never simply repeat Europe's antecedent development. Rather, with each new stage of the West's transformation, Russia had to telescope into two or three decades developments which at their point of origin had taken a half century or more. The result was that the pattern offered by the Atlantic West was usually simplified or distorted.[8]

This process became particularly acute when the Old Regime gave way to the new. In the eighteenth century, Europeanization for Russia meant replacing its traditional seasonal militia with a standing army equipped with the new sciences of artillery and fortification. The rise of the democratic idea in the West after 1789, however, redefined modernity, thereby making Russia's two principal institutions, autocracy and serfdom, out of date.

Seventeen eighty-nine, and still more Napoleon's armies, sent the same message to the serf-based monarchies of Prussia and Austria. The result was a "revolution from above" that echoed France's prior revolution from below. Yet east of the

Rhine this echo was muted by different historical conditions. In Western Europe serfdom had, of course, disappeared in the thirteenth century whereas it was re-instituted in Central Europe in the sixteenth; and Central-European economic civil society was only weakly developed. So the ideals of 1789 could travel east-ward only in transposed guise. In Prussia the result was the reform movement of 1807–1812, which accomplished, in filtered form, that part of the French revolu-tionary agenda that was compatible with autocracy and aristocracy: the abolition of serfdom, a modicum of local self-government, and universal military service. (Austria, though, was slower to react to Western pressure than Prussia: serfdom was not abolished until 1848, and the modest parliament "granted" that year was rescinded the next, unlike the Prussian *Landtag* of 1849, and did not reappear until 1867–1868.)

The shock of 1789 reached Russia twenty years after it hit Prussia, and it had the dual effect both of radicalizing Russian elite culture and of making the monarchy resistant to further imitation of Europe. The shock first produced the Decem-brist revolt of 1825, which was not a revolution, but a conspiracy of officers from the gentry mounted to introduce a constitution and end serfdom. The inevitable failure of this adventure produced a second, and opposite, response to the chal-lenge of the new Europe. During thirty years under Nicholas I, the hitherto en-lightened monarchy, which from Peter to Alexander I had emphasized Russia's belonging to Europe, now cut the nation off from Western contagion by cre-ating a cult of autocracy as the one true Russian way. Thus emerged the theory of a conservative Russian *Sonderweg* which would remain state doctrine until the end of the Old Regime.

At the same time, the Slavophiles put forth the ideal of a more open conser-vatism. Though opposed to Western constitutionalism, they wished to moderate autocracy by claiming "freedom of opinion" and an informal autonomy for "so-ciety," by which term they meant the nation's educated (and Westernized) elite. For to them the true Russian way was not individualism, but a consensual *sobor-nost'* — "conciliarity" in the church and "communality" in society—a principle of which the peasant commune was the prime exemplar. This is the first appear-ance of that institution in Russian social thought, and it was set forth—we are now at the time of the July Monarchy—in order to show that Russia had no need of the latest Western democratic innovation, socialism.

In response to the Slavophiles, the left of "society" updated the Decembrists' program. These "Westernizers" subdivided into two camps. The moderates be-lieved that piecemeal reform from above would eventually replace autocracy and serfdom with a constitutional polity, and so make Russia converge with the West. The radicals, on the other hand, echoing the avant-garde opposition to the July

Monarchy, sought that convergence in revolutionary socialism. Thus, on the eve of 1848, the Russian far left, at the same time as its Western mentor, precociously embarked on its own career of revolutionary anticipation.

The Western model, however, could not be taken over literally by these radicals; for in Russia, the democratic idea could refer only to the peasants—the *narod*, or "people." This circumstance soon yielded a specifically Russian radicalism eventually called *narodnichestvo*, or Populism.

Its foundations were laid by Aleksandr Herzen and Mikhail Bakunin. In the 1840s, like their later foe Marx, they went through a provincial version of German Left Hegelianism; then, again like him, they went west on the eve of 1848 in search of "the revolution." In the midst of its failure, the idea dawned that the West might not hold the key to humanity's emancipation after all. By 1849, taking a leaf from the book of the Slavophiles, they launched the theory that the most advanced Western ideal, socialism, might be realized in Russia earlier than in Europe on the basis of the peasant commune. That institution was already virtually "socialist," since property was not private but was periodically redistributed according to changing peasant needs. All that would be required to make the commune fully socialist, therefore, would be a revolution in which the wrath of the people would sweep away the autocracy and dispossess the parasitical gentry.

This alluring fantasy was buttressed by the more realistic proposition that the awesome Russian autocracy was in fact fragile. Given the brutality of the primitive two-class social system on which it rested, neither the enlightened elite nor the dehumanized people were attached to it. Nor was plausible evidence for this belief lacking in the long history of Russian peasant revolts, from the Time of Troubles at the beginning of the seventeenth century to Stenka Razin at its end, and on to Yemilian Pugachev in 1773–1775—all far mightier than the French jacquerie of 1358 or the German Peasants' War of 1525. It would therefore be far easier to ignite a revolution in Russia than in the West, where a solid bourgeoisie stood between the state and the people and dampened radical ardor by the half-way measure of property-suffrage constitutionalism. The politics of revolution in Russia would thus be supremely simple: the enlightened elite, the bearer of revolutionary "consciousness," would bring the idea of socialism to the "dark" people and, behold! Socialism itself would appear. Thus was born the radical version of Russia's Sonderweg in European history.

In more moderate form, the possibility of accelerating history through imitation translates as "the advantages of backwardness." One of these advantages was that Russia was able to close the gap with the West very quickly in high culture. Thus Russia's eighteenth-century "enlightened despotism" modernized its empire less by the expensive means of fostering economic development than by the cheaper recourse of educating the gentry for practicing the modern arts of warfare and bureaucratic government. This worked well until the very success of Europeanization made enlightenment a value in itself, and so, under Nicholas, created a gulf between the educated elite and its erstwhile autocratic patron.

There thus emerged that peculiarly Russian group, the intelligentsia, a name which it received toward the end of the century. Although the name meant the educated classes in general, and although the great majority of their members were not radical, it usually carried an oppositional connotation; and, as a practical matter, it was the radical minority of the intelligentsia that soon imposed its ideological hegemony over Russian society and culture. Until the Revolution of 1905, Russia's illegal, "shadow" politics, whether liberal or radical, would be almost exclusively the province of this intelligentsia.

This skewed situation may be considered one of the prime disadvantages of backwardness; for, to use Marxist terminology, Russia had created the "superstructure" of modernity before it acquired the "base." Or, as Joseph de Maistre, Sardinian Minister to St. Petersburg at the beginning of the century, pointed out to Alexander I in attempting to moderate the emperor's zeal for founding new universities: the great threat to the fragile Russian order would one day be a "Pugatcheff d'université."[9]

This prophecy began to resemble reality when Alexander II, shaken by Russia's defeat in the Crimean War, undertook a defensive revolution from above on the Prussian model of 1807–1812. This produced the Great Reforms of 1861–1864: the abolition of serfdom, a modicum of local self-government in the form of zemstvos, an independent judiciary—and in 1874 another modern institution, universal military service.

All the same, the result of Alexander's reforms soon confirmed Tocqueville's maxim that "the most dangerous moment for a bad government is when it starts to reform itself." For the terms of the emancipation—inevitably a compromise between gentry and peasant interests—failed to satisfy the peasants, and even more portentously the radical intelligentsia. Approximately speaking, the peasants got half the land, and had to pay for it in installments, whereas they had wanted "land and freedom," or all the land of the village without conditions. The radical intelligentsia had wanted this too, in part to do justice to the peasants, but in larger part to strengthen the base for a future agrarian socialism. Crying "swindle," therefore, the far left put forth the slogan "to the people," with the expectation that peasant bitterness would now overflow in revolution.

The great man of this new generation of radicals was Nicholas Chernyshevsky. He could not put appeals to revolution into print because of censorship, but, in his novel *What Is To Be Done* of 1863, he did give to generations of radicals the ideal portrait of the New People needed for revolution: single-minded, iron-willed activists, totally dedicated to the people's cause. He also championed "civic art," a code term for the subordination of all culture to politics; and he exuded hatred for pusillanimous liberals who rejected this militant worldview. Lenin had a special veneration for this predecessor, and expressed it in the title of Bolshevism's founding document in 1902.

Thus the intelligentsia's disappointment with the emancipation produced a crisis that led to an inverted pattern of politics which would endure until the early twentieth century. In 1862, there emerged the first socialist revolutionary society, Land and Freedom. In the same year, the gentry liberals, also disappointed by Alexander's concessions, demanded the "crowning of the edifice" of reform by the creation of a national representative body. The autocracy was able to contain the nobles simply by saying "no"; but it proved quite unable to counter the radical intelligentsia. The seed planted by Land and Freedom grew for the next twenty years, eventually creating a continuing movement of professional revolutionaries —a new breed in history and a veritable national "institution" down to 1917.

The Populists first "went to the people" with direct appeals for revolution; and when these failed, a part of the movement, organized as "The People's Will," launched a campaign of terror against the regime in 1879. Their strategy was to force the autocracy to convene a constituent assembly chosen by universal suffrage; and this body's inevitable peasant majority would then vote socialism into being. This tactic, in an odd way, did work, though not with the peasants. It affected above all the nonrevolutionary majority of society: both the liberal Ivan Turgenev and the reactionary Fedor Dostoevsky expressed awe and admiration at the revolutionaries' heroism. Indeed, the autocracy itself was moved to prepare, not a constitution, but a plan for a modest consultative assembly. Then, in 1881, the People's Will assassinated the emperor.

The legacy of the Populist phase of the Russian revolutionary movement was threefold. First, the emperor's assassination inaugurated twenty-five years of renewed reaction. This came, moreover, just as Russian society was beginning to break out of its two-class mold by developing economically and diversifying socially on the European model. Yet tsarism's answering reaffirmation of autocracy as the eternal Russian way prevented it from adapting politically to this evolving society—thereby inviting new revolutionary challenges.

Second, liberalism, based essentially on the gentry-dominated zemstvos, was placed permanently in a position of inferiority vis-à-vis intelligentsia socialism. This was in part because the socialist ideal was "higher" than mere constitutionalism, and in part because the revolutionaries could act illegally whereas the liberals were committed on principle to legality—and all politics were illegal in Russia until 1905.

This circumstance constitutes the principal particularity of the Russian political tradition down to 1917. Not only had the liberal and socialist movements emerged simultaneously in Russia in 1862, rather than sequentially as farther west, but for the next half century Populism eclipsed liberalism in Russia's "shadow" politics. Thus the "normal" historical relationship of liberalism to socialism was inverted. And inverting the traditional order of priorities could only open the way to a revolutionary grasp for instant socialism, thereby impeding progress toward "small-deeds" constitutionalism.

The final result of the Populist epic was to discredit Populism itself. The failure of both its democratic and its terrorist tactics showed that the peasantry was not revolutionary. And this failure in turn demonstrated that in backward Russia the objective social conditions for socialism were as yet lacking. To believe that the hand of history could be forced, or that subjective will would enable Russia to leap from one stage of development to another, was suicidal utopianism. Despite this relative realism, however, the radical intelligentsia continued to believe that at the time of historical "ripeness," revolution would at last arrive. In order to prepare for this consummation, one group of Populists, under Georgii Plekhanov, turned to Marxism in 1883.

It must be emphasized that Marxism did not come to Russia because industrialization had produced a proletariat. Marxism came to Russia because, after Populism's failure, the radical intelligentsia needed a new theory of revolution. For the primary commitment of the radical wing of the Russian intelligentsia, in all its phases, was neither to the peasants nor to the workers; it was to revolution.

The reason for this primacy of "the revolution" over its presumed popular beneficiaries was that the radical intelligentsia was moved not only by the wrong done to the people, but perhaps even more by the wrong done to themselves. Their governing emotion was thus a towering hatred of the "barbaric," "Asiatic," "Tartar," "lawless," (and so on) autocracy. For this "cursed" institution made them, the enlightened, eternal minors, deprived of that citizenship which the bourgeois West accorded even to its uneducated classes.

In the course of the 1890s, Russian reality put a "base" under the "superstructure" of the radicals' new theory. The autocracy's intensive drive for industrialization under Finance Minister Sergei Witte gave Russia a multiclass social order. Modern middling urban strata and industrial workers (by 1914, some three million) appeared alongside the gentry and the overwhelming peasant majority (in

1914, still 80 percent of the population). Indeed, the peasantry itself was at last awakened by these economic transformations, the zemstvos' schools, and universal military service. For the first time since the radical intelligentsia began anticipating revolution, the conditions actually existed for an assault on the Old Regime.

This propitious conjuncture for revolution, however, created a dilemma for Russia's new Marxist movement. We have already examined the birth of Lenin's idea of the party in the fin-de-siècle crisis of European Marxism. Nineteen-five would give that party a strategy for revolutionary action.

So long as the Russian Marxists were struggling against the revolutionary romanticism of the Populists, they remained united in applying Marx's logic of history to Russia literally: there would have to be two separate Russian revolutions, the first "bourgeois" and the second "socialist." As actual revolution approached, however, the Marxists had to devise a policy for worker participation in the lesser of these events. And on this issue they faced an acute dilemma. Since Russia was a "feudal" autocracy (or an "Asiatic" despotism) and at the same time a partially "capitalist" country with an emerging proletariat, what should be the role of socialists in a revolution that by definition could not be theirs? The solution that emerged was that, given the Russian bourgeoisie's "cowardice," the proletariat would have to play a "hegemonic" role in the revolution of its class enemy.

It is over the ambiguity of this political oxymoron that the Russian Social Democrats, after their organization as a party in 1903, divided into Mensheviks and Bolsheviks (the immediate cause of the split, of course, was disagreement over qualifications for party membership). The Mensheviks stuck to the two-stage theory of revolution fairly literally, and so interpreted "hegemony" as compatible with a tactical alliance with the liberals and a policy of caution. The Bolsheviks, emboldened by the ardor of combat, increasingly extended hegemony to mean, in fact, the telescoping of the two revolutions into one. Tactically, this led them to spurn collaboration with the liberals, and to seek instead an alliance with the now awakened peasantry.

In the heat of the battle of 1905, furthermore, it was not too difficult to integrate these apparent departures from "orthodoxy" into the logic of history. Thus Lenin concluded from the events of 1905 that in the struggle against absolutism it was legitimate for the proletariat to form an alliance with those "petty bourgeois democrats" who were the peasants. What is more, once the autocracy had been overthrown, the workers might ally with the "semi-proletariat" constituted by the poorer peasants in order to "begin the transition to socialism."[10]

Lenin produced his culminating rectifications of Marx's logic of history during

World War I with his theory of imperialism. Turn-of-the-century Marxism had been increasingly preoccupied with the consequences of the European powers' overseas rivalries, and in 1916 Lenin gave practical political point to this speculation. His theory of imperialism held that under twentieth-century conditions "colonial and semi-colonial" countries were the "weakest link" of international capitalism; world revolution could therefore legitimately begin in backward Russia.

The self-contradictory postulate of proletarian hegemony in a bourgeois revolution thus proved impossible to maintain amidst an actual revolutionary struggle. The breakdown of the Marxist schema in Russia, however, reflected a still more important fact: namely, there was going to be only *one* Russian revolution against the Old Regime, as had previously been the case everywhere else in Europe. The political superiority of the Bolsheviks over the Mensheviks was that they sensed that such a once-and-for-all break was the real nature of Russia's crisis. What is more, they understood that wagering on such a consummation was in the underlying spirit of Marxism, despite the fetters that the letter of that doctrine seemed to place on their actions. So Lenin resolved Marxism's dilemma in Russia by updating the doctrine's letter to make it correspond to the real revolutionary potential of the new century.

All of which is to say that Marxism does not offer an adequate theory of modern revolution. For the overthrow of an Old Regime is not a socioeconomic transition from "feudalism" to "capitalism," as Marx argued. It is a political, ideological, and cultural break with immemorial tradition; its essence is the passage from a corporate and hierarchical world that was simply given by history and/or divine ordinance to a world where men consciously order and mold their society. Seen in this perspective, such a transition—usually accelerated through violence, and sacralized by the blood of martyrs—by its very nature can occur only once in the life of a given Old Regime polity.

Perhaps the simplest terminology for designating such a once-in-a-millennium watershed is the distinction between "traditional" and "modern" societies. This distinction, to be sure, is very general, and entails no direct reference to a revolutionary break, whereas Marxist terminology does. By contrast, it has the merit of avoiding the Marxist fantasy of a two-stage modernity—capitalism and then socialism—and so fits the real endgame of all European Old Regimes. For the historical record is now clear: there is no such thing as "socialism," in the sense of a separate historical epoch following "capitalism." There is only the welfare state as a subphase of an industrial market economy. This said, the best dichotomy of all is simply Old Regime versus democracy (in the sense of constitutionalism combined with popular sovereignty); for the two terms of this contrast refer to the actual form that both traditional and modern societies took in European history.[11]

Thus, Lenin's telescoping of Russia's putative two-stage revolution does not mean that he had in effect reverted to Populism—a thesis often advanced to impugn his Marxist "orthodoxy."[12] We have already seen that his theory of the vanguard party derived from a specifically Marxist crisis of revolutionary praxis. To this must be added that this party's organization was directly borrowed from the centralized and hierarchal Social Democracy of Germany, not from the far simpler structure of the People's Will. And his policy toward the peasantry differed radically from that of the Populists: the latter wished to make the land the "socialized" property of all the peasants, whereas Lenin wanted state "nationalization" as a prelude to collectivization, to be achieved moreover by "class war" between the village "petty bourgeoisie" and the "proletariat" of poor peasants.

In view of these major differences between Leninism and Populism, it should be clear that those similarities that do exist between the two traditions are due, not to some covert filiation, but to the pattern of Russian backwardness leading to the telescoping of prior Western developments. Moreover, sensitivity to the advantages of backwardness was no monopoly of the Populists; before them, Marx had believed it of Germany.

Indeed, Marx, in his last years, explicitly extended this view to Russia. Once the Russian revolutionary movement emerged in the 1860s Marx followed it closely, even learning Russian to read Chernyshevsky. In the 1870s he became an advisor to the People's Will (after the crushing of the Paris Commune, only Russia offered an immediate prospect of revolution in Europe). And he was so impressed by the Russians' élan that in 1881 he conceded that if the Russian revolution triggered a Western proletarian upheaval, the peasant commune could serve as "the starting point for a communist development"[13]—in short, Russia could skip over capitalism. Although Plekhanov and Engels covered up this concession to "unlaw-like" history, the radical component of Marxism that prompted it could easily be awakened by a new revolutionary opportunity.

That opportunity was offered by the crisis of traditional Russia after 1900, an event the likes of which Europe had not seen since 1848. It confronted the Bolsheviks with a dilemma that Marx and the Second International never had to face: namely, what to do in a *successful* revolution against an Old Regime—a dilemma that forced the Bolsheviks to choose between the basic components of Marxism. Since the Anglo-French norm of historical development underlying their doctrine did not fit Russian conditions, they could not trust its logic to make Russia's one revolutionary chance yield socialism. So the Bolsheviks resolved the dilemma in the same way the Founder had first formulated his theory of the Party—by putting the spirit of Marx's class struggle ahead of the letter of his logic of history. Thereby they were able to make that revolution to end all revolutions, which other Marxists had anticipated in vain since the failure of 1848.

THE REVOLUTION OF 1905

Matters could reach this pass, however, only after the first round of the Russian revolutionary process, the "normal" European revolution of 1904–1907. Although this event is usually characterized as a workers' revolution, it was in fact liberalism's hour on center stage in Russian history.

With the political upsurge of the new century, the fifty-year eclipse of Russian liberalism by revolutionary socialism came to an end. Throughout the radical years 1904–1906, the leadership of the movement against autocracy was furnished by liberals, drawn in part from their traditional gentry base, but even more from the sophisticated intelligentsia of the now well-developed liberal professions. (Industrial capitalists were too dependent on the state to play much of a role in the opposition.)

Moreover, Russian liberalism—organized in October 1905 into a party of Constitutional Democrats, the Kadets—was considerably to the left of its Western counterparts, for it had to telescope into a decade programmatic developments that elsewhere had taken a century. Thus its social program advocated full rights of organization for the workers and compulsory alienation, with compensation, of some private land for the peasants. At the same time, for fear of the autocracy, the Kadets were wedded to a perilous policy of "no enemies to the left" toward the shooting revolutionaries. As for the revolutionary parties themselves— the two branches of the Social Democrats and the neo-Populists, organized in 1900 as the Socialist Revolutionary Party (SRs)—they played only a minor role in 1905. And they in no sense "led" the people.

The central demand of the revolution was constitutional democracy with universal suffrage, if possible achieved through a constituent assembly, but if not under a constitutional monarchy. Socialism was at no time an objective. This constitutionalist demand, moreover, furnishes the thread of revolutionary action. It began with the zemstvo congress of November 1904; it was carried to the street by the workers on January 9, only to end in the massacre of "Bloody Sunday"; and it culminated in the October general strike of the entire urban population which forced the monarchy to concede a Legislative Duma. The years 1906– 1907, finally, were dominated by the struggle between the Duma and the monarchy over their respective powers. This struggle ended with Prime Minister Petr

Stolypin's "coup d'état" of June 3, 1907, which cut back the suffrage to produce a Duma that would "work"; that is, be a junior partner of the monarchy on the Prussian model.

To be sure, the workers played a crucial role in the breakthrough year 1905 because of their concentration in key urban centers and their centrality in the general strike; but this did not make them the vanguard of the revolution overall, a role which remained with the gentlemen liberals. The workers' importance, moreover, did not derive from their social identity as a "proletariat," but from their political role as a plebeian combat force capable of exerting physical pressure on the system. In this, their role is analogous to that of the artisan sansculottes of 1792–1793 or the artisan "saints" of the New Model Army of 1647. The retrospectively touted Moscow December "insurrection" had no significant effect on the course of events. Overall, the liberal revolution enjoyed the support of most classes of the population, as was demonstrated in the October strike and by the Duma elections of 1906, held on something close to universal (male) suffrage, which was a clear victory for the Kadets.

Nonetheless, it was no accident that the liberals lost in this initial assault on the Old Regime. The first reason for their defeat is that they wanted genuine constitutional government and popular sovereignty while the autocracy was determined never to make such a concession; thus, periodic efforts to find a compromise that would produce a workable Duma always ended in failure. A lesser reason is that after the October Manifesto the opposition divided increasingly between the liberals and the politically weaker revolutionary left, while nationalist reactionaries emerged to challenge both. But the decisive reason, as suggested earlier, is that the monarchy kept control of the army, and so in any test of strength could always put down popular protest.

Still, decisive though this last factor was, we should not assume that if a disarmed monarchy had capitulated to the Kadets, then the constitutionalist revolution would have "won." A constituent assembly elected by universal suffrage would have produced a majority of land-hungry peasants susceptible to socialist leadership, a combination that the liberals could hardly have managed to keep within legalistic bounds. This pessimistic conclusion may be asserted with confidence on the basis of comparisons with earlier European revolutions: for it is most unlikely that 1905 could have established a constitutional order in Russia on the first try, when neither England nor France, not to mention Germany and Austria, had succeeded in doing so under much more favorable circumstances. In any event, the outcome of the failure of 1905 was to use up much of the constitutionalists' political capital before the next round of the Russian revolutionary process.

FROM FEBRUARY TO OCTOBER

The intrinsically unstable nature of the pseudo-constitutionalism produced by 1905 ensured that there would be a second round. And it began under maximal conditions for accelerated radicalization—in the midst of the world's first total war. For it must be emphasized that the revolution of 1917 as we know it was produced above all by the devastating impact of that war, not by "polarization" between the bourgeoisie and the proletariat, though such polarization obviously did exist. It was modern war that at last demonstrated the fragility of the state and social structures of tsarism on which the radical intelligentsia had wagered since the emancipation of 1861.

The war mobilized Russia's peasants into a multimillion man army, a concentration that for the first time gave them real political power, if largely negative. The war also disrupted the still fragile industrial economy, by 1917 creating severe shortages of food and fuel. And the war turned out to be a losing one, a circumstance that reignited the constitutional crisis: the monarchy used the wartime emergency to govern the country without the Duma, and the liberal opposition responded by demanding a government "of public confidence"—in effect, a prelude to constitution.

It was against this background that in February 1917, Petrograd was shaken by large-scale strikes protesting food shortages. When peasant soldiers refused to fire on the crowds, this street action escalated into a military mutiny, thereby depriving the monarchy of the shield that had protected it in 1905–1907. This mutiny became a revolution when the army command deserted Nicholas and the now frightened Duma liberals stepped in to form a Provisional Government.

This government was never able to govern, however, since the workers and soldiers, under socialist leadership, simultaneously formed councils, or "soviets," to monitor the "bourgeois" ministry—bodies that in fact had more authority than the nominal government. So the revolution of 1917, unlike that of 1905, began with the socialists, not the liberals, in the vanguard. Under the pressure of this "dual power" all the administrative and military structures of the state unraveled. With the state withering away, workers asserted their control over industry; the peasants moved to expropriate the gentry without waiting for the promised constituent assembly; and the peasant soldiers deserted the front en masse: rural Russia at last achieved its full measure of "land and freedom." By autumn the government had been thoroughly eclipsed by the soviets; yet these bodies, which were in effect permanent mass meetings, could not themselves govern. Given this descent into anarchy, it would be idle to insist that establishing a constitutionalist order in 1917 was out of the question. The real question then was who would pick up the pieces once the country hit bottom.

As we know, the Bolsheviks did so in "Red October." But the Marxist categories in which they enveloped that event, and which have dominated the debate over its meaning ever since, have obscured its real nature. In formal terms, this debate is between those who hold that October was a social revolution and those who claim it was a coup d'état. In fact it was obviously both: it was a coup d'état carried out against a background of social revolution, and the former was made possible only by the runaway pace of the latter. This does not mean, however, that the coup was the "law-like" product of its social backdrop. For 1917 was a peculiar kind of social revolution.[14]

That term usually means the displacement of one dominant social group by another, as when the Third Estate in 1789 displaced the first two in prominence, a process in which the social cause and the political result are intimately related. In October 1917, however, there were two distinct occurrences: socially, the yearlong descent into anarchy had at last run its course; politically, the Bolshevik party, acting through the amorphous soviet, successfully carried out a conspiracy to seize power. The empirical debate over October, therefore, is directed toward affirming or denying that the obvious gap between these two occurrences can be closed.

But this surface debate obscures the real issue, which is ideological: namely, was October a genuine proletarian revolution or not? (A matter on which once depended the legitimacy of the Soviet regime.) But this is, precisely, an ideological, not a historical question. For in plain historical fact there is no such thing as a proletarian revolution: in the entire history of capitalism, there has never been a worker seizure of power from the bourgeoisie. To this may be added that there is no such thing as a bourgeois revolution, either. To be sure, the French Old Regime was overthrown in 1789 in the name of the nation; but it was only the ideological gloss of the ultra-left in the 1840s that transformed that event into the birth date of the "bourgeois mode of production." In fact, both the bourgeois and the proletarian revolutions are not *events*, but *concepts*; and their function is to serve as the successive nodal points of that eschatological fantasy of mankind's exit from "pre-history" to its true history in socialism which had been haunting the left since 1848.

Yet in the midst of the horrors of World War I this fantasy was at its most plausible, and not just in Russia; millions would believe in it and struggle for its advent for decades to come. It was in the name of this fantasy that the Bolsheviks made October, and in its name that October's partisans thereafter so vehemently denied it was a coup. The real importance to October of the concurrent "social revolution" is that the anarchy it spawned alone made it possible for the Bolsheviks to get away with such a brazen action — without being shot for sedition like the Easter insurgents in Dublin the previous year.

The actual October insurrection, however, was derisory. It pales into insignificance in comparison with the Parisian June Days of 1848 or the Commune of 1871, the models for Marx of what a proletarian revolution ought to be. Even in Russia itself during 1917, far greater proletarian pugnacity had been displayed in February and in the July Days than in October. In fact, Lenin caught the working-class movement of 1917 just as its vigor was expiring, and the majority of Petrograd workers sat out "their" insurrection.

Indeed, there was no need for any insurrection at all, since the Bolsheviks had a majority in the Congress of Soviets ready to vote them power the next day. But Lenin insisted on an "armed insurrection" by the Bolsheviks alone, in part to avoid a coalition with other socialist parties, and in part because insurrection, ever since the Bastille, was the way that world-historical events happened. Still, the two decisive October days were no more than an amateur police operation of ragtag Red Guards and Kronstadt sailors against a Provisional Government now so weak that there was nothing worth mentioning to overthrow.

Thus, what triumphed in October was not a social class of flesh-and-blood workers, but a political party of ideologues purporting to incarnate the workers' revolutionary consciousness: Red October was a seizure of power by a metaphysical proletariat acting in the name of the empirical proletariat. Yet this seizure of power, though a vulgar "coup" in form, was ultra-revolutionary in content; for the Bolsheviks took power not just from the "bourgeoisie," but from society as such. By creating this void they assumed the world-shaking mission of filling it with a socialist order, which they indeed began forthwith to produce. And so the "October coup" came, in fact, to project a mythic force that would hold the entire twentieth century to moral ransom.

The question immediately arises: could Russia have avoided this grandiose yet terrible fate? As of the end of 1917, the options were perilously limited. What the majority of workers then wanted was a coalition soviet government of all socialist parties. Indeed, even if the Bolsheviks had not acted alone in October, such a soviet and socialist coalition would no doubt have taken over from the Provisional Government anyway. Even if the democratically elected constituent assembly (two-thirds socialist of one or another stripe) had been permitted to sit after its one meeting in January, this still would have meant the power of the same socialist and soviet parties. And these parties (in the feeble measure that the soviets or the assembly were able to govern at all) could only have done what the Bolsheviks in fact did after October: legitimize peasant seizure of the land, worker control of industry, and the disbanding of the army and thus effect a separate, disastrous peace.

These national calamities would surely have provoked the same right-wing backlash and civil war that they did in real history. In such a crisis, it is difficult to imagine the cautious Mensheviks or the loosely structured majority SRs organizing the "defense of the revolution"; so that task would have fallen anyway to the Bolsheviks and fire-eating left SRs. And against such a defense, the Whites—as is indicated by their actual performance, from General Lavr Kornilov in August 1917, to General Anton Denikin in the fall of 1919—were too distrusted by the "masses," especially the peasants, to prevail on their own. The Russian right would therefore have required effective outside support—not the limited aid which it actually received from the distant Allies, but that which would have been readily forthcoming from the Germans, who were already in the country with a real army. But the Germans, of course, lost the war. So, for want of a viable authoritarian solution of the right, the great Russian anarchy of 1917 and early 1918 had ended by late 1919 in an authoritarian solution of the left.

FROM WAR COMMUNISM TO THE NEP

This victory, however, did not at all correspond to the Marxist scenario, as revised by Lenin, for a socialist revolution. For, after a few years of intense expectation, neither the developed West nor the colonial East followed the Russian example. Still, this setback did not convince the Bolsheviks that Kautsky and the Mensheviks were right in condemning October as un-Marxist adventurism. And indeed, it was easy to find a plausibly Marxist counterargument in the thesis that the postwar "stabilization of capitalism"—by capitalism's very nature—would be only temporary, and that in the meantime the Bolsheviks owed it to the world proletariat to hold the Russian fort.

More troubling and urgent were the problems created within that fort by the revolution's isolation. The economic collapse begun by the war and aggravated by the social revolution of 1917 left Russia more backward than under the Old Regime. By 1918 the gentry and the urban middle class had been liquidated as cohesive groups, and Russia had become a rudimentary agglomeration of workers and peasants—a new type of two-class society, pitifully vulnerable, moreover, to coercion in its amorphousness. Yet this "un-Marxist" situation did not cause the Bolsheviks to rethink the rightness of October: the emergency, rather, brought their Marxism fully into its own as the demiurge of revolution from above.

By the summer of 1918, as the civil war hit full stride, the issue for the Bolsheviks was no longer world revolution, but survival. They responded with a pro-digious outburst of energy which, over the next eighteen months, created the essential elements of the Soviet system. The volatile soviets were purged of Mensheviks and SRs and transformed into mere administrative instruments of the "dictatorship of the proletariat," now growing into a structured Party-state. The rudiments of a centralized, nationalized command economy were created. And the whole system was backed up by a political police above the law.

In this coercive state-building the Bolsheviks were not seeking anything so trivial as power for power's sake, as is often alleged. They were consolidating power for the "radiant future" of socialism; and in that enterprise Marxism furnished the indispensable weapon of ideologically illumined political will. Hence, all the Bolsheviks' efforts to master the anarchy of the time and to combat the Whites were presented not just as emergency measures, but as destructive-creative class warfare; and so economic mobilization for the military struggle was transfigured to become the beginning of rational economic planning.

Military communism thus escalated into militant communism or War Communism, as the episode was called after it was abandoned in 1921. To be sure, the bold deeds of War Communism were in apparent contradiction with the Bolsheviks' concomitant premise that their revolution required a Western one to succeed. But the intoxication of class war obscured this contradiction in practice. So the Bolsheviks convinced themselves that in the heat of the internal class struggle they were forging the institutions of communism, and that their improvisations were in fact the first draft of a world order about to emerge from the international class struggle.

It is often alleged that the Bolsheviks were forced into these premature policies by the military emergency. This exculpatory rationalization, however, does not fit the dates of introduction of War Communism's chief measures. The Cheka (the first version of the KGB) was founded before there was any civil war at all; "class warfare in the villages" to extort grain from peasants and the nationalization of industry were all decreed when the civil war was still far off on the frontiers; and the culminating measures of War Communism, "the militarization of labor" and the abolition of money, appeared only after the civil war had been won.

What is even more important is that War Communism in fact represents Marx's real program of socialism as noncapitalism: the suppression of private property, profit, the market, and money. The military emergency led the Bolsheviks to do what they were ideologically programmed to do anyway; and it was premature only in terms of the Party's organizational ability to impose it on the country.

And so, with the precipitate action of War Communism the Bolsheviks took the principle of the vanguard party to its culmination. In opposition, the Party's vocation had been to substitute for the proletariat in seizing power; so it zestfully rode a wave of anarchy to get there. Once in power, the Party had to substitute as well for the logic of history since history had failed, on its own, to produce socialism out of capitalism's overthrow; so the Party now suppressed revolutionary anarchy by the dictatorial organization of the economy and society. Finally, the Party switched from one role to the other in all good conscience, because it was by definition the proletariat-and-the-logic-of-history rolled into one.

This same dialectical flexibility permitted the Bolsheviks to make another about-face in 1921. By that year, they were faced with a new crisis of survival; for the combined impact of civil war, epidemic, and War Communism had brought near-collapse in industry and famine in the countryside. The Bolsheviks were thus forced to retreat to the New Economic Policy (NEP) of a semi-market economy, as the only way to entice the peasants to produce a surplus which would permit the country to revive. And it must be emphasized that the NEP was a forced retreat from the Party's preferred policy. Indeed, the NEP was regarded at the time by numerous Bolsheviks (and of course their foes) as the defeat of the Revolution.

But soon some Party leaders made a virtue of necessity. Nikolai Bukharin, expanding on selected thoughts of the dying Lenin, argued that Russia might "grow into socialism through the market"—by which he meant that the peasants, especially the "kulaks," or well-off peasants, could be brought peacefully to collaborate in Russia's re-industrialization by offering them adequate goods at real prices. This retrospective rationalization of the Bolsheviks' forced option for the NEP has led to the second great debate about October's meaning: namely, was the NEP rather than War Communism the true Marxist-Leninist program? Or, put another way: could the "Bukharin alternative" have avoided the mass violence of Stalin's revolution from above?[15]

But this debate, too, ends in impasse, for it is never clear whether the contestants are talking about the empirical matter of economic development or about the ideological matter of divining the best road to socialism. Regarding the first issue, on the basis of the market's success in other developing countries, it may be confidently asserted that Bukharin's program of financing industrialization through a deepened NEP would have produced thoroughly satisfactory economic results. But this mundane purpose was not the point of Bukharin's program. For him, the market was not to be a permanent feature of socialism; it was only a transitional means to an ideological end, which was Marx's marketless, propertyless realm of noncapitalism.

Just as important, the "economist" view of Bukharin's program ignores its political consequences. For leaving the peasants their economic autonomy would
have eroded the Party's monopoly of power, just as it would have entailed (again
Bukharin's words) "advancing towards socialism at a snail's pace." But the monopoly of power for an accelerated march to socialism is what the vanguard party
is all about. Continuing the NEP threatened this monopoly and the crash "building of socialism," so Stalin cut off market experimentation at the end of the twenties. The real "alternative" to Stalin was not Bukharin; it was giving up the whole
impossible Marxist enterprise, and with it the Leninist Party.

STALIN BUILDS SOCIALISM

The moment of truth for the Bolshevik adventure came in 1929. In what
amounted to a new crisis of survival for the regime, the peasants, balking at artificially low state prices, withheld their grain from the market just as the great
industrialization drive of the First Five-Year Plan got under way. So Stalin reverted to the coercive methods of War Communism to collectivize the peasantry,
thereby ensuring the regime an adequate food supply without having to pay for
it. In the best Bolshevik tradition his solution was political and ideological, not
economic. And he could get away with this assault on the "idiocy of rural life"
because the Party now had far more numerous and better indoctrinated legions
than Lenin ever commanded.

With this Party-army Stalin succeeded in crushing the peasant autonomy that
had bedeviled the regime since October. Bukharin went along with the new
"general line" without a murmur of dissent, and even wrote Stalin's 1936 Constitution for him. Trotsky, in exile, held that though Stalin was bungling the job,
the line itself was still socialist—indeed, it had originally been his own. For to all
these true Leninists it was Party hegemony, not any one economic strategy, that
was the key to building socialism. As Trotsky once famously put it, "one cannot
be right against the Party, for history has given the proletariat no other vehicle
for its purposes."[16]

Stalin's quasi-military "revolution from above," however, could not be acknowledged for what it was; it was presented, rather, as still another class struggle
—of poor peasants against kulaks in the villages, and of the urban proletariat
against the kulak petty bourgeoisie. Indeed, Stalin declared that the nearer one
got to socialism, the more intense the class struggle became.

This thesis has been ridiculed as bad Marxism; in fact, it represents the inevitably perverse result of attempting to apply the impossible Marxist amalgam in
practice. To paraphrase Stalin's dictum in non-utopian form: the nearer one gets

to an unattainable goal—in the present instance, the "voluntary" collectivization of peasant agriculture—the more intense resistance becomes and the greater the need therefore of Party coercion. It is impossible to imagine either a neo-Populist Soviet government or a traditional Russian autocracy executing any such lethal policy toward the peasantry; for such Promethean coercion, Marxism-Leninism is indispensable.

By these means, Stalin at last "built socialism." On the foundation of collectivized agriculture, he went full steam ahead to accomplish a chaotic yet colossal industrial revolution. In the process, he transformed millions of peasants into proletarians; and he promoted hundreds of thousands of this expanded working class to be managers, military officers, and apparatchiki of a now all-encompassing Party-state. And so, by the mid-thirties, he had created a regime of institutionalized War Communism. Just like its predecessor it represented Marxism's real instrumental program: the suppression of private property, profit, and the market (though this time not of money).

To ensure that this achievement would endure, Stalin crowned it with the Great Purges of 1936–1939. This operation was not the aberrant rampage of a paranoid tyrant, as is too often asserted; it had a genuine function in the mature Soviet system. And this was to camouflage the fact that once socialism had been built, the result—from the horrors of collectivization to the chronic dysfunctions of the "command economy" in industry—hardly conformed to the promises of the regime's legitimating ideology. Since the ideology was indispensable to the system's survival, terror became necessary to hide the awful truth from the population—and indeed from the regime itself.

Stalin, therefore, resorting again to the principle that the nearer one got to socialism the more intense the class struggle became, launched a campaign to root out all "wreckers," Trotskyites, and other "enemies of the people." This time, of course, the "class struggle" was pure political metaphysics, without any relation to empirical fact, since all the "enemies" now were loyal Communists. Nonetheless, so potent was the Marxist-Leninist elixir of class struggle that it triumphed once again over mere reality. For Stalin indeed succeeded in largely replacing the old Party with a new one. It was appropriately composed of men who had come of political age after socialism had been built, who owed everything to the new system, who were the accomplices and beneficiaries of its crimes, and who would thus not question, like the oppositionists of the 1920s, the Leader or his handiwork.

With this second revolution from above of the 1930s the active role of Marxism, even in its debased Stalinist form, in molding the Soviet system came to an end. But this does not mean that the system ceased being ideocratic. For by

1939, the ideology had been cast in the concrete and steel of Magnitogorsk and myriad other achievements of the Five-Year Plans; it had been institutionalized in the triad of Party, Plan, and police; and it was codified as the One True Teaching (Solzhenitsyn's term) in Stalin's *Short Course* of 1938. To defend the fruits of this now reified and cold ideology, the masters of "really-existing socialism," as Brezhnev called it, for the rest of its existence viewed the world as divided into socialist and capitalist camps locked in permanent international class struggle.[17]

SOVIETISM AS REALLY-EXISTING MARXISM

But more was at stake in Stalin's crowning feat of cashing in one Party for another than defending specific features of his system. The ultimate issue was the fate of the Marxist enterprise since its inception in the 1840s. For the Party's pretension that Russia had actually reached socialism marked the first time that Marxism as a totality had been put to the test of praxis. The result, which Stalin went to such murderous lengths to hide, was to demonstrate that Marxism indeed offered an impossible utopia that had ended, as it only could, in failure and fraud. For this reason, after Stalin's death, dissidents referred to the Soviet system simply as "the Lie."

This failure, however, was not material, at least in the short term, for Stalin had in truth created industrial power sufficient to get Russia victoriously through World War II, and to compete for decades as a superpower in the Cold War. The failure, rather, was at the deeper level of the system's moral and ideological raison d'être—namely, the promise that socialism was the "radiant future" of mankind, the one just and egalitarian society, a promise that had fueled the titanic will making possible the regime's material success. And in the long term this moral and ideological failure would undermine that temporary success.

This failure, however, does not mean anything so simple as the judgment that Stalin in building socialism by violence had "betrayed" Marx, any more than Lenin had done so in creating a dictatorial party. The lack of a moral kernel in Soviet socialism, rather, means that Marx's instrumental program of abolishing private property and the market does not in fact yield his intended emancipatory results. So, in Marx's impossible system Stalin chose the only part that could be realized in practice—which was socialism as the instrumental negation of capitalism.

Thus the outcome of the world's first "proletarian" revolution was a cruel paradox. The defining characteristic of Bolshevism among twentieth-century Marxisms was to have privileged the voluntarism of the class struggle over the determinism of the logic of history. With this choice the Bolsheviks indeed succeeded in making the world's first Marxist revolution and in implementing its goal of socialism as noncapitalism, whereas their rivals could do no more than patch up capitalism with a social safety net. But the Bolsheviks achieved their dubious superiority only by fabricating an ersatz logic of history.

By the power of political will they first amended Marx's logic of history in Red October itself: for that event was not a proletarian revolution at all, but a Party and intelligentsia revolution. This vanguard of ideologues then proceeded to turn Marx's system completely upside down by acting as a "superstructure" engaged in creating the "base" that the real logic of history was supposed to have already produced. And once again political will, still camouflaged as class struggle, drove the Party—this time "to catch up with and overtake America"[18]—through a crash industrial revolution from above. The result was indeed an awesome assemblage of blast furnaces, tractors, and rockets that for a long time was frighteningly competitive with the "bourgeois mode of production"—but which lacked those accoutrements of "bourgeois democracy" that the real logic of history also provided.

It was in this truncated guise that Marx's transcendental doctrine reached the practical culmination of its fortunes. Guided by Lenin's vanguard, it landed on earth as no more than an inferior imitation of its capitalist adversary. For the Cunning of Reason had transformed it into a mere instrument for producing that industrial and proletarian society which was supposed to have produced *it*. Thus, with Soviet socialism Marx's "pre-history" ended, not in the human emancipation of communism, but in the institutionalized revolution of Communism.

And so, the Bolsheviks, by building socialism before Russia had attained capitalism, pushed the Russian pattern of telescoping history to the point of inversion. By the same token, they had inverted Marxism by making false ideological consciousness the demiurge of real social being. Hence, Marxism in practice turned out to be no more than a means for the modernization of a backward country.

Yet, at the century's end, it has become clear that Marxism was not all that successful in its only positive role. There have been far more effective—and humane—ways of promoting economic development. Before October, there was Witte's crash industrialization with the aid of the international market. And after October, there have been such East Asian "tigers" as South Korea and Taiwan, even the market Marxism of Deng Xiaoping's China.

Moreover, Marxism's ideological content matters greatly, because of its multiple perverse effects. For it breeds a stultifying hostility among the population to the psychological traits necessary for entrepreneurship, an activity stigmatized as "speculation." And this cast of mind is institutionalized and magnified a thousandfold by the inefficiency of a centralized command economy. In Marxism's capacity as official state dogma, moreover, it stifles critical thought and stunts society's capacity for innovation in every domain. But above all, Marxism's core program of abolishing private property and the market is a veritable charter for total despotism and the destruction of civil society.

Yet, at the same time, the rigidity of the One True Teaching makes this despotism a fragile one. For once reality has refuted the system's legitimizing postulate that socialism is more productive than capitalism, the ideology is discredited and the whole system is therefore demystified. This process, begun under Brezhnev, was brought to its culmination by Gorbachev's glasnost. With the ideological spell broken, a chain reaction was unleashed: the ideocratic regime lost its self-confidence; its will to coerce evaporated; and so the whole system collapsed like a house of cards.

This intrinsic hollowness explains why, when the Soviet regime collapsed, it left no usable heritage to Russia. No matter how bloody and destructive the English, American, and French revolutions often were, they all created institutions that have endured to this day, together with ideals whose moral appeal is still intact—a combination we now crudely summarize as "market democracy." The Russian Revolution, by contrast, when at last it gave up the ghost in 1991, left behind nothing but squalor, rubble, and wormwood.

And this is why it turned out—albeit perversely—to be the revolution to end all revolutions. For it at last demonstrated that there is no Second, Socialist Coming of 1789; that in real modern history there exists only the political republic; and that the attempt to transcend it with anything "higher" than a welfare state throws society back to a servitude worse than any known under the Old Regime.

Yet the combined heirs of the three Atlantic revolutions should not exult prematurely. For even after the failure of the Communist effort to transcend the classic democratic heritage, there remains the problem which initially inspired the socialist project: human inequality. So long as this problem exists—and there is no prospect of it disappearing in any conceivable future—utopian politics will remain with us. Who knows what good egalitarian cause may next be subject to millenarian and coercive perversion? The eternal return of the revolutionary myth, in new and unanticipated guises, can only be expected to haunt us.

Conclusion and Epilogue

THE EUROPEAN GREAT REVOLUTIONS

On the basis of the preceding discussion of the European Great Revolutions, of the list of actors, and of the general nature of the action involved, I wish to advance the following propositions:

1. The drama of a Great Revolution can occur *only once* in a given nation's history, not for any metaphysical reasons of historical necessity, but for the thoroughly mundane reason that any given nation has only one Old Regime to be liquidated, and that once this has been accomplished—or even attempted—a millennial historical divide has been irretrievably crossed. Moreover, the level of historical development at the moment of the revolution, the manner of its unfolding, and the proximate results, then determine, or rather govern, the given nation's future history, its style of politics, its communal myths, and its manner of coping with change—for example, legalistic, empirical, and reformist in Britain; ideological, dramatic, and radical in France; conservative and then catastrophic in Germany.

2. A Great Revolution is not essentially a socioeconomic phenomenon, but a political-constitutional and a cultural-ideological one. In other words, such a revolution does not mark the transition from one mode of production to another (e.g., from "feudal" to "bourgeois"), or from one stage of a country's economic development to another (e.g., from mercantile to capitalist, or from "traditional" to "modern"), although such transformations are obviously in some measure involved in revolution. A Great Revolution, rather, is essentially the general crisis of a total national system.

This is not to say that economic development is not a major force per se, or that it is not "revolutionary" (in the loose sense of that word) in its overall effect on society, mores, and culture. The point is, rather, that economic development is in no discernible way related to the timing or the manner of unfolding of a European Great Revolution. The two phenomena, in fact, occur out of phase with one another; and a Great Revolution can break out at the most diverse levels in the process of economic "development" from the seventeenth to the twentieth centuries.

To illustrate this lack of correspondence between political and economic configurations, we may note that the decisive period of the Industrial Revolution in England — say between 1780 and 1830 — occurred with an aristocratic, Tory government continuously in power (as, indeed, Marx was well aware). Still more striking is the fact that the Industrial Revolution in Germany was launched and nurtured through its crucial phase by the autocratic old regime of Prussia by means of the Zollverein. At the same time, the "bourgeois revolution" of 1789 in France was on the whole bad for business; for it severely crippled a previously thriving maritime trade, instituted a technologically stifling protectionism, and reinforced an archaic peasantry — all this to the point where France, in 1815, was relatively farther behind England economically than it had been in 1789, when the two countries were not far from parity. And the Russian Revolutions of 1917 (the "bourgeois" and the "proletarian" taken together) marked one of the greatest economic catastrophes of modern history. Indeed, it is quite possible to argue that there is a negative correlation between revolution and economic growth. At the very least, it must be recognized that Great Revolutions, though in some areas liberating and creative, are in others appallingly destructive and costly.

Perhaps the best way of formulating these relationships is to say that economic development is the necessary but not the sufficient cause of revolution, and that the sufficient causes lie in the overt political and ideological issues of the revolutionary events themselves, as perceived by the actors in those events. For economic development goes on almost constantly in modern history, and more often in periods of orderly change than of violent crisis, whereas revolutions are very rare occurrences. From this it follows that the unfolding and the outcome of a revolution are governed primarily by a special dynamic of crisis politics and ideological intoxication, and only secondarily by the long-term, slower-moving forces of socioeconomic development. In short, I am arguing that crisis politics and ideological afflatus — like the coercion to which they lead — have a logic of their own, which acts in relative autonomy from the socioeconomic matrix of the revolutionary event.

3. Similarly, a Great Revolution does not essentially mark the transition from the domination of one class to that of another (e.g., again, from "feudal" to "bourgeois" hegemony). Great Revolutions, rather, assume the epic dimensions they

do because they are "all-class" affairs—that is, events in which all, or almost all, of the significant social groups in the nation move against the monarchy either simultaneously or in very rapid succession. Only such a convergence of the whole of society against the sacred power of the monarchy can crack the immemorial structure of the Old Regime. This generalization I have derived by abstracting from the work of Georges Lefebvre, especially his *Coming of the French Revolution*. As a Marxist, Lefebvre set out to show that the French Revolution was a class struggle in which the bourgeoisie emerged victorious. Yet in closely analyzing the class character of the Revolution he demonstrated that it was, in fact, composed of the accumulation of an aristocratic, a bourgeois, a popular, and a peasant revolution. And this model is readily generalizable to 1640, to 1848, and to 1905–1917.

As a "control" of this assertion, we may note that when only one class moves against an existing regime, something other than a Great Revolution results. When the aristocracy alone moves, we have a Fronde. When the peasantry alone moves, we have a jacquerie or a *Pugachevshchina*. When the urban crowd alone moves, we have Gordon Riots or, at the outside, a Paris Commune. (It seems that only the bourgeoisie never has the imprudence to move all by itself.) Yet in none of these types of cases do we have revolution in the sense of any fundamental constitutional or social change: all such "one-class" movements fail, or at most result only in a consolidation of the existing order and system of authority.

THE TWENTIETH-CENTURY PARADOX

Once the initial target of European revolution—the Old Regime—no longer existed, the use of political violence in Europe could only assume a different form, nature, and purpose. We have seen that Red October turned out to be an ultra-left caricature of the modern revolutionary myth launched in 1789. Germany provided an ultra-right caricature of the revolutionary myth. Since German civil society was mature, propertied, and educated, the monarchical primacy gave way relatively easily to assembly sovereignty following the defeat in 1918; so the German November revolution of that year, even though it formally ended the Prussian Old Regime, cannot qualify as the "grand revolution," because that role had been preempted, and subverted, by the failed Revolution of 1848. Moreover, since German civil society had failed to make it to power on its own strength in 1848, the constitutional polity of 1918, born as it was by default, was fragile in the extreme. And this circumstance facilitated the second stage of Germany's twentieth-century revolution, the Nazi *Gleichsschaltung* of the 1930s, which at last leveled the Old Regime and "homogenized" society into a demotic *Volksgemeinschaft*. Thus, the military defeat of World War I at last

bore its full fruit in the "lumpen Bonapartism" of Corporal Hitler, whose movement offered a perverse expression of the national and socialist ideas of 1848.

Interwar fascism is the mirror image of Red October: the "people" as nation
or blood *Gemeinschaft* rather than the people as the masses; the chosen people
as the pinnacle of hierarchy of nations rather than the people as universal humanity; the absolutization of hierarchy and struggle as opposed to the absolutization of equality and fraternity. Both Communism and generic fascism are
perverse variations on those fundamental themes of modern politics first enunciated in 1789.[1]

The existence of a generic Communism can scarcely be questioned. It exists
everywhere a Leninist Party with the mission of "building socialism" is in power,
said socialism requiring the suppression of private property and the market in
favor of institutional dictatorship and a command economy. Even so, this formula has in practice yielded significantly different results from one case and
period to another. Thus, within the Soviet matrix there were marked fluctuations
in coercive power from Lenin's War Communism of 1918–1921, to the semi-
market New Economic Policy (NEP) of 1921–1929, to Stalin's "revolution from
above" of the early 1930s and his Great Terror of the decade's end and so on to
the perilous wartime and imperial postwar periods. Finally, in the Soviet case
the Khrushchev and Brezhnev eras are distinguished from Stalinism by diminished revolutionary vigor and a much-reduced level of terror.

Outside the Russian matrix, variations in the Leninist formula are even more
notable. The Soviets' postwar "outer empire" in Eastern Europe was significantly
different from the "inner empire" of the Union itself. There were no real revolutions in Eastern Europe (outside of Yugoslavia, which soon left the Soviet orbit),
but instead a diversified process of conquest and absorption. Postwar Poland, for
example, where the peasantry was never collectivized, is hardly comparable to
Russia under Stalin, or even to Romania under Nicolae Ceaucescu (which was
no longer really in the "outer empire"). And although the political police was
active everywhere, there was simply not space enough for real gulags.

When we move from the Soviet zone in Europe to the Communisms of East
Asia, we find greater differences still. Not only were all these regimes institutionally independent of Moscow, but each was different from the other. Kim Il Sung's
socialism meant a hermetically closed family dictatorship as surreal as that of
Ceaucescu; yet the "Great Leader" also retained the Soviet alliance as a shield
against China. Mao Zedong, in contrast, was Moscow's greatest enemy on the
left; so to prove his superiority over Khrushchev and his "capitalist roaders," he
outdid even Stalin's terror in seeking socialism through the Great Leap Forward
of 1959–1961 and the Cultural Revolution of 1966–1976. Ho Chi Minh, though

as authentically Leninist as his predecessors to the north, at least channeled his party's energy into a war his population supported. Pol Pot, finally, produced the demented reductio ad absurdum of the whole communist enterprise, as he attempted to out-radical not just Moscow, but Beijing and Hanoi as well. All these Communisms, moreover, varied in the intensity of their fury from one period to another, most notably as Maoism gave way to Deng Xiaoping's "market Leninism."

Still another variation on the generic Communist formula is introduced by the overlap of Leninism with nationalism, not only in the Soviet zone and East Asia but also in Cuba. It has often been noted that "proletarian internationalism" has been a very weak competitor to modern nationalism; and indeed, ever since European socialist parties in 1914 voted for war credits in their respective parliaments, in almost any crisis workers have put patriotism first. Consequently, it has been claimed that Stalinism was basically a new species of messianic Russian nationalism, that Maoism was an exacerbated Chinese reply to Soviet "hegemonic" pretensions, that Ho Chi Minh was a kind of Vietnamese George Washington, and that the sui-genocidal rampage of Pol Pot was a product of traditional Cambodian hatred of Vietnam. Obviously, also, Castro's revolution was a reaction to Yankee imperialism. And nationalism has, of course, played a role in all these cases. The real question, however, is whether that role is sufficient to demote generic Communism to secondary rank.

The answer depends on what we consider to be Communism's "social base." If we take the rhetoric of the "international workers' movement" literally, then worker addiction to nationalism argues against generic Communism's importance.[2] In fact, however, that "movement" has always been a movement of parties, not of proletariats. These parties, moreover, were founded by intellectuals and largely run by them, at least in their heroic phase, not by their alleged worker base; only later were these parties run by such ex-worker-apparatchiki as Khrushchev or Brezhnev. And by then, of course, the full administrative autonomy of the East Asian parties (and the relative autonomy of the East European ones) had fragmented Stalin's genuinely international movement into sovereign entities. Even so, each entity preserved its Leninist structure and goals.

Resolution of the question of nationalism prevailing over Communism also depends on historical period: in the case of Lenin's, and indeed Stalin's, Russia, the answer is definitely no; in the case of China after Mao it may still turn out to be yes. Yet we will not know for sure until we see how the last Leninist regimes disappear. An even deeper answer to this question, however, is that Leninist parties, whether united or at odds, have been able to master their populations' nationalism only so long as millenarian zeal lasted; but when zeal waned, nationalism returned to the fore. Indeed, the withering away of zeal is what explains the fate of both the former Soviet Union and the Yugoslav Federation. For in each case it was the prior death of the party that produced the collapse of the unitary state, with former apparatchiki, such as Nursultan Nazarbayev or Slobodan Milosevic, taking up the nationalist cause to retain power.

The burnout of institutional Communism in East Asia, together with the failure of all Latin American Communist movements—both developments of the late 1970s—at last makes it possible to examine the overall trajectory of Marxism. What is the balance sheet of the century and a half since the system's prophetic beginnings in the 1840s?

The great question posed by Communist history is why a doctrine predicting proletarian revolution in advanced industrial societies has come to power *only* in predominantly agrarian ones, by Marxist definition the least prepared for socialism. Or to put the problem in more general terms, Marxist theory rests on two bases: on the one hand, an objective logic of history leading implacably from feudalism to capitalism to socialism, and on the other a subjective proletarian consciousness (the class struggle) serving as detonator of the culminating revolution. But, in actual history, the logic of capitalist development and revolutionary worker consciousness have never intersected. Instead, socialist revolution has occurred *only* when the hand of history was forced by a vanguard of Marxist intellectuals standing in for the proletariat.

This outcome is often treated as an untoward paradox. The real problem, however, is why Marxist doctrine in fact ended in paradox. The most prominent answer is that its cult of the Promethean powers of industry made it an ideology for the crash overcoming of backwardness—at best a partial explanation. An equally frequent, and even less satisfactory, answer is that Leninist Communism was not genuine Marxism—an argument best treated as metaphysical exorcism to keep Marxism clean of Eastern Communist crime and thus eternally fit for criticizing dirty Western capitalism.

In fact, however, the vocation of Marxism as a doctrine for a "great leap" out of backwardness was built into the theory from its very inception. And this becomes apparent if we read its genesis in long-term historical context. Or in other words, of what "base" is Marxism the "superstructure"?[3]

It will be recalled that contrary to the usual perception, Marxism was not created as a critique of advanced industrial society. Rather, it was devised in the mid-1840s by a pair of intellectuals who hailed from then-preindustrial Germany. The pair, moreover, were moved in the first instance by the degrading spectacle of Germany's *political* backwardness vis-à-vis France and England: Germany still lived in the Middle Ages under a monarchical and aristocratic Old Regime (in their terms, feudalism) unchanged by the partial emancipation that bourgeois France and England had achieved, respectively, in the Revolution of 1830 and the Reform Bill of 1832. The solution for Germany, therefore, would be the leap of "permanent revolution" (as Marx put it in 1850), directly from feudalism to socialism. In the penultimate words of the *Communist Manifesto*, "The Communists turn their attention chiefly to Germany, because that country is on the eve of a bourgeois revolution that . . . will be but the prelude to an immediately following proletarian revolution."[4]

Germany could make this leap, moreover, because the very poverty of its real life gave it a superior capacity for theoretical understanding. Thus the *Manifesto* asserts that intellectuals will be the vanguard of Germany's coming telescoped revolution: "The Communists [as of 1848, only Marx and Engels] . . . have over the great mass of the proletariat the advantage of clearly understanding the line of march, the conditions, and the ultimate general results of the proletarian movement."[5] Moreover, as we have seen, the *Manifesto* spelled out that these results would be to "centralize all instruments of production in the hands of the State, i.e., of the proletariat organized as the ruling class," with all production "concentrated in the hands of the vast association of the whole nation" and "industrial armies, especially for agriculture," under a "common plan."[6] This, of course, is precisely Stalin's program of the 1930s, and the (unrealized) aim of Mao's Great Leap Forward.

And what of the paeans to the "revolutionary role" of bourgeois industry for which the *Manifesto* is now chiefly famous?[7] "The bourgeoisie, by the rapid improvement of all instruments of production, by the immensely facilitated means of communication, draws all, even the most barbarian, nations into civilization. The cheap prices of its commodities are the heavy artillery with which it batters down all Chinese walls."[8] In fact, however, these technocratic rhapsodies were not a description of Europe's as yet feebly developed industry. They were a projection by an awed and envious provincial of what borrowing from the Anglo-French West could do for his still-feudal homeland, a kind of verbal Crystal Palace anticipating the real one of 1851.

Marx's "permanent revolution," of course, never occurred in Germany, yet it did play out partially in Russia after 1917. And it did so in two sub-leaps. Lenin successfully engineered the theoretical vanguard's seizure of power; but his War Communism of 1918–1921 failed for want of the anticipated combined revolution with advanced Europe. So Stalin, no longer counting on the West in the short run, undertook a second leap to achieve "socialism in one country." Declaring himself the "Lenin of Today," he carried out a new October through the

Great Break of his "revolution from above" of 1929–1933. Thus the pattern was set for Marxism's ever more eastward leaps over backwardness (as well as into nationalism)—and its ever deeper descent into paradox.

It is only by taking account of this ideological trajectory through progressively more extravagant, and lethal, "leaps" that we can arrive at a real history of that dark doppelgänger of modernity which was Communism.

To such claims it will inevitably be objected that Marx never intended anything like the revolutions from above perpetrated by Stalin and Mao, that "he would turn over in his grave" if by some miracle he heard about them, and so on. Of course, he never intended any such terroristic programs; his aim was "human emancipation." His conscious intentions, however, are beside the point. The real point is that in his theory emancipation would result only from the full communization of society—an impossible program that cannot be implemented without mass violence. And he opened the door to such a politics with the illusion that an intellectual vanguard apprised of history's laws could engineer humanity's "leap from the realm of necessity to the realm of freedom."[9] As the old saying has it: he who wills the end wills the means.

Appendix I

REVOLUTION

What's in a Name?

In the modern consciousness, revolutions, like great wars, are accounted the high drama of history. They reorder the coordinates of legitimacy in the *res publica*; they seal the end of old regimes and inaugurate new orders; and they mark the turn from one era to another. For over two hundred years they have constituted the founding moments of nations, annually venerated on a July 4, a July 14, or the erstwhile anniversary of Red October, November 7. And in the aggregate, to their enthusiasts they have figured as milestones on the road to human emancipation.

The obverse of this progress, of course, is that revolutions, again like wars, precipitate political competition into overt violence, thus legitimizing methods that are normally the antithesis of civilized existence. And revolutionary founding moments—from the shot heard round the world on Lexington Green, to the fall of the Bastille, to the storming of the Winter Palace—have all been violent acts presaging continuing coercion. Revolution has thus been aptly described as "internal war."[1]

Yet, while wars are fairly clear-cut phenomena, events that may be plausibly termed revolutions have proved much more difficult to define. To be sure, custom has given us a convenient list of "grand revolutions"—England in 1640, America in 1776, France in 1789, Russia in 1917, and China in 1949.[2] But what do these upheavals have in common, whether in their programs or their institutional results, beyond high drama and the resort to force? Are movements personified by, for example, George Washington and Mao Zedong really members of the same historical genus or sociological family? In fact, efforts to bridge such gaps by finding a common structure of action, a shared pattern of stages, or other "regularities" have led with distressing frequency to "models" of revolution-in-itself that are either too abstract to tell us anything we did not already know or too forced to tell us anything at all. So why raise again the elusive question: what is revolution?

A first reason is that the close of a century marked as much by totalitarian revolution as by total war has at last accorded us a respite from such extreme turmoil, and hence a greater possibility of objectivity. An even more compelling reason is that the century's end has radically redrawn the boundaries of the subject: Red October, which hitherto capped the grand revolutionary series (China, conceptually at least, was an encore) is no longer a milestone on the road to anything: it now points only to the grand collapse of 1989–1991. Indeed, that most successful counterrevolution in history quite obliterated all of October's putatively "irreversible conquests": the "vanguard" Party, the "rational" economic Plan, and the "sword and shield" of both, the political police. Most of the world now goes on its way as if 1917 had never occurred; all its results have been repealed and its presuppositions refuted. By the same token, October's emulators and heirs, from China to Cuba, have become ghosts of their formerly haunting selves, progressively abandoning Marx for the market and retrenching behind the husks of Party and police. Surely, this quite unanticipated reversal must tell us something new about the world-historical course of revolution in general.

TOWARD DEFINING METHOD

But does revolution as such exist? Is there some sociological universal or Platonic idea undergirding "revolution" as a discrete historical phenomenon? It is possible to write general books about war: indeed, the father of history, Herodotus, has it as his central subject, as does his greatest ancient successor, Thucydides; General von Clausewitz and Admiral Mahan are notable modern classics.[3] But is it possible to do the same for revolutions? Alas, no indubitable classics come to mind. Our starting point here, then, will not be to propose still another general definition, conceptual scheme, or "model" of revolution designed to fit all events that have been customarily so designated.[4]

Similarly, it is hardly worthwhile to distinguish rigorously different kinds of violent political change, from revolt to rebellion to insurrection to revolution.[5] Even less fruitful is it to venture into the overlap between literal and metaphorical uses of our protean term, as expressed in the migration of the title for 1789 to the contemporaneous "Industrial Revolution," the seventeenth-century "scientific revolution," the fifteenth-century "print revolution," or the twentieth-century "scientific-technical revolution"—and so on to the postwar "green revolution" in third world agriculture or the "sexual revolution" in 1960s America.[6] Any change, in any aspect of human activity that is either sudden or brutal or deep or sweeping, can qualify as "revolutionary" in this extended sense, and no one conceptual net will ever be broad enough to catch them all in a coherent pattern.

The approach here, therefore, will be to proceed in the reverse order of march from all such semantic and a priori exercises, and to build instead from historical particulars to eventual generalizations. This method is in the spirit of Max Weber's principle that "the final and definitive concept cannot stand at the beginning of the investigation, but must come at the end."[7] Nonetheless, this approach requires a preliminary and provisional description of that investigation's aims, methods, and procedures.

In the present instance, such a description is best begun by examining the first historical particular relating to revolution; namely, the process by which the modern concept itself was formed. Although a priori definition of what revolution is has almost invariably proved to be as difficult as it is fruitless, tracing what people have meant by revolution at least furnishes us a preliminary delineation of what it in fact might be. This effort at *Begriffsgeschichte* (conceptual history), moreover, must be conducted as a critique—that is, as an analytical dissection of existing theories of revolution in order to determine not only what works, but especially what does not work. The function of such a triage is to isolate what the real problems are, as a precursor to devising more apposite concepts for addressing them. This exercise in definition by negation therefore takes the form of a brief intellectual history of our perceptions of revolution over the past two centuries.

To recall the by now well-known story, though the word "revolution" is a venerable one, the concept behind it is thoroughly modern, dating only from the end of the eighteenth century.[8] In late antiquity the substantive *revolutio* was formed from the Latin verb *revolvere*, meaning to roll back or to return to a point of origin. In this sense it was employed to designate circular or repetitive movements in nature, as in the waxing and waning of the moon. Saint Augustine was probably the first to use it in a figurative sense to mean the idea of bodily reincarnation or the repetition of providential patterns in historical time. For centuries the term was employed, in one context or another, primarily in a retrogressive or reiterative meaning. In this, it was of a piece with other backward-looking, pre-modern views of change, such as *reformatio* and *restoratio* in religion, and *renascita*, or rebirth, in art and letters. For, until the very end of the seventeenth century, even when Europeans were innovating mightily, as in the Renaissance and Reformation, they steadfastly believed that they were reviving the heritage of a golden age in the past, and that all their new departures were in fact restorations.

The most notable example of the pre-modern use of "revolution" is given by astronomy, as in Copernicus' "revolutionary" treatise of 1543, *De Revolutionibus Orbium Caelestium*. It is from this source that the term was first imported into political discourse, on the occasion of the "restoration" of Charles II in 1660, and in more durable fashion to designate the English "Glorious Revolution" of 1688, a term which at the time meant a return to the realm's "ancient constitution" allegedly violated by the king. Then, in the eighteenth century the political use of "revolution" came increasingly to describe any sudden or abrupt change in government, though without any normative connotation.

It was only at the end of the century, in the great watershed marked by the American and the French revolutions, that the term reversed its meaning, and, at the same time, took on a world-historical dimension. In the course of the paired convulsions of 1776 and 1789, revolution, once signifying return, now came to denote overturn and a radical new departure. It is only since this abrupt and hopeful passage to what we now call modernity—the first self-conscious transition from an old order to a new—that it has been possible to speak of revolution as a distinct genus of historical events.

The transformation occurred in two stages. The Americans began their rebellion by calling it a revolution in the old sense of a restoration of their historic liberties as Englishmen. But they ended it as an independent republic, and with the proud recognition that they had produced an order unprecedented not only in British, but in world history (a belief drawing on their earlier conviction that their new world would be a "city on a hill" for all God's elect). This sense of providential destiny was reinforced when, a scant six years later, their ally of 1776–1783, France, in its turn overthrew "tyranny," thus casting the American struggle as the first in a series that would someday liberate the world.

The French from the beginning knew that their convulsive leap from royal absolutism to popular sovereignty represented the overturn of a millennial national, indeed European, order, and that the trinity of liberty, equality, and fraternity was universal in its import. But they ended their ten-year trajectory from constitutional monarchy to universal-suffrage Republic to Bonapartist dictatorship with the consciousness that revolution was even more than that: it was historical destiny at white heat, unfolding like an irresistible force of nature. Thus one observer spoke of "the majestic lava stream of the revolution which spares nothing and which nobody can arrest."[9] Henceforth, both the teleological and destructive-creative aspects of revolution, just as much as violence, were indispensable components of the inaugural moment of modernity.

So, too, it is the French case that gave us the first terms for the comparative study of revolutions, the rudiments of a "model" for talking about revolution as such: Jacobinism and Mountain for revolutionary dictatorship; "marsh" or plain for the vacillating middle; Reign of Terror for the revolution's culmination crisis; Thermidor for the beginning of its end; and Bonapartism for its arrival at a full halt. In addition, this same trajectory produced those two great symbols of revolutionary polarization and internal war, the Red flag of civil violence and the White flag of Bourbon repression. Indeed, not even all our twentieth-century sociologizing has really displaced these ad hoc historical categories.

REVOLUTION AS POLITICAL LIBERATION

To nineteenth-century historians revolution was primarily a political phenomenon. It meant the overthrow of divine-right absolute monarchy in the name of liberty, individual rights (the right to property very much included), the rule of law, and representative government. In England, where 1688 had achieved these things for the oligarchic few—conquests the nineteenth century updated with the Reform Bills of 1832, 1867, and 1884—that gloriously moderate overturn always remained the good revolution. The violent prelude of 1640–1660, in the twentieth century given pride of historiographical place, was regarded as an unfortunate civil war and hence not incorporated into the national myth. (Thus England has no national day, that purpose being served instead by the queen's birthday, just as its seventeenth-century national anthem calls on God "to save the king/queen," not the nation.) The superiority of this essentially nonrevolutionary path to liberty is the message of Thomas Babington Macaulay's *History of England*, triumphantly concluded in 1848 just as the Continent was again succumbing to political violence. This "Whig interpretation of history," oriented to the lodestar of 1688, eclipsed the earlier Puritan Revolution down through the days to his nephew, George Macaulay Trevelyan, in the early twentieth century.[10]

The American Revolution, too, despite the ringing "all men are created equal" introducing the Declaration of Independence, was in fact basically about liberty, both individual and national; its central totem was thus appropriately the Liberty Bell.[11] Unlike in England, however, in America the violence of 1776 was enshrined as the founding national moment. Even so, the fact that this Revolution was essentially a War of Independence meant that for the United States the revolutionary overturn was completed with the institutionalization of the new nation's freedom in the Constitution of 1787. The Revolution was thus definitely not seen as an internal overturn, and its triumphant closure indicated that further fundamental transformation was unnecessary for national identity. Even such truly "revolutionary" transformations as the Civil War and the abolition of slavery could readily be accommodated within this perspective; the political outcome, after all, was the restoration of the Union. The historiographical result was a republican Whiggism codified in George Bancroft's multivolume *History of the United States* completed in the 1870s and offering the American story as "a beacon to the world."[12] Further, once tension finally abated between Britain and America after the Civil War, this version was integrated into a broader Anglo-Saxon Whiggism by Trevelyan, Rudyard Kipling, Teddy Roosevelt, and Winston Churchill. Both nations, moreover, considered their revolutions to be unique and therefore incomparable—in both senses of that word.

It was in France that the modern revolution for liberty first opened vistas onto something vaster and bolder than its initial political objective. The French Revolution from the beginning had been about the universal "Rights of Man and the Citizen," and in its republican phase it proclaimed not only liberty, but equality and fraternity as well, a democratic trinity offering not imminent closure but a continuing revolutionary potential. Hence the caesura of 1789–1799 not only produced an epochal break with the national—indeed European—past; it also brought the complete overturn of the previous existing internal order, now relegated to the graveyard status of ancien régime. By the same token, that past was forever after cut in two, unlike in England where the allegedly restorative revolution of 1688 harkened back to Magna Carta. Moreover, this brutal break with the old order meant that the French Revolution produced almost as many losers as winners, thereby dividing the nation over the issue of the Republic right down to the Dreyfus Affair at the turn of the next century, even to the Vichy regime of 1940–1944. Indeed, in the opinion of the major historian of the French Revolution at its bicentennial in 1989, François Furet, the grafting onto the French heritage of 1789 of the Bolshevik myth of 1917 prolonged this internal schism until the 1970s.[13]

It was the French case, therefore, that first generated what may be called a proto-science of revolution as such. To begin with, 1789 had a retroactive effect on the meaning of the English and the American revolutions. In England the convening of the Estates General caused religious dissenters, who were usually also political radicals, to reinterpret 1688 as a revolution analogous to that of France, and so to demand completion of 1688's alleged work by establishing full democracy. It was the activity of one such group, long organized as a "Revolution Society" founded to commemorate the tolerant legacy of 1688, that moved Edmund Burke to write his *Reflections on the Revolution in France*, sharply distinguishing the good British from the bad French type of revolution.[14] Even so, French events drove home to the English that they too had experienced something similar, replete with a royal execution—clearly, a deed never to be repeated. Yet it was only at the end of the century that S. R. Gardiner had made the Puritan revolution a positive part of the English story between 1603 and 1688, though hardly a constituent element of the national myth.[15] A similar differentiation soon appeared with the American Revolution. At first the alliance personified by Franklin, Jefferson, and Lafayette emphasized the similarities between the two overturns, and the participation of Thomas Paine in both events prolonged this continuity into France's Jacobin phase.[16] But soon the Terror, and then Bonaparte, brought out the differences. Thus by 1815 there were three types of revolution in the modern world. And this differentiation furnished the first basis for a comparative analysis of revolutions.

It was in France itself that this possibility was exploited most thoroughly. For the vicissitudes of national history — as the flame of 1789 was reanimated by the revolutions of 1830 and 1848 and the Commune of 1871 — meant that there could be no national Whiggism of any sort. Instead, there was a historiography divided: opinion ranged from the constitutional monarchist and moderate liberal François Guizot, to the radical republican and democrat Jules Michelet, to the liberal conservative and reluctant republican Alexis de Tocqueville, to the committed but disappointed republican Edgar Quinet, and on to the embittered conservative Hippolyte Taine.[17] Yet the very divisions of this historiography produced its richness, thus deepening the speculation about revolution in general.

The liberal generation of Guizot took the first step in this process by seeking the origins, and the legitimation, of 1789 in the "class struggle" waged by medieval municipal communes against their feudal or ecclesiastical overlords, a development later thwarted by the growth of royal absolutism, which was finally destroyed in 1789. Yet now that this grand breakthrough to freedom had been made, these liberals held that the Revolution of 1830 was to be the French 1688, a moderate sequel to 1789 that would close that upheaval with an ordered liberty.[18] But it was Tocqueville's refusal to share this illusion that first made the nascent comparative approach systematic. After 1830 he saw that closure of the process begun in 1789 would not come either early or easily to France. For the nineteenth-century revolution of equality, which we now consider indispensable to modernity, derived its irresistible force from a thousand years of European history, and so could not be stopped by the mere constitutional monarchy of 1830. As he put it in a famous passage:

The gradual development of the principle of equality is . . . a Providential fact . . . it is universal, it is durable, it constantly eludes all human interference, and all men as well as all events contribute to its progress.

Would it, then, be wise to imagine that a social movement, the causes of which lie so far back, can be checked by the efforts of a single generation?

Can it be believed that democracy, after having overthrown aristocracy and the kings, will stop short before the bourgeoisie and the rich?[19]

Thus for Tocqueville, revolution signified the leveling of the hierarchical structure of Europe's "feudal" Old Regime by the forces of egalitarian democracy.

His historical (or sociological) problem then came to be trying to determine why this epochal drive against the Old Regime, which was common to the whole of Europe, first produced overt revolution in France. This led him to continuous comparison with the less stringent Old Regime of England, the more stringent and laggard Old Regime of the Germanies, and above all with the world's first thoroughly modern nation, America.[20] "Whoever has studied and seen only France," he declared, "will never understand anything . . . about the French Revolution." It is "necessary to look outside of France . . . to understand why that great revolution, which was preparing simultaneously over almost all the continent of Europe, first broke out in our country rather than elsewhere."[21] Only in this way could he isolate the factor that made the French case so explosive; and this variable (to use a modern term) was the excessive centralization of the French Old Regime monarchy. With this step, the subject of revolution as such was first staked out.

It was this comparative sociological interest that led Tocqueville in the 1830s to undertake his famous investigation of democratic egalitarianism in America. Its subject was as much France as the United States, as is made clear by a bravura sociological history of the European Old Regime that introduces the volume:

> I look back for a moment at the state of France seven hundred years ago; at that time it was divided up between a few families who owned the land and ruled the inhabitants. At that time the right to give orders descended, like real property, from generation to generation; the only means by which men controlled each other was force; there was only one source of power, namely, landed property.
>
> But then the political power of the clergy began to take shape and soon to extend. The ranks of the clergy were open to all, poor and rich, commoner or noble; through the church, equality began to insinuate itself into the heart of government, and a man who would have vegetated as a serf in eternal servitude could, as a priest, take his place among the nobles and often take precedence over kings.
>
> As society became more stable and civilized, men's relations with one another became more numerous and complicated. Hence the need for civil laws was vividly felt, and the lawyers soon left their obscure tribunals and dusty

chambers to appear at the king's court side by side with feudal barons dressed in chain mail and ermine.

While kings were ruining themselves in great enterprises and nobles wearing each other out in private wars, the commoners were growing rich by trade. The power of money began to be felt in affairs of state. Trade became a political force, despised but flattered.

Gradually enlightenment spread, and a taste for literature and the arts awoke. The mind became an element in success; knowledge became a tool of government and intellect a social force; educated men played a part in affairs of state.

In proportion as new roads to power were found, the value of birth decreased. In the eleventh century, nobility was something of inestimable worth; in the thirteenth it could be bought; the first ennoblement took place in 1270, and equality was finally introduced into the government through the aristocracy itself.[22]

In such a centuries-long perspective, further movement toward democratic equality was inevitable; the only question was whether it would also be revolutionary. And as Tocqueville half-anticipated, 1848 revealed that the aftershocks of 1789 were far from over.

By 1848, then, the nineteenth-century concept of revolution as political liberty shaded off into revolution as the drive to social equality. The mechanisms of this momentous transformation are examined elsewhere in this book. Suffice it to note here that between the shocks of 1830 and 1848 socialism emerged as a magnetic idea; by the end of the century this idea had generated a European-wide movement poised to challenge the course of constitutional liberalism charted between 1776 and 1789.

Karl Marx, of course, was the greatest theorist of this movement—again a matter examined in detail elsewhere (see Chapter 10). Still, it is necessary to sketch here his theory of revolution, both because it marks the transition to the full "sociologizing" of revolution adumbrated by Tocqueville and because almost all the theorists discussed here and in Appendix II worked in his shadow.

Marx's concept of revolution took form in the years immediately preceding 1848, that is, roughly a decade after Tocqueville launched the idea of revolution as egalitarian democracy; its object was to determine under what conditions revolution might come to Germany. The historical data Marx used were the same as that of his French liberal predecessors. This point must be emphasized from the start: the challenge that produced Marx's theory was not emerging "capitalism" (a term which did not yet exist), as is commonly supposed, but the ambition to uncover the historical laws that would bring Germany into the revolutionary process inaugurated by 1789. To frame these laws, consequently, Marx appropriated from Guizot the principle of class struggle as the motive force of history.

In Marx's version, of course, this struggle is socioeconomic, not political. Moreover, he transformed the historical data underlying Tocqueville's tableau of Europe's class-by-class progression to equality into a rigorously structured dialectical march to the "bourgeois revolution" of 1789. And this lockstep logic, of course, he had taken from Hegel. The result is a theory of revolution propelling humanity from slave-holding to feudal to bourgeois and ultimately to socialist society. This theory, thus, is not comparative. Instead, it takes the form of a linear though dialectical development common to all Europe, indeed to the world. The theory, moreover, is a two-tiered construct of "superstructure" and "base" in which politics and culture become mere excrescences of socioeconomic forces.

The first part of the theory is sociological. In the famous words of the 1859 *Critique of Political Economy*:

> In the social production of their life, men enter into definite relations that are indispensable and independent of their will, relations of production which correspond to a definite stage of development of their material productive forces. The sum total of these relations of production constitutes the economic structure of society, the real foundation, on which rises a legal and political superstructure and to which correspond definite forms of social consciousness. The mode of production of material life conditions the social, political and intellectual life process in general. It is not the consciousness of men that determines their being, but, on the contrary, their social being that determines their consciousness.[23]

Out of this social process there then emerges the political overturn that will produce a new social order: "At a certain stage of their development the material forces of production in society come into conflict with the existing relations of production, or—what is but a legal expression for the same thing—with the property relations within which they had been at work before. From forms of development of the forces of production these relations turn into their fetters. Then comes the period of social revolution."[24] Its scenario was spelled out in the *Communist Manifesto*, published on the eve of the Revolution of 1848.

> Each step in the development of the bourgeoisie was accompanied by a corresponding political advance of that class. An oppressed class under the sway of the feudal nobility, an armed and self-governing association in the medieval commune; here independent urban republic (as in Italy and Germany),

there taxable "third estate" of the monarchy (as in France); afterwards, in the period of manufacture proper, serving either the semi-feudal or absolute monarchy as a counterpoise against the nobility, and, in fact, corner-stone of the great monarchies in general—the bourgeoisie has at last, since the establishment of Modern Industry and the world market, conquered for itself, in the modern representative State, exclusive political sway.[25]

Given this world-historical "logic," finally, bourgeois exploitation was destined to produce a second, higher 1789 in the form of proletarian, socialist revolution —though throughout the nineteenth century this outcome of course remained only a hope and anticipation.

Even so, by the century's end the history of past revolutions began to be rewritten from a socialist perspective. This movement was launched—not accidentally as we shall see—in the most backward European nation, Russia, in 1885 by Prince Petr Kropotkin's *The Great French Revolution: 1789–1783*, to be followed in the wake of 1900 by Jean Jaurès's *Histoire socialiste de la Révolution française*.[26] This turn-of-the-century reconceptualization of revolution as a social rather than a political phenomenon establishes another preliminary demarcation of our subject.

REVOLUTION AS SOCIAL UPHEAVAL

With the new century the socialist thought at last became father to the deed. In a prelude, democratic revolution for the first time spread beyond Europe, to Mexico in 1910 and to China in 1911. Then, in 1917 Russia's Red October raised the curtain on the century's central drama: for the first time a Marxist regime came to power and proclaimed the urgent aim of "building socialism." Henceforth, there existed two species of revolution, or were they in fact different genuses? In any event, 1917 sundered modern history into a grand "before and after" that indeed created antagonistic and irreconcilable worlds: socialist-proletarian insurrection was now pitted in a war to the death against a liberal-constitutional, bourgeois-democratic establishment. The very existence of red revolution thus constituted a declaration that 1776 and 1789 had been repealed and all their halfway measures and partial liberations annulled.

Liberalism's heirs were accordingly thrown on the defensive. As a sign of the times, the American republic, which had always thought of itself as a revolutionary guide, a subversive international force cheering on the Latin American revolts of the 1820s and the European upheavals of 1830 and 1848 (to be rewarded in 1889 by an enduringly established French Republic with the gift of the Statue of Liberty for the centennial of their paired founding national moments), now responded to the Bolsheviks as a barbarian force beyond the pale of civilization. The British adopted the even more vigorous policy of mounting armed intervention against them. And the French bourgeoisie, whose investment in Russian imperial bonds had been wiped out by the Bolsheviks' repudiation of tsarist debts, joined in the enterprise. Soviet Russia was not formally recognized by the French until 1924, the British until 1928, and the Americans until 1933. In fact, throughout the seventy-four years of Soviet Communism's existence, and despite the "Grand Alliance" of World War II, the Western democracies never genuinely accepted the Bolshevik regime as a legitimate order.

As part of the fallout from this change, there now existed a range of revolutions on which to build a grand subject. Concomitantly, revolutions—at least real revolutions—came to be regarded as social. In fact, most events that are now customarily called "revolutions" have occurred in the twentieth century. And almost all these revolutions have purported to be socialist. Indeed, the overwhelming majority of them were Communist.

This accumulation of circumstances, furthermore, transformed the subject of revolution from a historical into a sociological problem. The focus of analysis thus shifted from the particularities of a handful of upheavals, as in the nineteenth century, to the general, putatively universal, characteristics of what now seemed to be an endlessly recurring phenomenon.

The liberal reaction to socialist revolutions, however, was not simply an overreaction, as many throughout the past century held. This reaction testified to the very real fact that in the modern era there have existed two distinct families of revolution, as symbolized by the dates 1789 and 1917. And it is to the interaction between these two historical forces, not to some extended series of upheavals, that the subject of revolution-as-such really comes down. For some observers, modern revolution has been regarded as a progression from the first of these poles to the second. For others, the two have been seen as fundamentally antithetical. Yet for just about everyone, the problem of revolution has turned around these two grandest of grand revolutions. The polarity of modern revolution between the two mountain crests of 1789 and 1917 constitutes another preliminary demarcation of our subject.

THE WORLD BEYOND EUROPE

Does this genealogy of the revolutionary concept, then, mean that before the twentieth century there were no revolutions in China, India, and the Islamic world? Or, for that matter, in ancient Greece and Rome? The answer must be,

Eurocentrically, yes. True, in all these societies there was much political violence and extralegal change. But these transformations did not follow a pattern of action, or produce results, analogous to those found in modern Western revolutions.

Let us begin with the most surprising negative cases, Greece and Rome. Classical antiquity, after all, invented politics and gave us our basic political vocabulary: politics itself from the Greek *polis*, and of course "democracy"; "republic" and "citizen" from the Latin *res publica* and *civis*, meaning voting member of the *civitas*. Elsewhere on the planet, until the twentieth century, there existed only what Western philosophers from Aristotle to Hegel not inappropriately called "Oriental despotism." Yet the two societies that invented participatory politics had no word for revolution, for the good reason that they produced no transformations that could have given rise to such a term. In Greek, in famous passages in Thucydides and Aristotle, the word usually translated as "revolution" is *stasis*, from the verb to stand, meaning that factions in the *polis* (the *demos*, or people, and the aristocracy) "take a stand" and square off. In short, the term means civil war, but it carries no connotation of transition to a new order or a new age. In Latin the comparable terms are *bellum civilis*, or civil war, or *seditio*, which means just what its English equivalent does, or *res novae*, signifying approximately coup d'état. But again, there is no connotation of forward historical movement.

This view has been emphasized by such an authority on ancient history as Sir Moses Finley. True, as a Marxist he explains this absence by the fact that in antiquity "there was no revolutionary transfer of power to a new class (or classes) because there were no new classes." And it is quite true that, although there was much class struggle in both Greece and Rome, there was never a "genuine change in the class basis of the state." Indeed, whether one accepts this class explanation or not, it is indisputable that "ancient utopias were regularly static, ascetic and hierarchical, not the sort of image that could arouse popular enthusiasm in the name of progress."[27] This situation stands in marked contrast, not only to modern perceptions, but also to the medieval sense of teleology in human destiny—though in medieval society too there appeared no new classes.

Yet, the well-attested difference between ancient and later European mentalities has never prevented eminent historians, from Theodor Mommsen in the nineteenth century to Ronald Syme in the twentieth, from writing extensively about the "Roman Revolution," meaning the period from the Gracchi to Caesar, that is, from the republic to the empire.[28] Even so, the fact remains that this momentous transition was never perceived as the passage from a corrupt old world to a virtuous new one. Indeed, for many Romans the reverse was true: the despotic empire represented a great decline from the free republic. And this judgment fits quite naturally into the ancients' concept of history as cyclical, not linear and progressive.

The same cyclical pattern is characteristic of China before its contact with Europe. As Joseph Needham, another authority in his field, insists, China has followed a consistent pattern of change from one dynasty to another.[29] A given dynasty governs what it considers to be the empire of the world. This government is an autocracy resting on a mandarin class stemming from the aristocracy (or from the bureaucracy of eunuchs). Eventually, the system loses the population's confidence; peasant revolts ensue, often led by deserters from the mandarin class or by chiefs thrown up by the peasantry. In the national ideology, these defections demonstrate that the dynasty has lost the Mandate of Heaven. Hence it collapses, and on its ruins a new dynasty comes to power—only to govern with the same state forms as its predecessors. One can call these cycles "revolutions," if one wants to, but there is little point in doing so since they in no way resemble the paradigmatic European scenario of 1789–1799. Instead, as a succession of overturns that amounts to an eternal return, they offer a distinctive pattern of their own.

Similarly, we must note the lack of any plausible analogues to the modern European pattern of revolution in India. Of course, between the twelfth and the sixteenth centuries, successive waves of Muslim conquest did produce momentous change: the Islamization of a significant part of the subcontinent, and with it the leveling of the Hindu caste system.

But again, such leveling hardly resembles the later European mode of democratization. Nor will we find anything analogous to it in the Middle Eastern core of Islam. To be sure, the transfer of the caliphate from Umayyad Damascus to Abbasid Baghdad—which in fact has been called the Abbasid Revolution— represented a major shift of power from Arab and Sunni forces to Persian and Shiite ones.[30] Yet, even though this change had a millenarian dimension found also in European revolutions, this is far from enough to compare it profitably to what happened in France after 1789.

With the exclusion from consideration, then, of classical antiquity and the great Oriental empires, the subject of revolution is reduced to manageable proportions. Only by proceeding from such a relatively restricted number of cases is it possible to arrive at useful and verifiable generalizations. To summarize the parameters that have been brought out by this first approximation of method:

a. Before the twentieth century, revolution was a concept relevant only to the European cultural area, including the Americas. It was also, essentially, a political concept.

b. The concept and phenomenon of revolution spread to the rest of the planet only in the twentieth century as other cultures were subjected to European influence. Hence most upheavals that had been conventionally called revolutions have occurred in the twentieth century.

c. These twentieth-century revolutions have been regarded as social, not political in origin and nature.

d. Almost all twentieth-century revolutions therefore were socialist. Indeed, their socialism was overwhelmingly of the Communist, Marxist-Leninist variety.

e. These revolutions have been "theoretized" primarily by sociologists and political scientists, not by historians. Since the twentieth century was the revolutionary century par excellence, it is hardly surprising that revolution-as-such is a twentieth-century subject.

So large has this subject loomed in twentieth-century social science that one specialist has claimed for it the status of a separate discipline with the coinage "staseology," from the Greek *stasis*.[31] On the assumption that this subject really exists, this shorthand usage will be followed here. Appendix II is devoted to its twentieth-century history. And the emphasis will indeed be on history, for the analysis of revolution-as-such, just like the concept of revolution itself, has evolved over time.

In the natural sciences, relatively speaking and with all respect for the Heisenberg principle, the observer stands outside the subject examined. And even though the natural world has a history, it changes over time so slowly that the observer in fact works ahistorically. In the social sciences the observer is very much part of the social process he or she is observing, and both the process and observations are constantly changing in time. Hence, "staseology," and indeed all our social science explanations, are themselves evolving historical products. They are culture-specific. The fortunes of staseology, therefore, will be examined in this time-specific perspective.

Appendix II

HIGH SOCIAL SCIENCE
AND "STASEOLOGY"

All history is contemporary history.
—BENEDETTO CROCE

History is politics projected onto the past.
—MIKHAIL POKROVSKY

L'histoire est un roman vrai.
—PAUL VEYNE

What have been the results of the now decades-old social-science enterprise applied to the study of revolution? It is neither possible nor necessary to review here in any detail its voluminous production. For present purposes, our subject's main lines of development can be brought out by a sampling of viewpoints, with a focus on a few influential works marking the principal stages of what has been called, with a bow to Aristotle's vocabulary, "staseology."[1]

SYSTEMATIZING COMPARISON

The item that flags the transition from traditional history to sociology—and perhaps the work closest to being a classic—is Crane Brinton's *The Anatomy of Revolution*.[2] First published in 1938, revised a final time in 1965 and still in print, the book's conceptual scheme continues to be used to explain the course of the Russian Revolution, and even the Iranian Revolution of 1979.[3] A practicing historian of the French Revolution, the author aims in this general work to make his subject "scientific" and sociological. Given the fluidity of historical phenomena, however, he falls back on one of the softer natural sciences, pathology. Revolution thus becomes a "kind of fever," a conceptual scheme he applies to four prominent cases—England, France, America, and Russia—to see what "uniformities" they can yield. He is not seeking laws applicable to all revolutions, but simply some patterns of regularity capable of giving order to our social knowledge, patterns he expects "will turn out to be obvious, just what any sensible man already knew about revolutions."[4] In fact, his results resemble very much the familiar pendulum theory of revolution.

Revolution begins when the old order breaks down under the pressure of its increasing inefficiency, the criticism of intellectuals, and the defection of elites—all classic symptoms of crisis highlighted by Brinton's preferred sociologist, Wilfredo Pareto. The revolution's first stage is dominated by "moderates" seeking major change but not a wholly new order. The use of force, however, radicalizes the situation by raising up conservative foes of any measure of reform. The way is therefore prepared for the domination of a minority of "extremists" ready to defend the new order by all-out violence; these zealots—Cromwell, Robespierre, Lenin—impose on society a reign of terror and revolutionary purity. The constant tension generated by this generalized coercion, however, is too much for ordinary mortals to bear. This pressure produces a backlash, or a Thermidorian reaction; the fever breaks, and society returns to what the moderates had desired at the start.

This scenario is indeed a commonsense description of what goes on during a major European upheaval. And some of the specific parallels that Brinton finds are genuinely illuminating. One is the revolution's traumatic crescendo of regicide in both England and France. Another parallel he derives from the *dvoevlastie* (dual power) that existed between the Provisional Government and workers' soviets (councils) in Russia during 1917. Although dvoevlastie is at its sharpest in Russia, a similar polarity of "legal" and "illegal sovereignties" clearly existed in France as between the Convention and the Parisian sans-culottes organized in sections; in England as between Parliament and the Independents organized in the New Model Army; and even in America as between the Continental Congress and the "patriot" Committees of Correspondence. Here indeed is an important uniformity that does work.

Overall, however, Brinton's conceptual scheme has only limited explanatory power. It is basically a generalization from the French case, which is then projected onto the other three. It works quite well for England, which, as Burke, Guizot, and Tocqueville all well understood, was a kindred species of Old Regime. But the scheme is misleading for America and Russia. Indeed the author himself recognizes that in America, despite some "patriot" excesses, there was no Terror; and moderate, propertied gentlemen remained in control throughout.

The Russian case is even further from Brinton's norms. The moderates of 1917, the Kadets or constitutional liberals, were liquidated in a matter of months, not over the span of four years as in France. Conversely, the extremists, the Bolsheviks who seized power in October, then stayed there for seven decades, a performance quite surpassing the fifteen-month tenure of the Jacobins. There never was a Thermidor, whether in 1921 with the end of War Communism and the relaxation of the semi-market NEP, or in the mid-1930s between Stalin's collectivization and his Purges. True, after Stalin's death in 1953, revolutionary zeal dwindled away; but the institutionalized Party dictatorship created by Lenin retained power and its socialist goals remained intact until the crash of 1991. So the author, after seeking vainly between the editions of 1938 and 1965 a peg on which to hang his Thermidor, in the end gave up and labeled the Russian case "permanent revolution," without, however, explaining how this aberrant outcome of the Bolshevik fever came about.

To be sure, as of 1938, and even 1965, few in Western academe had a clear idea of what the Soviet experiment was like; so waiting for Thermidor was a perfectly plausible response. And if this eventually turned out to be a wait for Godot, it is because after Red October, "revolution" had surprisingly taken on still another meaning: it no longer signified upheaval or overturn; it now meant regime. Let it be noted here that this transfer occurs in most twentieth-century revolutions. When a Mao Zedong or a Castro spoke of "defense of the revolution" they meant defense of the ruling Party-state—another twentieth-century particularity in the expanding phenomenon of revolution.

Yet even if Brinton had all the information now available, his conceptual scheme still could not explain institutionalized revolution. For he never makes clear what the moderates and the extremists are moderate or extreme *about.* To be sure, he recognizes that the Puritan Independents were Calvinists, the Jacobins sons of the Enlightenment, and the Bolsheviks Marxists. Yet in his analysis they all act, not in terms of these belief systems, but only in their roles as moderates or extremists. That is, they are defined functionally, not ideologically; and in their functional capacity they are virtually interchangeable. Brinton's scheme, in short, is fundamentally ahistorical. His revolutions are conceptually the same, or at least analogous; but it should be obvious that, despite the common presence of fever, the American and the Russian cases are hemispheres apart ideologically and sociologically—or how could the Cold War have come about? And even the English and French cases, despite their close structural similarities, display major divergences that a functional approach cannot grasp—as British Whigs and French republicans have patriotically insisted ever since Macaulay and Michelet.

Revolutions thus do not repeat themselves. Nor can they be reduced to, or even minimally comprehended as, the unfolding of functional or structural patterns. Revolutions are always *about* something. Indeed, what they are about changes over time, as modern culture has moved from religious to secular concerns, and from political to social ones. Moreover, modern revolutions display a temporal or sequential pattern of development, as is apparent even from Brinton's limited sample.

This developmental pattern is that modern revolutions have become progressively more revolutionary: their outcomes moved from the oligarchic constitutional monarchy of England, to the moderate republic of America, to the radical leveling Republic of France, and to the Red Soviet Socialist Republic of Russia. By the same token, the prime actors in the revolutionary drama have been drawn from ever lower levels of the social scale: the leading roles devolved from landed gentry and substantial merchants, to liberal professionals and intellectuals, to artisans and industrial workers, and ultimately to peasants. In sum, the Western revolutionary process has *escalated* in intensity and ambition over time. Moreover, in this process of deepening, each revolution has learned from its predecessor and then radicalized the lessons learned, on a "higher," more democratic level.

There therefore exists not only a structural pattern of action *within* each revolution, part of which Brinton's metaphor of a fever catches quite well. There exists also a genetic pattern of revolutionary escalation, which Tocqueville and Marx spelled out in quite different ways in the mid-nineteenth century.

REVOLUTION AND HIGH SOCIAL SCIENCE

It is only after World War II that the systematic analysis of revolutions hit full stride. The first impetus to this development was the addition, in 1949, of China to the canonical list of great revolutions, thereby multiplying the effect of 1917 by two. This new escalation, moreover, for the first time brought the peasants to the fore of the world revolutionary process. This development had begun with the emergence of Emiliano Zapata in Mexico in 1910; it was carried a great step forward with the Russian peasant jacquerie that permitted the Bolsheviks to seize power, thus leading Lenin to present his party as a "revolutionary alliance of workers and peasants"; and the process reached its culmination with Mao's subordination of the workers to the peasants as the prime revolutionary class. This Chinese effect was further amplified by the unfolding Cold War, as Red Revolution continued to spread to Vietnam, Cuba, and Nicaragua, while at the same time spawning strong, if ultimately unsuccessful, Communist movements from Indonesia to South America. In the wake of this ruralization of revolution, "primitive rebels" and "peasant revolts" became increasingly popular social-science subjects.[5]

The second impetus to the transformation of the study of revolution came from the postwar institutionalization of the social sciences, especially in the American mega-university. These disciplines were now collectively promoted to the rank of the third great area of learning, on the same level as the humanities and the natural sciences; and they aspired to equal the latter in the rigor and certainty of their methods. Thus, "society," in its basic structures, functions, and component classes, was seen as a universal entity, susceptible to "value-free" analysis in terms of categories valid in any culture and any historical period. It therefore became imperative to fit the spreading phenomenon of revolution into these rigorous new categories. Brinton's prewar attempt at science soon came to be dismissed as a primitive, "natural history" approach to revolution.

This high social science literature falls into two broad types: structural-functionalism, which is an American synthesis of the European masters Weber and Durkheim; and socioeconomic class analysis, an approach obviously indebted to Marxism, without, however, being "orthodox." In the first category, we find the theory, already mentioned, of internal war. To flesh it out a bit in the language of the new social science, it comprises "four positive variables—elite inefficiency, disorienting social process, subversion, and available rebel facilities—and four negative variables—diversionary mechanisms, available incumbent facilities, adjustive mechanisms, and effective repression."[6] Any internal war, allegedly, can be explained by different patterns of interaction among these eight variables. Perhaps. But no historian has used it systematically on a particular revolution. Then, we have "frustration-aggression" theories, theories of structural "dysfunction," or of political and social imbalance and "disequilibrium," or of the institutional blockage of "modernization." And we have the behaviorist proposition that revolutions are not triggered by increasing misery but by "relative deprivation," that is, by the gap between peoples' expectations and their perceptions of their real situation.[7]

Some of this theorizing has been put to creative use in the study of actual revolutions. Historian Lawrence Stone has effectively employed both relative deprivation and, to a degree, internal war in analyzing the causes of the English Revolution.[8] Charles Tilly is a special case since he is both a historian and a sociologist, a practitioner of particular temporal and national fields and a theorist of revolutions in general. Thus, on the one hand, he presents us with a major case study, The Vendée, of an apparently self-contradictory, lower-class counter-revolution;[9] on the other, a theoretical treatise analyzing the uniformities underlining any process leading from social "mobilization" to actual "revolution."[10] There is no one pattern of revolution that is repeated in European history, but there is a mechanism of revolutionary change that underlies each specific upheaval. Tilly compares this to a traffic jam caused when diverse streams of traffic, each with its own separate causation, converge to create a great jam. That is, revolutions occur when various "normal" lines of causation converge (economic, demographic, constitutional, international, etc.). In the revolutionary situation two or more blocks of "contenders" make incompatible "claims" to control the state; thus "dual power" leads to a struggle and a revolutionary outcome. History enters into the model because the state, the economy, and society change over time: Tilly discusses the Dutch Revolt (the first bourgeois revolution), the English Revolution, the French Revolution, and the Russian Revolution. The Soviet collapse of 1989–1991 counts as a revolution, but not as big as the four grand revolutions. Culture and ideology do not exist in his model.

For the moment, suffice it to note that most historians—until well after World War II an untheoretical lot—have been forced by these various structural endeavors to be much more precise in framing their questions and answers.[11] Still, far too much theory amounts to abstract statements of things we already knew about politics and society. And just about all of it reduces lived experience to a kind of self-propelled mechanism that is "scientific" only in its internal conceptual logic (which is at times only the pseudo-precision of terminological overrefinement), not in its relationship to observed historical data.

Neo-Marxist theories of revolution are more interesting to historians, precisely because comparison by definition entails examining specific cases. The near-classic here is Barrington Moore's *Social Origins of Dictatorship and Democracy: Lord and Peasant in the Making of the Modern World*, of 1966.[12] A sociologist with a good empirical base in Soviet Russia[13] (like Brinton in France), Moore takes as his starting premise that the modern world is defined by the inexorable movement of all societies toward capitalism, a process that has entailed eliminating the inveterately backward-looking peasantry. His problem, then, is to determine under what conditions such "modernization" leads to democracy rather than to dictatorship, whether of the Communist or the fascist variety. And in attempting an answer he of course runs into the great twentieth-century paradox of class analysis: namely, contrary to Marxist expectations, socialist revolution has triumphed only in backward, agrarian societies, but never in advanced industrial ones, where the only revolutions have been fascist. Yet at the same time, as a quasi-Marxist, Moore remains committed to the proposition that all revolutions must be explained in class terms. He therefore seeks to resolve the modern

Marxist paradox by reshuffling the cards of social class and political regime to produce new correspondences between the two factors.

The model he comes up with sees three types of modernization: democratic capitalism in the West; authoritarian and ultimately fascist capitalism in Germany and Japan; and a Communist modernization from above that replaces capitalism in Russia and China. In each case, the outcome is determined not by the interaction of the bourgeoisie with the proletariat, as in classical Marxism, but by the interaction of the aristocracy with the peasantry.

In the first category, the "bourgeois democracies" (a term employed a bit apologetically, but nonetheless resolutely), there are three subcases: the unsurprising trio of England, France, and the United States. In the first, the aristocracy involves itself in commercial agriculture and so fuses with the bourgeoisie to limit the power of the monarchy; the peasantry is thereby eliminated through the enclosures of village commons, and the workers are left too isolated to revolt. The eventual result is a robust capitalism and an imperfect but still liberal democracy. In the French case, the bourgeoisie, less dynamic economically than in England, relies on the entrepreneurial peasantry and, partially, the workers to displace a largely pre-commercial and parasitic aristocracy and to destroy the monarchy. The result is a broad democracy but a weak capitalism because of the social weight of small peasant proprietors. In the American case, the Civil War plays the role of bourgeois revolution (sic!), destroying the commercial yet still "feudal" aristocracy of the South, thereby preparing the way for capitalism's triumph and a flawed but still real democracy. This last subset is manifestly absurd, a forced transatlantic projection of Moore's (and Marx's) paradigmatic economic case, England, in order to sustain an a priori pattern. All it really shows, as did Brinton's terminology, is that America is the odd man out of modern revolution.

Moore's second set of correspondences, Germany and Japan, offers a pattern of authoritarian modernization from above. The dynamic here is an aristocratic alliance with absolute monarchy to enserf the peasantry and so to enter commercial agriculture. This path leads to fostering advanced capitalism for national aggrandizement, and its ultimate outcome is fascist dictatorship.

In Moore's third set of correspondences, Russia and China, a weak aristocracy lives in overdependence on the autocratic monarchy, which it needs to subdue and exploit the peasantry. This produces a feeble, largely state-guided capitalist development, which in the wars of the twentieth century leads to national defeat. And this in turn produces a peasant explosion, led by disaffected intellectuals, which sweeps away the monarchy, the aristocracy, and the state-dependent bourgeoisie. The unavoidable task of modernization is then taken up by the disaffected intellectuals who have come to power amid the tumult. This Communist

and "totalitarian" dictatorship at last carries out the cruel but necessary liquida-
tion of "the idiocy of rural life."

Moore's model offers an intellectual construct as ingenious as it is ambitious.
It draws a multiplicity of variables into an internally coherent pattern and relates
them with apparent plausibility to a global range of cases. In both respects, it goes
far beyond Brinton's simple natural history; as a theoretical construct it rivals in
complexity the most comprehensive structural-functional models while surpassing them in fullness of factual illustration. Based as it is on extensive reading in
all the relevant European languages (it would be unreasonable to expect also a
knowledge of Chinese and Japanese), it often offers both challenging methodological observations and pertinent *aperçus* on social history, from the German
Peasants' War of 1525 to twentieth-century China and India.

But its greatest contribution perhaps is the inadvertent one of giving a truly
monumental example of what does not work in historical explanation. In fact,
Moore does a better job of discrediting Marxism than do most of its overt critics.
By using class analysis on a global scale Moore turns Marx's theory of history as
a progression from feudal to bourgeois to socialist society right on its head. Reactionary lords and retrograde peasants become the great revolutionary forces
of the modern world; the bourgeoisie emerges as the sole bastion of democracy, while the proletariat totally disappears from view; and the overall result of
twentieth-century revolution is dictatorship, not human liberation. Unwilling to
accept this grim outcome of modernity, however, Moore appends a final chapter on socialist India in the hope of finding some hints of a better future.

But Marxism stands or falls as a total explanatory system. Class struggle in
Marx's theory is the expression of a historical teleology by which the lower, exploited classes, by virtue of their very oppression, are the vanguard of a rational
reordering of the world into a society without classes. Wrenched from this context, class analysis becomes simply another form of structuralism, and not a very
useful one at that. It is certainly not enough to account for the grim paradox that
Moore's seven modern revolutions exemplify. So we must ask, what else is acting in modernity to produce such an untoward result?

A part of the answer lies in such contingencies as war, a factor Moore ne-
glects but without which the career of twentieth-century Communism is incomprehensible. A more basic factor still is the central defect of original Marxism,
which Moore preserves: the reduction of politics and culture to a mere superstructure of the socioeconomic base of society. Indeed, for Moore politics and
the state completely disappear from the revolutionary process; the only actors in
history's high drama are now faceless social classes. Hence the sole political force
mentioned in each national case is the monarchy, whose structure and mode of

operation, however, is never described or compared with other cases. But is the Mandarin Empire of the Manchus really comparable to the Old Regime of the Bourbons?

Just as crucial, no one in Moore's revolutionary process has an idea in his head: ideology, indeed culture in general, is totally lacking from his analysis. To be sure, Moore correctly points out that the peasants are not the supreme revolutionary class of the twentieth century because they have a vision or a program. In both Russia and China they were revolutionary only in the negative sense that their revolt sweeps away the old order; yet they were quite incapable of coming to power on their own or of building a state. All of this is quite true. But it does not automatically yield Moore's conclusion that the inescapable task of modernization then falls to disaffected intellectuals, a major actor in the drama but hardly a "class."

For where does this faceless body of intellectuals come from? What is the inspiration of their Communist program? And how could they get away with implementing it at such inordinate costs? These indispensable questions are not even raised; so by implication the modernizing mission of this intelligentsia is the automatic secretion of the socioeconomic process. Once again, therefore, the sociologizing of revolution has given us history as a self-propelled social mechanism. That this new mechanism is socioeconomic rather than structural makes it no less a ghostly abstraction than its rivals.

Filling the first of the gaps in Moore's model would appear to be the aim of his student, Theda Skocpol, in her work of 1979, *States and Social Revolutions: A Comparative Analysis of France, Russia, and China*, still the single most influential book in the field, and for many already a classic.[14] Skocpol's undertaking was announced under the slogan of "bringing the state back in."[15] Now this was a job that certainly needed doing. What is surprising, however, is that taking it on was treated as a methodological breakthrough. In fact, such straining to reinvent the wheel merely testifies to the low estate to which the sociology of revolution had fallen. It should have been self-evident from the start that there can be *no* revolution without a state to capture or to overthrow. Yet perhaps this point indeed came as news in a field whose base no longer lay in specific empirical cases but in the now elaborate accumulation of theory.

Skocpol's model covers France, Russia, and China. By a "multivariate" comparison of these three cases she aims to bring out a common *causal* pattern governing each.[16] In other words, this is "macro-history" at the highest level.

Before revolution, all three societies were similar "agrarian bureaucracies." This opaque term, taken from Moore, does not mean that bureaucrats tilled the fields, as one might imagine, but that the three cases were agricultural societies ruled by a bureaucratic monarchy. All three, moreover, were hard pressed by international competition from economically more advanced rivals: France by England, Russia by Europe as a whole, and China by the Western powers generally. This competition forced each agrarian state to undertake an "extraordinary mobilization of resources for economic and military development." This increased the tax burden on aristocratic landowners, who also staffed the royal bureaucracy. The nobles reacted to this pressure (a) by using their institutional leverage in the bureaucracy to demand control over the absolute monarchy (as with the French Estates General) and (b) by intensifying their own financial squeeze on the peasants. The conflict between nobility and monarchy at the top undermined the state apparatus, thus unleashing a massive peasant revolt from below against the landowners (as with the Great Fear of the summer of 1789). This agrarian revolution ultimately destroyed both the old social hierarchy and the state. Into the void then stepped "marginal elite political movements"—Jacobins or Communists—who rebuilt the state in even more centralized, rationalized, and bureaucratic form; and this strengthened state resumed and completed the task of modernization.

To fill the picture out, Skocpol has three negative "controls": seventeenth-century England, Prussia in 1848, and Meiji Japan. In all three cases, the peasantry was neutralized as a revolutionary factor by an early transition to capitalist agriculture, which broke up traditional rural communities. Moreover, the central governments of Japan and Prussia were independent of the landlord class, and so preserved the strength to act decisively against social discontent. Hence, the English and the French cases have nothing in common worth mentioning, and Japan was spared all revolutionary upheaval.

The key component of Skocpol's model and the common denominator of the three cases is the idea of the peasantry as the pivotal revolutionary force of modern history, and this of course comes from her mentor, Moore. Yet where did he get it? In part he derived it from the obvious fact of the peasantry's crucial role in the Russian, Chinese, and later third world cases. But this does not account for his highlighting a similar peasant role in eighteenth-century France. After all, France was Marx's paradigmatic political case, the one from which he derived the class struggle model of revolution and which he deemed the very quintessence of "bourgeois revolution"—a thesis Skocpol offhandedly rejects in favor of peasant hegemony.

The sources of this conceptual somersault are not far to seek. Moore got his idea of the peasant's revolutionary centrality from the great French Marxist historian Georges Lefebvre, who in the 1930s first analyzed in detail *La grande peur*

(The Great Fear) of 1789, a story now found in all accounts of the Revolution.[17] Lefebvre, as a latter-day Jacobin now attracted to Bolshevism, had been sensitized to the peasants' historic role by their obvious prominence in 1917 Russia. He therefore went back to his own national history to find something analogous, thereby giving 1789 a broader popular base than the bourgeoisie, and so making it appear an anticipation of its Russian socialist sequel.

Now, the peasants indisputably played an important role in 1789; but before Lefebvre this was never regarded as central. Although peasant disturbances of 1789 were mentioned in all nineteenth-century histories, they were never regarded as pivotal, even by such radicals as Kropotkin and Jaurès. Nor will one find in these authors the expression "Great Fear," for the good reason that it was not used in 1789 itself. So again we have the retroactive impact, the *Wechselwirkung*, of a later revolution on an earlier one, transference similar to the French Revolution's effect in revealing to the English that they had made an analogous revolution a century earlier. Nor is dating the term "Great Fear" just a terminological curiosity; rather, it points up the fact that it took the French over a century to discover the peasants' full impact in 1789, thereby indicating that these peasants could hardly have been the decisive force in bringing down the Old Regime. In fact, the regime was already dead before the peasants took to the field; that is why they could do so without fear of reprisal.

Indeed, Lefebvre himself puts the Great Fear in just this perspective in a work not cited by either Moore or Skocpol.[18] In his presentation, the fall of the Old Regime unfolds in four stages: the aristocratic revolution of 1788, which forced the convocation of the Estates General; the bourgeois revolution of May-June 1789 culminating in the Tennis Court Oath; the popular revolution of July 14 expressed by the taking of the Bastille; and the peasant Great Fear leading to the night of August 4 and the collapse of the estate system. This scenario, which fits the historical facts like a glove, offers a magisterial use of the class struggle model of revolution. Indeed, it is better than anything in Marx's own celebrated studies of French politics in 1848, *The Class Struggle in France* and *The Eighteenth Brumaire of Louis Bonaparte*.

Skocpol's hegemonic peasantry, therefore, represents a caricatured adaptation of Lefebvre. In fact, his work is used essentially to illustrate conclusions derived from her earlier study of China, from which she decided that, though "France was 'supposed' to be like England [both Tocqueville's and Marx's position], her absolutist Old Regime seemed in many ways similar to Imperial China."[19] After all, didn't Stuart England fail to produce a peasant big bang? This set of intuitions, Skocpol explains, derived from her "commitment to democratic socialism" which, in the effervescence of the 1960s and the Vietnam War, led her to develop a deep interest in East Asia. So the hegemony of peasant revolutionism she admired in China was projected onto the "bourgeois revolution" of France, and then onto the "proletarian revolution" of Russia. For France, however, the projection fails utterly, because it was indeed the nobles and the bourgeoisie, not the peasants, that brought down the monarchy and the estate system. So the first pivot of her triune model crumbles.

Another pivot falls through an elemental misreading of the international situation of her three agrarian bureaucracies. As every schoolchild ought to know, France, together with England, was one of the two superpowers of the eighteenth-century world. And even more than England, it was the intellectual and cultural leader of the radical Enlightenment. Moreover, as of 1789 the economic gap between the two rivals was narrow, some would say closing; it was the Napoleonic Wars that gave England an indubitable and enduring lead. The early twentieth-century Celestial Empire in China, by contrast, was heading for dissolution: it was so weak as to invite partition by intruding European powers; its economic gap with the West was enormous; and its culture was still largely premodern.

A third pivot falls with the particularities of the Russian case. In 1914, Russia was much nearer, militarily, economically, and culturally, to the earlier French case than to the later Chinese one. Moreover, the Russian monarchy's terminal crisis, unlike that of France, was not triggered by financial impasse and conflict with its aristocratic bureaucracy. It was brought about by defeat in modern war, a fact Skocpol notes without seeing the damage it does to her model's consistency. Thus, although Russia offers marginal similarities to China in this respect, it is quite unlike France, where revolution broke out in peacetime. And once the French Revolution went to war it conquered most of Europe in a few years, whereas Communist China has yet to take Taiwan.

With these three pivots gone, Skocpol's trio of agrarian bureaucracies hardly offers "comparable instances of a single coherent revolutionary pattern."[20] For her three cases do not offer a continuum of cognate yet partially different institutional forms of the sort Tocqueville found among the English, French, and German Old Regimes. Skocpol's method is in fact pseudo-comparative, a conceptually driven juxtaposition rather than a historically grounded structural kinship—in folk parlance, a comparison of apples and oranges.

Clearly, the common denominator of her cases, agrarian society, is too broad and undifferentiated to tell us anything about politics and the state, not to mention culture. At times this common denominator is diluted further by adding Ottoman Turkey and Mogul India to the list of "agrarian bureaucracies." But as of 1789 the whole planet was overwhelmingly agrarian. This includes the very "modern" United States to the tune of 98 percent, though American farmers, of course, even then were not the same as European peasants. Obversely, Tokyo was at the time the largest city in the world, equivalent to London and Paris combined. But politically, so what? Japan was still a species of autocracy. The same vagueness bedevils Skocpol's second conceptual common denominator, bureaucratic monarchy. If the Forbidden City of Peking, the Mogul Court, and Old Regime Versailles really commanded comparable state structures, what are the explicit equivalences between their various institutions, from the Mandarin class to *parlements?*

The perils of forced, noncognate comparison are more patent in the outcomes of her three revolutions. All turn out to be similar "bureaucratic and mass-incorporating national states," with variations to be sure, but each created by "educated marginal elites oriented to state employment and activities" who therefore built tough centralized new regimes.[21] In this perspective, Napoleon's empire, Stalin's "construction of socialism," and Mao Zedong's "mass mobilizing Party-State" are, give or take some details, equivalent. These comparisons are ridiculous on their face. Napoleon was a personal dictator, but his empire, and the Code he spread throughout Europe, represented an exemplary *état de droit;* and post-Napoleonic France developed into a liberal democracy, with a bureaucracy to be sure (we all know the textbook cliché about the institutional continuity amidst political instability in modern French history) — but what modern state is not bureaucratic? On the other hand, Stalin and Mao constructed regimes that ruled by institutionalized terror, at times veering to outright dementia. Their economic "planning" eventually had to be abandoned. And no evolution toward the rule of law or democracy was perceptible until almost the collapse of 1991.

Moreover, Skocpol repeats Moore's mistake of defining the revolutionary marginal elites solely in social and functional terms, without reference to culture — she may have brought back a state of sorts, but she continues to ignore ideology. She thus makes nothing of the fact that the Soviet and Chinese Communists were Marxists. Nor, finally, is there anything in her analysis that could later be used to make sense of the collapse of Communist "modernization" in the 1990s. It is now obvious that Communism did a very inferior job of modernization, and it was not very difficult to perceive this in 1979. Yet the Soviet and Maoist forms of modernity are treated as enduring achievements.

And this unquestioning assumption, common to most of the social-science literature on twentieth-century revolution, presents us with a final problem: must value-free social science also be amoral? Is not part of the problem of "modernizing revolution" the ethical one of what constitutes an acceptable level of human cost for the putative degree of progress achieved? This is routinely asked for earlier revolutions, especially the Terror of 1793. Yet in both structural-function-alist and neo-Marxist analyses of twentieth-century revolution this question is systematically absent. To paraphrase Skocpol's slogan, it is time to bring ethics back in to the study of twentieth-century revolutions.

BACK TO HISTORY, POLITICS, AND CULTURE

In sum, Skocpol surpasses even Moore in pursuing approaches that do not work. The latter's use of class analysis at least leads to three different sets of re-sults, and hence remains not too remote from the complexities of modern his-tory. The former, by contrast, dismisses the obvious English control case for her model with the comment: not enough peasants. In fact, the globe-straddling theories of both Moore and Skocpol produce results that are less useful than Brinton's modest uniformities of "fever" and "dual power." Indeed, the whole postwar social-science endeavor, structural-functionalist as well as neo-Marxist, has done surprisingly little to change the working historiography of the revolu-tions in its repertoire. This meager result stands in marked contrast to the deep impact that the nineteenth-century theorists Tocqueville and Marx have had on the major revolutionary historiographies.

So we are back again with the positive uses of conceptual failure in permit-ting us to define an adequate comparative method. Recall that the basis of such a method existed in Tocqueville's explanation of why modern democratic revo-lution broke out first in France, not elsewhere in Europe. It was by comparing the French Old Regime with cognate cases that he isolated monarchic central-ization as the decisive factor in producing the French Revolution.

This approach may be amplified by the example of the methodologically more self-conscious Weber. Weber's problem was to explain why capitalism arose first in Europe, not in some other civilization. He noted similar proto-capitalist forms of economic organization in all Eurasian higher societies—from China to India to Greece and Rome. What varied from case to case was the culture, which in pre-modern conditions meant religion. So he compared Confucianism, Hindu-ism, Judaism, and Christianity to isolate those aspects of Christian doctrine that predisposed the West to embark on the unending economic expansion of mod-ern capitalism. And these sources he found, of course, in Lutheranism's concept of a this-worldly ascetic "calling" and Calvinism's doctrine of predestination—a "Protestant ethic" which, when secularized, became the "spirit of capitalism."[22] The merits of this explanation are not the issue here. (Few historians would now defend it as originally stated, although some correlation between early capitalism and Protestant influence remains persuasive.[23] Certainly, Tocqueville's correlation between radical democracy and Old Regime works far better.) The point is that Weber's approach is the appropriate one for isolating any decisive historical variable. So, too, is his understanding that culture, in particular religion, is the first basis of European uniqueness.

NOTES

INTRODUCTION

1. *The Soviet Tragedy: A History of Socialism in Russia, 1917–1991* (New York: Free Press, 1994).
2. *Russia Under Western Eyes: From the Bronze Horseman to the Lenin Mausoleum* (Cambridge, Mass.: Harvard University Press, 1999).
3. For example, Chalmers Johnson, *Revolutionary Change* (Boston: Little, Brown, 1966). For a detailed critique of modern social science "staseology" (comparative analysis of revolutions), see Appendix II.
4. Max Weber, *The Protestant Ethic and the Spirit of Capitalism*, trans. Talcott Parsons (New York: Scribner's, 1958).
5. Ernst Troeltsch, *The Social Teaching of the Christian Churches*, 2 vols. (New York: Harper, 1960).
6. See Appendix I.
7. Alexander Gerschenkron, *Economic Backwardness in Historical Perspective: A Book of Essays* (Cambridge, Mass.: Belknap/Harvard University Press, 1962), especially the title essay (pp. 5–30).
8. This has already been tried by Michael Walzer for England in his *The Revolution of the Saints: A Study in the Origins of Radical Politics* (Cambridge, Mass.: Harvard University Press, 1965).

1. HISTORIC EUROPE

1. Alfred Weber, *Kulturgeschichte als Kultursoziologie* (Leiden: A. W. Sijthoff, 1935).
2. Martin Bernal, *Black Athena: The Afro-Asian Roots of Classical Civilization* (London: Free Association Press, 1987).
3. For the history of the term and the concept of Europe, see Denys Hay, *Europe: The Emergence of an Idea*, rev. ed. (Edinburgh: Edinburgh University Press, 1964); Frederico Chabod, *Storia dell'idea d'Europa* (Bari: Laterza, 1964); and Jean Baptiste Duroselle, *L'idée d'Europe dans l'histoire* (Paris: Denoël, 1965). For the specifically Western

Roman, or Latin, basis of historic Europe, see Rémi Brague, *Europe: La voie romaine*, 2d ed. (Paris: Critérion, 1993). For a perspective on Europe extending "from the Atlantic to the Urals," see Martin Malia, "A New Europe for the Old?" *Daedalus*, Summer 1997.

4. David Gress, *From Plato to NATO: The Idea of the West and Its Opponents* (New York: Free Press, 1998).

5. Georges Duby, *L'an mil* (Paris: Gallimard, 1980).

6. Richard A. Fletcher, *The Barbarian Conversion from Paganism to Christianity* (New York: Holt, 1998).

7. For the Orthodox east of Europe, see Dimitri Obolensky, *The Byzantine Commonwealth: Eastern Europe, 500–1453* (New York: Praeger, 1971).

8. Eamon Duffy, *Saints and Sinners: A History of the Popes* (New Haven: Yale University Press, 1997).

9. William H. McNeill, *Europe's Steppe Frontier, 1500–1800* (Chicago: University of Chicago Press, 1964).

10. N. P. Pavlov-Sil'vanskii, *Feodalizm v Rossii* (Moscow: Nauka, 1988).

11. For the optimism of the year 1000, see Duby, *L'an mil*.

12. Lynn White, Jr., *Medieval Technology and Social Change* (Oxford: Clarendon Press, 1962).

13. Dietrich Gerhard, *Old Europe: A Study of Continuity, 1000–1800* (New York: Academic Press, 1981).

14. For Europe's constantly expanding forces, see Robert Bartlett, *The Making of Europe: Conquest, Colonization, and Cultural Change, 950–1350* (Princeton: Princeton University Press, 1994).

15. Jenó Szúcs, *Les trois Europes* (Paris: Editions l'Harmattan, 1985).

16. *Romans 13, 1–7.*

17. Marc Bloch, *La société féodale* (Paris: A. Michel, 1994), p. 618.

18. Ibid., pp. 610–612, 618–619.

19. Ibid., pp. 617–618.

20. John Bossy, *Christianity in the West, 1400–1700* (New York: Oxford University Press, 1985).

21. Talcott Parsons, *The Social System* (London: Tavistock, 1952).

22. Mircea Eliade, editor in chief, *The Encyclopedia of Religion* (New York: Macmillan, 1987), and his *A History of Religious Ideas*, 3 vols. (Chicago: University of Chicago Press, 1978–1985), vol. 2, *From Gautama Buddha to the Triumph of Christianity*.

23. Louis Dumont, *Homo hierarchicus: The Caste System and Its Implications* (Chicago: University of Chicago Press, 1980), and his *Homo aequalis* (Paris: Gallimard, 1977).

24. Jaroslav Pelikan, *The Christian Tradition: A History of the Development of Doctrine*, 5 vols. (Chicago: University of Chicago Press, 1971–1989), vol. 1, *The Emergence of the Catholic Tradition (100–600)*, and vol. 3, *The Growth of Medieval Theology (600–1300)*.

25. Georges Duby, *The Age of the Cathedrals: Art and Society, 980–1420* (Chicago: University of Chicago Press, 1981).

26. Ernst Troeltsch, *The Social Teaching of the Christian Churches*, 2 vols. (New York: Harper, 1960), 1:234.

27. R. I. Moore, *The Origins of European Dissent* (New York: Blackwell, 1985), pp. 126–127.

28. Ibid., p. 127.

29. Marjorie Reeves, *Joachim of Fiore and the Prophetic Future* (London: SPCK, 1976).

30. For the impact of the military revolution, see Michael Roberts, "The Military Revolution, 1560–1660," in Michael Roberts, *Essays in Swedish History* (London: Weidenfeld and Nicolson, 1967), and Geoffrey Parker, *The Military Revolution: Military Innovation and the Rise of the West* (New York: Cambridge University Press, 1988).

2. HUSSITE BOHEMIA, 1415–1436

1. František Šmahel, *La révolution Hussite: Une anomalie historique* (Paris: Presses Universitaires de France, 1985).

2. František Palacký, *Geschichte von Böhmen*, 5 vols. in 10 (Prague: In Commission bei Weber, 1836–1867). These remarks on the historiography of Hussitism owe a debt to Ms. Jean Grant of the history graduate program at U.C. Berkeley.

3. George Sand, *Consuelo: La comtesse de Rudolstadt* (Paris: Garnier, 1959).

4. Jaroslav Goll, *Quellen und Untersuchungen zur Geschichte der Böhmischen Brüder*, 2 vols. in 1 (Prague: J. Otto, 1878–1882). Josef Pekař, *Der Sinn der tschechischen Geschichte* (Munich: Volksbote, 1961).

5. František Bartoš, *The Hussite Revolution, 1424–1437* (Boulder, Colo.: East European Monograph, 1986).

6. See, in addition to the short French version cited in note 1, František Šmahel, *Die hussitische Revolution*, 3 vols. (Hanover: Hahnsche, 2002). See also, in English, his chapter in Mikuláš Teich, ed., *Bohemia in History* (Cambridge: Cambridge University Press, 1998).

7. Frederick Heymann, *John Žižka and the Hussite Revolution* (Princeton: Princeton University Press, 1955), and *The Cambridge Medieval History*, vol. 8, *The Close of the Middle Ages* (Cambridge: Cambridge University Press, 1959), chs. 2 and 3 by Kamil Krofta.

8. Howard Kaminsky, *A History of the Hussite Revolution* (Berkeley: University of California Press, 1967).

9. John Klassen, *The Nobility and the Making of the Hussite Revolution* (Boulder, Colo.: East European Quarterly, 1978).

10. Thomas Fudge, *The Magnificent Ride: The First Reformation in Hussite Bohemia* (Brookfield, Vt.: Ashgate, 1998).

11. Šmahel, *La révolution Hussite*, p. 22.

12. For the rising power of the nobility see Klassen, *Nobility*.

13. Otto von Gierke, *Political Theories of the Middle Ages*, trans. with an introduction by Frederic William Maitland (Cambridge: Cambridge University Press, 1987).

14. The text of the declaration is in Heymann, *John Žižka*, ch. 10.

15. Eric Hobsbawm and Terence Ranger, eds., *The Invention of Tradition* (Cambridge: Cambridge University Press, 1992).

3. LUTHERAN GERMANY, 1517–1555

1. Thomas A. Brady, Jr., Heiko A. Oberman, James D. Tracy, eds., *Handbook of European History, 1400–1600: Late Middle Ages, Renaissance, and Reformation* (Grand Rapids, Mich.: William B. Eerdmans, 1996).
2. A. G. Dickens and John Tonkin, with Kenneth Powell, *The Reformation in Historical Thought* (Cambridge, Mass.: Harvard University Press, 1985).
3. Karl Kautsky, *Communism in Central Europe in the Time of the Reformation* (New York: Russell & Russell, 1959). The German original first appeared in 1894.
4. George H. Williams, *The Radical Reformation* (Philadelphia: Westminster Press, 1962).
5. Heiko Augustinus Oberman, *The Harvest of Medieval Theology: Gabriel Biel and Late Medieval Nominalism* (Cambridge, Mass.: Harvard University Press, 1963).
6. Philip Benedict, *Christ's Churches Purely Reformed* (New Haven: Yale University Press, 2002).
7. Hajo Holborn, *A History of Modern Germany*, 3 vols. (Princeton: Princeton University Press, 1982), vol. 1, p. 125.
8. Steven Ozment, *The Age of Reform (1250–1550): An Intellectual and Religious History of Late Medieval and Reformation Europe* (New Haven: Yale University Press, 1980), p. 231.
9. Johan Huizinga, *The Autumn of the Middle Ages* (Chicago: University of Chicago Press, 1996). The theme of the late Middle Ages as an age of anxiety has been updated and copiously documented in Jean Delumeau, *La peur en Occident, XIVe–XVIIIe siècles: Une cité assiégée* (Paris: Fayard, 1978), and *Le péché et la peur: La culpabilisation en Occident, XIIIe–XVIIIe siècles* (Paris: Fayard, 1983).
10. Heiko Oberman, "The Shape of Late Medieval Thought," in his *The Dawn of the Reformation: Essays in Late Medieval and Early Reformation Thought* (Edinburgh: T&T Clark, 1986).
11. Albert Hyma, *The Christian Renaissance: A History of the "Devotio Moderna,"* 2d ed. (Hamden, Conn.: Archon Books, 1965).
12. Hans-Jürgen Goertz, *Pfaffenhass und gross Geschrei: Die reformatorischen Bewegungen in Deutschland, 1517–1529* (Munich: C. H. Beck, 1987).
13. Hajo Holborn, *Ulrich von Hutten* (Göttingen: Vandenhoeck & Ruprecht, 1968).
14. Pierre Chaunu, *Le temps des reformes* (Paris: Fayard, 1975), p. 441.
15. Peter Blickle, *Communal Reformation: The Quest for Salvation in Sixteenth-century Germany*, trans. Thomas Dunlap (Atlantic Highlands, N.J.: Humanities Press, 1992).
16. A. G. Dickens, *The German Nation and Martin Luther* (London: Edward Arnold, 1974).
17. Bernd Moeller, *Imperial Cities and the Reformation: Three Essays* (Philadelphia: Fortress Press, 1972).

18. Thomas A. Brady, Jr., *Turning Swiss: Cities and Empire, 1450–1550* (New York: Cambridge University Press, 1985).

19. Blickle, *Communal Reformation*. Steven E. Ozment, *The Reformation in the Cities: The Appeal of Protestantism to Sixteenth-Century Germany and Switzerland* (New Haven: Yale University Press, 1975).

20. See Appendix I.

21. See above, Chapter 1.

22. Thomas Brady, Jr., *Ruling Class, Regime and Reformation at Strasbourg, 1520–1555* (Leiden: E. J. Brill, 1978).

23. Peter Blickle, "Memmingen—A Center of the Reformation," in his *From the Communal Reformation to the Revolution of the Common Man*, trans. Beat Kümin (Leiden: Brill, 1998).

24. Heiko Oberman, "Zwingli's Reformation Between Success and Failure," in his *The Reformation: Roots and Ramifications*, trans. Andrew Colin Gow (Edinburgh: T&T Clark, 1993).

25. Carter Lindberg, *The European Reformations* (Cambridge, Mass.: Blackwell, 1996), p. 169.

26. Steven E. Ozment, *Mysticism and Dissent: Religious Ideology and Social Protest in the Sixteenth Century* (New Haven: Yale University Press, 1973); Gordon Rupp, *Patterns of Reformation* (London: Epworth Press, 1969).

27. Hans-Jürgen Goertz, *Thomas Müntzer: Apocalyptic, Mystic, and Revolutionary*, trans. Jocelyn Jaquiery (Edinburgh: T&T Clark, 1993). Eric W. Gritsch, *Thomas Müntzer: A Tragedy of Errors* (Minneapolis: Fortress Press, 1989).

28. John Bossy, *Christianity in the West, 1400–1700* (Oxford: Oxford University Press, 1985), p. 109.

29. Eric W. Gritsch, "Thomas Müntzer and Luther: A Tragedy of Errors," in Hans J. Hillerbrand, ed., *Radical Tendencies in the Reformation: Divergent Perspectives* (Kirksville, Mo.: Sixteenth Century Journal Publishers, 1988); Hans-Jürgen Goertz, "The Mystic with the Hammer: Thomas Müntzer's Theological Basis for Revolution," in James M. Stayer and Werner O. Packull, eds., *The Anabaptists and Thomas Müntzer* (Dubuque, Iowa: Kendall/Hunt, 1980).

30. Claus-Peter Clasen, *Anabaptism: A Social History, 1525–1618: Switzerland, Austria, Moravia and Central Germany* (Ithaca, N.Y.: Cornell University Press, 1972). (For membership figures see Chapter 2.)

31. Roland Bainton, *The Reformation of the Sixteenth Century* (Boston: Beacon Press, 1952). George Williams, *The Radical Reformation* (Philadelphia: Westminster Press, 1962).

32. Blickle, *From the Communal Reformation*.

33. Peter Blickle, *The Revolution of 1525*, trans. Thomas A. Brady, Jr., and H. C. Eric Midelfort (Baltimore: Johns Hopkins University Press, 1981), p. 51.

34. Blickle, *Revolution of 1525*, pp. 78–86. See also his *From the Communal Reformation to the Revolution of the Common Man* and his *Communal Reformation: The Quest for Salvation*.

35. See above, Chapter 2.
36. James M. Stayer, *Anabaptists and the Sword* (Lawrence, Kan.: Coronado Press, 1972).
37. Williams, *Radical Reformation*, chapter 10.
38. James M. Stayer, "Christianity in One City: Anabaptist Münster, 1534–1535," in Hans J. Hillerbrand, ed., *Radical Tendencies in the Reformation: Divergent Perspectives* (Kirksville, Mo.: Sixteenth Century Journal Publishers, 1988).
39. Thomas A. Brady, Jr., *Protestant Politics: Jacob Sturm (1489–1553) and the German Reformation* (Atlantic Highlands, N.J.: Humanities Press, 1995).
40. I quote from memory Luther's frequently repeated criteria for the true church.
41. See, for example, Hans Ulrich Wehler, *Deutsche Gesellschaftsgeschichte*, 4 vols. (Munich: C. H. Beck, 1987–2003).
42. This view has been argued in a variety of forms. See, for example, A. J. P. Taylor, *The Course of German History: A Survey of the Development of Germany Since 1815* (New York: Capricorn Books, 1962), and Erich Fromm, *Escape from Freedom* (New York: Holt, Rinehart and Winston, 1969; first published 1941).
43. See above, Chapter 2.

4. HUGUENOT FRANCE, 1559–1598

1. The best survey of Calvinism as a European movement is Philip Benedict, *Christ's Churches Purely Reformed* (New Haven: Yale University Press, 2002).
2. Estimates vary. Quoting Huguenot sources of the period, Robert Kingdon gives a high figure of 15 percent or 3 million souls out of a population of 19 million; Robert M. Kingdon, *Geneva and the Coming of the Wars of Religion in France: 1555–1563* (Geneva: Droz, 1956), p. 79. Janine Garrisson, currently a major specialist of French Protestantism, gives 8.75 percent, or 1.75 million souls out of a population of 20 million; Janine Garrisson, *Les derniers Valois* (Paris: Fayard, 2001). Philip Benedict gives 10 percent, or between 1.5 and 2 million out of a total population of 19 million. Benedict, *Christ's Churches*, p. 137.
3. Pierre Imbart de la Tour, *Les origines de la reforme*, 4 vols. (Paris: Hachette, 1905–1935); Emile Doumergue, *Jean Calvin, les hommes et les choses de son temps*, 7 vols. (Lausanne: G. Bridel, 1899–1927).
4. Ernest Lavisse, *Histoire de France depuis les origines jusqu'à la révolution*, 9 vols. (Paris: Hachette, 1900–1911), vols. 4 and 5.
5. See, notably, Lucien Febvre, *Au coeur religieux du XVIe siècle* (Paris: SEVPEN, 1957).
6. Emmanuel Le Roy Ladurie, *L'état royal de Louis XI à Henri IV, 1460–1610* (Paris: Hachette, 1987).
7. Denis Crouzet, *Les guerriers de Dieu: La violence au temps des Troubles de Religion (vers 1525–1610)*, 2 vols. (Seyssel: Champ Vallon, 1990); see also his *La genèse de la Réforme Française, 1520–1562* (Paris: SEDES, 1996). This approach is also reflected in Philippe Erlanger, *Le massacre de la Saint-Barthélemy, 24 août 1572* (Paris: Gallimard, 1960). This volume in the series *Trente journées qui ont fait la France* has been redone by Crouzet as *La nuit de la Saint-Barthélemy: Un rêve perdu de la Renaissance* (Paris: Fayard, 1994). See also Natalie Zemon Davis, *Society and Culture*

in *Early Modern France: Eight Essays* (Stanford, Calif.: Stanford University Press, 1975).

8. Perez Zagorin, *Rebels and Rulers, 1500–1660*, 2 vols. (Cambridge: Cambridge University Press, 1982), vol. 2, ch. 10, "Revolutionary Civil War: The French Civil War."

9. Quentin Skinner, *The Foundations of Modern Political Thought*, 2 vols. (Cambridge: Cambridge University Press, 1978), vol. 2, ch. 8.

10. Kingdon, *Geneva and the Coming of the Wars*, p. 129.

11. Garrisson, *Les derniers Valois*, pp. 261–267.

12. Kingdon, *Geneva and the Coming of the Wars*.

13. Robert Kingdon, *Geneva and the Consolidation of the French Protestant Movement, 1564–1572* (Madison: University of Wisconsin Press, 1967).

14. This is the thesis of H. G. Koenigsberger in "The Organization of Revolutionary Parties in France and the Netherlands During the Sixteenth Century," in his *Estates and Revolutions: Essays in Early Modern European History* (Ithaca, N.Y.: Cornell University Press, 1971).

15. Lucien Romier, *Le royaume de Catherine de Medicis: La France à la veille des guerres de religion* (Geneva: Slatkine Reprints, 1978, originally published 1925). See also Michael Walzer, *The Revolution of the Saints: A Study in the Origins of Radical Politics* (Cambridge, Mass.: Harvard University Press, 1965).

16. Garrisson, *Les derniers Valois*, p. 128.

17. Robert Kingdon, *Myths About the St. Bartholomew's Day Massacres, 1572–1576* (Cambridge, Mass.: Harvard University Press, 1988).

18. Quentin Skinner, *The Foundations of Modern Political Thought*, 2 vols. (Cambridge: Cambridge University Press, 1978), vol. 2.

19. J. H. M. Salmon, *The French Religious Wars in English Political Thought* (Oxford: Clarendon Press, 1959).

5. THE NETHERLANDS' REVOLT, 1566–1609

1. John Lathrop Motley, *The Rise of the Dutch Republic: A History* (New York: Thomas Y. Crowell, 1901).

2. Pieter Geyl, *The Revolt of the Netherlands (1555–1609)* (New York: Barnes & Noble, 1958).

3. Volumes 3 and 4 of Henri Pirenne, *Histoire de Belgique*, 7 vols. (Brussels: M. Lamertin, 1922–1932).

4. Erich Kuttner, *Das Hungerjahr 1566: Eine Studie zur Geschichte des niederlandischen Frühproletariats und seiner Revolution* (Mannheim: Palatium Verlag, 1997).

5. Heinz Schilling, "Der Aufstand der Niederlande: Bürgerliche Revolution oder Elitenkonflikt?" in Hans-Ulrich Wehler, ed., *200 Jahre amerikanische Revolution und moderne Revolutionsforschung* (Göttingen: Vandenhoeck und Ruprecht, 1976) (*Geschichte und Gesellschaft*, 2 Sonderheft), pp. 177–231.

6. This is the case of the most important recent book on the subject, Jonathan Israel's *The Dutch Republic: Its Rise, Greatness, and Fall, 1477–1806* (Oxford: Clarendon Press, 1995).

7. Geoffrey Parker, *The Dutch Revolt* (Ithaca, N.Y.: Cornell University Press, 1977). See also Perez Zagorin, *Rebels and Rulers, 1500–1660, Volume II: Provincial Rebellion; Revolutionary Civil Wars, 1560–1660* (Cambridge: Cambridge University Press, 1982), ch. 11.

8. For the full constitutional history of the Burgundian Netherlands see H. G. Koenigsberger, *Monarchies, States Generals and Parliaments: The Netherlands in the Fifteenth and Sixteenth Centuries* (Cambridge: Cambridge University Press, 2001).

9. Heinz Schilling, *Religion, Political Culture, and the Emergence of Early Modern Society: Essays in German and Dutch History* (Leiden: E. J. Brill, 1992).

10. Kuttner, *Das Hungerjahr.*

11. Parker, *The Dutch Revolt*, p. 78.

12. Pirenne, *Histoire de Belgique*, 4:101–103.

13. Parker, *The Dutch Revolt*, p. 186.

14. Koenigsberger, "The Intervention of the Common People," in *Monarchies*, pp. 276–279.

15. Alastair Duke, *Reformation and Revolt in the Low Countries* (London: Hambledon Press, 1990).

6. ENGLAND, 1640–1660–1688

1. Edward, Earl of Clarendon, *The History of the Rebellion and Civil Wars in England Begun in the Year 1641* (Oxford: Clarendon Press, 1958).

2. To be sure, he, like Lord Clarendon, was writing an eyewitness account. Even so, his view represented the national consensus at a time when a Jacobite danger still existed in Britain. See Bishop Burnet, *History of His Own Time*, 2d ed., 6 vols. (Oxford: Oxford University Press, 1833).

3. Samuel R. Gardiner, *History of England: From the Accession of James I to the Outbreak of the Civil War, 1603–1642*, 10 vols. (London: Longmans, 1883–1884); *History of the Great Civil War, 1642–1649*, 4 vols. (London: Longmans, 1893); *History of the Commonwealth and the Protectorate, 1649–1660*, 3 vols. (London: Longmans, 1897–1901). See also Appendix I.

4. George Macaulay Trevelyan, *The English Revolution, 1688–1689* (London: T. Butterworth, 1938); *England Under the Stuarts* (London: Methuen, 1904) (this fifth volume of his *History of England* continued to bear the same title through many subsequent editions).

5. R. H. Tawney, *Religion and the Rise of Capitalism: A Historical Study* (London: J. Murray, 1926). See also his *The Agrarian Problem in the Sixteenth Century* (New York: Burt Franklin, 1912).

6. Christopher Hill, ed., *The English Revolution 1640: Three Essays* (London: Lawrence & Wishart, 1940), "I. The English Revolution, by Christopher Hill."

7. Friedrich Engels, *Socialism, Utopian and Scientific* (New York: New York Labor News, 1901). See also Eduard Bernstein, *Sozialismus und Demokratie in der großen englischen Revolution* (Stuttgart: J. H. W. Dietz Nachfolger, 1908).

8. See Appendix II.

9. G. M. Trevelyan, *English Social History: A Survey of Six Centuries: Chaucer to Queen Victoria* (London: Longmans, 1942).

10. Pokrovsky, of course, was referring to history as practiced by his ideological opponents. See George M. Enteen, *The Soviet Scholar-Bureaucrat: M. N. Pokrovskii and the Society of Marxist Historians* (University Park: Pennsylvania State University Press, 1978), p. 33.

11. Lawrence Stone's work on this subject culminated in his *The Crisis of the Aristocracy, 1558–1641* (Oxford: Clarendon Press, 1965).

12. J. H. Hexter, *Reappraisals in History* (Evanston: Northwestern University Press, 1961). In fact, Hexter allows some correlation between Independency and "mere" gentry.

13. Lawrence Stone, *The Causes of the English Revolution, 1529–1642* (New York: Harper & Row, 1972), and his "The English Revolution" in Robert Forster and Jack P. Greene, eds., *Preconditions of Revolution in Early Modern Europe* (Baltimore: John Hopkins Press, 1970).

14. Christopher Hill, "A Bourgeois Revolution?" in J. G. A. Pocock, ed., *The Three British Revolutions: 1641, 1688, 1776* (Princeton: Princeton University Press, 1980).

15. Conrad Russell, *The Crisis of Parliaments: English History, 1509–1660* (London: Oxford University Press, 1971). See also his later works *The Fall of the British Monarchies, 1637–1642* (Oxford: Clarendon Press, 1991); Conrad Russell, ed., *The Origins of the English Civil War* (New York: Barnes & Noble, 1973). Kenneth O. Morgan, ed., *The Oxford Illustrated History of Britain* (Oxford: Oxford University Press, 1984). A good state of the debate summary is G. E. Aylmer, *Rebellion or Revolution? England, 1640–1660* (Oxford: Oxford University Press, 1986).

16. Mark Kishlansky, *A Monarchy Transformed: Britain, 1603–1714* (New York: Penguin, 1996).

17. Lawrence Stone, "The English Revolution," in *Preconditions*, p. 57. Another proponent of the idea that the period 1640–1660 was indeed a revolution is Perez Zagorin, *Rebels and Rulers, 1500–1660*, 2 vols. (Cambridge: Cambridge University Press, 1982); he discusses the English case in volume 2, pages 130–186.

18. E. P. Thompson, *The Making of the English Working Class* (London: V. Gollancz, 1963). See also the somewhat dispirited attempt by his wife to keep up hope: Dorothy Thompson, ed., *The Essential E. P. Thompson* (New York: New Press, 2001).

19. For an intelligent, if at times somewhat too deliberately provocative, treatment of British and foreign absolutism, see Nicholas Henshall, *The Myth of Absolutism: Change and Continuity in Early Modern European Monarchy* (London: Longman, 1992).

20. J. C. D. Clark, *English Society, 1660–1832: Religion, Ideology, and Politics During the Ancien Regime* (Cambridge: Cambridge University Press, 2000).

21. G. Griffiths, *Representative Government in Western Europe in the Sixteenth Century: Commentary and Documents for the Study of Comparative Constitutional History* (Oxford: Clarendon Press, 1968). Otto Gierke, *Natural Law and the Theory of Society, 1500 to 1800*, trans. Ernest Barker (Boston: Beacon Press, 1957).

22. The classic statement of the relationship between foreign policy and domestic constitution is Otto Hintze, *Staat und Verfassung: Gesammelte Abhandlungen zur allgemeinen Verfassungsgeschichte* (Gottingen: Vandenhoeck & Ruprecht, 1962); see also

Felix Gilbert and Robert Berdahl, eds., *The Historical Essays of Otto Hintze* (New York: Oxford University Press, 1975). For a stimulating, if ultimately unsuccessful, attempt to fuse Hintze with Marx, see Perry Anderson, *Lineages of the Absolutist State* (London: NLB, 1974).

23. John le Patourel, *Feudal Empires: Norman and Plantagenet* (London: Hambledon Press, 1984).

24. R. J. Acheson, *Radical Puritans in England, 1550–1660* (London: Longman, 1990).

25. Conrad Russell, introduction to *The Origins of the English Civil War*, p. 14.

26. The relevant studies are Michael Roberts, "The Military Revolution, 1560–1660," in his *Essays in Swedish History* (London: Weidenfeld and Nicolson, 1967); Geoffrey Parker, *The Military Revolution: Military Innovation and the Rise of the West, 1500–1800* (Cambridge: Cambridge University Press, 1988) and his *The Army of Flanders and the Spanish Road, 1567–1659: The Logistics of Spanish Victory and Defeat in the Low Countries' Wars* (Cambridge: Cambridge University Press, 1972); William H. McNeill, *The Pursuit of Power: Technology, Armed Force, and Society Since A.D. 1000* (Chicago: University of Chicago Press, 1982); Bruce D. Porter, *War and the Rise of the State: The Military Foundations of Modern Politics* (New York: Free Press, 1994). For criticism of the standard view see Jeremy Black, ed., *The Origins of War in Early Modern Europe* (Edinburgh: John Donald, 1987), and Jeremy Black, *A Military Revolution? Military Change and European Society, 1550–1800* (Atlantic Highlands, N.J.: Humanities Press International, 1991). For the impact of all this on Russia, see Richard Hellie, *Enserfment and Military Change in Muscovy* (Chicago: University of Chicago Press, 1971).

27. J. G. A. Pocock, *The Ancient Constitution and the Feudal Law: A Study of English Historical Thought in the Seventeenth Century; A Reissue with a Retrospect* (Cambridge: Cambridge University Press, 1987). Glenn Burgess, *The Politics of the Ancient Constitution: An Introduction to English Political Thought, 1603–1642* (University Park: Pennsylvania State University Press, 1993). Christopher Hill, *Intellectual Origins of the English Revolution* (Oxford: Clarendon Press, 1965).

28. Stone, *Causes*, p. 137.

29. Zagorin, *Rebels and Rulers*, 2:130.

30. D. B. Robertson, *The Religious Foundations of Leveller Democracy* (New York: King's Crown Press, 1951); and G. E. Aylmer, ed., *The Levellers in the English Revolution* (London: Thames and Hudson, 1975).

31. The transcript of the Putney debates from the *Clarke Manuscripts* is given in A. S. P. Woodhouse, ed., *Puritanism and Liberty* (London: J. M. Dent, 1974).

32. Samuel R. Gardiner, *History of the Great Civil War, 1642–1649*, 4 vols. (London: Longmans, 1905), 3:290.

33. For a defense of the importance of sectarian radicalism in the English Revolution, see F. D. Dow, *Radicalism in the English Revolution, 1640–1660* (New York: Blackwell, 1985).

34. B. S. Capp, *The Fifth Monarchy Men: A Study in Seventeenth-Century English Millenarianism* (London: Faber, 1972).

35. Christopher Hill, *The World Turned Upside-Down: Radical Ideas During the English Revolution* (London: Penguin Books, 1991).

36. J. G. A. Pocock, *The Machiavellian Moment: Florentine Political Thought and the Atlantic Republican Tradition* (Princeton: Princeton University Press, 1975).

37. The classic biography of Cromwell is Charles Firth, *Oliver Cromwell and the Rule of the Puritans in England* (London: Putnam, 1901). The most prominent subsequent treatment is Christopher Hill, *God's Englishman: Oliver Cromwell and the English Revolution* (London: Weidenfeld and Nicolson, 1970).

38. John Locke, *Two Treatises of Government* (New York: New American Library, 1975).

39. Elie Halévy, *England in 1815* (New York: Barnes & Noble, 1961). It is highlighted in his *The Birth of Methodism in England* (Chicago: University of Chicago Press, 1971).

7. AMERICA, 1776–1787

1. Quoted in Gordon S. Wood, *The Creation of the American Republic, 1776–1787* (Chapel Hill: University of North Carolina Press, 1969), pp. 3–4.

2. François Furet, "L'idée française de Révolution," *Le Débat* 96 (September-October 1997).

3. Louis Hartz, *The Liberal Tradition in America: An Interpretation of American Political Thought Since the Revolution* (New York: Harcourt Brace, 1955).

4. Ray Allen Billington, *The Reinterpretation of Early American History: Essays in Honor of John Edwin Pomfret* (New York: Norton, 1968), and Jack P. Greene, ed., *The Reinterpretation of the American Revolution, 1763–1789* (New York, Harper & Row, 1968).

5. Eugene D. Genovese, *The Political Economy of Slavery: Studies in the Economy and Society of the Slave South* (New York: Vintage Books, 1967).

6. See Appendix I.

7. Edmund S. Morgan, *Inventing the People: The Rise of Popular Sovereignty in England and America* (New York: Norton, 1988).

8. George Otto Trevelyan, *The American Revolution*, 3 vols. in 4 (New York: Longmans, Green, 1899–1907).

9. Charles H. Lincoln, *The Revolutionary Movement in Pennsylvania, 1760–1776* (Philadelphia: University of Pennsylvania, 1901), and Carl L. Becker, *History of Political Parties in the Province of New York, 1760–1776* (Madison: University of Wisconsin Press, 1960, first published 1909).

10. Arthur Meier Schlesinger, *The Colonial Merchants and the American Revolution, 1763–1776* (New York: Columbia University, 1918).

11. Charles A. Beard, *An Economic Interpretation of the Constitution of the United States* (New York: Macmillan, 1913).

12. Vernon Louis Parrington, *Main Currents in American Thought*, 2 vols. (New York: Harcourt, Brace and Company, 1927), vol. 1: *The Colonial Mind*.

13. Merrill Jensen, *The Articles of Confederation: An Interpretation of the Social-Constitutional History of the American Revolution, 1774–1781* (Madison: University of Wis-

consin Press, 1940), and *The New Nation: A History of the United States During the Confederation, 1781–1789* (New York: Knopf, 1950).

14. Edmund S. Morgan and Helen M. Morgan, *The Stamp Act Crisis: Prologue to Revolution* (Chapel Hill: University of North Carolina Press, 1953).

15. Bernard Bailyn, *The Ideological Origins of the American Revolution* (Cambridge, Mass.: Harvard University Press, 1967).

16. Caroline Robbins, *The Eighteenth-Century Commonwealthman: Studies in the Transmission, Development and Circumstance of English Liberal Thought from the Restoration of Charles II Until the War with the Thirteen Colonies* (Cambridge, Mass.: Harvard University Press, 1959).

17. Perry Miller, *The New England Mind: The Seventeenth Century* (New York: Macmillan, 1939), and *The New England Mind: From Colony to Province* (Cambridge, Mass.: Harvard University Press, 1953).

18. Perry Miller, "From the Covenant to the Revival," in James Ward Smith and A. Leland Jamison, eds., *The Shaping of American Religion* (Princeton: Princeton University Press, 1961).

19. Alan Heimert, *Religion and the American Mind from the Great Awakening to the Revolution* (Cambridge, Mass.: Harvard University Press, 1966).

20. Bernard Bailyn, "Political Experience and Enlightenment Ideas in Eighteenth-Century America," *American Historical Review* 67 (January 1962): 339–351. The view of the revolution as essentially conservative is set forth most fully by Robert Middlekauff in *The Glorious Cause: The American Revolution, 1763–1789* (New York: Oxford University Press, 1982).

21. Gordon S. Wood, *The Radicalism of the American Revolution* (New York: Knopf, 1992).

22. Bernard Bailyn, *The Peopling of British North America: An Introduction* (New York: Knopf, 1986).

23. Fred Anderson, *The Crucible of War: The Seven Years' War and the Fate of Empire in British North America, 1754–1766* (New York: Knopf, 2000).

24. John Brewer, *The Sinews of Power: War, Money and the English State, 1688–1783* (London: Unwin Hyman, 1989).

25. J. G. A. Pocock, *The Machiavellian Moment: Florentine Political Thought and the Atlantic Republican Tradition* (Princeton: Princeton University Press, 1975).

26. Carl Bridenbaugh, *Mitre and Sceptre: Transatlantic Faiths, Ideas, Personalities, and Politics, 1689–1775* (New York: Oxford University Press, 1962).

8. FRANCE, 1789–1799

1. The best treatment of the Revolution's historiography is given in François Furet and Mona Ozouf, *Dictionnaire critique de la Révolution française: 1780–1880* (Paris: Flammarion, 1988). A convenient collection of opinion on the Revolution is Antoine de Baecque, ed., *Pour ou contre la Révolution, de Mirabeau à Mitterand* (Paris: Bayard, 2002). For a brief survey of the historiography of the Revolution to 1960, see George Rudé, *Interpretations of the French Revolution* (London: Routledge and Kegan Paul,

1961). For a detailed treatment of the historiography since World War II, see William Doyle, *Origins of the French Revolution* (New York: Oxford University Press, 1999).

2. Stanley Mellon, *The Political Uses of History: A Study of Historians in the French Restoration* (Stanford, Calif.: Stanford University Press, 1958).

3. Adolphe Thiers, *Histoire de la Révolution française* (Paris: Furne, 1845–1847, first published 1823–1827), and *Histoire du consulat et de l'empire*, 21 vols. (Paris: Paulin, 1845–1875). François Mignet, *Histoire de la Révolution française*, 2 vols. (Paris: Didot, 1824).

4. See Appendix I.

5. His major work, translated into all European languages, is François Guizot, *Histoire générale de la civilisation en Europe depuis la chute de l'Empire Romain jusqu'à la Révolution française* (Paris: Didier, 1840). See also Pierre Rosanvallon, *Le moment Guizot* (Paris: Gallimard, 1985).

6. Jules Michelet, *Histoire de la Révolution française*, 2 vols. (Paris: Gallimard, 1961–1962, first published 1847–1853).

7. Alphonse de Lamartine, *Histoire des Girondins*, 3d ed., 8 vols. (Paris: Furne, 1848).

8. Louis Blanc, *Histoire de la Révolution française*, 12 vols. (Paris: Langlois et Leclercq, 1847–1862).

9. The most useful English version of the book is *The Old Regime and the Revolution*, edited and with an introduction and critical apparatus by François Furet and Françoise Melonio, trans. Alan S. Kahan, 2 vols. (Chicago: University of Chicago Press, 1998–2001).

10. See Appendix I.

11. As quoted in English translation by Martin Malia, "Did Tocqueville Foresee Totalitarianism?" *Journal of Democracy* 11, no. 1 (January 2000): 185.

12. Edgar Quinet, *La Révolution*, 2 vols. (Paris: A. Lacroix, 1865).

13. François Furet, *La gauche et la révolution au milieu du XIXe siècle: Edgar Quinet et la question du jacobinisme, 1865–1870* (Paris: Hachette, 1986).

14. Hippolyte Taine, *Les origines de la France contemporaine*, 22d ed., 12 vols. (Paris: Hachette, 1899; first published 1876–1894).

15. F.-A. Aulard, *Histoire politique de la Révolution française: Origines et développement de la démocratie et de la République (1789–1804)* (Paris: A. Colin, 1901).

16. Jean Jaurès, *Histoire socialiste de la Révolution française*, 8 vols. (Paris: Editions de la Librairie de l'humanité, 1922–1924).

17. Albert Mathiez, *La Réaction Thermidorienne* (Paris: A. Colin, 1929) and *La vie chère et le mouvement social sous la Terreur* (Paris: Payot, 1927).

18. For a sketch of his career, see Richard Cobb, "Georges Lefebvre," in Richard Cobb, *A Second Identity: Essays on France and French History* (London: Oxford University Press, 1969).

19. J. Loutchitsky (I. V. Luchitskii), *La propriété paysanne en France à la veille de la Révolution (principalement au Limousin)* (Paris: H. Champion, 1912); *L'état des classes agricoles en France à la veille de la Révolution* (Paris: H. Champion, 1911). Russian scholars were the prime movers in launching both British and French agrarian history, in the former case when Paul Vinogradov (later Sir Paul Vinogradoff) inspired Frederic Maitland's *Domesday Book and Beyond* (Cambridge: Cambridge University

Press, 1897), and in the French case with the publication in French of the work of N. I. Kareev, which came directly out of the Russian populist—that is, agrarian socialist—tradition (Luchitskii was Kareev's student). See N. Kareiew, *Les paysans et la question paysanne en France dans le dernier quart du XVIIIe siècle* (Paris: V. Giard & E. Brière, 1899). See also Kareiew, "Les travaux russes sur l'époque de la Révolution française depuis dix ans (1902–1911)," *Bulletin de la Société d'Histoire Moderne* (1912), 2:132–143, and S. N. Pogodin, *"Russkaia shkola" istorikov: N. I. Kareev, I. V. Luchitskii, M. M. Kovalevskii* (St. Petersburg: Sankt-Peterburgskii gosudarstvennyi tekhnicheskii universitet, 1997).

20. Georges Lefebvre, *Les paysans du Nord pendant la Révolution française* (Paris: F. Rieder, 1924).

21. Georges Lefebvre, *La Grande peur de 1789* (Paris: A. Colin, 1932).

22. Georges Lefebvre, *The Coming of the French Revolution, 1789,* trans. R. R. Palmer (Princeton: Princeton University Press, 1947). Originally published as *Quatre-vingt-neuf* (Paris: Maison du livre français, 1939).

23. Georges Lefebvre, *La Révolution française,* 3d rev. ed. (Paris: Presses Universitaires, 1951).

24. C. E. Labrousse, *Esquisse du mouvement des prix et des revenues en France au XVIIIe siècle,* 2 vols. (Paris: Librairie Dalloz, 1933); *La Crise de l'économie française à la fin de l'Ancien Régime et au début de la Révolution* (Paris: Presses Universitaries de France, 1944).

25. Albert Soboul, *Les Sans-culottes parisiens en l'an II: Mouvement populaire et gouvernement révolutionnaire, 2 juin 1793–9 Thermidor An II* (Paris: Librairie Clavreuil, 1958).

26. See, for example, Albert Soboul, *La Révolution française,* 7th ed. (Paris: Presses Universitaires de France, 1981), an expanded version of his *Précis d'histoire de la Révolution française* of 1962.

27. Alfred Cobban, *The Social Interpretation of the French Revolution* (Cambridge: Cambridge University Press, 1964). In fact, he had already stated the essence of his position earlier and in shorter form in 1955 in *The Myth of the French Revolution: An Inaugural Lecture Delivered at University College, London, 6 May 1954* (London: University College, 1955).

28. Cobban, *Social Interpretation,* p. 162.

29. François Furet and Denis Richet, *La Révolution,* 2 vols. (Paris: Hachette, 1965–1966).

30. François Furet, "La catéchisme de la Révolution française," *Annales,* no. 2 (March–April 1971).

31. François Furet, *Penser la Révolution française* (Paris: Gallimard, 1978).

32. Augustin Cochin, *L'esprit du jacobinisme: Une interpretation sociologique de la Révolution française* (Paris: Presses Universitaires de France, 1979). The articles in this volume had originally been published posthumously in 1921–1924. (Cochin was killed in World War I.)

33. Crane Brinton, *A Decade of Revolution, 1789–1799* (New York: Harper & Brothers, 1934). In fact, Brinton's analysis, with its emphasis on ideological "fever," anticipates Furet's revisionism in many respects. Lefebvre's student George Rudé was also quite

aware of Cochin. See also Lord Elton, *The Revolutionary Idea in France, 1789–1871* (London: Edward Arnold, 1923).

34. See for example, François Furet and Mona Ozouf, *The Transformation of Political Culture, 1789–1848*, vol. 3 of Keith Michael Baker, ed., *The French Revolution and the Creation of Modern Political Culture*, 3 vols. (Oxford: Pergamon Press, 1987–1989).

35. Perhaps the best intellectual history of postwar France is Raymond Aron, *Mémoires* (Paris: Julliard, 1983). See also Tony Judt, *Past Imperfect: French Intellectuals, 1944–1956* (Berkeley: University of California Press, 1992).

36. Furet and Ozouf, *Transformation of Political Culture*. The very idea of "commemoration" was questioned in a number of articles by Furet gathered together by Mona Ozouf in *La Révolution en débat* (Paris: Gallimard, 1999).

37. Pierre Chaunu, *Le grand déclassement: A propos d'une commémoration* (Paris: Laffont, 1989).

38. Jacques Revel and Lynne Hunt, eds., *Histories: French Constructions of the Past* (New York: New Press, 1995).

39. The chief name here is Roland Mousnier, *Les institutions de la France sous la monarchie absolue: 1598–1789*, 2 vols. (Paris: Presses Universitaires de France, 1974). *Les hierarchies sociales de 1450 à nos jours* (Paris: Presses Universitaires de France, 1969). See also Pierre Goubert, *L'Ancien régime*, 2 vols. (Paris: A. Colin, 1969), and Denis Richet, *La France moderne: L'esprit des institutions* (Paris: Flammarion, 1973).

40. George Taylor, "Noncapitalist Wealth and the Origins of the French Revolution," *American Historical Review* 72, no. 2 (1967): 491, as quoted by Doyle, *Origins*, p. 17.

41. Joseph R. Strayer, *On the Medieval Origins of the Modern State* (Princeton: Princeton University Press, 1970), and *Medieval Statecraft and the Perspectives of History: Essays by Joseph R. Strayer* (Princeton: Princeton University Press, 1971).

42. Emmanuel Le Roy Ladurie, *L'Ancien Régime: De Louis XIII à Louis XV, 1610–1770* (Paris: Hachette, 1991), and *Saint Simon, ou, Le système de la cour* (Paris: Fayard, 1997).

43. Orest Ranum, *The Fronde: A French Revolution, 1648–1652* (New York: Norton, 1993).

44. Marc Raeff, *The Well-ordered Police State: Social and Institutional Change Through Law in the Germanies and Russia, 1600–1800* (New Haven: Yale University Press, 1983). See also Martin Malia, *Russia Under Western Eyes: From the Bronze Horseman to the Lenin Mausoleum* (Cambridge, Mass.: Harvard University Press, 1999), ch. 1.

45. Dale K. Van Kley, *The Religious Origins of the French Revolution: From Calvin to the Civil Constitution, 1560–1791* (New Haven: Yale University Press, 1996). Catherine Maire, *De la cause de Dieu à la cause de la nation: Le jansénisme au XVIIIe siècle* (Paris: Gallimard, 1998). Monique Cottret, *Jansénisme et lumières: Pour un autre XVIIIe siècle* (Paris: Albin Michel, 1998).

46. Dale Van Kley, *The Jansenists and the Expulsion of the Jesuits from France, 1757–1765* (New Haven: Yale University Press, 1975).

47. Chaunu, *Le grand déclassement*.

48. For Rousseau's audience see Robert Darnton, *The Literary Underground of the Old Regime* (Cambridge, Mass.: Harvard University Press, 1982).

49. See Keith Michael Baker, *Inventing the French Revolution: Essays on French Political*

Culture in the Eighteenth Century (Cambridge: Cambridge University Press, 1990), ch. 9.

50. Paul Hazard, *La crise de la conscience européenne, 1680–1715* (Paris: Boivin, 1935).

51. Ernest Tuveson, *Millenium and Utopia: A Study in the Background of the Idea of Progress* (Berkeley: University of California Press, 1949). Karl Löwith, *Meaning in History* (Chicago: University of Chicago Press, 1949).

52. J. B. Bury, *The Idea of Progress: An Inquiry into Its Origin and Growth* (London: Macmillan, 1920).

53. Daniel Mornet, *Les origines intellectuelles de la révolution française, 1715–1787* (Paris: A. Colin, 1954, originally published 1933). Robert Derathe, *Jean-Jacques Rousseau et la science politique de son temps* (Paris: Presses Universitaires de France, 1950).

54. Roy Porter, *The Creation of the Modern World: The Untold Story of the British Enlightenment* (New York: Norton, 2000).

55. Standard works on Enlightenment thought are Paul Hazard, *La pensée européenne au XVIIIe siècle, de Montesquieu à Lessing* (Paris: A. Fayard, 1963, originally published 1946); Ernst Cassirer, *The Philosophy of the Enlightenment*, trans. Fritz C. A. Koelln and James P. Pettegrove (Princeton: Princeton University Press, 1951); Peter Gay, *The Enlightenment, an Interpretation*, 2 vols. (New York: Knopf, 1966–1969).

56. Robert Darnton, *Literary Underground*, and *Edition et sédition: L'univers de la littérature clandestine au XVIIIe siècle* (Paris: Gallimard, 1991).

57. Jean Egret, *La Pré-révolution Française, 1787–1788* (Paris: Presses Universitaires de France, 1962).

58. William Wordsworth, *The Prelude: The Four Texts (1798, 1805, 1850)* (London: Penguin Books, 1995), p. 440. For Kant, Peter Burg, *Kant und die Franzoesische Revolution* (Berlin: Duncker und Humblot, 1974).

59. Patrice Higonnet, *Goodness Beyond Virtue: Jacobins During the French Revolution* (Cambridge, Mass.: Harvard University Press, 1998), p. 52.

60. Patrice Gueniffey, *La politique de la Terreur: Essai sur la violence révolutionnaire, 1789–1794* (Paris: Fayard, 2000).

61. Georges Lefebvre, "Saint-Just" and "Sur la pensée politique de Robespierre," in his *Etudes sur la Révolution française* (Paris: Presses Universitaires de France, 1963).

62. François Furet, *La Révolution: De Turgot à Jules Ferry, 1770–1880* (Paris: Hachette, 1988).

63. Ernst Kantorowicz, *The King's Two Bodies: A Study in Mediaeval Political Theology* (Princeton: Princeton University Press, 1957).

64. Hannah Arendt, *On Revolution* (New York: Viking Press, 1968).

65. R. R. Palmer, *The Age of the Democratic Revolution: A Political History of Europe and America, 1760–1800*, 2 vols. (Princeton: Princeton University Press, 1959–1964). Jacques Godechot, *Les Révolutions, 1770–1799* (Paris: Presses universitaires de France, 1986).

66. Garry Wills, *Lincoln at Gettysburg: The Words that Remade America* (New York: Simon & Schuster, 1992).

67. Susan Dunn, *Sister Revolutions: French Lightning, American Light* (New York: Faber

and Faber, 1999). Patrice Higonnet, *Sister Republics: The Origins of French and American Republicanism* (Cambridge, Mass.: Harvard University Press, 1988).

68. Pierre Rosanvallon, *La démocratie inachevée: Histoire de la souveraineté du peuple en France* (Paris: Gallimard, 2000).

9. FROM THE FIRST MODERN REVOLUTION TO THE FIRST ANTICIPATED REVOLUTION, 1799–1848

1. George Lichtheim, *Marxism: An Historical and Critical Study* (London: Routledge and K. Paul, 1964).

2. Jonathan Sperber, *The European Revolutions, 1848–1851* (Cambridge: Cambridge University Press, 1994). Wolfgang J. Mommsen, *1848, die ungewollte Revolution: die revolutionären Bewegnugen in Europa, 1830–1849* (Frankfurt: S. Fischer, 1998). Geoffrey Bruun, *Revolution and Reaction, 1848–1852: A Mid-Century Watershed* (Princeton: Van Nostrand, 1958). Lewis Namier, *1848: Revolution of the Intellectuals* (London: G. Cumberledge, 1944).

3. See Chapter 1.

4. Alexander Gray, *The Socialist Tradition: Moses to Lenin* (London: Longmans, Green, 1946).

5. Eric Hobsbawm, *The Age of Revolution, 1789–1848* (Cleveland: World, 1962).

6. *The Marx-Engels Reader*, ed. Robert C. Tucker, 2d ed. (New York: Norton, 1978), p. 475.

7. R. B. Rose, *Gracchus Babeuf: The First Revolutionary Communist* (Stanford, Calif.: Stanford University Press, 1978).

8. See "Kapital, Kapitalist, Kapitalismus," O. Brunner et al., eds., *Geschichtliche Grundbegriffe: historisches Lexikon zur politisch-sozialen Sprache in Deutschland*, 8 vols. in 9 (Stuttgart: E. Klett, 1972–1992), 3:399–454.

9. Karl Mannheim, *Ideology and Utopia: An Introduction to the Sociology of Knowledge*, trans. Louis Wirth and Edward Shils (New York: Harcourt, Brace & World, 1936).

10. Engels, *Socialism, Utopian and Scientific*.

11. See Chapter 8 and Appendix II.

12. For a classic critique of this laissez-faire revolution in the years around 1800, see Karl Polanyi, *The Great Transformation* (Boston: Beacon Press, 1944).

13. Pierre Rosanvallon, *Le moment Guizot* (Paris: Gallimard, 1985).

14. In addition to the general works cited at the beginning of this chapter, see, for a succinct introduction to events of 1848 in the context of the French revolutionary tradition, Lord Elton, *The Revolutionary Idea in France, 1789–1871* (London: Edward Arnold, 1959). Two recent histories of the revolution of 1848 in France are Philippe Riviale, *Un revers de la démocratie, 1848* (Paris: Flammarion, 2005), and William Fortescue, *France and 1848: The End of Monarchy* (London: Routledge, 2005).

15. The literature on "1848" in Central Europe is correspondingly vast. In addition to the classic work of Veit Valentin, *Geschichte der deutschen Revolution von 1848–49* (Berlin: Ullstein, 1930–1931), 2 vols. (Veit Valentin, *1848: Chapters in German His-*

tory [London: Allen and Unwin, 1940], is an abridged English version of his work), see Theodore S. Hamerow, *Restoration, Revolution, Reaction: Economics and Politics in Germany, 1815–1871* (Princeton: Princeton University Press, 1958); Frank Eyck, *The Frankfurt Parliament, 1848–1849* (New York: St. Martin's Press, 1968); Jonathan Sperber, *Rhineland Radicals: The Democratic Movement and the Revolution of 1848–1849* (Princeton: Princeton University Press, 1991). Wolfram Siemann, *The German Revolution of 1848–1849* (New York: St. Martin's Press, 1998), deals in some detail with the revolution in the "lesser Germanies."

10. MARXISM AND THE SECOND INTERNATIONAL, 1848–1914

1. Eric J. Hobsbawm, *The Age of Revolution: 1789–1848* (Cleveland: World, 1962).
2. Lenin quoting Kautsky in *What Is To Be Done?*; see Robert C. Tucker, ed., *The Lenin Anthology* (New York: Norton, 1975), p. 68. For the necessary distinction between socialism and the labor movement, see Selig Perlman, *The Theory of the Labor Movement* (New York: Macmillan, 1928). An ex-Menshevik who emigrated to the United States, Perlman came to reject all subordination of trade unions to socialist intellectuals.
3. Quotations of Marx and Engels here are from Robert C. Tucker, ed., *The Marx-Engels Reader*, 2d ed. (New York: Norton, 1978), unless otherwise noted. The most important and penetrating assessment of Marxist thought is Leszek Kolakowski, *Main Currents in Marxism: Its Rise, Growth, and Dissolution*, trans. P. S. Falla, 3 vols. (Oxford: Clarendon Press, 1978). His view of the metaphysical foundations of Marxism has been followed here. See also Shlomo Avineri, *The Social and Political Thought of Karl Marx* (London: Cambridge University Press, 1968). The tendency this book represents accepts the importance of the Hegelian substratum in Marxism, yet goes on to argue that, with time, the enduring legacy of Marx turned out to be social democratic reformism. This is probably the dominant view in the West. Kolakowski, however, argues that Marx led even more logically to Communism.
4. *Marx-Engels Reader*, p. 59.
5. "Contribution to a Critique of Hegel's Philosophy of Right: Introduction," *Marx-Engels Reader*, pp. 64–65.
6. The classic case for the secularization of religious elements in modern thought is given by Karl Löwith, *From Hegel to Nietzsche: The Revolution in Nineteenth Century Thought*, trans. David E. Green (New York: Holt, Rinehart and Winston, 1964). The classic rebuttal to Löwith is presented by Hans Blumenberg, *The Legitimacy of the Modern Age*, trans. Robert Wallace (Cambridge, Mass.: MIT Press, 1983).
7. H. Tudor and J. M. Tudor, eds. and trans., *Marxism and Social Democracy: The Revisionist Debate, 1896–1898* (Cambridge: Cambridge University Press, 1988).
8. For the main documents of Leninism, see *The Lenin Anthology*.
9. George Lichtheim, *Marxism: A Historical and Critical Study* (New York: Praeger, 1961), does the best job of situating Marxism in historical context, and in a comparative perspective from France to Russia, though the book is at its strongest for the

Marxist heartland of Germany and Austria-Hungary. Like Averini, Lichtheim tends to consider the early Marx and Lenin as immature versions of essential Marxism and to view reformist Social Democracy as its best expression. In historical fact, however, it is quite clear that until the end of his life, Marx believed that revolution was imminent, and in his last years that it could be started by a crisis in Russia.

11. RED OCTOBER

1. Johannes Sleidanus, *The General History of the Reformation of the Church from the Errors and Corruptions of the Church of Rome, Begun in Germany by Martin Luther; with the Progress Thereof in all Parts of Christendom from the Year 1517 to the Year 1556/Written in Latin by John Sleidan; and Faithfully Englished* . . . (London, 1689). Johann Cochlaeus (Johann Dobneck) was a Catholic humanist/publicist and opponent of Luther and the Reformation.

2. The author has discussed the Western historiography of the Russian Revolution and the Soviet regime at some length in two publications: Martin Malia, "L'Histoire soviétique," in Serge Berstein and Pierre Milza, eds., *Axes et méthodes de l'histoire politique* (Paris: Presses Universitaires de France, 1998), pp. 57–71; Martin Malia, "Clio in Taurus: American Historiography on Russia," in Gordon S. Wood and Anthony Molho, eds., *Imagined Histories: American Historians Interpret the Past* (Princeton: Princeton University Press, 1998), pp. 415–433.

3. John Reed, *Ten Days That Shook the World* (New York: International Publishers, 1919); Sergei Eisenstein, the film of the same name (called *Oktiabr* in Russian, 1928); and Warren Beatty, the film *Reds*, 1981.

4. The classic example is Leon Trotsky, *History of the Russian Revolution*, trans. Max Eastman (New York: Simon and Schuster, 1932).

5. The classic example is William Henry Chamberlin, *The Russian Revolution*, 2 vols. (New York: Macmillan, 1935).

6. The first treatment of the Russian Revolution as a long-term process is E. H. Carr, *A History of Soviet Russia, Volume 1: The Bolshevik Revolution, 1917–1923*, 3 vols. (New York: Macmillan 1951–1953). The series was continued by Carr and R. W. Davies down to volume 4: *Foundations of a Planned Economy 1926–1929*, 2 vols. (New York: Macmillan, 1971–1972), and then, by R. W. Davies alone, the volumes of his *The Industrialization of Soviet Russia: The Socialist Offensive: The Collectivization of Soviet Agriculture, 1929–1930* (Cambridge, Mass.: Harvard University Press, 1980); *The Soviet Collective Farm, 1929–1930* (Cambridge, Mass.: Harvard University Press, 1980); *The Soviet Economy in Turmoil, 1929–1930* (Cambridge, Mass.: Harvard University Press, 1989). This monumental opus indeed offers us a Bolshevik rather than a Russian Revolution. There is no upheaval at the beginning and society is virtually absent throughout; instead we are given a history of the Soviet regime and its policies. The whole is presented from a Bolshevik point of view, as a process culminating in the success of the "socialist offensive" of the First Five-Year Plan. Its basic perspective thus parallels Isaac Deutscher's equally influential *Stalin* (New York: Oxford, 1949, 1966) and his trilogy on Trotsky.

The second broad perspective to be offered is that of Theodore H. von Laue, *Why Lenin? Why Stalin?* (Philadelphia: Lippincott, 1964). In his view, the Revolution extends from 1900 to 1930 and is understood as a process of economic modernization. However, given what Von Laue considers to be Russia's basically non-European nature, this effort could end only in a despotic caricature of its Western model.

The third, and currently most influential, overview is Sheila Fitzpatrick, *The Russian Revolution* (New York: Oxford University Press, 1982, 1995). As with Carr and Davies, the Revolution begins in 1917 and culminates successfully in 1932. The emphasis, however, has shifted to social process; the Party is secondary and Marxism is virtually absent from the story. In the first edition the purges are dismissed as a "monstrous postscript." In the second edition, 1934–1935 marks an improbable "thermidor"; and the purges, though now included in the "twenty-year process of revolution," are presented merely as the tail-end of its turbulent but creative élan. The overall meaning of the Revolution is "terror, progress, and social mobility" (*The Russian Revolution*, 1982, p. 157).

An almost equally influential contemporary overview is Moshe Lewin, *The Making of the Soviet System: Essays in the Social History of Interwar Russia* (New York: Pantheon, 1985). Though not organized as a history, this work also posits a revolution extending from 1917 to the end of the 1930s. This revolution is also almost pure social process, with minimal attention to Party structure and Marxism. For Lewin, however, the "good" revolution ends in 1929; Stalin, though he succeeded with the industrial modernization of Russia, largely perverted the heritage of Lenin.

The most recent broad-gauge treatment is Richard Pipes, *The Russian Revolution* (New York: Knopf, 1990), and *Russia Under the Bolshevik Regime* (New York: Knopf, 1994). In this treatment, the Revolution extends from the student disturbances of 1899 to Stalin's death in 1953. Pipes' revolution is almost pure political process; society is virtually absent, and "ideology"—that is, Marxism—is dismissed as quite secondary. Instead, the guiding thread of the Revolution is the transmission of Russia's "patrimonial" despotism from the Old Regime to the New. The second volume takes the New Regime only to 1924, which makes it difficult to substantively argue the author's announced thesis of continuity from Lenin to Stalin.

7. This discussion thus privileges ideology and politics in explaining the Soviet experience, as does the author's *The Soviet Tragedy: A History of Socialism in Russia, 1917–1991* (New York: Free Press, 1994). The present treatment, however, expands on its predecessor by seeking to situate the Russian Revolution in comparative European perspective. A cognate ideological-political and European approach is that of Andrzej Walicki, *Marxism and the Leap to the Kingdom of Freedom: The Rise and Fall of the Communist Utopia* (Stanford, Calif.: Stanford University Press, 1995).

8. Alexander Gershenkron, *Economic Backwardness in Historical Perspective* (Cambridge, Mass.: Belknap Press of Harvard University Press, 1962). See the title essay.

9. Joseph de Maistre, "Cinq lettres sur l'éducation publique en Russie," in *Oeuvres choisies de Joseph de Maistre*, vol. 4 (Paris: R. Roget et F. Chernoviz, éditeurs, 1910), p. 191.

10. The concept of a proletarian-peasant alliance was first developed prominently by Lenin in his 1905 pamphlet *Two Tactics of Social Democracy in the Democratic Revo-*

lution, in Robert C. Tucker, ed., *The Lenin Anthology* (New York: Norton, 1975), pp. 120–147.

11. An excellent discussion of traditional Europe as a corporate and sacred order (what has been called here the Old Regime broadly conceived) is given by Dietrich Gerhard, *Old Europe: A Study of Continuity, 1000–1800* (San Francisco: Academic Press, 1981).

12. This is a staple of Menshevik criticism of the Bolsheviks. It has been repeated, in various forms, by such Western historians as Robert C. Tucker in the introduction to his *Lenin Anthology*, and Leopold Haimson, *The Russian Marxists and the Origins of Bolshevism* (Cambridge, Mass.: Harvard University Press, 1955).

13. From Marx and Engels's preface to the Russian translation of the *Communist Manifesto* (1882), as quoted in Andrzej Walicki, *The Controversy over Capitalism: Studies in the Social Philosophy of the Russian Populists* (Oxford: Oxford University Press, 1969), pp. 180–181.

14. The arguments for October as a social revolution are given in Daniel H. Kaiser, ed., *The Workers' Revolution in Russia, 1917: The View from Below* (Cambridge: Cambridge University Press, 1987); Ronald Suny, "Towards a Social History of the October Revolution," *American Historical Review* 88 (1983): 31–52.

15. The chief statements of the "Bukharin alternative" are Stephen Cohen, *Bukharin and the Bolshevik Revolution: A Political Biography, 1888–1938* (New York: Knopf, 1973); Moshe Lewin, *Political Undercurrents in Soviet Economic Debates: From Bukharin to the Modern Reformers* (Princeton: Princeton University Press, 1974). A much more nuanced analysis of the key decisions at the end of the twenties is given by Alec Nove, *Economic Rationality and Soviet Politics; or, Was Stalin Really Necessary?* (New York: Praeger, 1964).

16. At the Thirteenth Party Congress in 1924.

17. Those who doubt the enduringly ideological vision of the Soviet leadership should consult David Holloway, *Stalin and the Bomb: The Soviet Union and Atomic Energy, 1939–1956* (New Haven: Yale University Press, 1995).

18. "Dognat' i peregnat' Ameriku" was a slogan in particular currency during the ascendancy of Nikita Khrushchev. See William Taubman, *Khrushchev: The Man and His Era* (New York: Norton, 2003), another work that testifies to the Soviet leadership's enduringly ideological vision well into the post–World War II era.

CONCLUSION AND EPILOGUE

1. For a discussion and comparison of "generic fascism" and "generic Communism," see Martin Malia, "Judging Nazism and Communism," *National Interest* (Fall 2002): pp. 63–78. [The following discussion of "generic Communism" is drawn, with minor variations, from that text. — Ed.]

2. The position, notably, of Dan Diner, *Das Jahrhundert Verstehen: eine unversalhistorische Deutung* (Munich: Luchterhand, 1999).

3. The analysis of Marxism sketched here is developed at greater length in Martin Malia, *Russia Under Western Eyes: From the Bronze Horseman to the Lenin Mausoleum* (Cambridge, Mass.: Harvard University Press, 1999), ch. 4.

4. Karl Marx and Friedrich Engels, *The Communist Manifesto,* introduction by Martin Malia (New York: Signet Classics, 1998), p. 90.
5. Ibid., p. 66.
6. Ibid., p. 76.
7. See for example, Eric Hobsbawm's introduction to *The Communist Manifesto: A Modern Edition* (London: Verso, 1998). Hobsbawm assures us that 150 years earlier Marx foresaw present-day "globalization," which is of course the current expression of capitalism's "internal contradictions."
8. Marx, *Manifesto,* p. 55.
9. The phrase is Engels's. See Andrzej Walicki, *Marxism and the Leap to the Kingdom of Freedom: The Rise and Fall of the Communist Utopia* (Stanford, Calif.: Stanford University Press, 1995).

APPENDIX I. REVOLUTION: WHAT'S IN A NAME?

1. Harry Eckstein, *Internal War, Problems and Approaches* (New York: Free Press of Glencoe, 1964).
2. See the introduction to this book.
3. Carl von Clausewitz, *On War,* trans. Michael Howard and Peter Paret (Princeton: Princeton University Press, 1976). Alfred Thayer Mahan, *The Influence of Sea Power upon History, 1660–1783* (Boston: Little, Brown, 1898; first published 1890), and his *Influence of Sea Power upon the French Revolution and Empire, 1793–1812,* 2 vols. (Boston: Little, Brown, 1892). See also Raymond Aron, *Clausewitz, Philosopher of War* (Englewood Cliffs, N.J.: Prentice-Hall, 1985), and Peter Paret, *Understanding War: Essays on Clausewitz and the History of Military Power* (Princeton: Princeton University Press, 1992). On Mahan, see William Livezey, *Mahan on Sea Power* (Norman: University of Oklahoma Press, 1980).
4. As does the historian Charles Tilly, *From Mobilization to Revolution* (Reading, Mass.: Addison-Wesley, 1978).
5. The most recent general surveys of the problem of revolution are Michael S. Kimmel, *Revolution: A Sociological Interpretation* (Philadelphia: Temple University Press, 1990); Jack Goldstone, ed., *Revolutions: Theoretical, Comparative, and Historical Studies,* 3d ed. (Belmont, Calif.: Wadsworth/Thomson Learning, 2003); and Noel Parker, *Revolutions and History* (Malden, Mass.: Blackwell, 1999). Older but still relevant treatments are John Dunn, *Modern Revolutions: An Introduction to the Analysis of a Political Phenomenon* (New York: Cambridge University Press, 1972; 2d ed., 1989), and Mark Hagopian, *The Phenomenon of Revolution* (New York: Dodd, Mead, 1974).
6. I. Bernard Cohen, *Revolution in Science* (Cambridge, Mass.: Belknap Press of Harvard University Press, 1985), and Roy Porter and Mikulas Teich, eds., *Revolution in History* (Cambridge: Cambridge University Press, 1986).
7. Max Weber, *The Protestant Ethic and the Spirit of Capitalism,* trans. Talcott Parsons (New York: Scribner's, 1930), pp. 47–48.
8. The most complete discussion of the history of the term and concept "revolution" is Reinhart Koselleck, "Revolution: Rebellion, Aufruhr, Bürgerkrieg," in Otto Brunner,

Werner Conze, and Reinhart Koselleck, eds., *Geschichtliche Grundbegriffe*, 8 vols. (Stuttgart: Klett-Cotta, 1972–1992), 5:653–788. Still useful is Karl Griewank, *Der neuzeitliche Revolutionsbegriff* (Weimar: H. Böhlaus Nachfolger, 1955). For the term's usage in French, see Alain Rey, *"Révolution": Histoire d'un mot* (Paris: Gallimard, 1989). Christopher Hill, "The Word 'Revolution' in Seventeenth-Century England," in Richard Ollard and Pamela Tudor-Craig, eds., *For Veronica Wedgwood, These Studies in Seventeenth-Century History* (London: Collins, 1986), pp. 134–151.

9. Hannah Arendt, *On Revolution* (New York: Viking Press, 1963), p. 42, quoting Georg Forster.

10. Thomas Babington Macaulay, *The History of England from the Accession of James II*, 5 vols. (London: Longman, 1849–1861). See also John Leonard Clive, *Macaulay: The Shaping of the Historian* (New York: Knopf, 1973). For a classic critique of the Whig interpretation see H. Butterfield, *The Whig Interpretation of History* (London: G. Bell and Sons, 1931).

11. Garry Wills, *Lincoln at Gettysburg: The Words That Remade America* (New York: Simon & Schuster, 1992), shows that the famous opening of the Declaration of Independence acquired its modern meaning, and its centrality to the national myth, only with Lincoln's equally famous gloss on it in the Gettysburg Address.

12. George Bancroft, *History of the United States, from the Discovery of the Continent*, 6 vols. (Boston: Little, 1876). See also Merrill Jensen, "Historians and the Nature of the American Revolution," in Ray Allen Billington, ed., *The Reinterpretation of Early American History: Essays in Honor of John Edwin Pomfret* (New York: Norton, 1968).

13. François Furet, "La Révolution française est terminée," in his *Penser la Révolution française* (Paris: Gallimard, 1983).

14. Edmund Burke, *Reflections on the Revolution in France* (New York: Liberal Arts Press, 1955), p. 6.

15. His magisterial opus is Samuel R. Gardiner, *History of England: From the Accession of James I to the Outbreak of the Civil War, 1603–1642*, 10 vols. (London: Longmans, 1883–1884); *History of the Great Civil War, 1642–1649*, 4 vols. (London: Longmans, 1893); *History of the Commonwealth and the Protectorate, 1649–1660*, 3 vols. (London: Longmans, 1897–1901). It was Gardiner's intention to write the history of England from 1649 to 1660, but his death occurred before the work was completed (vol. 1, 1649–1651, 2d ed.; vol. 2, 1651–1654; vol. 3, 1654–1656). At the same time, he published a shorter popular version of his views under the title *The First Two Stuarts and the Puritan Revolution* (New York: Charles Scribner's Sons, 1907), first published in 1876, and also *The Constitutional Documents of the Puritan Revolution, 1625–1660* (Oxford: Clarendon Press, 1889).

16. Thomas Paine, *The Rights of Man: Being an Answer to Mr. Burke's Attacks on the French Revolution* (London: J. S. Jordan, 1791), simultaneously published in Baltimore and Paris.

17. On Guizot and Tocqueville, see notes 18 and 19 below. Edgar Quinet, *La Révolution*, 2 vols. (Paris: A. Lacroix, Verboeckhoven, 1866). Jules Michelet, *Histoire de la Révolution française*, 6 vols. (Paris: A. Lacroix, 1868–1869). Hippolyte Taine, *Les origines de la France contemporaine*, 6 vols. (Paris: Hachette, 1888–1894).

18. Pierre Rosanvallon, *Le moment Guizot* (Paris: Gallimard, 1985).

19. Alexis de Tocqueville, *De la démocratie en Amérique* (Oeuvres II) (Paris: Gallimard, 1992), p. 7. The "single generation" he refers to is Guizot and company; that is, the architects of the 1830 constitutional-monarchist "conclusion" to the French revolution.

20. Alexis de Tocqueville, *L'ancien régime* (Oeuvres III) (Paris: Gallimard, 2004), pp. 64–68, indeed the whole of ch. IV.

21. Ibid., p. 68.

22. Tocqueville, *De la démocratie en Amérique*, pp. 4–5.

23. Robert C. Tucker, ed., *The Marx-Engels Reader*, 2d ed. (New York: Norton, 1978), p. 4.

24. Ibid., pp. 4–5.

25. *The Communist Manifesto*, in *Marx-Engels Reader*, p. 475.

26. Pierre Kropotkine, *La grande révolution, 1789–1793* (Paris: Stock, 1909), and Jean Jaurès, *Histoire socialiste de la Révolution française*, 8 vols. (Paris: Editions de la Librairie de l'humanité, 1922–1924).

27. M. I. Finlay, "Revolution in Antiquity," in Roy Porter and Mikulas Teich, eds., *Revolution in History* (Cambridge: Cambridge University Press, 1986), pp. 53–55.

28. Ronald Syme, *The Roman Revolution* (London: Oxford University Press, 1962).

29. Joseph Needham, "Social Devolution and Revolution: Ta Thung and Thai Phing," in Porter and Teich, eds., *Revolution in History*, pp. 61–73.

30. M. A. Shaban, *The Abbasid Revolution* (Cambridge: Cambridge University Press, 1970).

31. Jean Baechler, "Conservation, réforme et révolution comme concepts sociologiques," *Esprit critique* 6, no. 2 (Spring 2004): 70–86.

APPENDIX II. HIGH SOCIAL SCIENCE AND "STASEOLOGY"

1. Jean Baechler, "Conservation, réforme et révolution comme concepts sociologiques," *Esprit critique* 6, no. 2 (Spring 2004): 70–86.

2. Crane Brinton, *The Anatomy of Revolution* (New York: Norton, 1938; reprint, New York: Vintage Books, 1965).

3. Robert V. Daniels, *The End of the Communist Revolution* (London: Routledge, 1993). Sheila Fitzpatrick, *The Russian Revolution* (New York: Oxford University Press, 1982 and 1994). Nikki Keddie, *Iran and the Muslim World: Resistance and Revolution* (New York: New York University Press, 1995).

4. Brinton, *Anatomy*, p. 26.

5. E. J. Hobsbawm, *Primitive Rebels* (Manchester: Manchester University Press, 1959). Eric Wolf, *Peasant Wars of the Twentieth Century* (New York: Harper & Row, 1969).

6. Harry Eckstein, "On the Etiology of Internal Wars," *History and Theory* 4, no. 2 (1964–1965): 133–163; Lawrence Stone, *The Causes of the English Revolution, 1529–1642* (New York: Harper & Row, 1972), p. 12.

7. The classic of the latter genre is Ted Robert Gurr, *Why Men Rebel* (Princeton: Princeton University Press, 1970).

8. Stone, *Causes*, pp. 12–17.

9. Charles Tilly, *The Vendée* (Cambridge, Mass.: Harvard University Press, 1964).

10. Charles Tilly, *From Mobilization to Revolution* (Reading, Mass.: Addison-Wesley, 1978); Charles Tilly, *Coercion, Capital, and European States, A.D. 990–1990* (Cambridge, Mass.: Basil Blackwell, 1990). See also Charles Tilly, *European Revolutions, 1492–1992* (Cambridge, Mass.: Basil Blackwell, 1993); Charles Tilly and Wim P. Blockmans, eds., *Cities and the Rise of States in Europe, A.D. 1000 to 1800* (Boulder, Colo.: Westview Press, 1994); Charles Tilly, ed., *The Formation of National States in Western Europe* (Princeton: Princeton University Press, 1975).

11. Peter Burke, *History and Social Theory* (Ithaca, N.Y.: Cornell University Press, 1993).

12. Barrington Moore, *Social Origins of Dictatorship and Democracy: Lord and Peasant in the Making of the Modern World* (Boston: Beacon Press, 1966).

13. Barrington Moore, *Soviet Politics: The Dilemma of Power; the Role of Ideas in Social Change* (Cambridge, Mass.: Harvard University Press, 1950).

14. Theda Skocpol, *States and Social Revolutions: A Comparative Analysis of France, Russia, and China* (New York: Cambridge University Press, 1979).

15. See Skocpol's introductory article under that title in Peter B. Evans, Dietrich Rueschemeyer, and Theda Skocpol, eds., *Bringing the State Back In* (New York: Cambridge University Press, 1985).

16. Skocpol, *States and Social Revolutions*, p. 36.

17. Georges Lefebvre, *La grande peur de 1789* (Paris: A. Colin, 1932).

18. Georges Lefebvre, *The Coming of the French Revolution*, trans. R. R. Palmer (Princeton: Princeton University Press, 1967, originally published under the title *Quatrevingt-neuf* [Paris: Maison du livre français, 1939]).

19. Skocpol, *States and Social Revolutions*, p. xiii.

20. Ibid., p. xi.

21. Ibid.

22. Max Weber, *The Protestant Ethic and the Spirit of Capitalism*, trans. Talcott Parsons (New York: Scribner, 1958).

23. David Landes, *The Wealth and Poverty of Nations: Why Some Are so Rich and Some so Poor* (New York: Norton, 1998).

INDEX